"Anyone who ever watched Alan Cutler during his time at WLEX-TV knows he's a unique but passionate person. He's also one of the hardest workers I have ever known. All that is evident in this great collection of memories and stories. Certainly you'll remember the Billy Gillispie encounter but savor other stories about UK sports and Cutler's love for the Kentucky Derby. Just a fun and interesting read."
    —Larry Vaught, Vaught's Views

"Alan Cutler was a Kentucky fixture by the time I came to UK. I always found him outspoken and honest, and his book is a reflection of the man. Proud to call him friend."
    —Hal Mumme, inventor of the Air Raid offense

"Even though I hold the record for working with Alan the longest in the WLEX sports department—believe it or not, I STILL haven't heard all of his stories! That's why I honestly can't wait to read his book. WLEX used to limit Alan to three minutes for a sportscast, and now he's got unlimited space to talk in a book? Look out!! I can't wait!"
    —Ryan Lemond, KSR

"CUT TO THE CHASE is not only an entertaining glimpse behind the curtain of UK sports, it's a testament to how the state of Kentucky and its people can win over anyone—even a born-and-bred New Yorker like Alan. Fans will enjoy Alan's stories from almost forty years covering the University of Kentucky, each told in the unabashed manner his followers have grown to love."
    —Tyler Thompson, Editor in Chief, KSR

"One reason I always looked forward to spending time with Alan on air was that Alan would only ask me fair questions and wouldn't let me off with the easy answer—all the while making me feel comfortable and at ease. I'm sure one book will not be enough for Alan to share all of his stories, so I'm already looking forward to book number 2.
    —Jack "Goose" Givens, UK great

CUT

TO THE CHASE!

Alan Cutler
with Dr. John Huang

Foreword by John Calipari

Cover Art: David Bryan Blondell

ISBN: 9798676513832

First Printing 2020

This book is a memoir. It reflects the author's present recollection of experiences over time. Although the author has made efforts to ensure that the information in this book was accurate at press time, the author acknowledges that errors or omissions can occur. The author does not assume, and hereby disclaims liability to any party for any loss or damage caused by errors or omissions, whether such errors or omissions result from negligence, accident, or any other cause.

"Every year we have two or three superstars. The rest of them aren't...so we don't tell them."

—Bear Bryant...Alabama quote from the 1960s

"History doesn't repeat itself, but men make the same mistakes."

—Bernard Baruch, American financier and political consultant

"What you see here, what you hear here, stays here when you leave here."

—Vince Lombardi, Green Bay Packers coach

"Common sense is king."

—Alan Cutler

Contents

Part 14—Going Out on Top

Foreword
By John Calipari

I t's been a while—nearly 40 years, as a matter of fact—since I first met him, but I can still remember the first time I crossed paths with Alan Cutler.

I was just getting my start in Pittsburgh as an assistant coach. He was fairly new to the area as a sportscaster, but he immediately stood out.

Huge smile. Goofy hair. Big personality. Said what was on his mind. My first thought was: *Who is this guy?!*

Alan and I would work together for a couple of years and moved on to the next step around the same time. I went to UMass and he moved back to Lexington where he would remain a fixture in the Lexington media for nearly four decades.

Our paths wouldn't cross again until 2009 when I took the Kentucky job. I can still remember the day I walked into the practice gym at the Joe Craft Center with all eyes focused on me. I had waited my entire career for an opportunity like this, but in that moment, when your dreams are coming through, there's an anxiety, a rush of emotions that felt like jumping out of an airplane.

This was the Kentucky job! And there I was, sitting up there trying to set the tone of what we were going to try to accomplish. I'm looking around the room and answering the questions and I see this familiar face. He's a little grayer than I remember, a few more wrinkles and a little rounder around the edges, but I know that face.

It's Alan Cutler.

Alan grabs the mic and starts to ask the question, and all of a sudden all that emotion—any anxiety I was feeling—disappeared. An immediate thought popped in my head and I had to ask it.

"Did you really chase him?!" I blurted out.

That "him" of course, was the former coach, Billy Gillispie, who I was taking over for. Alan, as you may have infamously seen, is the guy trailing him in a slight jog trying to get his questions in.

I had seen the video a couple of days earlier and I had the same thought I did so many years ago: *Who is this guy?!*

Fast forward to this past season. We're in the middle of conference play and it's late at night after one of our games. I can't remember what game it was or how we even did, but I'm sitting up there on the podium answering questions, counting down the time until I can get out of there, go home and get some sleep, and I look to my left and see this familiar face again.

His hair is all white at this point. He's got a full beard that looks a little bit like he's auditioning to be Santa Claus. And he's got this smile on his face as if to say, *did you forget about me?!*

After retiring a couple years earlier, Alan is back in the press room and this thought pops back in my head again: *Who is this guy?!?!*

I'm thinking, why in the world would someone return here after they had retired. Get away from this place! Go watch the game from your couch! What are you doing here working?!

But that's the thing about *who this guy is.* He loved his job, he loved being around people and he made no apologies for it.

Alan loved being the goofy guy who people gravitated to and felt comfortable opening up to in interviews. He loved asking the hard questions—even if it meant chasing someone down a hall. He loved covering sports, so much so that even after two years, he had to come back and see us.

What I found out over my time with Alan was he was a fantastic sportscaster. Whether you're talking about his time in Pittsburgh—covering everything from the Pirates to the Penguins, my Steelers, Duquesne, Pitt and high school football—his time in Lexington reporting on UK sports and the local sports scene, or his radio career with the Cincinnati Bengals, Alan has seen it all.

The one constant with every time Alan and I crossed paths is he's always had fun doing his job. He was thorough, fair with no agenda, objective and would ask the tough questions when he needed to. More than anything, Alan had a passion about him. That was clear to me in everything he did and why I believe he was so good at what he did.

Alan found his "why"—his motivation—a long time ago and came to do his job every day with a sense of pride and enjoyment. It was refreshing and why I believe Alan and I got along so well in a relationship where there can be natural friction. You knew what Alan was about, and agree or disagree with him, everyone can find common ground with him because of his passion and his approach.

Our media scrums aren't quite the same without him, but I know he's enjoying retirement as much as he did his job, if not even more so.

Maybe one day he'll write a book about all of his retirement journeys in this next stage—I've heard he's having a ball—but in the meantime, I'm looking forward to reading about all of the fun he had in his career.

Alan has had a Hall of Fame career, and I can honestly say there will never be anyone else in our media quite like *this guy*. Congratulations on a fantastic career and book!

Preface
by Dr. John Huang

Everyone in central Kentucky knows Alan Cutler.

Like me, Alan recently retired from the working world. Although outwardly we appear different as night and day, there's one big part of our lives that we do share in common—our connection to Kentucky and the sporting events which have defined our state.

It's only natural, then, that we join forces to tell you a story. When our retired worlds collide, it certainly has the makings for a darn good book.

My first memory of Alan Cutler was seeing him on a local Lexington newscast. Even then, he appeared larger than life to me. His cartoonish Groucho Marx mustache and his brash reporting style screamed stardom from the very beginning. I knew right then that Alan was a master of his craft—a talented sports personality with an uncanny gift for relating to people. Plus, he seemed to be a fantastic storyteller, a vital coup de grace for the making of a book people would flock to read.

Many years later, I had my first personal encounter with Alan when I put braces on his son's teeth. For a year and a half, I got to see the personal side of the guy that I had previously only known as that dude inside my TV screen. Looking past the theatrics of his outward celebrity mask, I saw instead a caring, compassionate, and concerned parent that only wanted what was best for his son. It was at that point that I knew his life story would definitely make for an interesting read.

"You should write a book," I casually mentioned to Alan during my first year on the UK media beat. "And I'll be glad to help you put it together."

He brushed me off immediately with his usual bravado. In his direct and emphatic style, Alan implied that no one would be interested. Plus, in my own insecure world, I thought that he felt my opinions had no credibility. I believed that in Alan's mind, I was a rich retired orthodontist, conducting bad interviews and writing impertinent columns.

Over the next year, I persisted in badgering Alan to start putting his thoughts together for the book. Imagine my surprise, then, when he finally agreed to do it. Don't get me wrong, he still had his doubts about the number of interested readers, but I'm glad I finally convinced him that he owed it to the people of Kentucky, to all of BBN, and to all his adoring fans and faithful followers to chronicle his over forty years of dedicated sports coverage.

The end product is something that we're both extremely proud of. It's a legacy that we hope will resonate with YOU, the reader. Sure, we've included well-known stories such as Alan's infamous chasing down of Billy Gillispie, but we've also shared some never-before-told tales that'll leave you surprised, stunned, and perhaps even shocked. I guarantee you'll bust a gut laughing at many of them. You may even shed a tear or two. But through it all, you'll finally get that much awaited glimpse of the wacky world according to Alan.

Memories fade over time. As crazy as some of these events, characters, and encounters appear to be, Alan swears they're all true—at least as he remembers them. We've both since discovered that it's not uncommon for different people to have totally different perceptions and recollections of the exact same event. Many of the conversations occurred decades ago. Although the ones we included were not intended to be an exact word-for-word transcript, we did the best we could to capture the feeling and meaning of what was said in all instances.

To be honest, Alan drove me nuts with his incessant fact checking follow ups. Through countless hours recording at his breakfast table, phone calls, text messages, video conferencing, verifying scores, dates, people, places, and times—through numerous rewrites, revisions, and additions—we compiled a story that we think you'll really like. It took us a couple of years to complete, but I'll have to admit that Alan was right…the devil really was in the details.

Even in retirement, you'll notice that Alan is as opinionated as ever. He's loud, he rambles, he speaks in staccato bursts. His narrative consists of an endless array of run on sentences, split infinitives, and reversed clauses. To make his words jump off the page in a readable format was a challenge that nearly killed me. And yet, I knew that in order to be true to everyone who buys a copy, this book had to sound exactly like Alan. It had to be Cutler telling you *HIS STORY*.

So here it is. Please, sit back, relax, and enjoy.

Introduction

Really? *LEXINGTON, KENTUCKY?* If you would have told me that I would spend more than half my life in Lexington, I would've told you that *YOU'RE OUT OF YOUR MIND!* What a great place it turned out to be.

Anyone growing up in New York as I did would never believe that Lexington is a great sports town. I had no idea when I moved here. I initially came to Lexington because I really needed a job...*AND THEY REALLY NEEDED ME!* My plan was to spend a few years in Lexington and then move to a much bigger TV market and closer to home. When I came back to Lexington the second time with my family, it was *BECAUSE* we decided to make it our home.

I grew up a New York Yankees fan. My hero was superstar centerfielder Mickey Mantle. Before our son, Jordan Joshua Cutler, was born, I told Judy, I wanted to name him Mickey Mantle. To show you who wears the pants in the family, that lasted about one second. Against her wishes, we ended up calling him J.J. rather than Jordan. As a teenager, J.J. told me the hair on his neck would stand up—whenever I called him Jordan—because he knew he was in trouble. Thank goodness, I almost *NEVER* had to call him Jordan.

I've always been lucky. As a kid, I was a dreamer. Everyone needs to *dream.* In my mind, *not dreaming* is one of the biggest reasons kids today face so much disappointment in life.

Andrew, my grandson, is six years old. He wants to be an astronaut. *That's dreaming!*

I began dreaming when I fell in love with sports. I was only five. Watching the Yankees on a black and white TV was special. I wanted to learn everything I could about my Yankees. That's one of the reasons I learned to read so quickly. In fact, I learned many life lessons that are still with me today just by listening to Yankees Baseball on the radio.

My dream was to eventually do radio play-by-play for the Yankees. I haven't yet put that on my resume, but I'm convinced my radio baseball play-by-play from the 1970s still remains by far the best thing I've done in my career. Occasionally, even the best dreams take an unexpected detour. I never dreamed of doing TV, but I ended up having a fabulous time in my forty-one years as a TV sportscaster. Without TV, I never would have met Judy. Without Judy, I wouldn't be the man I am today. God is much smarter than I am.

I've been really blessed. During my time in Lexington, I've been able to cover three NCAA Championship basketball teams under three different coaches. Sorry UCLA, Duke, North Carolina, and Kansas—Kentucky *IS* the New York Yankees of college basketball.

I started doing Kentucky Derby stories when I moved to Lexington in 1981. The Kentucky Derby is so much more than *the greatest two minutes in sports*. I've been privileged to interview the characters who make horse racing the *Sport of Kings*. 2018 was my last Derby—what a way to go out! Doing stories like where Triple Crown winner Justify came from, on a small family farm not far from Lexington—before he ran in the Derby—is really special. Talking to the people behind the scenes, that the public rarely if ever sees, has been a lot of fun.

I've loved the wonderful pure emotion of high school sports, and I'm proud of how I changed the coverage of high school sports in central Kentucky in the early 1980s. Today, everyone does expanded high school segments on Friday night. I convinced management that it wasn't about sports on Friday nights, but it was all about community involvement. Our high school show has been named the top sports program in Kentucky many times.

All this—together with having the top-ranked radio show in my time slot in Pittsburgh, Cincinnati, and Lexington—is something anyone would be proud of. Plus, being the host of the Cincinnati Bengals Radio Network and covering some terrific UK football players has made this a great run for a kid who couldn't hit a fastball—but continued to *dream big*.

Throughout my career, I never worked for any TV station. I worked for you—the True Blue fan. TV paid me, but I was always delivering for those that watched. There were times my aggressive philosophy caused some clashes with management, but that goes with the territory. You probably remember when I was chasing UK Basketball coach Billy Gillispie after he was fired. All I was trying to do was what I always did, working hard to get the story—nothing more, nothing less. It almost got *me* fired. More on that later.

Little did I know that my foundation as a broadcaster was set before I was ten years old. I've always considered myself a great listener, but most people don't believe me because of my *BIG MOUTH*. My big mouth paid off my mortgage, but my grandmother told me when I was five that there was a reason God gave us *two* ears and *one* mouth.

I learned as a kid by listening to Red Barber—one of the greatest baseball announcers. From 1934 through 1966, he did the play-by-play for the Cincinnati Reds, the Brooklyn Dodgers, and the New York Yankees. He and Mel Allen, also a great Yankees Baseball announcer, were the first broadcasters to receive the Ford C. Frick Award from the National Baseball Hall of Fame and Museum.

Barber taught me to be honest, while Allen—together with Phil Rizzuto, another wonderful Yankees announcer—showed me you could also have personality as a broadcaster. Part of the reason fans loved Phil Rizzuto was because he was a great Yankee shortstop—but a big key was he acted goofy like your crazy uncle. In other words, he was real.

These three men shaped my success as a broadcaster. What meant a lot to me was that in 1985, Mel Allen sat next to me as my guest for hours on KDKA radio. I got to tell him how much he and his partners meant to me when I was a kid. It made me feel great to not only spend time with one of my heroes, but he really appreciated hearing that directly from me.

My father didn't like the fact that I loved sports. He took me to one game in 1959, when the hapless Washington Senators beat my beloved Yankees 7-0. I will never forget walking into the stands and seeing a Major League field for the first time. I can remember that rush like it was yesterday. I was in *LOVE*. *That moment had a huge impact on my life.*

Just my luck—my hero, Mickey Mantle, who was often injured, didn't play that day. I always regretted that I never got to see Mickey Mantle play in Yankee Stadium. I compensated for missing out by listening to these great announcers with my transistor radio tucked under my pillow. If my father could hear the radio, he would tell me to turn it off. I would wait a few minutes and turn it back on. How ironic that my defiant attitude toward my father would serve me well later as a broadcaster.

Through the years, many up-and-coming broadcasters have asked me what they can do to be like me. My advice has always been the same. No matter what you do, be honest, be yourself, and work hard. It's really that simple.

One of my biggest fears in writing this book is that no one will read it. I was thinking about writing a book after I secretly decided to retire, but I was not close to making the commitment. I give Dr. John Huang a ton of credit for this project happening because he bugged me many times about telling my story. He started pushing me before he knew I was going to retire. He is responsible for "lighting the fire" and convincing me that there are people that would really enjoy reading the book.

If you happen to be someone who spent their hard-earned money to buy a copy, I want to thank you. I hope you enjoy it.

Over the years, I've been able to interview a lot of newsworthy people. I'm not trying to brag, but it's something I know I'm good at—it's a gift. People seem to open up to me, and I've accumulated a lot of interesting and entertaining stories along the way.

I put my heart and soul into this project.

That included a lot of soul searching.

At times it was fun. At times it was painful. It's called life.

Even though I'm so far from perfect—this book is as honest as I can be, and I had to dig deep a number of times to get there.

The stories I've included should make it fun for you to read. I think they're pretty cool. I hope you do too.

Part 1

The Early Years

1

Majoring in History at Cortland State

Being a history major has served me well. It's helped me tremendously in seeing things and understanding trends.

When it came time to choose a college, I picked Cortland State in upstate New York because they had a radio station. I knew that I wanted to go into radio, so every school that I applied to had to have a radio station.

I really wanted to go to Syracuse, which was easier to get into than Cortland State. Syracuse was known for having the best broadcasting school in the country—but it was too expensive. It was over five thousand dollars per year, and we didn't have the money. I never told my mother that's where I wanted to go because I didn't want her to feel bad. I also thought that as long as a school had a radio station, that's all I needed. I was just as "cocky" back then.

There were two freshmen who got shifts at the campus radio station right away. I was one of them—I got the last shift—the one no one wanted—Sunday morning at 8 am. It didn't matter what I did Saturday night, I was always there. I was playing records between 8 am and noon. The radio station couldn't even be heard off campus. Didn't matter. I'll never forget the first record I played was by Creedence Clearwater Revival. I stuttered on the air trying to say it because I was so nervous. I gave up and just said "CCR."

Cortland was really good at lacrosse. Little Cortland played in the NCAA tournament against the Naval Academy, so I went there to do the game. It was a perfect spring day. My play-by-play was broadcast on some huge speakers, there were kegs of beer, they were throwing frisbees, and having a big party. Cortland was down 10-6 with about five minutes left in the game. They made a great comeback and tied the game with less than thirty seconds to go. I'm going on and on about how Cortland came back to tie the game and how the game ended in a tie. I thought the game was over.

All of a sudden I see players walking back onto the field! Like an idiot, I said, "I guess they're playing overtime." I didn't know the rules—that there was overtime. How could I not know? My buddies told me at that point they wanted to shoot me. Thank goodness Cortland won, and I learned a valuable lesson about being prepared. This dumb mistake served me well. It made me want to outwork my competition…and I did. It might sound like a little thing, because as soon as Cortland won, no one cared about my mistake anymore—but this really bothered me.

I actually quit college for a semester because I thought it was a waste of time. It took me about two or three days to realize that was an egregious mistake. Instead of going back to sign up for the semester, I just decided to ride it out. I remember going to visit my friends about a month later, and I realized how much I missed school. I had great friends and ended up returning the next semester.

The semester off was a tremendous lesson. I got a couple of menial jobs that were tough to get. I was living at home and it was awful. My major was history because I liked history, and Cortland didn't have a major in broadcasting. The only thing I wanted to do was sports. I tried to get a job at a couple of radio stations, but they looked at me like I was a stranger. Too young, too much hair, and I didn't look the part. Plus, Long Island didn't have many radio stations that did sports, and you can't get a job in New York City doing sports with no experience.

I found that out the hard way. I took a tape to the New York Knicks while Dave DeBusschere—one of the great Knicks players—was then the general manager. Picture this. I've got long hair, I'm 185 pounds, and I'm wearing really tight white jeans and a pair of boots that have never been polished. DeBusschere comes out wearing a suit that had to cost a thousand dollars, and—I'll never forget it—he looks at me like *"I just left my office to get a tape from you?"* Marv Albert was doing the Knicks' play-by-play. He was one of my heroes and is one of the all-time great sportscasters. First time I met him years later doing TV in Lexington—he was cold as ice. Maybe I caught him on a bad day.

That same day at WINS radio, a terrific all-news station, Jim Gordon, who had done the New York Rangers and New York Giants broadcasts, said—"Kid, if you want to do this, you better go someplace small and earn your way back here. That's the only way you're going to do it." He was wearing a white shirt and a tie, and he had a big-time voice. He did New York sports for close to forty years. So, I thought that's what I had to do.

I went back to school with purpose. My goal was to spend more time at the radio station and get my degree. There were semesters I didn't do any class work at all. I was a good test taker. I liked my history classes. The classes I didn't like, I would cut as much as I could.

Just before I graduated, my family was gathered around the Thanksgiving table. My Uncle Aaron was a very successful businessman. He was moving to New Mexico to go into business with an old partner. I'm shoveling food in my mouth and just blurted it out with no premeditated thought, "Hey Unc, do you need help moving out west?" The look on the face of my mother was stupefying. When my uncle replied, "Sure," my mother looked at him and—I can picture it like it was yesterday, God rest my mother's soul—she looked like she wanted to kill him. Despite my mother's objection, that was it—I was going to help my uncle and move out west.

2

New Mexico, Here I Come

While helping my uncle make the move to New Mexico, I got to drive the big truck. My uncle rented a 35-foot truck that was pulling his cool 1931 Ford Model "A" with a rumble seat in it. What a classic car. I wasn't good with trucks, though.

During my break from college, I had a job with Frosty Fair Foods where I had to learn how to drive a truck. At 6:00 am every Monday morning, I would drive this big truck to the meatpacking industry in New York. The first time I had to back the truck in, some union guys were screaming and cursing at me like crazy because I didn't know what I was doing. I was way too slow backing the big truck in. The way the other guys whipped their trucks in and out around me, combined with me being cursed out, was intimidating.

What a trip. We had Mary (my uncle's girlfriend), three cats, her aunt—who was in her eighties, very weak and feeble—my uncle, and myself. We were traveling through Kansas late at night, and I'm driving. I had to do a U-turn underneath an overhang at a gas station. I remember my uncle asking me, "You think you can make it?" I thought I could make it, but I was wrong. There were long fluorescent lights hanging down, and I got stuck. There was nothing you could do, so my uncle told me to keep on going. There was glass everywhere.

My uncle left a note saying what happened, what hotel we were staying at, and that he would take responsibility. When we get to the hotel, I'm going out to get us some pop, and I see these two huge state troopers coming towards me. They figured out I broke the lights, and they wanted to throw me in jail. My uncle sees them and tells me to get inside and shut up. He tells them that *he* was the one driving. He calms them down, explains the whole situation, agrees to pay for the damage, and it's taken care of.

When we got to Albuquerque, I lived with my uncle, Mary, her aunt, and the three cats.

Back then you needed to take a test for the third-class license for a broadcasting job. The third-class test wasn't difficult. I took the test right after I graduated college while I was still in New York, and I was told I'd have the certificate in two weeks.

I went to an FM rock station off a street called—believe it or not—*Cutler Avenue* in Albuquerque, New Mexico and got a job as a part-time deejay working weekends at whatever the minimum wage was. I was so excited. I was supposed to start the following weekend, but I still hadn't received my broadcasting certificate. I told the program director the day before I was supposed to start that my license hadn't come in the mail. The guy then tells me that I shouldn't have told him. He said I made a mistake of being honest because now he wouldn't be able to hire me. My career was off to a great start. My license, which I still have today, came in the mail less than a week later.

I randomly went into all three TV stations in town to try to find a sports job. Once of the TV stations I walked into, I was lucky enough to find a local producer named Don McGuire. He ended up producing big-time sports on national TV, and I had a lot of respect for him.

I bugged McGuire by showing up every week. He finally told me what the deal was. I never figured out if he felt sorry for me or if he simply respected my determination. The station was going to have a tryout for a weekend sports anchor. McGuire invited me to try out for it but told me I wasn't going to get the job. There was a big Mexican community in Albuquerque, and he was told to find someone who is Mexican to fill the slot. However, he told me I could still make a tape, it would be a good experience for me—and if something happened down the road, McGuire would help me get a job in TV.

I had one sports jacket that my mother bought me for a wedding while I was still in college. It was an ugly plaid jacket, and it cost five dollars. Everything I owned back then fit in one suitcase. I'm sitting there with my shirt, tie, sport jacket, and all of a sudden I hear McGuire over the intercom, *"ALAN CUTLER COME TO THE STUDIO."* I started sweating like crazy. I was dripping in sweat, my hands were shaking—I had never experienced anything like that in my life. I did the tape, and I'm sure I looked like an idiot. Don told me that for a kid who hadn't done anything, the tape was good. He told me my tape was much better than the guy they were going to have to hire. I wish I had that tape today. I would put that on YouTube, and I'm sure it would get a lot of laughs.

By the way, the guy they hired ended up becoming the main sports anchor. I met him the day of the tryout. He was really nervous.

By this time, a couple of months had gone by, and I still hadn't found a broadcasting job. My uncle owned his own real estate agency and was very successful in buying, building, and selling homes. He offered to buy a business, work it with me, and set me up. I told him I wanted to be a broadcaster. He thought I was out of my mind, but if that's what I wanted to do, then he said I needed to go do it.

I probably shouldn't say this, but I went to the library and ripped out two pages in the broadcasting yearbook that had all of the phone numbers of the radio and TV stations in New Mexico. I then went to a Sambo's restaurant and put twenty-five dollars and twenty-five cents in quarters into a pay phone calling every radio and TV station that was on this list.

I found three potential job openings that had anything to do with sports. Only one was a true sports job. KRZE-AM was looking for someone to do Little League Baseball play-by-play in Farmington, New Mexico.

I was so excited!

I had never heard of Farmington, New Mexico.

I'm off to Farmington.

3

Little League Baseball in Farmington

I show up at 8:30 on a Monday morning hoping to get an interview with Dale Faulkner, the manager of the radio station. Dale didn't remember talking to me on the phone, but he was really desperate…I had the job in fifteen minutes. I made a whopping salary of one hundred dollars a week doing two games a night, six games a week.

I found a place to rent—by the week—over Snookers Pool Hall in downtown Farmington, a couple of blocks from the radio station. I often had to step around passed out locals—who had too much to drink—while cutting across a small park to get to work. The apartment was a dump. I had to walk up wooden steps that were partially broken. It was a rough pool hall. Living there was not my smartest move.

The radio station immediately started getting a lot of calls because they were upset that I wasn't properly pronouncing people's names. The secretary at the station, whose father owned the station, told me that if I wanted to keep my job, I had to learn how to pronounce Mexican names. So I sat there, and in fifteen minutes, she went through all the common Mexican names—and I learned how to pronounce them *ALL* correctly. Thankfully, she thought I was a nice, clean kid and was always watching out for me. Even though I was probably the only New Yorker in Farmington, New Mexico, I absolutely loved it. It was such a great time.

The station had a trade where you could get your hair cut for free. The second time I'd gone there, Harold, the owner, cut my hair and asked me where I lived. When I told him I lived over Snookers Pool Hall, he said, "You can't live there. It's not safe. You can't live there." He tells me that his sister has an empty room upstairs, and he offered to let me stay there for no more than what I was currently paying.

I moved next door to Harold. I quickly found out I was the only non-Mexican in the neighborhood—and I was fine with that. It was a tiny one-bedroom apartment with a broken window in the bedroom, and there was no refrigerator. To this day, my brother still gives me garbage about how I could be that dumb to rent a place without a refrigerator. I told my brother it was better than where I was living. Plus, Harold's sisters made the best chili I've ever had. I was happy.

One day, I heard a loud noise outside. I went outside, and Harold— who's maybe a hundred and fifteen pounds soaking wet—has a gun in his hands and screams, "Get back in the house!"

There were five or six Mexican guys in an old pickup truck...I saw a chain...I saw a sledgehammer...a couple of guys were holding a rifle— although no one pointed it at me. They were just screaming at Harold while Harold screamed back at them. They were yelling at each other in Spanish. I had no idea what was going on.

Harold later told me that I was lucky he had been there because those guys were coming to beat me up. *My kind* wasn't supposed to be in that neighborhood. Harold assured me that no one would ever mess with me and that I would be fine. For some reason, I didn't worry about it.

I loved doing Little League Baseball. The games would be on everywhere—stores in town, everywhere. It was interesting how popular it was. I loved doing baseball radio play-by-play. Professionally speaking, that's what I should have stayed with. I think I could have eventually done Major League Baseball for forty years. I was honestly that good— much better than anything I did on television. I was very descriptive, I could talk fast, I understood the game, I could be funny with people, and I was good right away. As a kid, I would turn the sound down on the TV and practice play-by-play doing Yankees games. When no one was around, I would just talk to the TV set.

This actually happened to me. "*High fly ball to deep right field, way back, it's going, going... oh, it's foul... oh, it hits a windshield... (pause)... (pause)... (pause)... that's my windshield.*" That foul ball actually cracked the windshield of my Chevy Vega. Before I went to Farmington, I had the car for about a week when the transmission went out. My uncle screamed and yelled at the dealership, and he made them give me a new transmission.

A star pitcher during my time in Farmington was 11-year-old Duane Ward. What are the odds? He ended up being one of the best relief pitchers in Major League Baseball and was a star for Toronto when they won the World Series in 1992-93. In two World Series, he was 2-0 with 5 saves and an all-world ERA of 1.13. He led the American League in saves in 1993. Before he went to Toronto, Ward pitched for Atlanta. The year I did Pittsburgh Pirate Baseball on TV, I walked up to him in the Atlanta clubhouse and told him my name. He gave me a big hug, and we had a great talk for about fifteen minutes. With this huge smile, he talked about the fun he had playing Little League Baseball, and that it was the most fun he'd ever had playing the game. That's the beauty of sports. It's about the love of the game and the people you meet along the way.

At the end of the Little League season, there was a tournament in Cortez, New Mexico. The radio station wanted me to do it, but they didn't want to pay me any gas money. They didn't have a station car, and I knew my car wouldn't make it there because it needed tires. The owner of the station, Boyd Whitney, told me he'd pay for the gas if I could sell sponsorships to a local tire store in exchange for some new tires. I'm twenty-one years old, have no idea who to call, so I opened up the Yellow Pages and called the tire places with the biggest ads. I got brand new tires because they listened to the games and knew who I was.

I go to Cortez, and the game is on an Indian Reservation. The umpires were terrible. A kid from Farmington hits a ground ball and clearly runs a step or two past first base, but they call him out.

Most press boxes for games like this were very primitive back then. You have to remember this was 1975. You had to walk up a ladder and pass your equipment to somebody else just to get it up there. The press box was shaky. The public address announcer, the official scorer, me, and one other person were all crammed up in an area that should have been for maybe three people. Plus, it's open. I have a *BIG MOUTH*. I was *LOUD!* As soon as I said, "Good afternoon," everybody stopped, looked at me from the stands, and asked themselves, "Who is this big mouth doing the game?"

I would say things like, "Hey, that umpire—what is he? Blind? He's crazy. The runner was safe!" Needless to say, people started booing me, cursing me out, yelling and screaming. I subsequently found out that the last time Farmington had played there, people in the stands had thrown rocks at the bus carrying the kids leaving the stadium because they had won. But, I respected how hard the local fans cheered for their players. This was a big deal to their community.

God bless my buddy Ken Wright. He had to have been about three hundred pounds, strong as an ox, and wore a lot of turquoise jewelry. His kid played on the Farmington team, so he became my protector. At the end of the game, he came to the press box steps and escorted me out. People were yelling and screaming and cursing at me, but they weren't going to mess with this guy. I had parked next to the bus. The bus driver waited nervously for me to get in my car, and we both floored it to get out of there as quickly as we could.

As baseball season ends, they give me a job playing records. I figured I could do this until I found another sports job. The room for the disc jockey was tiny. Back then, you would carry in a bunch of records for your shift. The guy who did the shift before me was a stoned-out hippie. I could smell pot on his breath. I walk in, set my records down, look up, and he teaches me the *best lesson* I ever learned in broadcasting.

I've told this story countless times to young broadcasters who have asked me about doing stand-ups for television. I walk into this tiny room, look to the right, and there's this centerfold from *Playboy* opened up on the wall facing the disc jockey. It's the only thing on the wall. I certainly wasn't expecting it. I look back and forth at the picture and the disc jockey.

He has a smile on his face and says to me, "You're wondering why I have that picture on the wall, aren't you? That's who I'm talking to. You see, I like that picture. That's a pretty girl. When I look at that picture, I'm smiling. As I'm looking at that picture while I'm broadcasting, I have a smile on my face, and I feel good. That's who I'm talking to. Kid, you better know who your audience is."

Wow! That's the best lesson I've ever had in my career.

It's simple. What you do in broadcasting is talk to that one person—your father, mother, sister, brother, your best friend, your girlfriend, your boyfriend, whoever—someone that you're comfortable with. That was the whole purpose of the centerfold picture up on the wall. And once you're talking to that one person, does it matter that a couple of other people are eavesdropping? No. It takes over the fear of the camera or the microphone.

The TV camera is my friend. I love the camera. Are you kidding me? The camera pays the mortgage. The camera pays the bills. The camera buys the groceries. Why would I not like the camera? Why would I be afraid of the camera? I'm going to be nice to the camera. I'm going to talk to the camera.

I wanted to do high school sports. Aztec was the town next to Farmington. It had one stoplight and a radio station. A small AM radio station was going to cover high school sports, so I went down there and quickly got a job. I lived in a tiny beat-up trailer in a really bad trailer park. I kept the same routine that I did in Farmington. On payday, I'd pick up a loaf of bread, peanut butter, a gallon of orange juice, a gallon of milk, a dozen eggs, and a six-pack of beer. I lived on that. I was so broke, there were two times I rolled into a gas station. Both times, I only had change to gas up the car. I had no money.

Twice I asked my uncle for fifty dollars. He always wanted to send me more, and we argued about it. We ended up laughing about it years later—but I always declined—and made sure I paid him back.

Here I am spinning country and western records that I knew nothing about. Little did I know the station was also going under. It got so bad that Stan, the station manager—a Vietnam vet and a big dude—tried to beat me to the bank to cash his paycheck by walking faster than me to downtown Aztec. When Stan started running, I stopped because I knew he had a wife and two kids—and it was more important for him to cash his check. Plus, I had enough gas in my car to drive to Farmington. I also knew a gal who was a bank teller in Farmington, so I was able to cash my paycheck there. My paycheck never bounced, but there were a couple of other young disc jockeys from Los Angeles—who also knew nothing about country music but were looking to get into broadcasting—who had checks bounce on them.

Around that time, I was asked to sell and broadcast a local basketball tournament. It was two to four games a day. During one of the sessions, I did a game next to Ted Foster, who ran a few radio stations in Durango, Colorado. He said, "Hey you're really good. What's your story?" When I told him about me being from New York, he said, "You can't stay here. I've got this friend, Barry Turner, who's looking for somebody. Why don't you give him a call?"

I called Barry Turner, who ran a couple of stations in Grand Junction, Colorado. He said he did have a job open—it was for the No. 2 newsman, but it would involve a lot of sports play-by-play. I told him I didn't have any news experience, but I would do anything he wanted if he let me do a lot of play-by-play. He just laughed and invited me up for an interview the very next day.

4

Crazy Hours in Grand Junction

It took some effort for me to make it to my interview in Grand Junction. It was about a four-and-a-half-hour drive one way, and I still had four games to call in New Mexico before driving up to Grand Junction that night. Then I had four more games back in New Mexico the very next day. Barry Turner told me to be there at 8:30 in the morning. He said he would either hire me or not by 9:30 so I would have enough time to drive back and call my games.

At the time, I had this 1965 Cadillac that I had bought for five hundred dollars. I loved that car. I drove through the night with a lot of snow on the ground. That first drive to Grand Junction was majestic. I slept in the car for a couple of hours before my interview. Sure enough, I got there on time, I got the job, and I'm on the road back to New Mexico in no time.

I'm heading through Montrose, Colorado, and I get pulled over for speeding. Like an idiot, I'm going ninety-five to a hundred miles per hour. The cop tells me he's taking me to jail. I've got on the same tie and my awful looking cheap plaid jacket—the same one I used when making the demo TV tape in Albuquerque—and I say to the cop, "I don't have time to go to jail." Not kidding—that's exactly word for word what I said.

The look on the cop's face was priceless. It was a *really stupid* thing to say, but I go on to tell him the whole story about working at the station in New Mexico…how the place was going broke…how I just got this new job…and how I have to go back and call this basketball tournament…and how I'm coming back to live in Grand Junction, Colorado…and that he can hear me on radio on Monday. The cop then says, "That's the wildest story I've ever heard. OK, no ticket. Go the speed limit, but just go."

I showed up to call my games ten minutes before the tip-off. The two guys who owned the station—who I've never met before—were very surprised to see me. I told them I had just gotten a new job but was coming back to do the games. They told me not to bother because they would do the games and I was *FIRED!*

I said immediately back to them, "No, get the hell out of this seat. It's *MY* tournament. You're going to pay me the sales commission, you are going to pay me my talent fee, I'm going to do the tournament, and then I'm gone. Now get the hell out of my seat."

I was loud. REALLY LOUD. People were staring at me in this small high school gym that was packed. The two guys who owned the station got up and walked out. I did the games, they paid me my money, and I went up to Grand Junction, Colorado.

When I get to Grand Junction, I'm the No. 2 person in the news department. I don't know how to type. I don't know anything about news. All I know is that there's a guy in front of me, and we're going to split the high school and college games.

I ran around like crazy. The guy in front of me didn't last too long after I got there. After he left, they named me news director for two radio stations—what a joke! I had no idea what to do. I had to do two live half-hour newscasts a day that I had to produce by myself. Between live and taped shows, I had to do more than fifteen newscasts a day. It was non-stop work...but I had a great time. It was a great education.

The Grand Junction Eagles were a semi-pro baseball team made up of college stars. Some eventually made it into the Major Leagues. Paul Molitor, a very fast shortstop who looked like he could hit line drives in his sleep, was on the team the first summer I was there. He went into the Baseball Hall of Fame in 2004.

Bob Howsam was the General Manager of the Cincinnati Reds and one of the top baseball executives of his time. He came to Grand Junction like so many other scouts looking for players in the Junior College World Series. The first two days of the tournament, I called four games each day by myself without a color man. Try being on the air from 8 am until midnight with only a short break between the day and night sessions. Don't forget that I also have a big mouth. Howsam walks into the booth and says to me, "Young man, you are one of the finest baseball announcers I've ever heard." Without missing a beat, I hit my cough button and said, "Hire me." He told me to call him. I did just that after the tournament was over...and he never got back to me.

Decades later, I went to Cincinnati to cover a reunion of the Big Red Machine—one of the greatest baseball teams ever—and there is Bob Howsam, who never got enough credit for putting that team together. I always said that if I ever saw him again, I'd tell him I'm still mad because he never got back to me. At the reunion, he was sitting by himself, and there was no one around him. I felt sorry for him. I went up to him to do an interview...and I never said a word about Grand Junction or the call.

When I wasn't doing games at night, I would also cover city council and school board meetings. *BORING!!* I knew I wanted to get out of news, and the deciding factor was Chris Chambliss of the Yankees hitting one of the greatest home runs ever against Kansas City in the playoffs. Bottom of the 9th and Chambliss' home run in 1976 sent the Yankees back to the World Series for the first time since 1964. Where was I when it happened? Sitting in my Cadillac outside of the city council meeting trying to listen to the game while waiting for them to make some decision on something that I can't even remember. I'm missing the Yankees game? That's it—I'm getting out of news!

That fall, Fruita Monument High—one of the three teams I called high school sports for—ironically had a game back in Farmington, New Mexico. I drove down to do the play-by-play. As luck would have it, Ernie Hall of Hall's Texaco—a good friend—had a son who played on the football team, so he and his wife were also going to the game.

To get to Farmington, you had to drive through Durango. I used to call it "the descent into Durango, Colorado." It was a tight, twisting, winding road with, at some points, no guardrails. If you went off the road, you were done.

A car on the other side of this two-lane road swerves and is heading right towards me. My reaction wasn't what anyone would normally do. You would normally swerve away from the car, but my instant reaction—because I had been on this road many times—was just the opposite—to turn into the car. If I turned away, I would have driven off the side of the mountain—and I'd be dead.

The accident ended up not being my fault because the collision happened on my side of the road. The impact pushed me back towards the open edge of the road with a long drop-off—another ten feet, and I would not have survived. They closed the road down for a couple of hours to get everything cleaned up.

I wake up in the hospital with a concussion and my shoulder in a sling. Two huge cops are standing over me. I remember one of them saying, "Do you know how lucky you are to be alive?" God bless Ernie Hall and his wife, who were also standing outside my room seeing if I was OK.

I was extremely lucky. I was in my boss's car—wearing a seatbelt which didn't work. My forehead hit the windshield, and my shoulder hit the steering wheel. My torn rotator cuff ruined my shoulder for life. I decided not to get surgery because back then, the doctor said if the surgery got messed up, I would lose total use of my arm. I had six months of physical therapy exercises just to be able to lift my arm over my head.

Twice, years later, I ended up having total reconstructive surgery on my shoulder—the second time because I ripped everything again. In spite of all that, it could have been much worse—so I still consider myself lucky.

As bad off as I was, I convinced the doctor to release me from the hospital so I could still make it to the game in time. Thanks to Ernie Hall, I made it. Picture this—I had a head bandage on, and blood had trickled through. I had my arm in a sling. Both coaches heard about my accident and met me on the field while the teams were warming up. I looked like Rambo without the muscles. The players from both teams surrounded me, and the coaches used me as their pregame motivational speech. Hey, if Cutler could show up here after being in an accident where he's lucky to be alive, then you can give everything you have, they said to their players.

The only thing I remember from the game was that it was one of the hardest hitting high school football games I've ever seen. The game was decided in the final seconds.

My boss ended up getting mad at me because his car was totaled. I had a screaming match with him over the use of the company car. He didn't want me to ever drive the company car again. Whoa! Here I am—I'm lucky to be alive, it's not my fault, and he's worried about his company car.

I've always wondered, "Why me?" Why did I survive that car accident? I should not have survived. This was pure luck, and I never understood why in that moment I was calm and literally turned the steering wheel towards the other car.

Once again, God took care of me.

Back in Grand Junction, between high school football and basketball, college basketball, semi-pro baseball, and the Junior College World Series, I ended up doing 130 to 140 live play-by-play games a year. *IT*

WAS GREAT! I was also making three dollars a story—beer money—stringing news stories for KOA in Denver. KOA was the No. 1 station, and I was their correspondent on the western slope of Colorado.

I was twenty-two years old and now the news director of two radio stations, KQIL-AM and KQIX-FM. There was a salesman at the station who we thought was trying to get rid of the general manager. The rumor was he was going to fire a bunch of people including a couple of my friends.

I have no idea where I got the guts to do this, but I went to a couple of people and told them what was going on. "Here's the deal," I said. "I'm willing to walk into the general manager's office and tell him we are all willing to quit unless this guy gets fired because he's trying to take your job and get a number of us fired."

The salesman in question ended up leaving.

Then I did another stupid thing. I walked into the general manager's office and demanded they put me in sales, or I'd quit. I didn't have another job. I didn't know anything about sales. All I knew was that I sold some tires once so I could call a baseball game in New Mexico. They were paying me $750 a month, plus $25 a game, plus the $3 per story I did for KOA radio in Denver. I was living high on the hog compared to Farmington, but I saw some salespeople at the station who were making really good money. I figured I could do what they did, and of course I'd still be doing all that play-by-play.

Not only did they put me in sales, but they quickly named me operations manager for both stations. In less than six months, I hit the board No. 1 in sales.

When my boss went out of town, I hired the No. 1 morning radio personality from across town without my boss's permission. When I told him, my boss went crazy on me. When he found out I only had to pay the guy $150 more a month than he was making, he came over and gave me a hug. Remember, this is the same man whose car I totaled in the car accident. By the way, the deejay—Robert St. John—stayed in Grand Junction. He was really good and a perfect example that there are some very talented people broadcasting in small towns.

I played a major role in rebuilding two radio stations. When I decided to leave, they offered me five percent of the gross to stay. They told me there would be more down the road while also offering me a huge raise. I was just twenty-five years old, but I turned it all down because I was ready to do something else. I was having a great time, doing all the sports I wanted to, but after three and a half years, I was just ready for another adventure.

5

The Road to Boise

After three and a half years in Colorado, I got a job doing play-by-play for the University of Wyoming. Not only would I do radio play-by-play, I would do sports on TV as well. Pete Williams—the NBC-TV correspondent—was the news director at KTWO Television. Little did I know that he didn't want me to get the job. He thought the color commentator on the Wyoming games, who had been at the station for a long time, should have gotten the position. He was right. I showed up, and there was a battle because I got hired instead. I walked into a mess.

The guy who owned the TV station, Jack Rosenthal, owned a small part of the Chicago Cubs. He told me not to worry about it, to do a good job, and he would eventually help me get a job in a bigger city. Since he didn't really run the place on a day-by-day basis, everyone I dealt with was cold as ice to me because they didn't want me there. It was ridiculous. They wanted this other guy to get the job. The other guy was furious at me also. He wouldn't even say "hi" to me in the hallway.

It was my fault for not doing due diligence. I left a really good job in Colorado in hopes of doing big-time sports as one of the youngest broadcasters in the country. I thought I had everything going for me. I was going to do the WAC—University of Wyoming sports. I knew I was good at play-by-play. I figured I would be here a couple of years and eventually move up to a much bigger place.

Instead, they ended up getting rid of me. When I found out, I barged into the general manager's office while he was on the phone. I wasn't very nice about it. I told him the least they could do was to give me three months severance pay. I should have asked for six. Jack apologized and wrote me the check right away.

19

Now I go back to Grand Junction. They had hired three people to replace me. In other words, it took three people to do all the jobs I had been doing. It was obvious I couldn't go back there.

I found out there was a TV sports job in Boise, Idaho. I asked my buddy, Dave Hopkins, who was the main news anchor at the only TV station in Grand Junction, to let me make a tape. To heck with my ugly cheap plaid jacket this time around—I put on a golf shirt, totally unbuttoned, with my Star of David hanging out. I took five pieces of wire copy and ad-libbed a sportscast. I did it in one take and sent it to Boise.

Paul Reiss, the news director of KBCI-TV in Boise, liked my tape. He also happened to be *desperate*. He needed someone immediately to be the sports director. He didn't seem to mind that I basically had no TV experience. Paul had made some phone calls and knew that I worked really hard. I told him that me not working hard would never be an issue. When he asked me how much I wanted to be paid, I told him I wanted fifteen hundred dollars a month. I didn't think that was a lot of money—even back in 1978—but he said he couldn't do that. He countered with five. I froze for a moment trying to figure out what he meant by five. He said, "Five dollars an hour, and I'll raise you fifty cents in three months *if you survive*. You want the job or not?" I took the job. Paul told me to be there on Monday.

By this time, I had gotten rid of my Cadillac and replaced it with a cargo van because I knew I would be traveling around the country. It was a really dumb thing to own because it ate up gas like crazy.

I started on the air and didn't know what I was doing—but I had a great time. The most money I ever made in Boise was $7.15 an hour. They never paid overtime. If you had to work extra, too bad. Work was fun—so I worked. Boise was great. I loved Boise. Still do. I would get to the station a little after ten o'clock every morning, make any phone calls I had to make, rip the wire copy, and get ready for the day. I'd leave at 10:45 to go play basketball and lift weights at the YMCA, come back to the station by 1:30, and start my day. I had a great time.

One day, I received a letter about a really good boxer who was in jail. I called the warden and asked if I could do a story at the jail. I got to the jail with my photographer, and I'll never forget the sound when the jail door closed behind us. I wasn't worried about my safety, but it was still very eerie. As we're walking into the gym with a couple of guards, the inmates began cheering us like crazy. It made me a bit uncomfortable as a chill started running up and down my spine. When we finished the story and put it on TV, I was told that everyone at the jail really liked it. The warden told me it lifted their spirits.

Less than a year later, there was a riot at the jail. They were setting fires in buildings, and a couple of guards were taken hostage. The warden called me and told me that the inmates wanted *me* to be the mediator. Think about this—I'm a kid from New York, and this is way out of my comfort zone—but because the inmates decided they trusted me because of the boxing story, they wanted me to help them mediate. The warden was so desperate that he called me. I never forgave Paul Reiss, our news director, for not letting me do it. I was furious because this was such a big story that even Walter Cronkite—then the lead anchor on the CBS evening news—sent a Learjet from Los Angeles to Boise to pick up some of the riot footage we had filmed. It ended up as the lead story on CBS that night.

The cops wanted a copy of our tape because Mark Montgomery, our terrific chief photographer, got there first and had footage of some of the inmates burning parts of the jail down—but KBCI-TV refused to release it to them. That's a pretty normal procedure because TV stations didn't want to get in the habit of giving their footage to the police. To me, that's sad because we should be able to help in these situations. But, if we did it one time, our lawyers said they could request anything we had whenever they wanted it.

My boss knew he was going to be jailed for the refusal. The Boise police treated my boss with respect. He was fine, but he did end up spending the night in jail. This was a big story nationally. One hostage was released after some very intense negotiation, and the second hostage was rescued when an assault team was finally sent in. The inmates, meanwhile, inflicted nearly two-and-a-half-million-dollars-worth of damage to the jail.

Since the station didn't allow me to cover the story, they sent a reporter named Bob Loy. Bob was a reporter who was nerdy, but he did a good job. I was known for being a bit of a prankster, so I decided to pull one on Bob.

One of the other reporters tells me that Bob is impossible to deal with because his head's getting too big from all the publicity he's getting. I go to the back of the newsroom, call my own station, and ask to speak with Bob Loy.

I'm doing all this off the top of my head. I had no idea what I was going to say. Bob picks up the phone, I go under the desk to talk, and I say, "Bob Loy? Ed Rhoden, WCAU news in Philadelphia. I'm the assistant news director. I've seen your story about the Boise prison riot.

You did a great job. Have you ever thought about working in Philadelphia?" (By the way, I knew no one named Ed Rhoden.)

Bob gets all excited, so I ask him to send me his best four or five stories for review. I'm totally full of it as colleagues around me are trying not to laugh. When we finally hang up the phone, Bob Loy is so excited that he can't contain himself and walks out of the newsroom.

About a week or so later, Bob calls the station in Philadelphia asking for Ed Rhoden. When he made the call, one of our reporters—thank goodness—heard the call and got close to Bob so she could hear what was going on. Bob is told that there's no Ed Rhoden working there. "Who are you?" they ask him. Bob immediately figures out that he was pranked.

Before he knew it was a prank, Bob convinced his wife that they were going to move and sell their house. That was probably the best laugh I had in Boise, Idaho. Cruel, I know—but funny.

When he figures out he was pranked, Bob slams the phone down, looks directly at me, and before he walks out, he says, "I hope you pranksters had a good time." He slams the door behind him, and everyone in the newsroom starts laughing hysterically. Afterwards, I never talked with Bob ever again about the prank.

One other time, a consultant comes to the station. He's a former news director who should have retired. He says to me, "Young man, let me tell you something. You're the kind of person people are either going to love or hate. You're polarizing."

He's supposed to be a consultant, so I told him to tell me something I didn't already know.

"You're pretty brash," he responds back to me. "That's your pitch?" I ask him. "I'm a New Yorker in Boise, Idaho. I look different. I sound different. I'm aggressive. Some people aren't going to like me right away. I will grow on some of the people. Some people will never like me. You don't think I know that?" The guy just sits there for a second before he gets up and walks out.

The next day, Paul Reiss, our news director, asks me what I did to the guy for him to hate me so much. When I told him the story, we just both laughed. Had the guy given me some constructive criticism, I would have gladly listened to what he had to say. I still had a lot to learn. Paul told me to just keep doing what I was doing.

Jim Criner was the coach of Boise State when they won the NCAA Division I-AA Championship in 1980 in a wild game, 31-29 over Eastern Kentucky. Back then, reporter involvement was the thing to do.

You have to understand, I was 185 pounds back then, so I went to Criner before the season and asked him if I could do a week of stories on Boise State. All I asked in return was to take one snap as quarterback at the end of the week with everyone in full pads.

The last day, I remind Criner of our deal, and he says there is no time to do it. I raise my voice and tell Criner *in front of his whole team* that it's now time for my one snap. It was the end of practice. Looking back, I can't believe I challenged any coach like that in front of his team. He didn't have any choice. The players loved it that I stood up to Criner. They were happy to help me put my pads and helmet on.

I got in the huddle, and one of the players wants me to throw a pass. He explains the play and tells me how to call it at the line of scrimmage so it looks like I know what I'm doing. Two guys on the right side were supposed to go downfield. I take the snap, drop back, and get ready to throw the ball. I'm aiming for the first guy who ran a simple down-and-out pattern about ten or twelve yards toward the sidelines. I throw the ball as hard and as far as I can towards him. The throw was so bad it ended up being great. I hit the second receiver—who I never saw—who was going deep—down the field—right in stride. He scores a touchdown, and everybody goes absolutely nuts.

I later admitted to everyone that I was throwing to the short guy. I missed him by about twenty yards. You gotta be kidding me. If we tried this a hundred more times, I couldn't have hit that deep receiver. Criner comes over and he's laughing like crazy. The whole episode turned out to be a fun experience for everyone involved. I played that tape on TV for three to four days afterwards. I wish I still had it.

Outside of work, I loved the social scene in Boise. Gene Harris was one of the greatest jazz piano players of all time. He was a self-taught musician from Michigan, who had toured, recorded dozens of albums, and ended up moving to Boise. He performed in the Idanha Hotel about three blocks from the TV station, and I used to go listen to him play music three to five times a week. My spot was right next to his piano—great fun.

I still listen to Gene all the time. There was a moment when we were either going to become good friends, or he was going to think I was a jerk. He asked me to play golf after having a lot of laughs in between sets while he was playing piano. One time, we were at Warm Springs Golf Course. Gene is a big man with crazy strong hands, and when he hits it, he can hit a golf ball a long way. I sneak behind him and roll a ball between his legs at the exact moment he's about to hit his drive. I'm not kidding—he hit both balls. There was a pause because he had to figure out what happened, but then he literally fell down laughing.

There were three or four bars in downtown Boise that young people would go to. On a Friday or Saturday night, you'd just walk around from one of these places to the other. I met a young lady named Judy, who would soon change my life, in a bar called Humpin' Hannah's. She later told me the only reason she even came over to talk to me that night was because she was a Groucho Marx fan. I was standing there with my curly black hair, mustache, and smoking a cigar when she came up and asked me, "Has anybody ever told you how much you look like Groucho Marx?"

I was pretty cocky back then and was a bit taken aback that Judy didn't know who I was, even though I was on TV every night—so I told her I was a taxicab driver. Little did I know that both Judy and her best friend, Karen, had both worked as taxi dispatchers. Karen actually drove for the cab company that I claimed I was working for. What are the odds? Judy starts asking me questions, and I'm just making things up. She never bought it for a second.

We struck up an interesting conversation, but that was the end of that. Occasionally I would run into her, but we weren't dating or anything. She had a boyfriend. One day she told me she was leaving town. She asked me if I would write to her if she wrote to me. I said, "Sure," figuring she was never going to write to me.

She actually wrote me, and I wrote her back. I didn't think too much about it until I was walking around on a typical Saturday night just having a good time, and I saw her there at the same bar, Humpin' Hannah's, where we had first met. She had come back to town, split up with her boyfriend, and shortly after that, we became good friends.

It took a while before Judy found out what I really did for a living. She was talking to her dad one night after work at her parent's house. He was watching our newscast when the sports came on. Judy suddenly hears my voice, looks over at the TV, and says, *"Hey! I know that guy!"* Prior to that, she really had no idea who I was, other than the fact that I looked very different from any guy in Boise, Idaho. The rest—as they say—is history.

Even though my father-in-law never liked anyone else that Judy dated, he and I developed a great relationship. He loved to come visit us even after Judy's mom passed away. Judy later told me that her dad had huge respect for me. She said he loved having conversations with me, was always so proud of everything I had accomplished, and was always impressed to hear stories of what I did. My relationship with my father-in-law was so important to me because I had never had that type of relationship with my own father.

When I left Boise, Judy and I dated long distance, and our phone bills were outrageous. One month, mine topped $230. I remember saying to her, "It'd be cheaper if we just got married rather than having to pay all these big phone bills." *HOW ROMANTIC!!* It was a typical stupid comment by me, and she kind of laughed, but there was obviously something about our relationship that was special. It was really weird. I didn't feel like I wanted to date anyone else.

By this time, I was already working in Lexington. We decided to take a vacation together because it was either put up or shut up time. We knew we couldn't keep up our long-distance relationship. I flew back to Idaho, and Judy and I drove to the beautiful resort town of McCall. We were sitting on top of a little mountain, overlooking the water, with a six-pack of beer when I asked her to marry me. She said yes, and thirty-seven years later, she still puts up with me.

Judy gave up her whole life in Boise to start a new life with me in Lexington. She left her parents, her friends, and a good job to come to a place where she didn't know anyone but me. It wasn't easy. She walked away from her whole life to live with a workaholic. If Judy hadn't done what she did, there was no way I would be in Kentucky today. One, I never would have come back to Lexington. And two, I would have taken the job at ESPN that was offered to me twice—or one of the many other jobs that I turned down—and I never would have worked in Pittsburgh. My life would have been completely different. It's because of her that I was lucky enough to have ended up staying here in Lexington.

6

Mustache Desperation!

The truth is that Channel 18 was *desperate*, but so was I when I got hired to be the sports director on TV in 1981. I had decided to leave Boise because I trusted a friend who was the program director in beautiful Grand Junction, Colorado. He somehow convinced me to do a sports talk show for a small radio station in Monroeville, Pennsylvania, not far from Pittsburgh.

Before taking the radio job, I called Magid Associates, a big-time media consultant. Barb Frye, Vice President of Talent Services, told me not to take the radio job because she was going to find me a major market job in TV. I had already turned down a job anchoring in New Jersey, which would have put me into the New York market, because I was stubborn and stupid. I trusted my friend Dick and went to Monroeville instead.

Dick and I were friends, he was a lovely person, and his wife was a doll. That's the way it was in Colorado. I show up to do a sports talk show and discover that he'd become an alcoholic who was in the process of getting divorced. Two days after I got there, I realized I had made a horrendous mistake. After a couple of weeks, people were leaving the radio station because the place was falling apart. My first paycheck was half of what Dick told me it would be. I walked into his office yelling and screaming.

After about a month, I knew this was the dumbest thing I had ever done in my career. I had to get out because I guessed I wasn't going to have a job in six weeks or less. There were two TV sports jobs listed in Broadcasting Magazine—one of them was in Dallas, and the other was in Lexington, Kentucky. I asked about the job in Dallas, but Barb at Magid didn't think she could get it for me. She did think she could help me get the job in Lexington, and quickly at that. She overnights a tape to LEX18, and the day after that I get a call from John Ray, the news director.

You have to understand that I'm a loud New Yorker. I had never been to Lexington and knew almost nothing about Kentucky. At first glance, me being in Kentucky makes no sense.

I knew the history of the Kentucky Colonels of the ABA because I was a big ABA fan growing up. Dr. J, superstar Julius Erving, played against us in high school in New York. I once saw him take his last step at the free throw line and drop the ball in the basket. He could really fly before his knees got bad. You couldn't dunk back then in high school. If you did, it was a technical foul. Dr. J was a huge name in the ABA.

Obviously, I knew who Adolph Rupp was. I thought I knew how big college basketball was in Lexington—but I was wrong about that. I didn't realize how big it was until I moved here. Did I know the intricacies of Kentucky? No!! Nevertheless, I fly in and have a fun day with the management team. We go out to dinner that night, and John Ray says the job is mine. He told me he'd call me by four o'clock the next day.

Four o'clock comes...and there's no phone call. Five after four...no phone call. Ten after four...no phone call. I'm going nuts, so I call John up and he answers, "John Ray, hi Alan, how are you?" Just like that. *Are you kidding me?* I went off on John. "Look, if you don't want to hire me, I don't care," I blasted back at him. "But you said you were going to call me by four o'clock. And if I can't trust you to do what you say, I don't want to work for you. If you wanted me to work for you, you would expect me to be that honest and that prompt. If there's a problem, you owe it to me to tell me what it is." Those were my exact words.

The problem was that Harry Barfield, the general manager, who I ended up becoming very close to, didn't trust me. Now you have to understand that I didn't look the part. My hair was getting longer. I hadn't gotten a haircut, and by then, my mustache was long. John told me that Harry didn't think he could control me. He liked my energy and my personality, but he was afraid about how far I'd go on TV. Later on, once Harry got to know me, he enjoyed me taking strong stands on topics my competitors on TV wouldn't touch.

I took a deep breath, asked John if I could put him on hold, looked around the newsroom of the radio station, got back on the phone and told John that I would *shave my mustache* and get my hair cut really short if that would make Harry more willing to hire me. "If I tell you I'm going to shave my mustache, then I'm going to shave my mustache," I said. "And if you don't understand that if we get together that I'll be the most honest person you will ever work with, then we can't do this."

John puts me on hold, and after what seemed like an hour—but it was really about 10 minutes—he tells me *NOT* to shave my mustache. As it turns out, Harry just wanted me to trim it. "Make sure we see your lip on the mustache," John said. "Get a haircut, but don't cut your hair completely off. There'll be a plane ticket for you in the Pittsburgh airport. I'll see you tomorrow. Just do what I tell you, and you'll be fine."

When I hung up the phone, I sat there staring at it, partly because I was shocked at what I said to John. And two…I thought *this just might work out.*

When John Ray picked me up at the airport, he looked at me, nodded his head in approval and said hello. He never said a word about the change in my hair or "stash."

When I walked down the hall towards Harry Barfield's office, assistant general manager John Duvall looked at my "stash and hair." He also nodded and said hello. He also never said a word about the hair.

I walk into Harry's office, he puts down his White Owl cigar, nods, smiles and says. "Cutler, how are you? Good to see you. Sit down." No one said a word about my hair and "stash." I had a contract in my hands in about ten minutes. I've never read a contract so quickly. I never tried to counter for more money. I was *desperate*—but, luckily for me, so were they.

Here's the rest of the story on why I got hired.

Tom Hammond was LEX18's main sports anchor. Tom Hammond left and became one of the top TV network sportscasters. I can't tell you the number, but LEX18 looked through a lot of tapes, and they couldn't find anyone to replace Tom—either they couldn't afford them, or they got turned down, or they didn't like the tape. This search went on for a long time. THEY WERE DESPERATE! John Ray later admitted they were desperate. I don't get hired in Lexington if they're not desperate.

I'll never forget when I first met Mark Sok, who was the weekend sports anchor. "You're Alan Cutler," he said. "Nice to meet you. By the way, I don't know who you are. I don't care how good you are. *PLEASE* take this job."

Sok was tired of working seven days a week all by himself.

I was desperate. LEX18 was desperate. That's how it all began.

Part 2 (1952-1980)

Memorable Stories from the Past

7

The Mickey Mantle Story
that Shaped My Life

Jim Bouton wrote a book called Ball Four in 1970 that changed sports. Previously, there had been this unwritten rule that you couldn't talk about the personal side of athletes and what they went through. In his book, Bouton—who pitched for the New York Yankees—put in some wild and crazy stories about the Yankees...including my hero Mickey Mantle. To say they weren't flattering would be a huge understatement. Bouton broke the code of silence.

Ball Four was powerful. The New York Public Library had it on their list for *Books of the Century*. It was the only sports related book on that list.

Baseball commissioner Bowie Kuhn called *Ball Four* "detrimental to baseball," and he did everything he could to make Bouton sign a statement stating that the book was fictional. Bouton didn't give in.

For years, Bouton was hurt that the Yankees wouldn't invite him to their annual Old-Timers' Day, which is one of the great events in baseball. The Yankees finally gave in, but it was only after Mickey Mantle had passed away.

A hundred years ago when Babe Ruth played, sportswriters knew he liked to have a good time. They would joke about things he did, but most turned a blind eye when it came time to bang on their typewriters. Grantland Rice, one of the great sportswriters during Babe Ruth's time with the Yankees, believed it was his job to make heroes out of athletes.

In today's world, Babe Ruth—who made the Yankees pay him more money than Herbert Hoover, the President of the United States—would have trouble being Babe Ruth. Babe's logic on his huge salary? He had a better year than the president.

Today, Ruth, who hit a record 714 home runs and also doubled as a great pitcher, wouldn't be nearly as protected by the media. It was easier being Babe Ruth back then than it would be today because today's media would put a lot more pressure on a superstar like him.

Here's a sad story about "the Mick" (Mickey Mantle) that had a lot to do with my workaholic attitude.

1968 was Mickey Mantle's last year. Everybody knew he was done. Mickey admitted that he drank too much. Plus, his knees were shot. I just happened to be watching this Yankees game on TV. They were playing Baltimore. Mantle, who was the Most Valuable Player of the American League three times and made the all-century team in 1999, hit a two-run pinch-hit home run to win the game. To me, it's one of the most exciting plays in sports. I'm cheering like crazy because it's Mickey Mantle.

Here's what I didn't know. The night before, Jim Bouton told me that Mickey Mantle got so drunk that one of his teammates gave the cabdriver fifty bucks to put Mickey in his cab and haul him back safely to his hotel room. When the game started the next day, Bouton said Mickey stayed in the training room, wrapped in a towel, hung over and sleeping.

Around the fifth inning, Ralph Houk—the Yankees Manager— knows he's going to need a pinch hitter later in the game. He also knows that Mantle is sleeping off a hangover, so he decides to get him ready. Houk was a tough guy, but rather than go wake up Mickey Mantle, he sends somebody else to get him.

Mickey's not very happy to be woken up. He slowly gets his uniform on, comes out of the dugout, goes up to the plate…and BOOM…hits a home run! Not only does the Yankees' bench go crazy, but Baltimore's bench can't believe it either. Bouton said that everybody in Baltimore's dugout knew that Mickey was drunk and hung over.

Mickey comes back to the dugout and sits down. A couple of his teammates pick him up and push him out of the dugout to wave to the fans one more time. Mickey Mantle often gets credit for making popular those celebrations you see today, where baseball players come out and wave to the fans in the stands. This would be his last time in Baltimore, so when Mickey waved to the fans, they gave him a standing ovation out of respect. It was their way of saying goodbye to him.

One of his teammates pounds him on the shoulder and shouts, "Mickey, Mickey, Mickey, how'd you do it, how'd you do it?" …Mickey says, "I hit the *middle* ball."

Here's what's sad. Despite Mickey Mantle hitting 536 home runs over the course of his illustrious eighteen-year career with the Yankees, he never took care of himself. He was an alcoholic. Alcohol, at times, has been a huge problem in sports—and especially in baseball back then.

After he retired, Mickey had a lot of regrets about what he could have done if he had just taken better care of himself. You see, Mickey's father, Mutt, died at thirty-nine from Hodgkin's disease. Mickey, who was crushed when his best friend died, thought he wouldn't live long, so he was a big party man. Mickey Mantle is one of the greatest base-ball players of all time, yet he was hounded by the fact that he never lived up to his potential. One of the greatest players of all time could have been *THE GREATEST* player of all time. The point of the message is that whoever you are and whatever you do, be the best you can be. Whatever your God-given ability is, try to squeeze the most out of it.

That's the motto that I've tried to live by. Even at the end of my career, I was still trying to get better. I'd rip my stories apart looking at what I could have done better. Even with my big ego, I was always looking at my work very critically and trying to make it better.

Be the best that you can be. No regrets allowed.

8

Hebrew School with Jerry Seinfeld

One of my best friends in college was Carnac. I loved Carnac. He was a good writer, but he partied too hard and flunked out on purpose. Every year, when I went back to New York, we would get together...and then all of a sudden, I couldn't find him.

Carnac used to go to local comedy clubs on Long Island in New York. He remembered seeing Jerry Seinfeld, the famous stand-up comedian and TV sitcom star, many times early in his career. He said Seinfeld was terrible. Fine—a lot of people aren't very good when they start out.

Fast forward many years later, and I'm talking to my mother on the phone. She asks me if I remembered going to Hebrew school with Seinfeld. I didn't. Hebrew school was after regular school, and I would go a couple of times a week. At that time, we lived in Massapequa on Long Island in New York.

Up to that point, I had never watched Seinfeld's show. From that point on, after the conversation with my mother, I became a big fan and watched the show all the time.

9

"Mahvelous" Billy Crystal

I grew up playing basketball with Billy Crystal. Yes—the actor and comedian. Billy is four years older than me. We both grew up in Long Beach on Long Island in New York. We both lived close to East School, an elementary school where we played ball. In those days—you just headed over to the court. Kids don't do that today. I've driven by that court for over forty years, and rarely now do you ever see anyone playing. From the time I moved there in the eighth grade until the time I left for New Mexico, I played ball at East School. I loved that place.

Billy Crystal was a good basketball player. When I was around fourteen years old, my friend Bobby Everett and I were just sitting at the East School courts after playing ball. I was drinking a Nedicks orange soda and eating Twinkies—that was my go-to snack. Bobby had his RC Cola and Ring Dings. Billy comes over and starts doing the funniest Howard Cosell/Muhammad Ali impersonation I have ever heard.

Ali is the most popular boxer of all time, and Cosell was a lawyer who became the most important and by far the most outspoken sportscaster of his time. They had a wonderful act together. I was a big fan of both.

Fast forward to 1977, and I'm in Colorado Springs calling a baseball game for the Grand Junction Eagles. After the game, I'm in a fourth class hotel watching this small black and white TV when the *Howard Cosell Roast* just happens to come on.

The show's almost over and here comes Billy Crystal. They almost didn't put Billy on because the show was running late, and the producer didn't know if he would be able to fit him in.

Fortunately they did, because Billy Crystal does the exact same Howard Cosell/Muhammad Ali impersonation *word for word* that he did

35

testing me and Bobby Everett at East School. I'm screaming at the tiny TV with my face just a couple of inches from the screen. I was freaking out that this was Billy Crystal doing the exact routine he was doing when we were kids. It's not a stretch to say that Billy Crystal's life changed after that routine.

I've never contacted Billy Crystal. He probably wouldn't even remember me if I did. But it's still pretty neat to say that Bobby and I, after playing basketball at East School, once served as his props.

10

A Punch in the Gut from Larry Brown

Larry Brown was the all-time leading scorer at Long Beach High, where I went to high school. He went on to be a star for North Carolina. As a coach, Larry Brown is the only one in the history of basketball to win both an NCAA national championship (Kansas in 1988) and an NBA title (Detroit 2004). He was enshrined in the Basketball Hall of Fame in 2002.

There were pickup basketball games in the summertime in Long Beach that attracted some terrific talent. People would come from all over to play in these games. Lew Alcindor, before he became Kareem Abdul-Jabbar, even showed up. That was before my time. A lot of players would play basketball and then spend the rest of the day at the beach, which was an easy walk from the basketball courts.

In 1968, while I was still in high school, I frequently played against former college stars—some of them with big bellies—who were in their 40s and 50s. There was this one guy who played for St. John's, who was a couple of inches taller and about seventy pounds heavier than me, who never missed a hook shot. I've never understood why more guys don't shoot hook shots. I don't know why it's not taught more. You can't block the shot. All you have to do is work on making it. I've said this for decades. It's just stupid why more guys don't use it.

Larry Brown shows up. It's the same year he was named the MVP of the ABA All-Star game. He arrives in a sports car wearing a basketball jersey and shorts. He immediately inserts himself into the game and takes over the entire court. After all, he's Larry "frickin'" Brown—returning home as a triumphant ABA All-Star hero. Larry knows everyone on the court except me.

We're playing for a few minutes against his team, and I go up for a rebound. I feel a guy behind me, but I don't look to see who it is. I stick my butt out to block him out. That's something that nobody does today anymore—another lost art. I had to do it because I couldn't jump, and I wasn't big. What I didn't realize was that I had boxed out Larry Brown. I pushed him away. It was no big deal. Just playing ball.

I remember the guy from St. John's saying to me in a gruff voice, "Kid, watch yourself." After about five minutes, I'm going up for another rebound and Larry Brown sneaks behind me, takes his fist, and punches me in the stomach as hard as he could. I never saw it coming. It wasn't even his elbow, but his fist that he buried into my stomach.

I couldn't breathe. I was pretty mad. I didn't want to get into a fight with Larry Brown, but I wasn't going to back down either. The guy from St. John's puts his hands up and gives me that "don't do it" look. It took me a while to regain my composure—but I did, and we went back to playing. Larry played a couple more games before he took off. He never said a word to me.

Fast forward to a few years ago. Larry Brown shows up in Lexington to visit UK coach John Calipari. He and Cal are good friends. In fact, Larry Brown's the one who helped Cal get back on his feet after he was fired from the New Jersey Nets job. When Brown was the head coach in Philadelphia, he got himself thrown out of the game against New Jersey on purpose, and had Cal, one of his assistant coaches, coach the team. The players won that one for Cal. So I asked DeWayne Peevy, the UK Basketball SID at the time, if I could meet with Larry Brown during his visit.

We met after practice. Brown had a big smile when I told him his cousin, Arnie Hittleman, was my soccer coach in high school. I then tell Larry the story about him punching me in the stomach. He listens patiently, then grabs my arm and says, "I'm really sorry." I start laughing and tell him he doesn't need to apologize. He apologizes a second time. For me, since the day it happened, it's always been a funny story.

We talked about Long Beach for a few minutes, and then Larry Brown wanted to know how Cal was doing. Cal's his guy, so we spent the next ten minutes or so just talking about Cal.

The next time I saw Larry Brown, he didn't remember my name, but he did say, "Hey Long Beach, good to see you."

11

I'm an IDIOT!

I refused to get a telephone when I worked TV in Boise, Idaho. My thought was that I worked so many extra hours, and they refused to pay me overtime—which was illegal—and they were paying me nothing...that if they needed me they could come knock on my door. They never had to do that because I was always at the station. When I worked Boise State football games on Saturdays, they never paid me for that either. They were supposed to pay me or give me a comp day, but they refused to.

In the process of looking for other jobs, I didn't want to use the station phone because I didn't think it was the right thing to do, even though others were doing it—and I also didn't want anyone to know my business. I would make my phone calls at a payphone that was outside at Kmart and about a block from my apartment. I remember being there in the wintertime, putting quarters in, freezing, and making phone calls. Crazy—but it's true.

Shirley Barish was a powerful agent. She told me that she loved my resume tape. She had this deep, gravelly voice—and liked to call people "honey." She told me she was going to get me my next job. Shirley also told me that I was "limited,"—that I couldn't work out west—because I was from New York. I sounded eastern, I looked eastern, and she saw me ending up in a major city back east. She didn't see me working in Portland, Seattle, or Los Angeles. She saw me working in New York, Boston, or Philadelphia. She could see me being the No. 1 person in one of those big markets after a couple of stops, but she couldn't see me being the No. 1 person out west. She was surprised I was in Boise. When I told her they were desperate when they hired me—she had a good laugh.

I got a call from Shirley one day, and she told me the public TV station in New Jersey was starting a newscast. Remember, I'm making no money at all. I was offered the job, and it was a lot more money than I was currently making, but they didn't want to fly me in until I signed the contract because they were trying to save money. They offered me $25,000 a year to be the sports director on TV Monday through Friday. The only catch was they wanted me to "tone down my act."

What does that mean? *I'm real.* They told me I had to be more conservative on TV. "Honey, just do this, and I'll get you into New York City," Shirley said. "You'll go there for two years, and I'll have them put in the contract that you can go to New York City. Just do this." I'm an idiot because I told Shirley that I didn't want to tone my act down— "I just want to be me." Shirley pleaded with me to listen to her. She tried to convince me that I didn't need to change *everything* about me— just a tweak here and there.

I turned the job down. Who knows what would have happened, but it would have gotten me just outside of the New York area. When I told my brother I turned the job down, he said, "Are you an idiot?"

Maybe I was an idiot—but I was just that stubborn that I was GOING TO BE ME. My life could have been totally different. 1 could have bombed, or I could have made it big in New Jersey. For years when I went home to visit, I would watch their newscast and always wonder what an idiot I was for turning that offer down.

After that, there was no more Shirley. She wouldn't pick up the phone when I called or return any of my phone calls. I called her at least six times. Her secretary felt sorry for me because I told her that I was sorry and asked her to tell Shirley that I was sorry and that I should have listened to her. Shirley wanted to control my career and I didn't listen, so she was done with me. That one hurt. A friend of mine called me—someone who Shirley had helped become quite successful—and cursed me out. He said I was the dumbest New Yorker of all time— that Shirley was going to make my career…but we were now finished.

12

No Filming at Lambeau Field

It's 1980—I'm in Boise doing TV sports, and I get flown in to be the sports director of a local TV station in Green Bay, Wisconsin. In a station like that, when they fly you in, they're normally doing it with the thought process that they're going to hire you. TV stations often have small budgets for flying talent in. They told me they were flying me in and unless the interview goes poorly, the job is mine.

I was in New York on vacation when the news director asked me to come to Green Bay. They fly me in, take me around town, show me what apartment they suggested I live in, and give me all kinds of advice to help make the transition easier.

They took me to Lambeau Field. Ohhhh! I'm thinking to myself—the Green Bay Packers! I walked around the field and was in heaven. This is the home of Vince Lombardi for crying out loud. I was excited. Sure, it was cold in Green Bay. I'm not a fan of cold weather, but it didn't matter. I can live here for two to three years before getting a big-time job. That was my thought process. I'm even thinking about how this will make up for turning the job down in New Jersey. I couldn't stop smiling as I was walking on the field.

I went out to lunch with the general manager, and everything's good. When I go back to speak with the news director a second time, everything's fine…and then it all falls apart on a dime.

They wanted me to do a weekly fishing report—OK, I was fine with that. In fact, I started a fishing report here in Lexington when I first came here. True story. Everybody said I was crazy. I had my weekend sportscaster, Mark Sok, help me do it—and we had a lot of calls and letters about how much people liked it.

Anyway, I told them that I'd be glad to do the fishing segment one morning every week. I didn't mind working extra hours. If I had to go out in the morning on a day that I'm anchoring and working until midnight, I was fine with that. If there were no interviews for me to do, I could just have the sports photographer go out and get the shots we needed.

It suddenly got very quiet in the room. I can remember it like it was yesterday. The news director is staring at me. *What happened?* It turns out that the station didn't have a sports photographer. They expected me to shoot all of my own sports. They weren't going to help me get any video. This was a sports director's job Monday through Friday, and you had to shoot all your own stuff!

I told them the interview was over because I'm NOT going to be the photographer in addition to the job they hired me to do. I work so hard and put in so many hours—I'm not going to shoot—I planned to spend my time on the phone chasing down stories. "You might as well have someone take me to the airport," I said. The news director started turning white. He said to me in a tone that wasn't friendly, "I can't believe you don't shoot." I snapped back, "I can't believe you didn't ask me."

They told me everybody at this level shoots. Green Bay is a much bigger TV market than Boise. They were surprised I didn't shoot in Boise. The station in Boise never asked me to, and I wouldn't have done it if they did. I wouldn't have taken the job. I'm not going to be a shooter. *It's not negotiable.* There are too many places in this country where I can get a job without shooting.

I thanked them for flying me in and told the news director to take me back to the airport. The news director looked nervous. I figured the general manager would get on his case because they wasted money on a plane ticket that they never should have bought. I think he was about to yell and scream. I went to shake his hand, and he sheepishly stuck his out. I thanked him again, grabbed my bag, walked into the newsroom and went up to the assignment manager and told him I wasn't going to be working there. I needed a ride to the airport.

I did the same thing in Dallas and Tampa Bay on interviews I was flown in for jobs that I knew were mine. I knew that if you let TV management push you around before you get there, you are finished. Besides, I was just being honest. TV management, like a lot of businesses, don't like their employees being "real" with them.

I'm sitting in the airport for a couple of hours before my return flight, drinking a cup of coffee, when I hear over the airport PA sys-

tem, "ALAN CUTLER, YOU HAVE A PHONE CALL." Green
Bay's not the biggest airport in the world, and I've never been paged in
an airport before. Who could possibly be calling me? My mother
knows I'm in Green Bay. Judy knows I'm in Green Bay. My brother
and sister knew I was in Green Bay. Who was going to page me? Plus, I
was on vacation. Remember, there were no cell phones back then.

I pick up the phone at the airport service desk, and it's the news director of the TV station in Green Bay. Earlier, they had offered me
$17,500 a year to be sports director. I know that doesn't sound like
much, but it was a raise over what I was making at the time in Boise.
Plus it was NFL Football, and I was closer to a lot of major markets
that would find out who I was. I also did my homework before I
showed up. I knew they weren't going to pay me $50,000 a year, but I
was expecting to be making $24,000 to $28,000 just walking through
the door based on some phone conversations I had with people about
what the market would pay.

I wasn't happy with the $17,500. He had offered it to me at the be-
ginning of our meeting. I was going to wait until the end of the day to
ask for more. Usually if everything went well, they'd come up with a
second offer if you asked.

The news director told me over the phone that he'd up his offer to
$22,500. I asked him if they would pay me that AND get me a photog-
rapher for the weekly fishing report. When he said "No," I thanked
him and told him he could double my salary and I still wouldn't work
for him. It's not what I wanted to do with my life. It's not something
I'm good at. I want to break stories. I want to get to know people. I
don't want to shoot.

He couldn't believe I was turning him down again. The simple fact
was that I wasn't going to shoot. It was not a negotiating ploy. It then
got really quiet on the phone. I said thanks, and I put the phone down.

I turned down a lot of jobs.

13

The One Time I Drank

My last time on TV in Boise, Idaho was on a Friday. I had a lot of friends in the newsroom. They convinced me to go out after the six o'clock news and have a drink before coming back to the station to put the final show together. Since I knew it was going to be my last show, I'd already put most of the show together the night before. It consisted of all the fun things I had done during my time there—such as Boise State beating Eastern Kentucky to win the national championship, along with other goofy stories. So, the tapes were already cut and ready to go.

The problem was that a whole lot of our TV crew went to a bar a couple of blocks from the station before the final show. I didn't just have one drink that evening...I didn't have two drinks...I had enough that a couple of friends had to walk me back to the TV station. How stupid could I be? The fact was that I had never drank and gone on TV before. Plus, the crew from the late news was planning to take me out *after* the show.

I got back to the station at about a quarter after nine. Scripts were due before 9:30 for the ten o'clock newscast. The director was upset and started yelling at me, wondering how I was going to write a script for the news. I told him to relax. I'd just give him a list of the tapes we were doing and cue him on the air when it was time to go to the next tape. He had directed my shows for a long time, and I thought we'd be fine. There was no script.

Because it was my last show, they gave me a ton of extra time. By then, everyone at the station who I had been partying with had packed the studio. The show goes off, and for most of the show, it's one of best shows I've ever done. I'm thinking that I'm leaving Boise with a resume tape—it was so good. I wish I had a tape of the show.

Then, about five minutes in—which is way longer than I'd usually get to do a sportscast—I made one mistake. I fumbled a word but quickly managed to get it back together and finished with a bang, as the people who were watching in the studio started clapping. I was mad because I almost had a perfect ad-lib for a seven-minute show without a script—especially in my condition. The director did a fantastic job. There was just that one minor little flub. I was so mad at myself while everybody there was cheering.

I'll admit—I was excited and scared before I went on that night. *You don't drink and then go on TV.* That was one wild day.

14

Late with the Logo—Jerry West

One of the best things about doing my job was getting to meet some of my heroes—and getting to see them as real people. I put Jerry West on that list. He was as clutch as anyone who ever played in the NBA. He was the co-captain of the US Olympic team that won the gold in 1960. He was a very good defensive player—but he was famous for his offense. He still holds the all-time record for most points averaged in a playoff series—46.

I cursed at the greatest shot that Jerry West ever made—that went against me—and screamed at the TV set. In 1970, during the NBA Finals against my New York Knicks, West hit a 60-footer that sent the game into overtime. I had never yelled at a TV any worse than that. When Duke's Laettner hit the shot against Kentucky in the NCAA Tournament, I didn't scream. I was heartbroken for those kids. There's a difference.

Jerry West is not only the logo, or the symbol for the NBA—he's not only in the Naismith Hall of Fame as a player—he also doubles as one of the best NBA executives of all time.

While he was the general manager of the Lakers, he came to Lexington to do some scouting. I was covering the game at Rupp Arena and asked for an interview. I asked if he had three minutes for an interview. He quickly declined.

"No, not now, I'm working," he said, "But if you want to meet me tomorrow, I'd be happy to. I'll meet you at 11:15 at the Marriott where I'm staying."

The next morning, I walked in with the camera at 11:10 thinking I'm cool. West is sitting in a big chair. I walk up to him and before we can shake hands, he says to me, "You're late."

I'm speechless. Remember, this is Jerry West. Are there ten better players in the history of the NBA? This is an idol of mine. This is my hero. This is a guy who did everything right in my eyes, and he's telling me I'm late.

I sort of stumble around and manage to tell him that I thought the interview was scheduled at 11:15.

"I've been sitting here since 11:00," he tells me. "I'm always fifteen minutes early."

I apologized profusely and assumed he didn't want to do the interview. Boy, was I wrong.

"Sure, I'll do the interview," he said with a smile.

It ended up being a great interview. He made some wonderful comments about the history of Kentucky Basketball. He obviously followed Kentucky and knew a lot about them. I don't think we talked for long, about four minutes, but I used every single soundbite over a few days—which rarely happens.

Generally speaking, a lot of NBA people are guarded when they come on camera because they don't want to say too much about a particular player. They are careful to not give away trade secrets. But as an executive at his level, Jerry West was a lot more open and honest than I anticipated. Here I was, just a local guy—and he's one of the greatest superstars of all time being kind, caring, considerate, funny, and very open.

I'll never forget it. I was late—even though I was five minutes early.

15

Happy Chandler's My Old Kentucky Home

One of the most interesting people I've ever met is Happy Chandler. He was a lovable old man...who was full of *bleep*... was really smart... who accomplished so much... who knew how to play politics... who lost a lot of political battles... who loved a fight. He was so *happy* and appreciative that someone like myself—who had a thirst for learning about Kentucky's history— started to pay attention to him even as he got older.

As people get older and are forgotten—especially if they were somebody famous—they can be very appreciative if you paid any attention to them. It has nothing to do with sports. It's just a trait in people that I've seen a number of times. I recognized that in Happy.

Happy made enemies quickly because he didn't back down from strong and controversial issues he believed in. He was one of those guys that you either loved him or you hated him. He loved telling stories, and I was what you would call "fresh meat." I was a new audience for stories that Happy had told countless times. I soaked it all up. I often wondered—and I mean this with no disrespect—how many of the things he told me were true. Happy liked to amplify. If he caught a fish, it was a big fish.

Here's something else you probably didn't know about the man who was a senator, a lieutenant governor, served two terms as governor of Kentucky, and was one of the strongest and most successful baseball commissioners who was voted into Baseball's Hall of Fame in 1982.

With a great deal of pride, Happy bragged about being the scout for the Centre College Praying Colonels football team located in Danville, Kentucky. On October 29, 1921, Centre defeated Harvard 6-0 in what is considered one of the greatest upsets in college football history. Harvard had won the national championship in 1919 and 1920, and they

48

didn't lose any games during those seasons. Happy had diagrammed plays and taken copious notes on Harvard leading up to the game, which helped Centre secure the victory. The story goes that Happy Chandler brought the game ball back to campus on the train.

A lot of people have forgotten about Happy Chandler. Almost no one remembers that he coached the UK women's basketball team back in 1923.

Happy left the Senate in 1945 partly because he got a huge raise when he became baseball commissioner.

Happy Chandler was regarded as a players' commissioner. He started baseball's great pension system and approved the contract for Jackie Robinson to join the Brooklyn Dodgers in 1947. I sat in Happy's house in the early 1980s, and he told me he prayed about that decision. "I couldn't meet my maker some day and know that I didn't allow those boys to have the same opportunities as the white boys," he told me.

Branch Rickey, the Dodgers general manager, deserves the most credit because he spearheaded bringing the Black athlete into baseball, and he handpicked Jackie Robinson to be the first African American to play in the Major Leagues. Jackie Robinson was picked for his temperament and for the man that he was—there were better African American baseball players at that time. Jackie Robinson was a great athlete, but many believed that baseball wasn't his best sport. He was also a star in track and in football. He had a great baseball career—but he was picked because of his ability to handle the barrage of threats that were sure to come his way. He was picked because he also understood that he wasn't allowed to answer back for three years when confronted. Later in life, he became a strong vocal advocate of civil rights.

Jackie was also named the Most Valuable Player in the National League in 1949 and enjoyed a six-year period where he was one of the best players in baseball.

Branch Rickey picked Jackie Robinson, but Happy Chandler approved the contract. Almost all of the baseball owners were still opposed to integration at the time this decision was made. Here's something that Happy was really smart about. If he could see a trend of something that was going to happen, he was going to be the one to push it through because he wanted to take the credit. He was never afraid of taking criticism. It was like something that lit a fire in him.

One of the first stories I did for ESPN was in 1981 when the Negro League Hall of Fame had a reunion in Ashland, Kentucky. Satchel Paige was there in a wheelchair with tubes in his nose when I interviewed him. I was in awe of talking to Satchel Paige, one of, if not *THE* greatest, pitchers of all time.

Paige was by far the biggest star in the Negro Leagues. He was famous for telling his infielders to sit down because he was going to strike the batter out. He was upset that Jackie Robinson was picked to be the first African American to play in the Big Leagues.

In his autobiography he said, "Signing Jackie like they did still hurt me deep down. I'd been the guy who'd started all that big talk about letting us in the big time. I'd been the one who'd opened up the Major League parks to colored teams. I'd been the one who the white boys wanted to go barnstorming against."

On July 7, 1948—his forty-second birthday—Paige became the oldest player to debut in the Major Leagues. He went 6-1 with an outstanding 2.48 ERA in half of a season, helping the Cleveland Indians win the World Series. At the age of forty-two!!!! He pitched one more season with Cleveland, then played for three years with the St. Louis Browns. At age fifty-nine on September 25, 1965, Paige became the oldest player in Major League history, marking the occasion by throwing three scoreless innings and allowing just one hit for the Kansas City Athletics. He finished his Big-League career with a 28-31 record, 32 saves and a 3.29 ERA. I remember the rocking chair he sat in—in the bullpen.

Hearing all those barnstorming stories—and how all in the Negro League lived their lives, and what they had to go through eating in separate restaurants, and not drinking from water fountains—made a big impression on me. I didn't know a lot of this stuff growing up in New York. Up until all the protests happened in the sixties, I didn't really have a good understanding of what went on in the South at all. When I heard those stories, I was shocked. How could people treat other people like that?

Happy Chandler always wanted to be remembered as a champion for changing what was then called the color line. But I also remember how Happy used the N-word, which got him kicked off the UK Board of Trustees in 1988. They did the right thing. At that time, people talked a certain way and that was accepted, even though it shouldn't have been.

One of the reasons I love living in Kentucky is because the Commonwealth is rich with great characters. And being on TV, I was able to meet so many of them. Happy Chandler was such a character, even well into his eighties. I remember once while I was visiting with him in his home in Versailles, Happy invited me to sit down right next to him. "Partner, come here, feel my bicep," he would say as he flexed his muscle. "I'm the strongest old son of a gun in Kentucky." And then he'd start laughing. He had a big laugh.

Here's another quote from one of the TV interviews with Happy that I'll never forget. He was talking about how he felt about all the people who didn't like him. "The one who is bitter is the one who loses," he said to me. "Besides, I outlived all those sons of bitches."

The second to the last time Happy Chandler sang *My Old Kentucky Home* in Rupp Arena—I was on the court. After he was done, I walked around the court in front of everybody and gave him a big hug. It was the best rendition of *My Old Kentucky Home* that I've ever heard. It was with power, feeling, guts, and soul. It's one of the most moving things I've seen in all my career in Lexington. The place went crazy. There were old-timers who had tears in their eyes. That was Happy's way of belting out his love for the Commonwealth. I also thought that that was his way of saying goodbye.

There's no doubt that Happy Chandler loved Kentucky as much as anybody I've ever met.

16

Adolph And Herky Rupp

I never met Adolph Rupp. The Baron of the Bluegrass won 876 games, four national championships, 27 SEC regular-season championships, and 13 SEC tournament championships from 1930-1972. He was forced to retire in 1972—long before I arrived in Lexington.

One of the best stories I ever did on television was with Herky, his son.

I really liked Herky. As direct as this book is, I hesitate to tell you that I always felt sorry for him. He tried to do the right thing. Being the son of Adolph Rupp and spending his entire life defending his father wore him down. Being related to Adolph Rupp wore a lot of people down, and I'll bet most of you reading this didn't realize that.

I could care less that John Calipari makes eight million dollars a year coaching UK Basketball. I actually think it's a bargain for everything that he does. Yet, there are coaches who make two million that I think are vastly overpaid. At times, Calipari's kids have gone through a ton of garbage on social media. This kind of thing drives me crazy. They seem to handle it well, but it's *NOT right*. These are people's children. It's family. Scream at Rupp. Scream at Cal. Scream at Tubby. *BUT LEAVE THEIR FAMILIES ALONE!*

You just can't understand unless you've walked a mile in their shoes. That comment you will see a lot in this book. I'm not just talking about immediate family members either. It's even been difficult at times for Chip Rupp, Herky's son, being Adolph Rupp's grandson. More on that in the next chapter.

I'm a peanut compared to those guys in regard to publicity, but there's a reason I kept my family out of everything I did at LEX18. When my son, J.J., was winning many national championship trophies in karate as a kid, WLEX-TV's Ryan Lemond more than once asked me why I didn't do a story on him. *No way!!* I didn't want to expose him. He had to deal with all that stuff enough at school. J.J. was at basketball camp once, and one of the campers wanted to know what kind of car his dad was driving. *Why would you want to know what kind of car I'm driving?* BECAUSE I'M ALAN CUTLER. If I were the insurance salesman next door, no one would care. So I was always very conscious of keeping my family out of it when I was on TV.

In Herky's basement, he showed me letters—and there were many dating back to as early as the 1950s—that they sent to the FBI *threatening Rupp* if he ever recruited African Americans—although that wasn't the term used in the letters. As I read some of those disgusting letters, not only did it make me angry, but it made me think about how similar these letters were to what Hank Aaron got before he broke Babe Ruth's home run record, and some of the awful things Jackie Robinson had to go through breaking the color line in Major League Baseball. *No one should have to deal with this.*

When it came to Hank Aaron and Jackie Robinson, to say they got hundreds of times more hate mail would be a very low figure. What they went through was *TONS worse.* Unless you experience something like it, I don't think it's possible to understand what all these men and others went through.

I was honored that Herky trusted me enough to show those letters to me. He told me no TV camera had been in his basement before I interviewed him that day. That footage is something else I should have saved.

I once did an hour-long segment about race on my sports talk show on WLW radio, the best radio station in Cincinnati—and I was followed all the way home to Lexington. The car stayed most of the night by my house. I kept a baseball bat by my bed and didn't get any sleep. The same thing happened the next night after I did another show. Same car...and it looked like the same two people. I didn't tell Judy about it for quite a while, and I probably shouldn't have said anything at all. The crazy things that go through your head. And again, I'm nobody compared to Rupp, Aaron, or Jackie Robinson.

I didn't sleep for three to four days. It made me wonder how many sleepless nights Jackie Robinson and Hank Aaron and others had.

I don't care what you believe or what you look like—or the color of your skin—*NO ONE* should have to deal with it.

I called Darryl Parks, who I liked. He was my boss at WLW, and he

CUT TO THE CHASE!

taught me a lot about doing a talk show. I told him what happened, and he blew it off. "Cutman, Willie gets threats all the time. It's no big deal." Willie is Bill Cunningham, who has been a very strong personality on WLW for a long time. As I hung up the phone, I was ticked off.

People often form opinions without researching all the facts. I think we all have been guilty of that. One of the greatest debates in the history of Kentucky sports has been whether Adolph Rupp was a racist or not.

I think Adolph Rupp was a product of his time. Initially I was shocked when S.T. Roach, the very classy late great African American basketball coach at Dunbar High in Lexington, told me he never met Adolph Rupp. I was speechless because Dunbar had a lot of very talented African American ball players. Why didn't Rupp try to recruit them? Did Adolph Rupp not establish a relationship because he knew people *wouldn't allow him* to recruit them? Yet, on the other hand, Adolph Rupp had an African American basketball player on his high school basketball team before he came to Kentucky.

Herky told me that his father would recruit his grandmother if she could win for Kentucky. It's not cut and dry. To me, whether Rupp was a racist is a debate that will live on.

Rupp was far from perfect. And this won't be popular. I believe if Rupp thought he was going to recruit some of S.T. Roach's best players, he would have reached out to him. But because he either couldn't, or wasn't going to, or wasn't allowed to—he wasn't going to waste his time.

That's the part I've struggled with. I believe that Rupp believed that he "couldn't" recruit Black athletes, *but I blame him for not being much stronger and not trying to*. He was Adolph Rupp for crying out loud. He had a lot of power. He could have helped change a lot of things in the South.

What's sad is, if Rupp did the right thing, I'm absolutely convinced he would have won one or two more NCAA championships because there were so many great Black basketball players in Kentucky—much more back then than today.

If that sounds cold—and it probably does—I think that was on Adolph Rupp.

17

Rupp—The Head Coach at Duke?

One of the most fascinating things about Rupp is that after he was forced to retire at Kentucky, Duke offered him—and he accepted—the head coaching job with the Blue Devils. The deal was that Herky would be his assistant and then become head coach when Adolph retired. Can you imagine how all of the history between Kentucky and Duke changes if that had happened?

Think about this. Kentucky's national championship 94-88 win against Duke in '78, the Laettner shot in '92, and the time Kentucky rallied to beat Duke in the '98 NCAA regionals on their way to their seventh national title—how would that all have changed had Adolph Rupp become the coach at Duke? It's crazy to think about. Absolutely crazy!!

Here's why Rupp never wound up at Duke. After he accepted the job, Herky told me he lost his farm manager. Rupp's farm was a major source of income for his family. In August before the season, when it was time for Rupp to move to Duke, he called and told them he couldn't come because he had to find a farm manager. That was his priority. When Herky told me this on camera, I was speechless. I was shocked Rupp didn't go.

I assumed that Herky Rupp had regrets about that. He said he would have loved to have gone with his father and eventually become the head coach at Duke, but it wasn't something that consumed him or that he gave a lot of thought to. He told me he had a good life, and he was happy.

Joe B. Hall, who became the UK coach after Rupp, said many times that replacing a legend is one of the toughest things to do. When legendary UCLA head coach John Wooden retired, Joe said UCLA should have hired him. "Why ruin two lives?" Joe said jokingly. "You never want to be the person following the legend. You want to be the person following the person following the legend."

Here's another debate I've also encountered about Adolph Rupp. Coaches back then were dictators. Do you think Rupp would have been able to coach in today's environment? There is no way he could treat players today the way he did back then. No way!! I'd like to think that he would have changed with the times.

Rupp was smart and did a lot of things that were way ahead of his time. I've talked to many of his former players who told me that no one but Rupp talked in practice. There were unique drills that Rupp would have the players do. At times he did drills where he didn't want the ball to bounce at all. He definitely had his way of doing things. Ralph Beard, one of UK's greatest players, told me there were times all you heard was the sound of the rubber from their sneakers hitting the floor. He told me it was a beautiful sound, and they did the same drills over and over until they were really good at it.

I've interviewed a lot of Rupp's former players. I can't remember one telling me that they didn't hate him when they played for him. Many said that years later, they understood and accepted it. Some told me that years later, they *still* hated the man. And some of these former players were in their seventies when they told me that.

Could Rupp have handled coaching today? Just like the racist question, you'll have to decide for yourself.

What might seem a little crazy to you is that Chip Rupp, Herky's son, also had to deal with some issues because he was the grandson of the most famous man in Kentucky.

18

A Chip Off the Old Block

In the early 1980s, I did a TV feature on a very good high school player. His name was Chip Rupp. I was very surprised how calm and mature he was. Although Chip was a very good basketball player, he knew that wasn't the reason I wanted to do the story. I wasn't sure they were going to let me do the story. But, coach Al Prewitt, one of the great ones, told me after the interview that he trusted me.

Chip's grandfather, Adolph Rupp, was UK's winningest coach ever.

Chip started his college career at Vanderbilt, but he wasn't the star on Henry Clay's 1983 State Champion team that beat Carlisle County 35-33 in triple overtime on a shot at the buzzer by Greg Bates. I can still picture Bates' winning shot off his offensive rebound. It remains one of the top fifteen sporting events I covered for TV. The tension at Rupp Arena that day was tremendous.

In 1984, during the Sweet Sixteen, Chip hit two free throws with nineteen seconds left which led Henry Clay to a 70-69 win over Pulaski County.

I want you to try and picture yourself being Chip Rupp—the grandson of Adolph Rupp, arguably the most famous person ever in Kentucky.

"I never understood his fame or notoriety," Chip told me. "He was just my grandfather. We would play *Go Fish* (a card game) for hours. He was never too busy for me." That's Chip talking about what it was like for him as a kid.

Normal certainly would not be the word Chip uses to describe his childhood. "I grew up in a fishbowl," he said. He told me his grandfather had to stop coming to his elementary school basketball games because the crowds were too wild when he was there.

Chip said he's never told this story before, so you're getting another exclusive by reading this book. "In the early 1970s, we received two different kidnapping threats," he explained. "This was around the time of Patty Hearst. They were worried that I was going to be abducted. I had a teacher who would escort me to our car. It was not something they did with any other students. I think they thought my grandfather had a lot of money."

In 1974, Patty Hearst, a nineteen-year-old college student was taken by a group of armed men and women with their guns drawn. Patty's grandfather was the newspaper magnate William Randolph Hearst.

Here's another story about Chip that you may not know. Adolph Rupp III—nicknamed "Chip" at birth—turned down a scholarship at Kentucky because the Wildcats' head coach at the time, Joe B. Hall, quietly told him he was going to retire at the end of the season. Not knowing who his coach was going to be, Chip went to Vanderbilt to play for another former player of his grandfather—C.M. Newton.

To many, Adolph Rupp was a racist. In 2006, the movie *Glory Road*—which was all about Texas Western, with an all Black starting five upsetting all white Kentucky 72-65 to win the NCAA Championship in 1966—exemplified that point. No matter what you thought of the movie, Texas Western's win changed basketball forever. African Americans started receiving opportunities on the court that they always should have had.

Herky, Adolph's son, swore that his father was not a racist. He said Adolph wanted to win more than anything. Herky believed his father would put five people of any color on the court in order to win.

Remember, in the late 1920s—while coaching high school ball—Rupp started William "Mose" Mosely, the first African American to play basketball at Freeport High. In the 1960s, Rupp tried to recruit Wes Unseld and Mike Redd, two great players from Louisville. They were the first two African Americans to be named Mr. Basketball, the award that goes to the best player in Kentucky. Redd won it in 1963 and Unseld in 1964. Unseld, like Rupp, is in the Naismith Memorial Basketball Hall of Fame.

Former UK great Kenny "Sky" Walker played for the Washington Bullets with Wes Unseld. Sky says during a plane ride that Unseld told him that his parents didn't want him to go to Kentucky because of how rough it could be being the first Black basketball player at UK, and because of the racism that existed in the many places they would travel to in the South.

"My grandfather wanted both [Unseld and Redd] and didn't get either," Chip Rupp told me. "It crawls all over me. He's been dead for years, and they keep bringing it up."

"My dad [Herky] went to his grave fighting...," Chip continued. "It bothered him his entire life. He [Rupp] wasn't a saint by any means. Right is right and wrong is wrong. I'm tired of defending him."

When Chip told me that, I got sad. Again, try and walk a mile in his shoes. Chip has always been classy about this controversial subject. I don't know many who would have been as classy as either Herky or Chip on this very sensitive topic. I don't think I could handle myself with the class they have shown.

The year Adolph died, Chip went to Atlanta with him for the Final Four. It was just the two of them. Chip didn't know his grandfather was terminally ill. Rupp was giving a speech at the NABC (the National Association of Basketball Coaches) which was started by Phog Allen— who Rupp not only played for, but he ended up breaking Allen's all-time record for most wins.

"It was one of those Jimmy V moments," Chip explained. "He knew it was going to be his last speech. I remember it brought out some rousing applause. That was March of 1977. He died two days before my birthday."

"I still have his favorite chair from his living room," Chip continued. "He was a fun-loving guy. He had a very caring side, and I got to experience that. Every holiday, he would call up and make sure Santa came by."

Chip and his dad Herky have something else in common. Adolph made sure that Herky scored the first bucket at Memorial Coliseum, and he also told Chip to score the first basket at Rupp Arena before the team held their first practice. That's quite a legacy.

19

The Truth Behind Ralph Beard

Ralph Beard was on the cover of *Sport Magazine* and *Sports Illustrated*. He was also named to the All-NBA team for the 1950-51 season playing for the Indianapolis Olympians, a team that was built around former UK stars.

Beard, who was All-State in four sports at Male High school in Louisville, came to Kentucky at 140 pounds to play football—fullback for Bear Bryant. When Ralph told me that, I just stared at him and shook my head. With a big smile on his face, Ralph said he dislocated both of his shoulders on the first play of football practice, so it was on to basketball.

Ralph Beard gained fame by shutting down Bob Cousy, the superstar from Holy Cross, who was at that time considered the greatest guard in the game. After three years as a consensus first-team All-American at Kentucky (1947, 1948, and 1949) and as part of the 1947-48 UK "Fabulous Five," Beard was on his way to becoming one of the best professional basketball players of all time before he lost his professional career in the infamous Kentucky gambling scandal. They put Ralph in jail in 1951. Beard looked me in the eye and told me that he took the money, but he never shaved points. "Cutler, as a kid I couldn't rub two wooden nickels together," he said to my TV camera. "I had no money. I took the money but played basketball." As a kid, there were times he didn't know where his next meal was going to come from.

Alex Groza, the starting center and captain of that team which won the NCAA championship in 1948 and 1949, was also a three-time All-American, twice the most outstanding player in the NCAA Final Four, and the leading scorer on the Gold Medal 1948 US Olympic team. He was also banned for life in the NBA due to the point shaving scandal. His life was also *never* the same.

In November of 1983—a couple of years after I arrived in Lexington—Earl Cox invited me to the first reunion in a long time for the "Fabulous Five." After they won the NCAA championship in 1948, they then led the USA team that won the Olympic Gold Medal. The "Fabulous Five" consisted of Ralph Beard, Alex Groza, Wallace 'Wah Wah' Jones, Kenny Rollins, and Cliff Barker (who spent sixteen months as a prisoner of war after the B-17 bomber in which he was serving as a gunner was shot down over Germany during World War II).

There was a party for the "Fabulous Five," and Earl Cox invited ME! I got there after the 11 pm news. Earl Cox was a very powerful sports columnist back then. This was one of the hundreds of WOW moments for me in TV. That night, someone poured me a tall bourbon. I sat there, didn't say a word, and I just listened to the stories.

I wish I had a tape recorder because everyone was drinking, telling stories about Coach Adolph Rupp, and having a great time. I could feel both the love, as well as the anger and frustration. I wasn't expecting the anger and frustration. It was very strange. There's no question that the '48 team was one of the greatest basketball teams ever assembled. They were national collegiate champions and represented America in the Olympics, but no one really remembers. I think that's partly because of the scandal, partly because it was so long ago, and partly because TV stars like Dick Vitale rarely seem to mention them. Unfortunately, they've been lost in history. I'm a history major, and one of things that bothers me about sports is that not many people seem to care about what has gone on in the past.

Ralph Beard was a Kentucky boy from Louisville who stayed home and became a successful salesman. He's one of the nicest guys you'll ever meet. He made a horrible mistake that he had to pay for the rest of his life.

"Yes, there are days that I go for five minutes during basketball season that I don't even think about it" Beard said, when I did a story on him in the early nineties. "If taking the money admits guilt, then I'm guilty. If influencing the score of a basketball game for one second constitutes guilt, then I am the most un-guilty person in the whole world because I loved basketball. That was my life. I'm sixty-four years old, and I will feel that way until the day they hit me in the face with a spade—because that [playing basketball] was the only thing I really ever wanted to do. I was banned at twenty-three and [have had] a long time to think about it."

Ralph gave credit to Betty, his wife, for saving his life. There was a time when things were so dark, he considered suicide.

If the point shaving scandal happened to Ralph Beard today, things may have worked out differently for him. He certainly would have had a lawyer who would have done a much better job defending him. At that point in history, Ralph Beard had no defense. It was a tragic ending to a great career for a talented star.

Before we left, Ralph took me into his kitchen. He had a small plastic table for two. He told me that one of the highlights of his day was having coffee there with Betty.

On the wall right next to the table was a large frame of his 1948 gold medal. I got emotional when he showed me.

I felt awful for Ralph. Yes he did something really stupid. Yes he was wrong. Yes he shouldn't have taken the money. We've all done dumb things. But, if you believe him that he never altered the outcome of a game—and I do—to me the punishment didn't fit the crime.

What really gets me angry is if Pete Rose would have been so open and honest about his gambling issues like Ralph Beard was, I believe he would already be in Baseball's Hall of Fame.

20

In Prison with Tom Payne

Tom Payne was the first and only African American to accept a basketball scholarship from legendary University of Kentucky coach Adolph Rupp. Payne, who didn't start playing basketball until he was a sophomore at Shawnee High School in Louisville, averaged 17 points and 10 rebounds in his only season (1970-71) with the Wildcats. He played in the NBA for the 1971-72 season after being drafted by the Atlanta Hawks. He should have had a great career in the NBA.

Instead, in 1972, Payne was first convicted of rape in Georgia. In 1977, he was sent to Kentucky to stand trial for another rape that had occurred in 1971. He was tried and convicted of rape and two counts of detaining a female (attempted rape) and received a life sentence.

Payne was paroled in 1983. Three years later, he was convicted of rape again in California. He was paroled for that in June 2000 but was returned to Kentucky for his parole violation. After spending thirty-two years in prison for rape, Payne made parole in 2018.

Before I could do my 2004 TV story on Tom Payne, I called the Green River Correctional Complex in Central City and was told that no interviews could be done unless Tom's brother approved it. Darrell Payne is a lawyer and was teaching at Northern Kentucky University. We talked on the phone, and Darrell said we had to meet in person.

In all the years I'd been doing this, I'd never met with anyone for hours in person to do a story—NEVER.

I would refuse to meet with people who wanted to come to the station to talk about doing a story. My thought was that if they came to the station, I would have to spend too much time with them. I would always talk, however, to anyone on the phone.

Darrell drove down from Northern Kentucky, and we met for

hours at a local restaurant before he would allow me to go to the jail to do the story. He asked me point blank, "Are you going to ask my brother about all the rapes that he was in jail for?" I told him point blank that I would. If I was going to do the story, he couldn't tell me what to ask or what to do. I told him I wasn't doing the story to destroy his brother. His brother needed to be remembered, and I wanted to do an update.

I wasn't sure he was going to agree to it, but he did. Tom Payne admitted to me that he "had hurt people." He never admitted that he raped anyone.

It's a really sad story. It's past awful for the women involved. There's no excuse for what he did. But, this was a human being that could have become anything he wanted. He came from a good family. For him to be the first African American at Kentucky, and the pressure he was under—I don't think many understand. To go on the road and hear all the racial slurs—even here in Lexington—there's no excuse for how people treated him.

There might be people who will either skip this chapter or be angry that we included it in the book. But it's history, and I'm a history major. One of my favorite quotes—it's in my top three—is "History doesn't repeat itself, but men make the same mistakes."

That quote by Bernard Baruch, an advisor for presidents from Woodrow Wilson through John F. Kennedy, has affected my life *tremendously*. I've always looked at how things that happened in the past relate to how they would happen today. It allowed me to gain a whole new perspective when doing a story.

No one wants bad history brought up. I get it, I understand it, I respect it. But we shouldn't forget.

We shouldn't forget that slaves were sold in downtown Lexington.

We shouldn't forget that six million Jews were slaughtered by Adolf Hitler.

We shouldn't forget all the atrocities that go on today and have gone on forever.

We shouldn't forget. It's important to tell Tom Payne's story.

When I walked into the correctional facility with Brian Gilbert—my friend and a terrific photographer—Payne was shooting baskets in the gym. At seven feet two inches, he appeared to still be in good shape. He was just lightly shooting around while we made small talk. It was uncomfortable for both of us.

Then they put us in a room that I will never forget. It was amazingly tiny. Tom, a small table, myself, and Brian my photographer right behind me. Brian didn't have much room. I was shocked, but also happy there wasn't a guard with us.

Payne talked like a gentle giant with a lifetime of regrets. But, you're asking a man about his life and why he's in jail. I didn't know how he was going to react. I'll never forget when we left the jail. Brian and I both had felt uncomfortable about being put in such a tight room with a person we believed might never get out of jail.

I remember before doing this story, I was talking to Bruce Carter, my news director. "You know we're going to get hate mail and calls about the story," I said. Bruce never flinched. He told me to go for it.

I didn't save the emails I received afterwards. In fact, I saved so little of my career, it's embarrassing. But if you can use your imagination, you might get a glimpse at all the names I was called. Tom Payne was called every name that could be associated with his actions—and then some. They wanted to know why I was giving airtime to a *blankety-blank* rapist. Some of the phone calls were so rough I had to put the phone down on people. Some I slammed the phone down, some I told they had to change their tone or otherwise I'd hang up. I wasn't going to let anyone yell at me or call me names.

Here's the story that ran on LEX18.

> Cutler Narration: He's 7'2", weighs 290 pounds. Is still considered by some to be an animal. Ironically, he comes across as a reflective, gentle giant. A man who was convicted of rape three times. A man who knows he blew a great opportunity.

> Payne: If I would have took advantage of what I could have at U of K. If I would have appreciated the opportunity to play for U of K—the great opportunity that God had given me and used it the right way, then I could have ran for senator. I could have been the first Black man to run for mayor of Louisville. I think like that.

> Cutler Narration: The sixties were turbulent times. Adolph Rupp was getting heat for not recruiting African Americans. Many great Black athletes from the Commonwealth were going to Louisville and Western Kentucky. Payne, who was

already 6'10" when he started playing organized basketball in high school, signed with UK in 1969. He stayed one year before taking the money and going to the NBA. It's one of the biggest regrets in a lifetime full of them. At UK, Payne set a rebounding record and was almost a leading scorer.

Payne: You feel like the whole world was against you.

Cutler Narration: Getting booed and being the target of all kinds of racial slurs from hometown fans still hurts. Being announced as the starting center for the first time remains the highlight of his life.

Payne: I didn't think many people wanted to see me start.

Cutler: Because of your race?

Payne: I think that was it.

Cutler Narration: When Payne left UK, he heard the whispers that many thought that he thought that Rupp was a racist. Number one, he doesn't believe that. And number two, he'll tell you that Rupp was just a product of the times.

Payne: I like to focus on the fact that he had the courage to put me out there. I like to focus on the fact that Jack Givens came after that, and they won an NCAA title.

Cutler Narration: Payne believes he paved the road for other African Americans to play at Kentucky.

Payne: If he was a racist, was he the only racist? He must have been getting support. He had to be getting support. There must have been other people who supported him, so why would we pick him out? Because he was the head coach. I think it's unfair.

Cutler Narration: Payne would love to talk to former teammates—especially Jim Andrews. You could feel the anger Payne had admitting to being nasty on purpose.

Payne: You're a white guy, you're getting my position. That's how I thought then. You don't like me and this and that. And I don't like you. Because I took potshots at him as far as a player. I mean if I could elbow him, I'd elbow him.

Cutler Narration: When Payne played for Kentucky, he had no idea how special it was. Years later, he realized being a Cat kept him going.

Payne: In my heart, I'm a Wildcat. In other words, I have survived because I went to Kentucky. There have been a lot of things that happened to me in prison and stuff, that if I hadn't been a Wildcat—you understand what I'm saying? A Kentucky Wildcat.

21

The Original Twin Towers?

There are a lot of great players that people forget about. One of the best underrated players with UK Basketball is Jim Andrews. The 6'11" center from Lima, Ohio was first-team All-Southeastern Conference in his last two years at Kentucky. During that time, he averaged a double-double. As a junior, he averaged 21 points and 11 rebounds a game. As a senior, he averaged 20 points and 12 rebounds a game.

How Andrews got to UK is a funny story Joe B. Hall loves to tell. He stopped in Lima, Ohio to get gas on his way to Findlay, Ohio on a recruiting trip. At the gas station, Joe B. asks a guy if there are any good ball players in the area. The guy tells Joe B. that some big guy who is averaging 36 points a game is playing tonight. That's how Joe B. discovered Jim Andrews. Ironically, Andrews was thinking about going to Tennessee.

Andrews' greatest moment from 1970-73 at UK was a game-winning shot against Tennessee in which Adolph Rupp called the play. But, what happened before the game was also talked about a lot. It was cold the night before, so they allowed students to camp out in Memorial Coliseum. But, for some inexplicable reason, they gave out oranges to the students. What?? It's called payback. In Tennessee, they threw oranges at UK players during warmups. Ray Mears, the Tennessee coach did some wild and crazy stunts for attention—like having a basketball player on a unicycle ride around the court juggling basketballs before a game. So, when the unicycle came out onto the floor of Memorial Coliseum for Tennessee, a lot of oranges ended up on the court. Gee, that's so surprising.

Former UK great Mike Pratt, who played at UK from 1968-70, remembers Tennessee fans throwing oranges at UK players when they came out on the court and during warmups. He also remembers the time UK fans tossed them at Tennessee at Memorial Coliseum. He said that Rupp then took the microphone and asked fans to stop. But when he came back to the bench, he winked at the players. There was plenty of gamesmanship going on.

Can you imagine the national publicity any school would get today from ESPN with a story like that? Because of that, think about the scrutiny school officials would have been under? Somebody might get fired. I'm laughing. The good old days.

A few years ago, Jim Andrews name was rekindled because Julius Randle—the former Kentucky star and first-round pick in the 2014 NBA Draft—started the season with seven consecutive double-doubles (points and rebounds). He tied Jim's record. Julius, when he failed to get his eighth double-double, said it was an honor to be tied with Jim. It was a classy comment by Randle.

Tom Payne, the first and only African American to play for Coach Rupp, took his relationship with Jim Andrews the wrong way. If you think about it, what competition did Payne really have when he started playing basketball in high school? Tom Payne was a great athlete re-cruited by powerhouse schools like Kentucky and UCLA. Tom Payne and Jim Andrews ended up as teammates at Kentucky.

When you come to Kentucky, you have to fight for your position. Jim Andrews was battling for playing time by being physical in practice, and Payne took it the wrong way. Payne thought that Andrews didn't like him. He was concerned that there were some racial overtones be-hind the normal, physical part of practice. To Andrews, it was just competition.

Andrews told me that anytime someone threw any racial language at Payne, his teammates would defend him. The problem was that Tom Payne admits he was immature and took that competition the wrong way. Still, what Tom Payne went through—not just in Lexington but traveling on the road in the Southeastern Conference—was past *disgust-ing*.

Jim saw my story about Tom Payne in prison. From that story, he told a friend they were taking a road trip, and they visited Tom Payne in prison after all those years. Subsequently, Jim and Tom rekindled their relationship and became friends. They tried to see each other once or twice a year when Payne was in jail. Jim even attended Tom's moth-er's funeral. He's also gone to Tom's parole hearings. That relationship all started because of my story.

"I went for two reasons," says Andrews. "One, it was to pay respect to Tommy's mother. And I also had developed a close relationship with Darrell Payne, his brother."

Andrews discovered that Mrs. Payne was a remarkable woman. He says she demanded that each of her children and grandchildren attend college in pairs so they could look after each other. "She had a grandchild that when it came time to go to college didn't have a family member to attend with her. So Mrs. Payne went with her and got another degree as her granddaughter got her degree."

One final tidbit about Jim. He told me that Joe B. Hall wanted to play him and Tom Payne together. They would have been the original twin towers at UK before Rick Robey and Mike Phillips and before Sam Bowie and Melvin Turpin. But Coach Rupp didn't want that. Jim said that Rupp would make up his mind in the summer about who was going to start. Consequently, Jim didn't get to play a lot during that sophomore season, and his averages were rather pedestrian that year.

Jim was drafted in the seventh round of the NBA draft and ended up playing in Italy for a number of years.

22

The Quarterback Club

When it comes to a player who is the most respected by different generations of UK football players, Derrick Ramsey has to be No. 1. He's been very close with many UK quarterbacks going back to the 1940s. The strength of this bond might surprise you.

"Babe" Parilli

Ramsey, who was the first African American quarterback at UK in 1975, told me many times that "Babe" was the best quarterback to play at UK. That's Vito "Babe" Parilli, a two-time first-team All-American who led UK to a 13-7 win over Oklahoma in the 1951 Sugar Bowl. The Sooners had won 31 games in a row and were No. 1 in both polls at the time. Back then, they decided who was No. 1 even before the bowl games were played.

In 1990, Jeff Sagarin's computer ranking said that UK was the No. 1 team in 1950. Kentucky was ranked 7th that year before they beat Oklahoma, who was the king of college football. UK's only loss was 7-0 to Tennessee. They finished the season at 11-1.

When "Babe" left UK, he was No. 1 in the history of college football in TD passes, completions, and passing yards. "Babe" was so good, they said he had "Houdini Hands." There were defensive players tackling UK players who didn't have the ball because he was so good at faking out the defense.

"Babe"—who's in College Football's Hall of Fame—was a first-round draft pick in the NFL and played pro football for eighteen years. He held the New England Patriots' touchdown record until it was broken by the greatest—Tom Brady.

I interviewed "Babe" a number of times when he came back for UK reunions. He was a great guy who told me that the best thing he ever did was come to Kentucky. I loved talking to him about the New York Jets. In 1969, I went to a number of their games thanks to my uncles Aaron and Arnie. Babe was the backup quarterback to the great Joe Namath when the Jets shocked the world and beat the Baltimore Colts in the Super Bowl.

Many UK fans would say that Tim Couch was UK's greatest quarterback. I'm good if you pick Couch over "Babe" or Derrick Ramsey. Couch brought the fun back to UK Football with Coach Hal Mumme in the 1990s. "Babe," meanwhile, was 28-8 as the starting quarterback when he played for the greatest coach of his time, Paul "Bear" Bryant.

The entire story about why "Bear" left UK has never been told. We'll leave that for someone else's book.

Derrick Ramsey

Here's what I want to tell you about Derrick Ramsey. Unless you've walked a mile in a man's shoes—you don't get it. I can't imagine putting up with the garbage thrown at Ramsey.

Sounds crazy, but after winning two state championships in football at Florida, Ramsey moved to New Jersey where he believed it was easier for an African American to get a scholarship. After Ramsey wins two more state titles—one in football and one in basketball—he comes to UK.

Ramsey loved his UK coach, Fran Curci. At 6'6, 220 pounds, and super tough—my friend still gets a bit defensive about his arm. "I could throw Cut," he tells me. "But Fran wouldn't let me because we didn't need to. Do you want stats, or do you want wins? I'm all about winning."

That last word sums up Ramsey perfectly— "winning." Ramsey is a winner who likes to help others learn how to win.

Ramsey, who played nine years in the NFL as a tight end and won a Super Bowl with the Oakland Raiders, will always believe that if he played for UK today—and was allowed to throw the ball, with African Americans *finally* getting a chance to play quarterback in the NFL—that he would have been a first-round draft pick to play quarterback.

Ramsey does have one regret. He wishes he had gone to Canada to play quarterback—even if it meant giving up his Super Bowl ring. But, who doesn't either have regrets or say to themselves, "What if?" For me it was turning down ESPN—not once, but twice in the 1980s after so many of my stories were on their network. I'll always believe because of my strong personality, that I would have either become a big star or would have gotten fired.

Ramsey believes there were four or five African American quarterbacks in college when he played for UK that should have gotten a chance to play in the NFL. He wonders what some of the long-time respected owners of NFL teams really think about not giving some of his peers a chance to play quarterback simply because of the color of their skin. Ramsey will always believe it cost some teams a chance to win more. Do some of those owners now believe it because of all the great African American quarterbacks playing in the NFL? Or did some of the owners really believe it back then—but didn't have the guts to do the right thing?

Ramsey has been a successful athletics director and worked for two Kentucky governors heading important cabinet positions. Helping young people getting jobs and getting the proper education has been a big part of Ramsey's life.

"It's not that I'm that damn smart," he said. "But I had so many good people in my life that I couldn't fail. When I help someone, I tell them I don't want a penny from you. All I ask is for you to pull someone up with you."

Ramsey is being modest. He is that smart.

Ramsey was the quarterback and is still the leader of the 1976 UK team that went 10-1, won the SEC Championship, and finished 6th in the national polls. Even with all his success, there was a big problem because of the color of his skin.

"It was tough, Cut," he admitted to me. "They [UK fans] didn't want me. My celebrity has grown over the years. They now realize how tough it is to win nine or ten games in the SEC."

Can't you understand why Ramsey felt that way? Ramsey says that when he got booed against West Virginia, he told the fans where they could go. He also said there were two sacks of mail waiting for him in Lexington afterwards. Ramsey says there were thousands of letters, and most of them were hate letters. Even when UK won their next game 34-10, he remembers being booed. He was called all kinds of names. "Monkey, shut up," they said. There were other racial names that he was called—but I won't put it in the book.

Can you imagine walking a mile in *those* shoes?

"They were booing me because I'm a brother," he continued. "For years, these folks didn't know how to take me. Was I a militant or what? I was approachable...*BUT*..."

I have always found Ramsey to be very smart, funny, strong, and honest. I respect him as much as anyone I've ever talked to at UK.

It's tough to say who is the biggest winner in the history of UK Sports, but for my money, no one tops Ramsey. Plus, you have to remember how bad UK football was when he got here. And, that takes nothing away from some of his great teammates.

As one of my heroes, sportscaster Howard Cosell, used to say, "Sports is a microcosm of society."

Pookie Jones

Pookie Jones had a very good career playing quarterback at UK. After leading UK to the Peach Bowl in 1993, he played minor league baseball and spent a little time in the Canadian Football League—but his shoulder was a problem. Pookie always handled himself the right way. He was always quick to smile.

Like Ramsey, let's see if you can walk a mile in Pookie's shoes.

"I've had the N-word dropped on my voice message," Pookie said to me. "I've never told anyone. I was raised in Murray, Kentucky. Ninety percent of my friends were white. I just wanted to represent myself and the community. It didn't register with me. Coach Curry told me that you can't control idiots. Ram (Ramsey) gave me a shoulder to lean on. He was always a person I could reach out to—even today."

"Pookie, we would talk frequently," says Ramsey. "He cried after a game. I told him, 'Pookie, they can never see you like this again.' He's one of my favorite kids."

Bill Ransdell

The quarterback bond between Ramsey and Bill Ransdell is also extra special.

From 1984 until Rich Brooks took over as UK's coach, Ransdell's claim to fame was that he was the last quarterback to win a bowl game. From 1984 until 2011, he was the last UK quarterback to beat Tennessee. And from 1984 until 2018, he was the last UK quarterback to beat Florida.

Ransdell's dad played for UK. Playing for Kentucky was Bill's dream. Yes, Ransdell would have loved to have played for Hal Mumme and throw the ball a ton, but his respect for Coach Jerry Claiborne was off the charts. Like Pookie, Ransdell also loved Derrick Ramsey.

"I remember getting sweat bands and chin straps from Ram," says Ransdell. "Ram was always gracious to me. He was the one I looked up to. I've reached out to Ram, and he's always called back."

Ransdell is still upset that somehow he lost the sweat bands and chin straps Ramsey gave him about ten years ago. Later, when Ransdell made the UK Hall of Fame, having Ramsey shake his hand and say, "Welcome to the club," meant the world to him.

"To visit with him and talk to the Babe [Parilli], that's just icing on the cake. Ram was my guy. Humble. All about the team. No ego."

You could feel the pride and smile when Ransdell talked about his teammates—his brothers.

"We fought at times, but we loved each other."

Freddie Maggard

Don't ask me who my favorite Kentucky player is that I've covered. It hurts to leave someone out. But Freddie Maggard has to be on any short list that I come up with during my time on TV.

I've always been so jealous of Freddie—happy for him, but jealous. You see his dad, Big Fred, was his hero. I had no relationship with my father—and that's being kind. I would trade much more than my small TV pension, which I really appreciate having, just to have the relationship that Freddie had with his father.

It just so happens that Big Fred is one of the greatest ever in Kentucky. Big Fred hit not one, but two game-winning shots in the 1956 Kentucky Sweet Sixteen to bring Carr Creek back—when they were down by one. Carr Creek's graduating class in 1956 had forty-two students.

Not only that, but in one of the games that Big Fred hit a shot, Carr Creek beat King Kelly Coleman, the greatest high school basketball player ever in the state of Kentucky. King Kelly not only remains as the all-time leading scorer in Kentucky, his 4,337 points was a national record at the time. He was also named Mr. Basketball as the best player in the state in 1956. In one of the games of the Sweet Sixteen Tournament, Coleman scored 68 points.

It's tough for me to visualize what it would be like to grow up in eastern Kentucky when Big Fred was a child. There weren't many basketball goals or basketballs, so Freddie tells me that Big Fred had to use a foam ball with an oatmeal box with the bottom cut out for the goal. That's how he honed his shooting skills.

"My dad is my hero," he said. "Always has been, always will be."

March was Freddie's favorite month with Big Fred. They both loved the Sweet Sixteen State Basketball Championship. And they both loved rooting for any mountain team that made it to Rupp Arena.

Here's what's crazy. If you compare the conversation I had with Bill Ransdell and the conversation I had with Freddie Maggard—talking about Derrick Ramsey—they're *EXACTLY* the same! Like Ransdell growing up, Freddie's hero was…Derrick Ramsey. Freddie to this day still calls Derrick, "Mr. Ramsey." Ramsey doesn't like it, but Freddie won't stop. It's done totally out of respect.

All the UK quarterbacks that are close will occasionally get together. Freddie tells me that when Derrick Ramsey walks into the room, the other quarterbacks will stand up out of respect.

When Freddie Maggard was a kid, he would paint the number twelve on his T-shirt and play like Derrick Ramsey. When Ramsey played at Kentucky, Freddie would often arrive early to watch Ramsey warm up. He would then try to get an autograph from Ramsey after every game—just like Bill Ransdell.

"He's one of the most intelligent people I know," Freddie recently said to me about Ramsey. "I value his leadership more than anyone I've ever known—other than my dad."

Wow! As far as Freddie is concerned, when it comes to former players, it's Derrick Ramsey's program when you talk about UK Football.

Freddie started playing quarterback at UK in 1989 for both Jerry Claiborne—who he loved—and Bill Curry. He'll do anything to help anyone, especially if they're from eastern Kentucky. When asked, he said, "Eastern Kentucky means everything to me. It's who I am. It's my heritage. It's my family. It's everything to me. I'm very proud of Kentucky. I'm extra proud of southeastern Kentucky. It would have been blasphemy if I wore a jersey other than Kentucky. My goal always has been to show others in eastern Kentucky that if I can do it, you can do it. If I can get a scholarship to play football at the University of Kentucky, so can you."

One of the great things about sports is the bond it creates with your teammates that often lasts a lifetime. That's especially true with the UK quarterback club—even though they played on different teams at different times.

The bottom line is this: I have no idea what the pressure is like to play quarterback at schools like Kentucky.

Don't think anyone outside of quarterbacks will really know.

But these guys do—and that understanding lasts a lifetime.

23

The World According to Joe B. Hall

With all the pressure in 1978—because they were expected to win it all—Joe B. told his basketball team, "You'll party for the rest of your lives. Let's get this done."

Because of all the reunions and places they've been, I've gotten to know the guys on that championship team. Joe B. often doesn't get enough credit for being the motivator he was.

Before they played Duke in the national championship game, Joe B. put on the blackboard what the team was going to do after they won, and he described how they were going to celebrate. Think about that. The pregame talk wasn't about Duke, and it wasn't about what the team needed to do to beat Duke—it was all about how the team was going to *act and celebrate* after they won.

James Lee, a senior forward on the championship team, told me, "We knew we were going to win anyway, but it was nice for Coach to say." He then let out his usual big, hearty laugh. Lee's dunk to seal the NCAA Championship was a perfect ending.

"I don't have the words to describe the total feeling, but it was there...totally !!!!!" Joe B. said after the championship win.

The difference in coaches' salaries today versus back in the seventies is astronomical. Kentucky basketball coach John Calipari's most recent contract extension pays him eight million a year. People are often shocked when they learn how little Joe B. was paid by comparison.

His initial contract in 1972 was negotiated moments before he was introduced as the Kentucky head coach. As they were walking up the stairs to the sixteenth floor of the Patterson Office Tower, Joe B. told University of Kentucky President Otis Singletary that they hadn't completed their deal. Joe B. informed Dr. Singletary that he had previously been told that he would start at the same salary Adolph Rupp was paid when he left—$65,000 a year. Dr. Singletary told Joe B. that it wouldn't work. He was told he'd get paid $22,000 a year, and there would be no negotiations. Joe agreed, and subsequently proceeded to win the school's fifth national championship six years later.

"When we won in '78, I got a letter from [athletics director] Cliff Hagan that said, 'Congratulations, this was one of the greatest years in the history of Kentucky Basketball,'" Joe B. told me. "'And, we're raising your salary to $45,000.' I've got the letter. I've got it laminated on a plaque. It didn't matter to me. I never took a job for money. Never asked for a raise. Whatever I was paid, I was satisfied with it."

You have to understand where Joe B. came from—Cynthiana, Kentucky. He didn't grow up with a silver spoon. "You know when you cut tobacco for a penny a stick, you've hit the height of making money."

Joe retired in 1985—after thirteen seasons as the UK head coach, a 297-100 record, eight SEC regular season championships, one NIT championship, 3 NCAA Final Four appearances, and one NCAA championship.

Reggie Warford, the first African American basketball player to graduate from the University of Kentucky, told me with tears in his eyes about the time in 1975 at Madison Square Garden when Joe B. first put five African American players out on the court at the same time. Reggie says that they all looked at each other to remember that moment. Joe B. Hall was a huge part of that cultural transition. In my mind, he doesn't get enough credit.

Joe B. always calls Adolph Rupp "Coach Rupp." It's done out of respect.

As far as being a Kentucky boy, here's what Joe B. said. "There is no place I'd rather be or be from than Kentucky. I think it's such a grass roots, basic way to grow up and have an understanding of people—and have an opportunity to love what you do and live in peace with your fellow man."

I hope people spend an extra few seconds on that last paragraph.

That's Joe B. Hall's love letter to his life in Kentucky.

24

Kevin Grevey—"The Old Man Was Right"

Kevin Grevey was a two-time SEC Player of the Year and a consensus first-team All-American. On March 31, 1975, in the NCAA Championship game, Grevey scored 34 points as Kentucky lost to UCLA 92-85. That was also legendary UCLA coach John Wooden's last game.

John Wooden was the first person ever to be enshrined as a player (1960) and a coach (1973) in the Basketball Hall of Fame. The 5'10" guard was a three-time All-American at Purdue and started his coaching career at Dayton High School in Dayton, Kentucky. The *Wizard of Westwood* won ten NCAA national championships in a twelve-year period at UCLA, including seven in a row—a record that will never be matched.

Here are a couple of things everyone forgets about that game in '75. To get to the national championship game, UCLA had to come back and beat Louisville 75-74 in overtime. I can picture the shot right now—on a Richard Washington basket with less than five seconds to go. Without that shot, Kentucky would have been playing Louisville for the national championship. Think about that!

Grevey and his teammates were ticked off that everyone was cheering for UCLA. After the Bruins beat Louisville, Wooden told his team that he was retiring after the next game. Once word got out about that, the *whole world outside of Kentucky* wanted UCLA to win. Grevey felt like UCLA had gained a tremendous advantage.

It bothers Grevey that UK beating Indiana 92-90 in the NCAA Mideast Regional Final seemed to be forgotten by the time UK played for the NCAA Championship. Indiana had not only beaten UK 98-74 during the regular season, but they had won thirty-four in a row, and were ranked No. 1 nationally. IU coach Bobby Knight called it his best team ever, even though his team the following season had a perfect record. IU star Scott May was dealing with a broken arm that year, and he just wasn't the same player as before.

Late in the championship game, Kentucky was called for a foul on UCLA forward Dave Meyers that many old-timers reading this book do not believe was a foul. It changed the complexion of the game. Kentucky players still feel that they got robbed in '75. They went from the joy of beating Indiana and Bobby Knight in the Mideast Regional Finals to the grief of losing to UCLA and John Wooden in the national championship game.

Years later, Grevey was still mad at John Wooden for announcing his retirement prior to the championship. He thought it was a selfish position for Wooden to take.

In the mid-nineties, Grevey was working as the color announcer on a CBS Westwood One national broadcast during a UCLA versus Notre Dame game at Pauley Pavilion. Joel Meyers was doing the play-by-play. For the pregame show, the two start going down memory lane by talking about all the UCLA championship banners hanging from the rafters. When they get to the 1975 banner, Grevey tells a national audience, "That last banner should be at Rupp Arena. If Coach Wooden hadn't retired the night before the game, I believe the banner would be at Rupp Arena."

Everyone, including Joel Meyers, couldn't believe Grevey said what he said on the air. Remember, Grevey was in Pauley Pavilion telling listeners that UCLA's banner really belonged someplace else because of what John Wooden did. That shows you how angry he still was. Networks *do not want* freedom of speech with their announcers.

During a commercial break, Grevey asks Joel Meyers if Coach Wooden ever came to the games. Little did he know that Wooden was sitting behind him. Grevey wanted to say "hi" to John Wooden but wasn't even sure that Wooden would remember him. After the game Grevey went up to Wooden, but before he could say anything, Wooden says, "You know, Grevey, if you played some defense, you guys might have won the game." Wooden then turned his back to Grevey, as if to say he was done with him.

Kevin Grevey is quick-witted and really good with one-liners. When I asked him what he said back to Wooden, he told me that he didn't respond because "the old man was right."

That's one of my favorite UK stories. People forget that when you lose a game like that, it stays with you for the rest of your life. I've had a lot of coaches tell me that the losses stay with you a lot more than the wins.

In 2003, Kentucky played UCLA in the John Wooden Classic in Anaheim. ESPN called Grevey up and asked him if he would talk about the 1975 game as part of the pregame show. After Grevey agreed, ESPN called back the next day and told him there had been a change of plans—they didn't want Grevey to do the show after all. When Grevey asked them why, ESPN told him that when John Wooden learned that he would be on the show, he wasn't happy about it.

Despite still holding a grudge over everything that happened back in '75, Grevey told me that "there probably wasn't a more solid guy than John Wooden." I give Grevey a lot of credit for that attitude.

Over the years, John Calipari has made a big deal about having players working out in the morning on their own. Remember the *Breakfast Club* with Michael Kidd-Gilchrist? Kevin Grevey, as a senior at UK, was coming in early in the morning and at night to get in extra shots. He knew he had to do that if he wanted to be a first-round draft choice and play in the NBA.

One day, Cliff Hagan, then the UK athletics director—who was a consensus two-time first-team All-American at UK, is in the National Collegiate Basketball Hall of Fame, the Naismith Memorial Basketball Hall of Fame, won the NCAA Championship and the NBA Championship, and was a five time NBA all-star—invited Kevin Grevey to join his noontime "basketball club." Cliff Hagan has always stayed in unbelievable shape. He's playing tennis well into his eighties.

Even back in his forties and fifties, Cliff Hagan was tough to beat in a half-court game of basketball. He's always been strong. In the 1990s, I ran into Cliff many times at the place where I worked out. He would work out for hours and hours and hours at a time. He was amazing, and one of my favorites I've covered at Kentucky. He never worked out on campus because he was still mad at Kentucky for how they got rid of him as athletics director during the basketball scandal of the eighties. It was sad that one of the great names in UK history elected to go to a private club because he didn't like the way the university treated him.

Grevey told me that during those noontime workouts, Cliff Hagan "kicked his ass." Here Grevey was, an All-American, and he can't beat a guy more than twice his age in half-court basketball. Hagan had a hook shot that no one could stop. "Plus," Grevey added, "In half-court basketball, do you think any fouls were called?"

Cliff even invited me to take him on in some of those noontime sessions. I told him the truth—I was really bad at hoops.

In 1975, Grevey became the first-round draft choice of the Washington Bullets. Wes Unseld—an NBA MVP and a member of the Naismith Memorial Basketball Hall of Fame was also on the Bullets when Grevey was a rookie. Unseld was a huge star from Louisville with a very strong personality.

Adolph Rupp had made an in-home visit to Unseld when he was recruiting him to Kentucky back in the 1960s. Rupp was under pressure to recruit an African American player. Unseld wasn't a fan of the culture at Kentucky. As the story goes, Rupp heads back to Memorial Coliseum and tells everyone that Wes Unseld might be the best Puerto Rican player he's ever seen.

Grevey and Unseld became very good friends, but initially, there were some natural problems. First of all, Unseld, who was the rookie of the year and MVP of the NBA in 1969, didn't like rookies. He wouldn't call Grevey by his first name. He called him "Rook" instead. He did that to everybody. Secondly, Grevey went to Kentucky—and Unseld didn't like Kentucky. Because of that, Grevey had to prove himself to Unseld even more.

In the NBA back then, Grevey likes to talk about how NBA teams would supply cigarettes and beer in the locker room. *WHAT?* Yes, they would supply cigarettes and beer for the players.

Rookies back then were also required to carry basketballs around for the entire year. Can you imagine former UK star De'Aaron Fox, as a rookie, carrying balls around for the Sacramento Kings wherever they went? Not in a million years. Kevin Grevey had to carry six balls in the bag all year—to practice, on the airplane while on the road, to practice on the road.

Here's something else that happened to Grevey. On road trips, other players would order meals in their hotel rooms and charge it to Kevin's room. It wasn't unusual for him to have to pay an extra two or three hundred bucks for meals alone. He couldn't do anything about it. It was just part of the rookie hazing that went on.

On one occasion before a road trip, Unseld calls out to Grevey, "Hey Rook, make sure you take enough beer for the trip." Kevin doesn't want to disappoint, so he packs the remaining beer from the cooler into the bag of basketballs he's been tasked to carry. When they get to their destination, Grevey discovers that the basketballs in his bag are soaking wet—with beer. Coach K.C. Jones goes crazy. He starts yelling and screaming at Grevey, telling him he owes the team $150 for the six ruined basketballs. And now they can't practice—which suited Wes Unseld because he hated practice as much as former NBA superstar Allen Iverson hated practice.

When they get back on the bus, Unseld started laughing. He loved the fact that he didn't have to practice. He told Grevey that ruining those basketballs was really smart on Grevey's part. Unseld then passed around a hat to collect the $150 fine Grevey needed to purchase new basketballs. "After that, he started calling me Kevin," Grevey recounted.

Grevey and Unseld played together for six years. They won the NBA Championship in 1978. Unseld was MVP of the championship series.

Before Unseld's last game, the players got together and bought Wes a nice retirement gift—a big recliner. Grevey wanted to add something special. He presented a gift that he told Wes came directly from Adolph Rupp. It was an autographed picture of the Baron.

The truth was that Grevey and his dad had stopped one time at a gas station, saw this "cheap" picture of Adolph Rupp, and decided to buy it. Grevey asked his father to dig this picture out of his basement and gave it to Unseld as a gag gift. He asked his dad to inscribe on the picture as follows: "To Wes Unseld, the greatest Puerto Rican to ever play basketball, Best Regards, Adolph Rupp."

At the banquet, Grevey gives Unseld the picture of Rupp. Unseld takes a look at the inscription, smashes the picture, and starts chasing Grevey around the banquet room. Everybody at the banquet was laughing like crazy.

When Grevey told me that story, I laughed like crazy too.

25

The Goose was Golden

No one will ever forget Jack "Goose" Givens scoring 41 points when Kentucky beat Duke 94-88 to win the 1978 National Championship. Fifty years from now, that will still be called one of the greatest clutch performances of all time. After all, how many people are going to score 41 points in an NCAA championship game fifty years from now?

Part of Jack's performance was just Jack being ridiculously hot. Part of his performance was just his teammates being unselfish. You have to remember that Kentucky had five starters who averaged in double figures.

Since point guard Kyle Macy had the ball in his hands—he knew when he had to take over, and he knew when somebody was hot to give them the ball. Kyle Macy was as pure of a point guard as Kentucky has had. I didn't say the biggest, strongest, or fastest—but when it comes to the purity of point guards, Kyle Macy was special.

Macy didn't miss a field goal. But he only took three shots because he was giving the ball to Goose. UK found a hole in Duke's zone. Kentucky was smart. Keep feeding Goose.

Jack was Mr. Basketball at Bryan Station High School. He was a Parade All-American. Jack played basketball at a time in Lexington that was about as good as it has ever been. In all my years here, basketball in Lexington has never been as good as in the early seventies when Jack played against James Lee and many other terrific players in town. The old-timers will tell you that was the best of times.

What most people don't remember about that championship run was Kentucky coach Joe B. Hall making one of the gutsiest or craziest coaching moves in the history of the NCAA Tournament.

It happened during Kentucky's first-round game against Florida

State in the Stokely Athletic Center in Knoxville. Heavily favored to win the national championship that year, No. 1-ranked Kentucky suddenly finds itself down 39-32 at halftime.

Kentucky had played horribly in the first half. Joe B. Hall goes into the locker room and kicks a water bucket and goes crazy. He then decides to sit three of his biggest stars. He benches All-Americans Givens, Rick Robey, and senior guard Truman Claytor. In their place, he inserts seldom-used substitutes freshman Fred Cowan, sophomore LaVon Williams, and junior Dwane Casey.

What you can't forget is that Joe B. was still trying to replace Adolph Rupp. Replacing a legend is a tough thing to do. Had Kentucky lost that game, who knows what would have happened to Joe B., the coach? Who sits three stars on a team ranked No. 1 when you're expected to win the NCAA Championship? To have the guts to do it—that's coaching.

Fortunately for Joe B., the ploy worked as the quicker, smaller lineup was a better match with Florida State and the deficit disappeared quickly. The starters were allowed back on the court and completed the convincing beatdown as UK outscored the Seminoles 53-37 in the second half for the 85-76 victory.

The only other coaching move I can think of that comes close to what Joe B. did was when Alabama coach Nick Saban changed quarterbacks in the 2018 National Championship game. Replacing Jalen Hurts with true freshman Tua Tagovailoa in the second half against Georgia with his team trailing 13-0 may be the gutsiest coaching move ever. Alabama came back to win 26-23.

When Joe B. benched his starters, some of the players told me they thought he lost his mind. I'm sure there were two million assistant coaches for the University of Kentucky—called True Blue fans—who thought he had lost his mind.

From 1974-78, Goose scored 2038 points, ranking him third on the all-time scoring list at UK behind Dan Issel and Kenny Walker. He was drafted No. 16 in the first round of the 1978 NBA draft by the Atlanta Hawks. He was kind of a "tweener." I thought the Hawks gave up on him too early after just two years in the league.

The night before fellow Kentucky player Charles Hurt's funeral, Goose said something to me that was like getting hit with a pie in the face. It was just before I was going to interview him on camera. "Alan, you watched me grow up," he said. "You know how I feel about this."

But the truth is that I never covered Jack while he was playing. It's just that I've been around Goose so much and done so many things with him on TV—that's how he felt towards me.

We all forget that they may be great basketball players, but these guys are just people. They're no different from the rest of us, except they can play in front of 24,000 people and make fans yell, scream, and cheer. But they go through the same problems as everyone else. And I think people often forget when they boo, curse, and belittle, that these guys are just people. Because I've gotten to know so many of these athletes so well, I try never to forget that.

There's a difference between criticizing someone and ripping someone. I've tried hard not to rip an athlete. I've always tried to be conscious that these players are people too.

26

UK's Greatest Artist

While I was working in Grand Junction, Colorado in the 1970s, Fruita Monument High made it to the state tournament. I went to Denver to call their games. They only played one game. They were blown out by a Denver team whose star was named LaVon Williams. This is the same LaVon Williams who ended up coming to Kentucky. He was one of the three seldom-used players put into the game against Florida State during that 1978 championship run.

The first time I met LaVon Williams in Lexington and told him the story about doing the play-by-play of his game in Denver, his look was priceless, and we had a big laugh.

LaVon is an artist. He's soft spoken and sensitive. LaVon Williams, if he had not gone to Kentucky but to a school where he would have played more, I think he might have played in the NBA for a long time. But when you have talent like Mike Phillips and Rick Robey in front of you, it's tough to show off your skills.

One of my pet peeves is when people get upset at a player transferring or leaving because they're not getting enough playing time. That ticks me off. People saying that a player should stick around and be loyal to their favorite school is ludicrous. It's selfish. Coaches leave all the time and break contracts. Plus, the scholarship isn't for four years, it's renewed year by year. That's how I broke the story that Rodrick Rhodes, one of the biggest disappointments I've ever seen at UK, was leaving. His scholarship wasn't renewed.

There have been a number of quarterbacks in the last ten years who transferred and then made it to the NFL simply because they got a chance to play. It's tough making the NFL if you're a backup. LaVon Williams was a Parade All-American in high school. People will remember him—if they remember him at all—as a nice backup at Kentucky when he got a chance to play.

How about not only if you get to play, but if you get to *feel comfortable* playing? If you know you're only getting two minutes—now you're uptight. You're supposed to hustle and do all the right things, but you can't do anything well if you're uptight. I think there are a lot of athletes who never made it because they didn't get the opportunities to be themselves and show what they were capable of. If you screw up once, it helps to know that you're not going right to the bench.

When you come to a school like Kentucky, the competition in practice is fierce. But it's different when you go in a game. It's just different if you know you're only going to get a few minutes.

This is NO rip on Joe B. Hall. I get why he started Robey and Phillips.

I'll give you football examples too. I've always been convinced that Jared Lorenzen was good enough to be a starter in the NFL—if he ever got a chance to play and relax. Andre' Woodson never got comfortable either. I watched him on TV playing a preseason game, and he was not comfortable. It's his fault for not getting comfortable, but my point is that it's hard getting comfortable when you know you're only going to get a few snaps to show what you can do. Most of the time in NFL preseason games like that, the coaches have already decided whether you're going to make it or not even before you get in the game—unless you really surprise them.

Whether they admit it or not, coaches, in general, also have different sets of rules for different athletes. Everyone does not get treated the same way. There are certain athletes that can make a mistake and get away with it, and there are certain athletes if they make a mistake, they're going right back to the bench.

LaVon Williams at Kentucky just wasn't the right fit. That's not a negative toward anyone, but he needed to be at a school where he could have played a lot. If LaVon played at UK today, I'd bet the odds are really good he would have transferred. If LaVon transferred to Colorado or a school close to home and played thirty minutes a game, I believe his life would have been different. Can't prove that, but to me it's obvious.

If this were 1978, Kyle Wiltjer would probably have stayed at UK instead of transferring to Gonzaga where he had a great career. Kyle always appreciated his time in Lexington, playing for Cal and with his teammates—and he loves Kentucky to this day which is wonderful—

but he also loved playing for Gonzaga where he was very successful.

I don't believe had Wiltjer stayed at UK that he would have ever seen the same kind of playing time he did at Gonzaga. Players want to play. Let's not overlook the obvious. Wiltjer was a McDonald's All-American in 2011 and the SEC 6th Man of the Year at UK in 2013, but he made All-American at Gonzaga and is playing pro ball in Spain after a short NBA career. Plus, he felt much better about himself playing ball at Gonzaga. In reality, he had the best of both worlds. Wiltjer learned a great deal at UK, and the practices against so many NBA players helped his game...and then he got to sit out a year, got stronger and got in better shape, and became a star at Gonzaga.

Part 3 (1981-1984)

Lexington, Here I Come

27

Joe B. and Denny

Istarted out on the wrong foot at LEX18 in 1981 by ticking off Harry Barfield, our general manager. Louisville had won the national championship in basketball the year before. Besides the obvious—covering UK for their media day—I did something Lexington TV stations didn't do back then. I went to Louisville's Basketball Media Day.

Louisville's Hall of Fame coach Denny Crum was special. During his brilliant career with the Cards from 1971-2001, he compiled a 675-295 record, went to six Final Fours, and won National Championships in 1980 and 1986.

Media Day at Louisville was also different back then. I walked on their practice court, and believe it or not, no one was talking to Denny Crum. I was shocked. So, I walk over to Crum and say, "Denny Crum, I'm Alan Cutler, the new sports director at LEX18 in Lexington. Nice to meet you. Do you have a minute?" And he says to me, "*Are you lost?*" We had this big laugh because at that time, Kentucky refused to play Louisville. I told this story to Crum years later. He didn't remember but laughed again when I told him.

I made a *BIG* issue out of Kentucky not wanting to play Louisville. To me this was a *BIG story* that was a no-brainer. Back then, people that didn't like me used to say I would stir things up just to stir things up. I would take on issues many others wouldn't touch. I never stirred something up for the sake of making an issue. Never had to.

When I was doing sports talk on weekends at WLW in Cincinnati, program director Darryl Parks—who was a big-time radio geek—asked me more than once to stir things up whether I believed it or not. I wouldn't do it.

Back to Denny Crum. I asked Crum about playing Kentucky. He responded by saying, "We'll play them anywhere, anytime. They're the ones who don't want to play us. They refuse to play us." He was *really strong.*

I come back to the station, and I'm running into the newsroom to slap it all together after 4:30 pm. That's late getting back to the TV station. It's a tight deadline putting the show together, and it's a *rush* because I know I have something special. *Crum just ripped UK, da-da-da-da-da.* The whole newsroom stops because of the way I ran into building, and John Ray, our news director, comes out of his office and asks me if I'm going to air that. "Word for word," I replied. "Good," he answered and walked away. Back then, I was also stringing for ESPN. They were excited to get the story too. Although ESPN wasn't big back then, it still helped to get a lot of people talking.

Obviously, word gets back to Kentucky coach Joe B. Hall. My interview with Crum is the talk of the town. Next time I go to UK's practice, I get a really cold shoulder from Coach Hall. Really cold. It's a small circle of media around Joe B. I ask a question without knowing how he would respond. He gives me a really short answer—really curt, to the point, and that was that. And I'm thinking, OK, he's ticked off.

After the media session is over, I ask Joe if he wants to talk about it. He tells me sternly, "You don't understand. You're from New York. You don't understand. This is how we do it. This is how Coach Rupp said we would do it, and this is how we do it. We have nothing to gain by playing Louisville."

I responded, "Joe, I'm not from Kentucky. I don't claim to know everything about Kentucky Basketball. I'm reading books about Kentucky Basketball. It makes no sense to me why you don't play Louisville. It would be one of the great rivalries in basketball. That's my opinion. I'm not going to change it. You don't have to like me for it. I respect who you are. You can be mad at me, but I'm treating you with respect."

There is another side to Joe B.'s comment about doing things the way Coach Rupp did it. Yes, Joe B. was all about tradition, but he took over the program, and for his sake, I hope he ran it his way. I wasn't always sure of that. It's tough to be as successful as you can be if you don't do it your *own* way. You aren't being yourself. No one gets the pressure he felt succeeding a living legend. Try walking a mile in his shoes.

Hall surprised me by asking why I didn't come to him first. I told him, "I don't believe I need to come to you with anything first when

I'm going to talk to anyone else." He turns and quickly walks away. *Why would I ask him first?* If I ask Joe B. before going to Louisville, everyone in the Lexington media would hear his answer—and it might then make some of the Lexington media go to Louisville's media day too. I wanted the exclusive with Crum—and I got it! Denny made it a much bigger story, and that was exactly what he wanted to do. It was a terrific story.

Now, I wonder if my relationship with Joe B. will ever be good. I remember him turning and walking away like it was yesterday. Next time when I showed up with a camera—he was fine. In other words, he had his say. That's what's great about Joe. It was the only time we ever had a problem. Later, when we talked about it, he admitted he was mad. He didn't like my answer, and I didn't like his answer. But it was done respectfully. He wasn't going to back down, and neither was I. We both said our peace, and it was good that we had it out. Joe was terrific. He's old school—so respectful.

I have strong feelings towards Joe B. Hall. He's a class act.

Regardless of their personalities, one of the lessons you learn as a reporter early on is that you don't back down. Lots of coaches like to intimidate you. Respect them, but hold your ground.

28

Media 101

When I first arrived in Lexington, it was much easier covering UK Football and Basketball than it is now. It was also a lot more fun. Today, there are way too many rules for the media. I don't blame UK. Part of the rule changes happened because of new coaches wanting stricter rules—meaning less access for the media. Also there are so many more media outlets trying to get stories. The internet brought about a huge influx of media types.

Back in 1981, for basketball, you could go to practice any day that wasn't game day to talk to the players. There weren't many in the media, so it was easy getting a one-on-one interview. Today, you don't get the opportunity to know Cal's players like you did Hall's, Pitino's, or Tubby's. Back then, players got to know you and if they liked you, they trusted you. Today there is very little trust. Back then, it was easy to get to know the players as people. Many of those players have remained friends. Back then players trusted me.

Through the years, there have been a number of times when I thanked a player at the end of their career for talking to me after a loss. Everyone knows that it's much easier talking after a win. I covered a lot of bad UK Football teams that had some terrific players who were really good guys. There were so many heartbreaking losses. Many players answered questions after those losses with a lot of class. I was on Kentucky Sports Radio right before I retired. I mentioned this on the air, and former UK quarterback Jared Lorenzen called in to say he's seen me thank players during interviews on many occasions. Jared told me, "I kept it real."

Interviewing players today is also different from the good old days. Today, they usually bring out just two or three basketball players for the media to interview. In the old days, you could talk to anyone in the locker room after the game. Today, UK has to use a stopwatch to keep track of time during these sessions, and there are so many media people surrounding a player that it can even be difficult for your photographer to get a good clean shot.

There are also times a player has a bad game and they don't want to talk to the media. Other times, UK may prevent a player from talking about a particular issue by not making them available. That's wrong! What happens to an athlete who goes on to the NBA? You can't hide there. The media is much tougher in the NBA. When Calipari talks about getting his players ready for the NBA, he should tell the players they *have* to talk to the media even if they don't want to. It's a practice that will serve them well when they are making a lot of money. The pressure of the media in pro sports has gotten to many athletes. Practice, practice, practice—the players need to practice with the media. Many improve light years from the first time they talk to you to the time they leave school.

Plus, I know there were players kept from the media until an issue cooled down. But you have to realize that the next time the athletes talk to the media, it'll obviously be brought up. Players often would rather just get those questions over with as soon as possible. That should be stressed by UK. Why have that issue hanging over your head when you know you are going to have to eventually face the media?

This isn't just a basketball issue. It applies to football also. When you go out in the real world, if you can handle dealing with the media in good times and bad, it can give you a huge leg up on others in your profession. Thinking on your feet and dealing with questions that can be good or bad will ultimately help you succeed.

I think, generally speaking, that the media in Lexington treats athletes with kindness. I think they should because the athletes are college kids. I've been tougher on coaches. They're getting paid—it's what they do for a living…but a kid is a kid.

Nowadays, not only is it hard for the media to establish relationships with the players, it's also difficult for them to get to know the coaches. Today, with the huge amount of media covering Kentucky, it's impossible for any coach to get to know everyone who covers them. Coaches don't like to admit it, but there are times they enjoy their relationship with someone in the media. I've been very lucky in that way.

The truth is that coaches don't really want to get to know *everyone* in the media. If you're John Calipari, do you think you really want to get to know 100 reporters? Of course not. Plus, the media is oftentimes considered the enemy. Sometimes if a coach believes a certain reporter is against them because of what they've done, I can see why they feel that way. And other times when a coach feels someone is out to get them, they can be way off base. I've seen coaches who were paranoid.

Cal doesn't want to deal with the media, but he knows he has to. He's really good with the media. Just like every other smart coach, Cal uses the media to his advantage. Cal likes to get his message out through the media. Sometimes his message is for his players. Sometimes it's for the fans. And, yes, sometimes it's for the media.

Any coach that doesn't use the media to put out their spin is wasting a potential resource. Billy Gillispie said that all he wanted to do was stay in his office and look at tape. This is Kentucky Basketball, so it was a dumb thing to say...but I respected his honesty. It also showed that Gillispie was clueless to the size of this program, and yet another reason why he never should have been hired.

The secret to successful reporting is that if you want to get something from somebody, you had better give them something back. It's THE secret of reporting. That's what got me ahead when I moved to Lexington in the 1980s. It's a lot tougher to get ahead today.

A lot of people don't want to dig for things. I remember my old photographer, Robin Lynch, telling me that I used to live on the phone.

My wife often called me to the phone by saying, "Your work wife is calling."

There are also media types that don't want to report on the negative. They are fans. I've called them "jock sniffers." Truth is, I stole that term from an old photographer at KDKA-TV who didn't like sports. If you're a jock sniffer, it's really difficult for me to respect what you're doing. Coaches don't respect jock sniffers, but they know they are harmless. The good news is that it's a much smaller group than it was when I started.

29

Howard Schnellenberger—Oh So Close!

Howard Schnellenberger, an All-American at Kentucky in 1951, was a star wide receiver for Coach Paul "Bear" Bryant. He was known as one of "Bear's Boys"—a disciple of the legendary Bear Bryant. Schnellenberger put the University of Miami on the football map, taking over a program that was a "have-not" and winning the national championship in 1983. There are many who believe that had he stayed at Miami, he would have gone down in history as one of the greatest football coaches of all time and could have won many national championships. Two of his successors—Jimmy Johnson and Butch Davis—both won national championships based on the foundation that Howard built.

Howard was a very smart offensive coach. It's forgotten that he was the offensive coordinator for Bear Bryant when Alabama won three NCAA championships. He was also the offensive coordinator when Don Shula's Miami Dolphins were undefeated in 1972. Both Shula and Schnellenberger were assistant coaches at Kentucky in 1959.

Howard *always* wanted to be the head coach at the University of Kentucky. He should have been the head coach but was turned down multiple times. It's baffling when you consider that a Kentucky boy—a huge star at Kentucky, and a big-time coach—never got the chance to coach at the flagship school of his home state. Some things in athletics make no sense. Although he'd never admit it, and I've tried multiple times to get him to say it, I know it will bother Howard until his last breath that he was never the coach at Kentucky.

In 1981, after Fran Curci had been fired, there were all kinds of rumors as to who the next Kentucky head football coach would be. I got a call from LEX18's Sue Wylie, one of the great female pioneers in broadcasting history. Her show, *Your Government*, had guests that included Ronald Reagan, Ted Kennedy, Jesse Jackson, and all the big political players in Kentucky.

Sue was eating lunch at the Lexington Country Club one afternoon and called me. "Alan, there's a guy here with a big mustache," she says to me over the phone. "He's smoking a pipe, and someone says he's a football coach. Ralph Gabbard and Cliff Hagan are also here." Gabbard was the president and general manager of Channel 27, and Hagan was the Kentucky athletics director. I slam the phone down and start screaming to our assignment editor, "I NEED A PHOTOGRAPHER RIGHT NOW!"

We run out the door and head over to the Lexington Country Club. The problem is that the club is private. I walked in with a photographer and went right up to the table where Howard's sitting. As he says hello, I'll never forget the look on Ralph Gabbard's and Ralph Hacker's face. Hacker served on the UK Radio Network for thirty-four years, many of them as the analyst beside legendary play-by-play man Cawood Ledford.

"Alan just barges in and there we were," said an amazed Hacker to Earl Cox of The Courier-Journal.

Howard hesitates and tells me he's just having lunch with some friends. I ask him directly if he's going to be the next football coach at Kentucky. He laughs, picks up his pipe, and at that moment I get a tap on the shoulder. It's one of the club managers reminding me that this is a private club and politely asking us to leave.

As we're leaving, I'm told that I can't shoot any video anywhere on their property. So we respected their request by shooting our video just *outside* the country club. We stayed just off the grounds, on the sidewalk, for about forty-five minutes and got the shot of Howard Schnellenberger getting in his car and driving past us. That twenty-second segment was the only video of Howard being in Lexington. It was a HUGE story. We played that video many times.

Cliff Hagan was not only the athletics director, but he had been a University of Kentucky basketball All-American at the same time Howard was starring in football. My sources had told me that Hagan, who I really like, wanted to have final say—as athletics directors often do—over the football program. Howard Schnellenberger, being Howard—was a very strong personality who also wanted more control than the wonderful man who would become the next coach.

Kentucky hired Jerry Claiborne, a great man who did a really good job. Claiborne was a very good player at Kentucky under Bear Bryant.

He was also at UK when Cliff Hagan played for Adolph Rupp and also—like Howard Schnellenberger—was an assistant coach for Bear Bryant.

I believe that Howard Schnellenberger was the one who should have been hired instead of Jerry Claiborne. That was the best opportunity for Kentucky to become a consistent Top-25 program. People often thought I was out of my mind, but ever since I arrived in 1981—although the support for football wasn't equal to basketball, or nearly the support that the other big-time powerful football teams in the SEC have—I always thought Kentucky should have tasted a lot more success. I stand by that today. Mark Stoops is finally proving me right.

I believe that athletics directors often hire the wrong coach. They don't take enough heat for that. Some of Jerry Claiborne's players, who loved him, won't like me for saying that...and I'm ok with that.

This would make a good debate. Which program was worse? Louisville when Howard took over or Kentucky when Mark Stoops took over? I go with Louisville. I just happened to cover Howard's first game as head coach at Louisville when they played at West Virginia. In 1985, I covered West Virginia, Pitt, and Penn State football for KDKA-TV in Pittsburgh. Louisville was awful.

After the game, Howard was walking into his locker room, he sees me and asks, "What are you doing here?" I tell him about moving to Pittsburgh and he says, "This is much worse [his team] than I thought it would be." He told me he'll talk to me as long as I want, but he needed to shower first because he was afraid he'd say the wrong thing. He was that upset.

When Howard got to Louisville, they were not only giving away tickets, but there had been talk about dropping to 1-AA football, a huge step down. He did one of the best jobs in the 1980s turning Miami around. He did one of the best college coaching jobs in the 1990s turning Louisville around.

Don't forget, however, that Jerry Claiborne is in the College Football Hall of Fame.

Both men deserve a great deal of credit for turning around bad football programs.

It still makes *no* sense to me that Howard didn't coach Kentucky Football.

As a footnote to both of these men, there are two things that stand out for me. One, I have a tremendous amount of respect for both of them. Two, the admiration they showed when they talked about their wives, Beverlee Schnellenberger and Faye Claiborne, only added to the respect I already had for them.

30

Freezer Bowl

It's January 10, 1982, and not only do I remember it like it was yesterday, but just thinking about it makes my toes freeze. The Bengals were playing the San Diego Chargers for the right to go to the Super Bowl. My photographer, Harold "Fat Man" Williams, and I went to cover the game. I remember the car they assigned us had no heater. There were plenty of "warmer" cars available, but the box where the keys were kept was locked.

On the way up to Cincinnati, we stopped to get a soda. I put fifty cents in the machine, and the soda came out frozen. *It was that cold.*

We got to the game and, with the wind chill, the temperature registered at *fifty-nine degrees below zero.* There were some brilliant kids who went shirtless in the stands.

The Bengals offensive linemen had decided the week of the game to wear short sleeves to intimidate the Chargers. When I interviewed them after the game, their arms were burned beet red. You could see exactly where their sleeves had ended and where their skin had been exposed to the brutal cold.

Right before kickoff, I remember Bryant Gumbel—a big shot at NBC Sports—strutted past me wearing this huge fur coat. I thought Gumbel did a great job.

On this day, thinking on my frozen feet paid off. Back then you could walk the sidelines, so I went on San Diego's side behind their bench because I knew that almost all the media on the sidelines would be on the Bengals' side. I stood by one of the big heaters used to keep the players warm. Obviously, you are *not allowed* in the bench area. When players came off the field, they would go stand directly in front of the heaters before taking a seat on the bench.

I purposely had my press pass so that you could just barely see the tip of it coming out of my jeans with all the layers of clothing I had on. For over three quarters of the game, I stayed right by one of the big heaters speaking with a security cop as if I were part of the San Diego staff. Players would come off the field to come stand by the heaters, and I would just casually acknowledge them as if I were part of the team. "Hey man, nice play," I'd yell out to them. They would respond, so the security guy didn't think twice that maybe I wasn't supposed to be there. I must have had very short conversations with over twenty players. They didn't know who I was. They just wanted to get warm.

In the fourth quarter, for some reason, this cop suddenly asks to see my pass. I show him my *press* pass, and he immediately wants to kick me out of the stadium. I plead with him to let me stay in front of the heaters, but he won't have any of it. He laughs as he says, "Get out of here." So for most of the fourth quarter, I watch from the Bengals' side of the field—freezing.

The Bengals, coached by Forrest Gregg, won 27-7 that day. For what it's worth, I always thought Don Coryell, the Chargers' head coach, was one of the great coaches. He never got enough love with his *Air Coryell* passing offense.

The Bengals' quarterback, Kenny Anderson, should have been in the Hall of Fame a long time ago. In his sixteen NFL seasons, Anderson completed 2,654 of 4,475 passes (59.3%) for 32,838 yards and 197 touchdowns. I've said this on radio many times that if Kenny Anderson played for the New York Giants, he'd have been in the Hall of Fame a long, long, time ago.

Man, it was cold.

31

Fishing with Bobby Knight

This isn't breaking news. Bobby Knight—the legendary, bombastic former head basketball coach of the Indiana Hoosiers—is a *strange* man. At times, his opinions are brilliant. At other times, his opinions are so bad it makes you wonder how he could believe some of the things he's saying. The thing about Bobby Knight that I've never understood is how he could win three national championships and demand that his players perform with great discipline—but he was a hypocrite, not being able to control himself better.

This was crazy. We go to Indiana, and I'm covering my first Kentucky at Indiana game on December 22, 1982. Joe B. Hall was UK's coach. Kentucky was ranked second in the nation, and Indiana was ranked fifth. I did something you couldn't do now—I snuck behind the Indiana bench a couple of times late in the game to hear what Bobby Knight was saying. That would be a "no-no" today.

Indiana has the game won, and Bobby Knight takes a timeout at the end of the game just to congratulate his team and to tell them, "You guys did a great *bleeping* job." When his players heard those words, they exploded with orgasmic jubilation. Indiana, led by Randy Wittman's 17 points, wins 62-59.

Afterwards, Bobby Knight comes into the press area. I ask a question. I don't remember what I asked, but I know it wasn't in a bad tone of voice. "I'm not answering," Knight says. "I'm going fishing. I'll see ya." He then walks away, and all these guys from Indiana want to break my neck.

Even though I didn't do anything wrong, the press from Indiana were chirping at me really bad because they had so little time with Knight. I had to tell one of them who got in my face to get the *blank* away from me. Fortunately, he did, and the Indiana media left me alone.

Generally speaking, coaches are usually very good at listening to your tone of voice. If you have a bad tone when you're asking what they perceive to be a negative question, a little bell rings in the back of their head and they can go off—sometimes loud, sometimes nasty, sometimes snippy. You can ask a tough question in the right tone of voice, and most of the time you get a good answer.

When I asked Bobby Knight the question that day, there was nothing wrong with my tone of voice. Bobby Knight didn't know who I was, and he didn't care. He probably instantly figured out I was from Kentucky, and he didn't want to deal with me. He didn't want to do the press conference, and he just decided to walk out. I shouldn't have been surprised. Knight was just being Knight.

32

Sam Bowie Shoots Air Balls

When I got to the TV station in Lexington in 1981, there were two tapes in the sports closet that had the game highlights from the year before. I sat down and watched both of those tapes multiple times. I have never seen a big man who could dribble, run, jump, shoot, and block shots like Sam Bowie could when he was healthy. The running part was amazing. I've never seen it before for a big man—and never seen it since. The long alley-oop dunks were the best I've seen covering Kentucky.

After a stellar career as a McDonald's and Parade All-American at Lebanon High School in Pennsylvania, Bowie got off to a quick start in his freshman year at UK. During that 1979-80 season, the 7'1", 235-pound center averaged 12 points and 8 rebounds for the Wildcats. The next year—his sophomore season—Bowie averaged 17.5 points and 9 rebounds per game while being named a third-team AP All-American.

Then Sam had all those knee and leg injuries. Due to a stress fracture in his left tibia, Bowie missed the entire 1981-82 season. When his recovery didn't go the way Kentucky had hoped, Bowie also sat out the 1982-83 season as a medical redshirt. He was able to return for the 1983-84 season, where he averaged 10.5 points and 9 rebounds while being named to the second-team All-American squad.

If you compared the highlights from the year before I got to Lexington and those from Sam's last year, he was a shadow of what he used to be. He should have been one of the greatest players of all time. If he was healthy, Joe B. Hall might have won another NCAA championship. That would have put Joe B. Hall in the Hall of Fame.

When Sam got drafted by the Portland Trailblazers as the second pick in the 1984 NBA draft, I knew he wasn't the same player. If I knew he wasn't the same player, I've always wondered—what was

Portland thinking?

Here's a part of sports that I hate. Sam Bowie has gone down in history as one of the biggest draft busts in the NBA. It's not Sam's fault. It's Portland's fault. Portland is the idiot that didn't draft Michael Jordan. They didn't draft Michael Jordan because they had Clyde Drexler, and they didn't see the need for two players who played similar styles. How many NBA Championships would Portland have won with Drexler and Jordan? I've been following the NBA since 1960. It's the dumbest decision ever—not drafting Michael Jordan. Sam Bowie has taken a lot of crap in his professional basketball career that wasn't his fault. It's not right.

Fast forward to after Sam retires. He comes over to our house, and my son J.J.—who couldn't have been more than six at the time—is trying to shoot baskets next door. He couldn't really shoot the ball at a ten-foot rim, so he was basically just dribbling. Sam goes over, picks J.J. up, and lets J.J. dunk the ball a few times. I told Sam he didn't have to entertain my son, but Sam was having a good time. J.J. was having a great time. He had no idea who Sam was. He just knew two things— Sam was the tallest man he'd ever seen, and he was having a lot of fun playing with Sam.

When they were done, I picked up a ball and tossed it to Sam. He was about ten feet away from the basket when he shot an air ball. *What?* I tossed him the ball again, he shot it, and it's another air ball. "Sam, you OK?" I ask. He says back to me, "Alan, I haven't picked up a ball in a year."

Sam had a chance to go back to the NBA, but he chose not to. He says the Chicago Bulls—Michael Jordan's team—brought him in just to play backup center for ten or fifteen minutes a game. They were also going to pay him a lot of money for not a lot of work. Jordan told him that they were going to win an NBA championship either way—with or without Sam. Sam turned it down. He didn't need the money...and he no longer loved the game.

I always thought it was sad. You look at a guy like Sam Bowie, and you quickly see how his injuries robbed him of his joy for the game. I'm not so sure how much Sam loved basketball after he got hurt. I can understand why the love would disappear. He could have gotten a potential NBA championship ring, but Sam didn't care. I respected the fact that he just didn't want to play basketball anymore.

Karl-Anthony Towns, if he stays healthy, is going to be in the NBA Hall of Fame. I don't doubt it. At his pace, his numbers over twelve to fifteen years will get him there. Sam Bowie, before his knees and legs got brittle, was a much better basketball player. Sam could shoot better, block shots better, run the court much, much better, and handle the ball better. As I say that, I'm enjoying watching Karl-Anthony Towns play.

But that's how good Sam Bowie was.

33

Charles "Atlas" Hurt

In my career, the three most chiseled athletes I've ever talked to and interviewed were Charles Hurt, Herschel Walker, and Bo Jackson. Charles "Atlas" Hurt wasn't a shooter, but he left UK No. 1 all-time in field goal percentage at 59 percent. I actually thought he could have played pro ball as a defensive specialist off the bench. Another mistake by the NBA. He could have definitely played today because the really good NBA teams think of extra players as specialists.

Charles Hurt played for UK from 1979-1983. He could have scored more if he played on a bad team, but Kentucky didn't need him to score. He didn't take a lot of shots, but he never took bad shots. He was smart and efficient.

I remember covering a game in Auburn. Wesley Person and Charles Barkley were on that team. Early in the game, Hurt was covering Barkley who was named one of the fifty greatest players in NBA history in 1996. Hurt boxed out "The Round Mound of Rebound," and Barkley went flying—literally flying. And this was when Barkley—who's in the NBA and College Basketball's Hall of Fame—was really heavy (He once blamed chocolate cookies for him topping 300 pounds). Barkley was furious, runs after Hurt...and just 113 seconds into the game, Barkley gets thrown out for deliberately hitting Hurt's head from behind. Derrick Hord hit a shot at the end to win the game for UK. Auburn probably would've won the game if Barkley didn't take the bait.

I'll never forget Barkley talking to the media after the game. What are the odds of a college player talking to the media today after getting tossed? A hundred to one—and I'm being optimistic.

Barkley admitted he deserved to be thrown out. "More like I was made a fool of," he said to me after the game. You don't hear athletes say that every day. But, that's part of the charm of Barkley—who in his own way is a great broadcaster. He doesn't hold back.

There was a theory that Hurt had set him up, that he purposely got Barkley mad. When we lost Hurt to complications from leukemia in 2016, I talked to Kenny "Sky" Walker. The former UK great had a big smile on his face saying that Hurt knew what he was doing getting under Barkley's skin.

Hurt was picked by Milwaukee in the sixth round of the 1983 NBA draft. Later he played basketball in Japan. He joined the Army in 1987 and went on to have a great military career. He was way too young when he died at the age of fifty-five.

His death was shocking. Here was a great high school basketball player—a two-time All-Stater who led Shelby County to the 1978 State Title—being taken away from us so soon. I was surprised to be the only TV camera there for his visitation. Many of his former teammates came in from all over to say goodbye. Many hadn't seen each other in a long time. I just wished the reunion had taken place under happier circumstances.

34

The Big Dipper

I used to do a lot of live shots when I anchored for LEX18. I can't remember where I was this particular time, but I was doing a live shot and made an egregious mistake. I took a big swig of soda—with bubbles—just before going on the air. It was a dumb thing to do, and for obvious reasons, I never did it again.

There are two things in broadcasting you don't do. You don't eat popcorn when you're doing radio baseball play-by-play because you just can't talk. I made *that* mistake in my first job in Farmington, New Mexico. And you don't swig soda before going on the air.

It was a story about Melvin Turpin, whose nickname was the Big Dipper. I had taken a swig of soda and had saliva in my mouth seconds before going on the air. People were convinced that instead of me saying, "Big Dipper," I said, "Big *Blank* (rhymes with stick)." I probably watched that tape close to a hundred times, and I don't think I said it—but whatever comes out of my mouth is my responsibility.

This thing just took off like wildfire. What I eventually learned was that you just have to laugh it off. But I was stupid. At first I was mad at everyone who was busting my chops because I honestly thought I said, "Dipper," but it didn't come out that way. If you have something in your mouth and you're talking, your mouth can become compromised.

I got very defensive about it which only made it worse. When I got back to the station, people were clapping, calling me names, and giving me a really hard time. I kept denying that I ever said it, but I simply wasn't going to convince anyone that I didn't. The mistake I made with the Big Dipper helped me tremendously later on in dealing with the Billy Gillispie situation. I should have resorted to humor right away. That would have defused the situation, and it wouldn't have been such a big deal.

Shooting from ten to fifteen feet, Melvin Turpin was a wonderful shooter for a big man. While playing for the University of Kentucky from 1980-84, the 6'11" center out of Lexington Bryan Station High School scored 1,509 career points while shooting 59% from the field. As an All-American during his senior season, he averaged a team-high 15.2 points per game and led the Wildcats to the Final Four.

Melvin was also a very kind and considerate person. It was well documented that Melvin had a weight problem. I was the one who broke the story that Coach Joe B. Hall had a student manager following Melvin around at night to make sure he wouldn't go out and eat pizza. Fast food establishments in the area were told that they were not to feed Melvin.

I had a friend at the TV station who lived in Melvin's neighborhood. He told me that since everyone loved Melvin, Melvin would just visit neighborhood homes and get plenty of food.

Melvin Turpin should have played in the NBA for a long time. Big men who can catch the ball and turn and shoot are worth their weight in gold.

I was in the Stokely Athletic Center on January 31, 1983, the night Melvin put up 42 points against Tennessee. Melvin couldn't miss, hitting 18-22 shots from the floor and grabbing 12 rebounds against the Volunteers. After a while, tenth-ranked Kentucky just gave Melvin the ball, and he would seemingly score every time down the court. It was a magical evening despite unranked Tennessee pulling out a 65-63 upset.

Melvin needed someone to help him out with discipline and structure while in the NBA. You can blame Melvin himself for not having it, but I blame the teams. If I'm an NBA team and I make an investment in a player, I'm going to take care of that player. In the NBA, players are commodities. If you're signing somebody to a big contract, isn't it in your best interest to take care of your investment? That's what players are—they're investments. That may sound cold, but that's reality.

When the Washington Bullets drafted Melvin with the sixth overall pick in the 1984 NBA draft, they should have been smart enough to know that Melvin was a lovely person who needed some help. They should have assigned somebody—paid them fifty thousand dollars a year, or whatever—and they would have gotten millions more out of Melvin. If I'm running the team and I see that Melvin is getting heavy and can't move as well, I'm going to do something about it. Melvin just needed some TLC—some tender loving care. The NBA has since gotten much better about watching over their talent.

A couple of years before he died, I'm driving down Richmond Road in Lexington and someone is honking their horn at me like crazy. I turn around, and there's Melvin in this small, old, beat-up car. I hadn't seen him in years. When Melvin played here, I interviewed him for what seemed like a hundred times. I really liked him, and he liked me.

Melvin knew that I thought of him as a kind person who just happened to be seven feet tall. We were right by a car dealership on Richmond Road. I can remember it like it was yesterday. Melvin was four hundred pounds then, so I don't know how he even got into that tiny car—but he gets out of his car, comes over to me, and gives me a big hug. I was far from skinny back then—but Melvin puts his arms around me, picks me up, and tells me how happy he is to see me. He's not letting go. It's like one of those special moments. That was Melvin's way of saying that I was his friend. I've had some terrific relationships with players over the years, but I've never been hugged like that by anyone.

Here's something that's really sad. Someone gave Melvin a menial job after his playing days just so he could have a couple of dollars in his pocket. Melvin should have had someone manage his money. He should have had a personal trainer watch over his health. He should have retired with a lot of money. Like a lot of other athletes, Melvin simply didn't know how to deal with fame or fortune.

On July 8, 2010, I was in Salt Lake City on my way to Idaho when I get a phone call from my colleague, Mary Jo Perino, telling me that Melvin—who was only forty-nine years old—died by suicide from an apparent self-inflicted gunshot wound. After the call, I just stood there and started crying. It was just so sad.

You never know the pain someone is feeling in their heart. Just writing this chapter has me very emotional.

35

The Pure Emotion and Passion
of Paul Andrews

This will always be one of my favorite moments as a reporter. The score is tied 51-51. North Hardin has the ball with seconds left. They throw a long pass towards their basket. Paul Andrews intercepts the pass, takes three dribbles, throws up a shot past half court that goes in, and Laurel County wins the 1982 State Championship 53-51.

Paul said that there was no pressure on his shot because the score was tied. "I wasn't thinking," he said. "My first instinct was to grab the ball and the game would go into overtime. The right thing to do would have been to just let the ball go out of bounds."

"My wife teases me, because so often when we go out, someone will come up to us and tell me they were at that game. Rupp Arena only holds 23,000 people, but on that night, there were evidently 50,000 people there because everybody tells us that they saw me hit the shot."

To get to the state championship game, Laurel County had to beat Virgie. If you remember, Paul Andrews hit the winning free throws with two seconds left. Virgie was a really good team, and its star was Todd May—Kentucky's Mr. Basketball.

Todd May's story is a really sad one. I thought he was going to be one of the great UK players. He was 6'9" and could shoot with either hand. He was unbelievable. He comes to UK, gets homesick, and goes back home. Todd May should have been an NBA star for a *long* time. He had game—but he was country. Lexington was too big for him. He didn't like the hugeness of UK, even though he grew up a UK fan. It was really sad. It's one of the saddest things I've seen living in Kentucky. If you talk to Joe B. Hall, he'll tell you that's one of the saddest parts of coaching—seeing somebody who doesn't make it who should have made it big.

Todd May could have put UK over the top. Kenny "Sky" Walker, an All-American at UK, will be the first to tell you that May could do things that he couldn't do. May just never gave UK a chance. He played in only four games. Some of the greatest unknown secrets in sports involve the number of athletes who think about transferring early in their career and then don't do it.

For decades, the semifinals and finals of the Kentucky High School State Championship were played on the same day. You had to play two games on Saturday. I always thought that was really stupid. Their reasoning was that they were saving people money on hotel rooms while allowing everybody to still make it to church on Sunday. I get that.

I can't tell you how many times that I believed teams lost the state championship game because too many players cramped up. Cramping has played such a huge part in those games that it's not even funny. Paul Andrews was even dealing with cramps that night.

It's always been my opinion that the KHSAA was doing this all wrong. I used to call The Sweet Sixteen the greatest show on earth on TV. It's about as pure of a sporting event as you can find in America. When you play all year and have worked your whole life to get to the championship game, dealing with cramps shouldn't be the issue. You're asking players to do something that they just never do. Some teams have to play four games in three days with all that pressure. Then on Saturday, you're playing the two biggest games of your life. When they finally moved the championship game to Sunday, I was very happy.

Back to Paul Andrews. So, the shot's going up, and I'm on the baseline behind Paul on the floor. Paul throws the shot up. It's just a heave. About half way through—I remember it like it was yesterday—I thought the thing had a chance. I didn't say it was going in—but it had a chance.

I remember Rupp Arena just going dead silent. Paul remembers the silence also. As the ball is going down, I think to myself, "holy *bleep*, this ball's going in." The shot goes in, and I literally helped pick up and drag my photographer, Harold "Fat Man" Williams—who weighed over 300 pounds—onto the court. It was an adrenaline rush. Harold somehow kept the shot steady and did a great job.

When I got to center court, right after he hit the shot, Andrews was on his back, screaming. I stick the microphone in his face and do the interview. "Paul how'd you do it?" I asked. We played that interview for days. No one else had their camera at center court. The pure emotion after that shot was as good as it gets on any level of sports. That's why I love getting interviews right away when you can. The yelling, screaming, and the pure emotion of the moment isn't the same five or fifteen minutes later.

I covered national championship games. But, did they go down to the last second? Kentucky had to come back to beat Utah in 1998, but it wasn't a last-second win. Nobody thought Kentucky was going to lose to Syracuse in 1996. When Kentucky beat Kansas in 2012, I never thought Kansas was going to win. There was tension in those games, but when it comes to raw emotion, there's nothing else I've ever done or been a part of that matches that moment with Paul. Plus in those NCAA championship games, local cameras aren't allowed on the court immediately after the game.

Paul Andrews, for us, was a hall of fame moment.

Paul Andrews had a nice career at Kentucky. Since the very first time we talked, he's always been a class act. He's now the CEO of Brook Hospitals in Louisville. He's very successful. He's one of the most successful former UK athletes in any sport.

One of the things I think is really cool about Paul is that he's always deflected a lot of the accolades associated with hitting that shot. He made sure people knew the victory was a team thing. That's just the way Paul was—and still is.

36

Swimming with Herschel Walker

In the early 1980s, the NBC-TV stations had gotten together to give an award out honoring the Athlete of the Year in the Southeastern Conference. As sports director of LEX18, I went to the banquet as the station representative.

The first time I went, the banquet was held in Birmingham, Alabama. I went to the pool the day of the event, and Herschel Walker just happened to be there. Herschel played college football for the University of Georgia, earned consensus All-American honors three times, and won the Heisman Trophy in 1982.

Chris Collinsworth, future NFL wide receiver for the Cincinnati Bengals—and future NBC-TV star—and Olympic swimmer Rowdy Gaines were also sitting by the pool as they were representing their schools—Florida and Auburn. Did you know that Chris Collinsworth's dad was on the bench playing basketball for Kentucky when they won the national championship in 1958?

These guys were just sitting around the pool, cracking up, and having a good time. You could tell that they were all getting along great. Athletes have said many times that the thing they missed most when they retired was the camaraderie—the kidding that goes on in the locker room, the boys being boys, the goofing around, the yelling and screaming of athletes giving their teammates a rough time—that is tough to get anywhere else.

I don't know how it all started, but Herschel wasn't going into the pool under any circumstances. I heard one of the guys call over to him, "Hey Herschel, why don't you get in the pool?" Herschel declined several times, but they were persistent in asking him to get in the water. Finally, after the ribbing had gone on for a little while, Herschel turned to them and said, "Don't you know my people don't swim."

If you said that today—oh my gosh—people would go crazy. But Herschel was just being funny. And in that group of athletes, it was hilarious. Now somebody may read this and perceive it to be racial. It wasn't. I get that not all jokes are harmless. But when Herschel made that comment, everybody was laughing.

There are many things that go on in a sports locker room that are politically incorrect, but most athletes love it. And that's the part about sports that I think the public doesn't understand. What really stinks is, we've become so politically correct that we miss out on so much of the kidding that used to go on.

For example, the Rat Pack. Frank Sinatra, Dean Martin, and Sammy Davis, Jr. were all great friends. I'm a big Sinatra fan. I listen to him all the time. I've even done yoga listening to Sinatra. If someone went on stage in Las Vegas today and did the same kind of ribbing and kidding that went on between the three of them, I think they'd be in serious trouble. Sammy Davis Jr. called himself a one-eyed Jew. He gave it to Frank, and Frank gave it to him.

By the way, Herschel finally did get in the water. He didn't do a good job swimming. Some athletes are just not good swimmers. Instead, Herschel started doing push-ups by the side of the pool. He was famous for doing five hundred push-ups and a thousand sit-ups at one time during a workout. I watched Herschel Walker that afternoon do two hundred push-ups by the pool. He did them so fast that it still remains one of the most amazing things I've ever seen. He wasn't even tired afterwards.

37

Charles Barkley—
"That Means They Love Me"

Charles Barkley wanted to play basketball at Kentucky. Kentucky thought he was too short and too fat, so they never really considered recruiting him. Growing up in the South, Barkley—like many other kids at the time—thought Kentucky was the mecca of college basketball.

Auburn came to Rupp Arena in the early eighties. Barkley was 6'4" and really heavy back then. I have *never ever, ever, ever* seen a human being that big and that wide jump like he did. He had two dunks where his elbows got above the rim—*above the rim!* People were booing him and jeering him the minute he walked out on the court.

After the game, I went to the opposing team's locker room. I probably did that more than any other reporter back then. Barkley came in, and I kneel down in front of a big crowd that has already gathered around him. "Charles, did you hear the people booing you?" I ask him.

"Yes," he answered me.

"What did that tell you?" I ask him.

Barkley pauses. It was a well-timed comedic pause, followed by a giant smile. When he did this, I immediately knew he could eventually be great on television. He turns to the TV camera and says, "That means they *LOVE* me." Everybody in the room just started laughing. Barkley wasn't afraid of the Rupp Arena crowd. He wasn't afraid of the hugeness of the moment.

I can't tell you how many times I saw teams come into Rupp Arena and choke and fold. They'd be down ten to fifteen points in the first ten minutes of a game. They would then settle down and play Kentucky fairly evenly, but by then it was too late. Those first few minutes ended up being the difference in the game. They were intimidated before the ball was ever thrown up.

Barkley was never intimidated. Whatever that certain something "it" is, Charles Barkley had "it." He just always had it. He always had a big mouth, he always told you his opinions, he always just had it.

There was the time Kenny "Sky" Walker made Barkley cry. Kenny hit the game winning shot in the SEC Tournament just before the clock ran out. Barkley sat on the court crying after the shot went in.

Walker and Barkley are friends—and when given the chance, Kenny still likes to rub it in.

38

Channel 27 Looking
to Replace Rob Bromley

I wish this headline never was in the *Lexington Herald-Leader*. I was a big part of that story. While I was the sports director at LEX18, I was offered the chance to get rid of my competitor, Rob Bromley.

I thought that sucked for two reasons. One, I felt bad for Bromley, who ended up working for Channel 27 for forty years. And two, I eventually had garbage thrown at me by LEX18 management, so I could relate to what Rob went through.

More on this later in this chapter. But first, there are some things in here I don't think Rob ever knew.

I was the sports director for KBCI-TV in Boise in 1980. Back then, getting interviews from opposing teams was like driving a Fred Flintstone car. There was no technology. Today you can get a story in five minutes. Back then, it took what seemed like forever to get interviews long distance. To cover a team like Idaho State, the sports information director would send us interviews once a week on an old, ratty, three-quarter tape that sometimes wasn't usable. Monday's press conference tape wouldn't arrive until late Wednesday afternoon. A photographer would pick the tape up at the bus station. No kidding. That was how we covered Idaho State. You couldn't drive to Pocatello to get what you needed. Plus, Idaho State recruited in Boise, so they needed the exposure on TV. By the way, former Cincinnati Bengals coach Marvin Lewis was an All-Big Sky linebacker for Idaho State back then.

In 1980, Boise State was in the NCAA Division I-AA National Championship. They were playing Eastern Kentucky University. I didn't know where EKU was. I look it up and find out that Richmond is close to Lexington, so I called the CBS affiliate in Lexington in order to trade interview tapes. Rob Bromley, of WKYT-TV gets on the phone, and he's happy to make the trade. I had to get permission to put my tape on an airplane. It wasn't a big deal if I had to spend five dollars to put my tape on a Greyhound bus, but an airplane was more expensive. That's how we traded tapes. That was my first encounter with Rob.

This isn't a negative commentary on Rob Bromley. We went through some of the same things. Trust me—Channel 27 wanted to get rid of Rob Bromley multiple times. Trust me—LEX18 wanted to get rid of *me* multiple times.

I'd been at LEX18 for less than two years. All of a sudden I started getting unsolicited phone calls for jobs from TV stations all across the country that I never applied to. I asked one news director in a major market who called me how he found out about me. Initially, he didn't want to tell me. But I told him if he didn't tell me how he got my tape, the conversation was over. That surprised him. He admitted it was Channel 27. The rival station was trying to get rid of me.

This happens more than the public realizes. If there's someone that's hurting another TV station, they would send your tape to a consultant who shops the talent (Tape? No such thing today. It's all online). I know LEX18 did the same thing. Channel 27, whether they want to admit it or not, marketed me.

Ralph Gabbard was the president and general manager of Channel 27. Remember, I'm the sports director of LEX18. Ralph Gabbard's first words when we finally met face to face about taking over his sports department were, "You're killing me." Honestly, that made me feel great.

Ralph Gabbard had built Channel 27 into a powerful TV station. Part of his strategy was taking away the Kentucky Basketball TV contract and coaches shows from LEX18 before I moved to Lexington. Gabbard thought he owned UK sports news and wasn't happy that this new kid—who didn't have the access his people did—was kicking his tail when it came to UK sports. I respected Ralph Gabbard. He was one of the top broadcasting executives ever in Kentucky. Just because someone works at another TV station doesn't mean you can't respect what they do. I've never played that game. If you're good, you're good—it doesn't matter where you are.

In 1982, just before the tipoff of UK being upset 50-44 in the NCAA Tournament by Middle Tennessee, Ralph Gabbard took the media seat next to me and introduced himself. It was the only time I ever sat next to a TV general manager covering a UK Basketball game. Obviously, it wasn't by accident. By the way, that was a really bad loss. UK didn't have anyone with double figures in that game. They shot 37%, and they scored only 14 points in the second half. They also had a ton more talent than their opponent. They played like a very uptight team. It was one of those games UK never should have lost. Joe B. Hall took a lot of heat for losing that game—and he deserved it.

I didn't realize it at the time, but Gabbard was trying to figure out who I was as a person. Seconds before the tip-off, he holds up a pencil and says, "Joe B. is so uptight you couldn't stick this up his *blank*." We laughed. I was shocked to hear that because Gabbard didn't know me at all. He was testing me. That became obvious as the game went on. We talked a lot throughout the game. I'm sure that conversation had a lot to do with him trying to hire me.

To my second conversation with Ralph Gabbard. It's a normal day at 5:35 pm—I'm scheduled to go on TV at 5:50 pm, and I'm sitting at my desk. I remember it like it was yesterday. Ralph Gabbard calls me and says he wants to talk to me about hiring me. I was shocked. We met a couple of times to discuss his offer. I was still under contract with LEX18, but he wanted me to be the Monday through Friday main sports anchor at his station. He also wanted me to do the UK coaches shows that Bromley was doing and whatever play-by-play they did.

I asked him what *he* wanted to do with Rob Bromley, who was the main sports anchor at Channel 27. Gabbard replies back to me—and I quote—"Do whatever you want." I was surprised to hear him say that. Whether I wanted to fire Bromley, or make him the weekend sports anchor, or whatever, Gabbard's answer was always, "Do whatever you want." Wow!!

I became uncomfortable with Gabbard because of Bromley. First of all, I wasn't looking to go to Channel 27, although I did still listen to his pitch. Gabbard even had a lawyer in Washington look at my contract to check out my non-compete clause. He told me that if I had to sit out for six months or a year, Channel 27 would pay me for sitting out. When he said that, I couldn't tell what was more important—getting me out of LEX18 or hiring me at Channel 27.

I never agreed to go to Channel 27 even though Ralph Gabbard's offer was a lot more than I was making at LEX18. To be honest, I expected a much better offer.

I had turned down more money than that in Grand Junction, Colorado years before to run two radio stations, sell advertising, and continue doing a ton of radio play-by-play. At this time, I was already starting to get the itch to move on from Lexington. I was in line for better jobs in much bigger markets which would pay me more than what Gabbard was offering. I didn't need to go across town. I was just listening to him.

Earl Cox, the most powerful sports columnist in the state with the *Louisville Courier-Journal,* did a big Sunday feature on me. I was really surprised. The picture they took of me on the sidelines of a UK Football game was typical for me back then—hat on backwards, cigar in my mouth, and too many buttons unbuttoned on my shirt.

This is what Earl wrote:

"Despite his looks—[Alan Cutler] is turning Lexington television upside down. As sports director of WLEX-TV, Cutler is Lexington's most recognizable television personality, according to Ralph Hacker, general manager of radio station WVLK."

"Cutler has broken so many stories that sports fans are getting scared not to watch because they are afraid they'll miss something. A report making the rounds in Lexington is that one of his competitors may lose his job because of the job Cutler has done."

Cox was talking about Bromley. I was surprised he wrote that.

Here's what Oscar Combs, then the owner of *The Cats' Pause,* a subscription publication spotlighting University of Kentucky sports, told Cox about me:

"He works hard and hustles, and he is great at making contacts. Alan even had the story when Cliff Hagan [UK director of athletics] mailed the contract to the University of Louisville for the UK/U of L game. On hard news, no one is better."

Hacker and Gabbard owned the rights to UK Basketball and Football for their radio and TV stations. Hacker's comments blew me away.

"Alan is a personality, a hustler…if there's a story about to break, he works it. People notice that and now they are calling him. When you hustle, you deserve to get the story. People in Lexington are starting to respect him totally," Hacker told Earl Cox.

Here's where it gets hairy. Susan White was the TV writer for the *Lexington Herald-Leader* newspaper. She came to the station and did an interview with me. She wrote in her article that *I* was the one who called Channel 27 rather than the other way around. *I HIT THE ROOF!* There were people at LEX18 who believed that Channel 27 had Susan in their back pocket. I never bought it, but I still told Susan that what she wrote was a *blank blank blank blank blankety blank lie.* I went crazy. It was a lie—an absolute lie. Not true!

I've never done that to anyone doing a story. Never!!! And I couldn't believe anyone would do that to me.

Down the road, Susan White called me about doing another story. I said no and hung up on her. She kept on calling back. I finally said okay, but that I would bring a tape recorder to the interview and if she lied, I would rip her on TV. I did the story.

Back to my problem with Gabbard and LEX18. Now I get called into Harry Barfield, the LEX18 general manager's office. Harry went crazy on me because he said I *never* should have called Ralph Gabbard. He never yelled at me like he did that day. I just let him go. When he was finished, I told him what the deal was. "One, I have never lied to you," I said. "Two, I'm not going to lie to you now. Three, Ralph Gabbard called *me*. And four, you ought to be *ashamed* of yourself because you know I've never lied to you." The last part didn't sit well with Harry.

When Harry said I shouldn't have talked to Channel 27 at all, I got really angry and told him that I would talk to anybody who wanted to talk to me. He might not like that, but I didn't care—and I told him that. I wasn't going to work for Channel 27, but you never close the door on anything. During the entire negotiations with Channel 27, I figured Gabbard would at least work harder to get me a job in a much bigger TV market. There was never a point in these negotiations that I actually wanted to go work for Channel 27. I'll admit that I did enjoy being courted and someone telling me how good I am. Who doesn't like that? And yes, I was curious as to what was going to be offered.

Harry went crazy again. By the time we were finished, at the end of the conversation—as God is my witness—he offered me a fifteen-hundred-dollar raise. It remains one of the weirdest conversations in my career. We're yelling back and forth at each other, and at the end of our meeting, he wants to give me fifteen hundred dollars. He's got that cheap White Owl cigar in his mouth, and he's offering me more money. Before I left his office, we shook hands.

A couple of days later, Mindy Shannon, our female anchor, had this huge smile on her face as she sat down to go to work. She had flowers on her desk too. After the early newscast, I sat down by the desk next to Mindy and purposely got really close to her and the flowers. Me sitting that close to Mindy made her uncomfortable—but I didn't want anyone else to listen—and remember I have a big mouth.

"Mindy, I have this crazy feeling that you just got a fifteen-hundred-dollar raise," I said. She blushed like I've never seen her blush. She then asked me how I knew. I told her the whole story, and her jaw dropped like never before. Harry didn't want to pay me more money than Mindy, so he gave both of us a raise. Mindy did manage to say "thank you" with a nice smile as I walked away.

Within a couple of months of me declining Gabbard's offer, I started getting those phone calls from all over that I told you about earlier. I was offered the No. 1 job in Dallas based upon what Gabbard did. I turned it down because the contract was going to be awful—but that's neither here nor there. Dallas wasn't the only major market I turned down.

The next time I saw Rob Bromley was at a press conference at the Hyatt Regency in downtown Lexington. By then, what happened with me and Channel 27 had been in the newspaper. It wasn't the only article written about Bromley's future. People were talking. I asked Rob if he had a minute, and he looked at me with fire in his eyes.

"Rob, I'm going to tell you this for your benefit, not mine," I said. "I'm going to tell you this because Ralph Gabbard is going to get you. He called me, and he offered me your job, and he said I could do anything I want with you. If this was happening to me, I'd want someone to tell me. That's the God's-honest truth."

I thought I was being a nice guy. Bromley and I weren't friends, but there was no bad blood on my part.

Bromley said he didn't believe me. That *really* ticked me off. I didn't have to tell Bromley anything. Most people wouldn't have said anything. Rob turned away sheepishly from me, walked away, and we never talked about it again. That was over thirty-five years ago. For a long time, he never said a word to me. In fact, for most of the time we competed, we rarely talked.

Fast forward to today. I respect Rob. He's always handled himself with class. He is quiet, and a little bit shy. He worked hard and did a good job. When Rob got in the Kentucky Athletics Hall of Fame, I congratulated him and told him how happy I was for him. He deserves it and earned it. I also expect that I'll never join him. I'm not popular with a number of people who do the voting. I'm good with that. The truth is, and many who know my large ego won't believe this, I wanted to get in and to see the look on my kids' faces. Having my family be proud of me means everything. The politics to get in? They can kiss my.... If they called today, I would say, "no thank you—not interested in joining." It should have already happened.

On my last day on TV, Rob agreed to be part of Lee Cruse's funny story about putting me out to pasture—on Derby Day. I didn't see the story until it was on TV, and standing with Lee had us both fighting back tears.

Rob and I are just very different. Everybody's got their own style. Back in the day, I lived for breaking big stories. Back then it seemed like I lived on the phone. Back then I beat WKYT in the ratings when it came to breaking stories.

I developed a system for breaking stories that ended up working much, much better than I thought it would. I would go on TV and say "sources tell me"—I couldn't believe all the sources that told me things. If their bosses knew what they told me, their job might be in jeopardy. Many times I questioned myself and wondered if I could ever do that. But the big stories kept on coming while I was anchoring. People trusted me. That was the key.

Some of those "sources" from the 1980s and 1990s are still friends.

Some of those "sources" from the 1980s and 1990s are gone.

Some of those "sources" never liked me, but they trusted me.

For some of those "sources," I was able to trade information to help them out with stuff that I couldn't or wouldn't put on TV.

Some of those "sources" told me they talked to me because they trusted I would be fair with them.

One of my favorite "sources" was someone who bled Blue as much as anyone. I wasn't going to say his name, and for years I've told this story without saying his name. But I did in a speech where his daughter is the one who asked me to speak. Judy Covington not only liked what I said about her father, she is the one who told me I was her father's favorite.

So, here we go.

Russell Rice would call, quickly and quietly tell me what was going on, and then quickly—and I mean quickly—slam the phone down. And I mean slam the phone down! It was crazy. It was something that you would expect to see in a movie—only it was real. And he was connected...really connected.

Russell Rice was the sports information director at UK for eighteen years. He was also a respected newspaperman. The first book I took out of the library when I moved here in 1981 was his—*Kentucky Basketball's Big Blue Machine*.

While I was anchoring and breaking stories, I would often offer my opinion and make a strong comment after breaking the story, or any UK story. That was how I operated. You really couldn't ask any of the sports anchors who followed me to do that. All of that was me and my strength. Very few people in any TV market were doing what I was doing.

When Bruce Carter became our news director, he refused to let me rely on my sources for my stories. He wouldn't let me say "a source said this" or "a source said that." He would frequently ask me whether the source would be willing to defend me if the station wound up in court. He knew the people giving me these kinds of tips and stories would never be willing to talk if they were forced into that type of legal situation. And the odds were tiny at best that something I did would come to that, and he knew that.

What really ticked me off was what happened the day John Calipari got hired. I was obviously happy to break the big story but quietly got very angry at my boss. Until I put this in the book, I had never told this to anyone. One of my sources—as good of a source as it gets—tells me on the phone to go with Calipari coming to Lexington. Everyone at LEX18 was on pins and needles waiting for the actual announcement. I'm guessing that it was the same way over at WKYT Channel 27.

When my source told me that Cal was going to be the new head basketball coach at the University of Kentucky, I screamed across the newsroom twice that we need to go with the story. You almost never break into programming for a sports story. This was different. My news director, Bruce Carter, asks me if I'm sure. After all, it's his call. He decides to go with it. It turns out that we beat WKYT by less than five minutes on the story.

The newsroom on a day like that is a rush. It was a lot of fun, but it aggravated me that in one of the biggest stories of that year, I was able to use "my sources"—but on all the other times, the station felt my sources weren't good enough. When I drove home, instead of being really happy that I broke this huge story, I was *cursing* out my boss.

My goal was to get it out of my system before I got home. I always did my best to not bring the emotion of work home with me. I didn't even tell Judy what happened. She found out about it just like you did—by reading this chapter.

Since I couldn't say, "sources said this or that," I stopped making phone calls chasing those sources and stories down. Why bother? It takes a lot of time. I was still working too many hours, but not nearly as much as I was when I anchored. Sometimes it can take hours and a number of phone calls to get the right story. If I came across something that was good, but I had to protect my source, I just stopped asking if we could go with it. That decision by LEX18 to not let me use my sources hurt our news department. They never understood how bad that decision was.

I understand that my news director was covering his own...you know what. He didn't want lawyers involved. He didn't want his boss all over him if I made a mistake. But we all make dumb mistakes. His biggest mistake was not trusting me. But he's the boss, so ultimately it was his call. LEX18 never understood my relationship with sources or with the public.

I won't mention his name, but someone in management asked me before I left if I could pass along to Keith Farmer—the main sports anchor and the new sports director at LEX18—all my sources. Keith's a really good guy who I fought hard to get hired back at LEX 18—but you can't do that. And that person should have known that. I told that person I couldn't pass along my sources, and he just had this blank look on his face. It just showed me how clueless at times management can be.

Afterwards, I told Keith about that conversation, and he understood. Keith knows that anytime he needs help, I will always be there for him. I know he would do the same for me.

This whole ordeal with the sources was one of the really frustrating parts of working at LEX18. I'll be honest, it made me think about leaving. But as you get older, you can't be moving your family all over the place. Also, as you get older, no one wants you anymore. Prior to age forty, I received a lot of calls from TV stations. After age forty, it was like they lost my number.

The truth is, I felt stuck at LEX18, so I tried to be positive and remind myself how lucky I was to be able to do what I was doing. Despite the difficulties, I still found a way to have fun. I really got into being a storyteller. My career took a different turn. I dove into it and really enjoyed it. Since retiring, I miss telling stories more than anything else about TV. I've always felt blessed to be able to do what I love.

Anyway, I digress. If you've made it this far into the book, you know I go off on rants all the time.

Back to Bromley and Gabbard in the 1980s. Gabbard was so upset at his sports department, they had meetings about what they should do. In 1983—and this makes no sense—WKYT hires Rick Van Hoose to break stories and compete with me. Rick's a young broadcaster with a lot of potential, but he was still a student at UK. Gabbard was desperate. I laughed when I found out. To put a college kid in that position wasn't fair to Rick.

Fast forward to 2011, UK is in Houston playing in the NCAA Final Four. A lot of media ended up eating at the same Mexican restaurant. Rick Van Hoose, who has since been an award-winning news anchor at WLKY for decades, was there. After all these years, he tells me the story on how he got hired by WKYT to do sports. He confirmed that Gabbard was tired of getting beat by me. They gave Rick a camera and told him to go out and get Kentucky stories. With a big smile, he thanked me for helping him get his first job. I knew the story back then, but it was fun to hear it from him.

It was obvious the first time I saw Rick on TV, I knew he was going to be successful. I remember him as the young kid on the block. He's now called "Grandpa."

I can't tell you how many times people I've known who have worked at a place for a long time have to occasionally go through some garbage. It's called life. Whether it's a steel mill or a doctor's office, if you work anywhere for a long time, odds are you're going to have ups and downs.

I've had ups and downs. Rob Bromley had ups and downs. It's not a negative shot at either one of us. Everything we do is amplified more because we're on TV. I'm not complaining—I had lots of fun.

Here's the bottom line. I'll repeat it—I respect Rob Bromley and always thought he was a class act. Just because you are competing with someone doesn't mean you can't respect them. I know my intensity through the years bothered a lot of people—even at my own TV station. I'm competitive. I can't change, and don't want to change who I am. I'll never apologize for the fact that I wanted to beat Rob to every story. It was never personal with Bromley, but to me WKYT-TV was the enemy, and Rob just happened to work there.

There were a number of articles about Bromley and me. The *Lexington Herald-Leader* was all over this story. Problems involving TV personalities always sell newspapers. My point is that this isn't just *ME* talking about the story. I felt bad for Rob. The *Herald-Leader* pushed it *HARD!*

October 10, 1983–the headline in the *Lexington Herald-Leader* said, "Channel 27 Looking to Replace Bromley."

In the article, Bromley said he didn't know what was going to happen.

Ralph Gabbard, the general manager of WKYT, had no comment on Bromley's future or me.

I said I was offered the job at Channel 27 and couldn't take it because of my contract—even though I was never going to go because I had my sights set on bigger TV markets.

Gabbard's "no comment" was his way of saying what I said was true. It's a good thing he did because I would have ripped him like crazy—on the record—and I always believed he was smart enough to know that.

When I moved to Lexington, Channel 27 was a big-time power. They had much more than twice the audience as LEX18 and WTVQ combined. When that *Herald-Leader* article was written, LEX18 was No. 1. The turnaround was amazing in just the few short years I was in town.

39

They Don't Make 'Em
Like Harry Anymore

Harry Barfield, the president and general manager at LEX18 when I was first hired, was different. If Harry told you something, then that was it—you didn't need it in writing. If he looked you in the eye and told you he was going to do something, his word was golden. I trusted Harry tremendously, and I'm not the kind of person that trusts management very easily. I just don't—with good reason. Going back to 1975, I've seen a lot of crap in management.

I've said it before, regarding management—they're just people. They rise to a high level where they make a lot more money. Some of them are wonderful people, and some of them are turds. But they're no different than anyone else—except they have more power and make more money. And I've seen how the power can get to their heads. Their egos are a lot worse than they often realize. I knew I had a big ego. I dealt with many people in management who were in denial of their egos, and it affected some of their decisions.

Harry Barfield came to LEX18 as the No. 2 sportscaster and rose to become the president of the company. He was hard working and honest. His life was his family and LEX18. He wore a white shirt and tie every day to work. He was old school.

I had been at the station a year or so when Harry did a commercial for something. I was like, WOW! He had a great broadcasting voice. When he got behind the mic, he was really good. I remember walking into his office and accusing him of being a sandbagger. He just started laughing. That was my way of telling him that he was really good. I had no idea.

Harry died of a stroke in October of 1991. When we had the fiftieth anniversary of LEX18, the station put on a huge party. The video they did of the fifty years of the station was wonderful. Harry's kids came to the party. They came over to me and said that the only reason they showed up was to tell me that their father said I was his favorite. That's what he told them, and they wanted me to know. I was fighting back tears.

They don't make 'em like Harry anymore.

40

Fat Man and Mike Barry

I consider colleagues Mike Barry and Brian Collins like brothers. Mike was the main news anchor, and Brian was our weatherman at LEX18. I nicknamed Brian "Fat Man." I'm not sure why. I asked him once whether I was insulting him by calling him that. "Hebe," he said (he was the only one to call me that because I'm Jewish). "I love it. And if you don't call me Fat Man, that either means you're mad at me or you don't love me anymore." Although he was older than me, he was like a kid brother.

There's a second Fat Man. Harold Williams—a very strong Christian. Anytime I said something with my potty mouth, which was daily, he would give me a look. I actually tried to clean up my language around him because his looks were ridiculous. He often said he appreciated me trying to change my vocabulary, but I still needed to do much better. Fat Man, the photographer, ended up being my sports shooter for a few years. He was very good, and as different as we were, we became what I would call good station friends. I've been so lucky with having so many wonderful photographers. I'm not sure how I was that lucky. He showed up at my retirement party and I hadn't seen him since 1984—it meant the world to me. He's just a great human being.

One day at the station, Fat Man and Fat Man were standing by Brian Collins' desk, and they both started screaming at me. "Hebe, which one of us is Fat Man?" they asked. "You better make up your mind." Everybody in the newsroom started laughing. They both said I better keep calling them Fat Man, but that I'd also better delineate which one is which. They both loved the nickname. In today's society, you start calling someone Fat Man, and you're probably in the boss's office. Back then, it was a term of endearment.

I've lost thirty pounds in a month eight times in my life. How I've done it wasn't always very smart. But *pills or drugs never had anything to do with it*. One of the times was before I entered college. There's soft serve ice cream in New York called Carvel. I ate it seven days a week—and not much else—and I lost over thirty pounds in one month. It's a fun diet when you're young and play sports and your metabolism is quicker.

I said to Brian "Fat Man" Collins, "If you only eat ice cream for dinner and eat a very light breakfast and lunch, you'll lose weight." I never thought he would do it. So he became a freak on Wendy's Frosty. He started going through the drive-thru so much that they'd just start giving it to him for free. He lost twenty pounds pretty quick. Then when he put the weight back on, he still kept the Frosty on his diet.

Brian Collins and Mike Barry have something in common. I've seen a lot of alcohol problems in broadcasting. I don't know if it's the pressure or the deadlines, but it's here. Mike Barry, in my mind, had everything—smart, a really good writer, honest, terrific judgment, and calm under pressure. I wish I had his voice. He was a really good news anchor and had anchored in much bigger markets. I had no idea he had an alcohol problem.

I knew Brian Collins had a problem with alcohol. I knew he had a problem with it in the past. I knew his father had a problem with it also. There were times I saw Brian and wondered how he was going to do the show that night. He was always somehow able to fake it. I tried to talk to him about it, but he told me to mind my own business. It's the only time I heard him use that tone of voice to me. I knew he was in trouble. He wouldn't listen to me like he did with the ice cream diet.

The station finally got rid of him because of his drinking problem. Brian was fortunate that Channel 27 picked him up after he was let go. He was very well known in the community—he went to so many schools, made so many public appearances, and was such a nice guy. I was so happy that Channel 27 picked him up. But that drinking problem came back at Channel 27. Judy and I went to see him just before he died, and I felt guilty that I didn't keep trying to help him.

On the other hand, I had no idea that Mike had a drinking problem. I was clueless. I never saw him when I thought he was drinking. We had a tiny bathroom in the old TV building—Mike admits that he would hide beer under the trash liner. One day, Mike disappeared. You have to understand that Mike Barry had a beautiful wife and a beautiful home. You would look at him and say, "This dude has everything, and he seems happy."

Mike runs away and gets into all kinds of trouble. The station liked him so much that they were willing to put him through rehab. He refused.

Eventually, thank God, he ends up at *The Healing Place* in Louisville. They saved his life. He then became an instructor, and now not only is he the CEO and founder of *People Advocating Recovery in Kentucky*, but he's been to the White House twice, attended congressional hearings, and testified before hearings in Kentucky. He's also gone all over America talking about this disease. He's turned his life around and uses his gift—his big booming voice—to help others.

What's also amazing is that Mike found his soulmate twice. Dona Barry is also a recovering alcoholic. They make a great couple. I don't think the three of us have ever been together where we didn't laugh a lot.

He sent me a long letter years before he became CEO. I cried reading it. I never told Mike that. He said, "Cutler, you don't understand. If I have another sip of wine, I'm going to die." I've never forgotten that. I wish I saved the letter. I always thought you could just have enough discipline to push the bottle away. Brian and Mike have both convinced me that alcoholism is a disease.

As I've told Mike, I'm so proud of him. Truth is, I'm so proud of Mike and Dona.

41

Johnny Majors—Is It True?

When Johnny Majors was the coach at Tennessee, I did a live TV interview with him on Friday night—the day before they played Kentucky in Lexington. Today, there's no way that could happen. The visiting coach of a big-time school is not going to talk to you live the day before. Will they talk to ESPN? Yes. How about a local TV person? No way!

I was at the studio, and he was at the hotel where they were staying. Majors was wearing a really expensive suit. He's dressed perfectly. I was a little nuts back then. I asked him a couple of little things about Tennessee. After he answers, I didn't plan on asking this—which is normal for me—I then blurt out, "Hey Coach, there are a lot of rumors that you have a drinking problem. Is it true?"

He takes the mic, throws it down on the floor, gets up and says he's "not answering that," and walks out.

The next day at the football game, I got chewed out by the Tennessee sports information people. I probably deserved it, but there *WERE* all kinds of rumors. I was pretty direct back then.

What I always found fascinating about this story is that it never affected my relationship with the Tennessee people for the rest of my career. When we saw each other three to four times a year at Kentucky/Tennessee games and at the SEC Tournament, we remained professional, cordial, and they would share information when they could.

I always found that interesting. Tennessee and Louisville might be bitter rivals with Kentucky, but some of the folks who run their sports information departments are terrific.

I remember meeting Louisville's Kenny Klein in the mid-1980s. He's now their Senior Associate Athletics Director for Media Relations.

I told him, "Look—I could care less about the UK/Louisville rivalry when it comes to both of us doing our job." Kenny not only gets along with everyone, not only does he try to help if he can—but I'll never forget him walking around with beer in their press area after UK played at Louisville. There's nothing like having a beer on a deadline getting your story back to the TV station while my photographer edits what I've put together.

I will also never forget the elevator ride to the UK press box the day after the Johnny Majors interview. As the doors were about to open, I took a deep breath because I knew I was going to get it, and I knew I had to take it.

Forget about my question, what Tennessee did to Johnny Majors is past disgusting.

Majors was a two-time SEC Player of the Year, and in 1956 finished second to Paul Hornung for the Heisman Trophy—there are many who believe he should have won it.

Majors was a superstar for Tennessee who returned home after winning the national championship at Pittsburgh in 1976. Think about this. The year before Majors was hired, Pitt was 1-10. Training camp that year was so rough that there were five buses taking players to camp. They returned to Pittsburgh with only three. It's one of the great coaching jobs in the last fifty years.

It's not just that they fired Majors in 1992—and I thought that in itself was baloney. I like to call it equity in the bank, and no one at Tennessee ever had more of that—especially after winning the SEC in 1990. But, it was how they did it that stunk. In 1992, Majors missed three games due to a heart attack, and he wasn't fully recovered when he came back. Tennessee had some bad losses after he got back...and they dumped him.

If they would do that to Johnny Majors—*WOW*...no one is safe.

Even though Majors was angry and bitter for years about what his Tennessee did to him, his love for the state didn't stop him from going home in 2007. He lived the rest of his days in the house on the hill overlooking his beloved Tennessee River until he died in his sleep in 2020.

In 1981, the whole world knew that UK Coach Fran Curci was getting fired. Even Curci knew. It got so bad towards the end of the season that Fran wouldn't talk to the media, so I interviewed a picture of him (yes, an actual *photo* of Fran Curci) to make a story. Wish I had the tape. It was funny. Curci, who I've always liked, is wearing Governor

John Y. Brown's overcoat. Before the game, he shakes Johnny Majors' hand and says, "Johnny, we're going to kick your a-- today."

There are certain games where the sound is different if you are walking the sidelines. The pads were really popping on both sides that day.

Quarterback Randy Jenkins—who is often forgotten but played in some big games—threw two touchdown passes to lead UK (who was down 10-0) to a 21-10 win.

Part 4 (1984-1987)

My Time in Pittsburgh

42

Miserable in Pittsburgh

In 1984, I left LEX18 because of money. I ended up taking a job I never would have taken the year before—and never should have taken. *My fault.* Going to one of the best stations in America turned out to be a *dumb mistake* on my part.

I know sportscasters from cities all over America—like Boise, Idaho and Albany, New York—that combine multiple sources of income so they can make a really nice living and don't have to move around so much.

I thought that was going to be an option for me at LEX18 because of how popular I had become and how I quickly grew to like Lexington. My first choice, however, was always just to move to a much larger market.

I should have been able to make a nice living in Lexington, but LEX18 made what I consider their own *dumb mistake.* Management, of course, is *never* wrong.

LEX18 was stubborn, so I left.

This part was my decision. When UK Football and Basketball were playing, I averaged over seventy-five hours a week. I'm serious. I didn't even take dinner breaks, which wasn't good for my marriage and later my family. It's a *huge* regret. I've apologized to my family many times for not being around enough.

I loved my family. I loved my job. But with the hours I put in, I often made eight dollars an hour to be the sports director. Others were making a lot more money than me, even though I believed I was the main reason for the huge change in the TV ratings. I'm sure there will be many who don't agree—I don't care.

Please understand I worked with a lot of talented people. It wasn't all me. That would be ridiculous to think that.

Judy and I were working, not spending much money, and renting a small house in a mediocre neighborhood because that's what we could afford. It would have taken years to save enough for a down payment on a decent house in Lexington. To me, that was the last straw. Like everyone else, I wanted to buy my family a nice house.

The second reason I left was because I was young, I knew I was good, and I wanted to end up in New York, Chicago, or Los Angeles. That isn't a negative comment towards Lexington. I just wanted to work in a larger city, to make a lot more money, and to cover major league sports.

Almost anyone in the media who is not from Kentucky and comes to work at LEX18 has no intention of staying when they walk in the door.

When I left, sales manager Joe Oliver—who wasn't a friend—told me I personally cost him $250,000 by leaving, and that I should have come to him and he would have gotten me a big raise. I had trouble believing that figure...and why would I go to him to get a raise?

A couple of other things really bothered me during this time. The first was clothing. There was a clothing chain called Dawahares. One of the owners offered to outfit me from head to toe. All they wanted in return was a small mention at the bottom of the screen at the end of the newscast. I thought the idea was more than fair. I wasn't making any money, so I didn't want to spend my own money on clothes.

I was known as an awful dresser for my entire career, and I earned that reputation. However, I really did want to look nice. I realize many who worked with me will laugh at that, but it's true. I wanted to dress like Cawood Ledford, the legendary radio voice of the Wildcats for thirty-nine years. The classy Cawood was always the best dressed man on press row.

No one is going to believe this, but it's true. I can be really stubborn when I believe I'm right.

I pitched the Dawahare's proposal to Harry Barfield, the general manager, and he told me LEX18 doesn't do clothing trades. He told me about a sportscaster who abused his fifty-dollar clothing trade in the 1950s, so now the station won't allow it. What? A fifty-dollar trade? In the 1950s? That's crazy. I was literally speechless.

After Harry told me that, I promised him that one—I would never cheat, and two—I'd bring him the receipts of what was spent if that made him happy. He then said that if they did it for me, they would also have to do it for everyone. His reasoning was *ridiculous*. As mad as

I was, it gets worse.

I go back to Dawahares. They can't believe the station wouldn't go for it. They then offered to outfit all four of our main anchors. All they wanted in return now is to hold the mention on the bottom of the screen for as long as the credits are rolling at the end of the newscast. That's for both the 6:00 and 11:00 pm newscasts Monday through Friday. I assumed Harry would change his mind. Once again, it's more than fair. Harry tells me again that the station won't do it. Not only was I upset, I told Harry I would never spend money on clothing for TV, and I bolted from his office.

Here's the second thing that bothered me. While I was doing TV, I wanted to make money on the side. I loved doing radio, and I was approached a number of times. Radio always helped me tremendously because I never made a lot of money in television.

Radio put my kids through college.

I was offered a local radio gig doing commentaries. I could tape it on the phone at night. This takes no time—ten minutes or less—and I knew that it would be good for the TV station.

I was hoping to use the extra money to put a down payment on a house in a year or two, or save it for when we needed our next car. I'm like most reading this book—if I can eliminate a car payment the next time we get a car, that would be a bigger raise than I was ever going to get working for LEX18. I went to Harry, and he told me that the station wouldn't let anyone make money on the side. That was the rule. I asked him again a second time after another radio station called, and he told me "no" again.

If that wasn't bad enough, here comes strike three. WVLK radio offered me a job. At that time, WVLK and Channel 27 were joined at the hip. They had UK games on radio and TV. I quietly called them the Big Blue Mafia. Why would they try and hire someone from a rival TV station? It made no sense at all. There was obviously something else going on there, but they asked me to do a sports talk show.

I go to Harry for the third time, and he tells me "no" again. I lose it. I said to Harry, "You don't pay me any money, you won't let me make money on the side, and I'm already working way too many hours. You can't expect me to stay here." I turn around and storm out.

At that moment, I was gone. Without that thought, I don't believe I would have taken the job in Pittsburgh. I would have waited a little longer. It was just a matter of where and when.

I started getting calls from stations around the country, even though

I hadn't sent any of my resume tapes to them. I turned down a number of TV jobs. I was very direct with people. I frequently told news directors that I didn't want to waste my time or their time. If they didn't talk about salary on the phone, why spend any more time talking? Another case of me being too cocky. I shake my head at some of the *dumb* things I did. But, I didn't want to have to move three more times to get my dream job.

The job I took at KDKA-TV had nothing to do with WKYT sending out my resume tapes. I wasn't cocky on the phone about money when I spoke with them...MISTAKE!! I *REALLY* just wanted out of LEX18 at that point.

It's the weekend sportscaster job with KDKA in Pittsburgh, one of the most respected TV stations in the country. When I was flown in for the interview, John Sanders, the main sports anchor, was supposed to be there. I was very uncomfortable taking the job without meeting him. They let John do Big East Basketball and a lot of games on TV when he was supposed to be anchoring sports. That surprised me.

KDKA told me that John was gone about half the time. The station told me they wanted to bring in someone with "more" personality to fill in for John when he was gone. That excited me. John Sanders was similar to Rob Bromley, the long-time sports anchor at Channel 27 in Lexington. They're both good in their own styles. Neither one is very flowery, and neither one has much on-air personality.

I'm laughing right now because I'm thinking about Bill Currie (not the UK Football coach), who ended up being my weekend radio partner for years on KDKA-AM, a great station. I was the straight man in the show if you can believe it. Bill was known as the "Mouth of the South." He wore plaid jackets with polka dot ties. He once said, "Watching John Sanders on TV was like watching paint dry."

Back to the job offer. I was promised that I would become the weekend sports anchor and fill in anchoring during the week, but they wouldn't put that in the contract. They also weren't offering me enough money, so I turned the job down.

I had an agent, a really good dude named Steve Poricelli, who told me he would get me more money. He also offered to forego his commission—and even then it still wouldn't be much more than I was making in Lexington. I didn't want him to do that, but he made me promise that I would use him for my next job which he thought would be for a lot more money. Why not? I liked Steve, and he worked hard to get this deal done. Steve not only convinced me to take the job, but he got me the extra money. All the sports anchoring I was promised wasn't put in the contract, and he convinced me that I should trust KDKA. I'm tired of trying to make a decent living in Lexington, so I take the job.

I learned a *very* valuable lesson the hard way. My gut told me not to take the job, but I did it anyway. I had turned down a number of jobs, so why take this one when they refused to put in writing what they promised me? *Big Mistake!!!*

I told Harry that I was leaving LEX18, mainly because I'm putting in all these hours for the station and not making any money. He tried to get me to stay by offering to adjust my salary, but it was too late. I told him not even to throw a figure at me because he had plenty of chances to adjust my salary. I told him that even if he doubled my salary, I was leaving because of the principle. I turn and walk out. We didn't say another word to each other for weeks. I should have at least listened. Another *dumb* mistake.

I got emotional on my last day at the station. I walked out of the newsroom towards Harry's office, and Harry's walking toward me to say goodbye. "Hey Cutler," he says. "You're not leaving without us shaking hands and saying 'goodbye' properly. We need to talk. Our relationship has been too good." I have tears in my eyes now because I was thinking the same thing. We were both walking to see each other at exactly the same time.

The day before I was to start at KDKA in Pittsburgh, I went in to fill out my paperwork. After the 6 pm news, I finally got to talk to John Sanders. "Hey John, I'm not here to stab you in the back," I say to him. "I'm here to hopefully become pretty good friends. I'll never go after your job. I'll never go after you, but I'm going to get what I was promised—being the weekend sports anchor and doing all the fill-in anchor work when you're gone." I even told him I hoped to go to New York and anchor when my contract was up.

At that moment, John Sanders wouldn't look me in the eye, and he turned his head.

I went back to the hotel that night, very upset, and told Judy that we just made a big mistake. Sanders doesn't want me there. John Sanders and I were cold as ice for the entire time I was in Pittsburgh.

Shortly after I started, I found out that Mark Sok—my weekend sports anchor in Lexington—had a brother whose best friend growing up just happened to be a really good TV news reporter for KDKA. His desk was close to mine. Mark tells me that I've got a big problem because he heard the sports department didn't want me there. They decided that they didn't like me even before I got there. Management at KDKA even told me why I was moving in front of two other sportscasters.

The sports department hated me, but the truth was that KDKA hired me because they were looking for someone with more personality than those guys. That was management's call. The decision to move me in front of two other people was made *before* I was hired. If it wasn't me, it was going to be someone else. The people there should have looked at themselves in the mirror. The two on-air sportscasters I was put in front of ended up leaving.

So, the long and the short of it is that I ended up spending over three years of my life in a place where nobody wanted me. It was miserable, but I still found a way to have fun. I covered some great college football games at Pitt, West Virginia, and Penn State—and hockey with the Pittsburgh Penguins. I covered Doug Flutie as many as three times in a season. I've never seen a college quarterback with better timing with his receivers. He was so much fun to watch.

I also had a great deal of fun on my weekend radio sports talk show on KDKA radio...and our daughter Jenna was born during my time there. I did my best to ignore the rest of the sports department. They did their best to ignore me. You don't show that you're bleeding in situations like that. I did my own thing and trusted no one.

43

Franco Harris Scoop

When I got to Pittsburgh, Franco Harris, one of the Pittsburgh Steelers' all-time greats who's in the Pro Football Hall of Fame—and who's far more popular than the mayor—was in a contract dispute. He's thirty-four—that's really old for a running back, and there is very little tread left on his tires. The Steelers want him to break Jim Brown's all-time rushing record (he's less than 400 yards away). Franco ran for over a thousand yards the year before, and the Steeler offensive line would do anything to get him the record, but there is a huge ugly battle over the contract.

I got really lucky. The first week I'm at KDKA, Franco's agent—lawyer Bart Beier—has just been interviewed on the 6 pm news. It's raining. I'm leaving the same time he is. He asked me if I could give him a ride to his office. He told me it's about five minutes from the station. I agreed to give him a ride. I'm parked in the big parking structure next to the station. When we get there, we couldn't find my car! I had already heard stories about cars being stolen in downtown Pittsburgh, so I'm really starting to worry about my 280Z. We walk up and down numerous levels of the garage looking. Beier is trying to calm me down when even he thought we weren't going to find the car. When we finally found it, we had a good laugh.

As loved as Franco Harris is, Beier was convinced his client couldn't get a fair shake from the local media because of the power that the Rooney family has. The Rooney family, one of the great sports owners of all time, really wanted Franco to stay. It's past silly that they couldn't work it out.

As Beier left my car, I told him that if he could get me an exclusive interview with Franco, I promised that the story wouldn't be one-sided, and that I would let Franco talk. I never expected he would call, and I

147

didn't tell anyone what we talked about.

Beier called me late the next morning and said I would have the exclusive with Franco. I rushed into the news director's office and told him the whole story—that this is pure luck and unless they back out, I have one of the best sports stories of the year. I was also concerned that Franco would change his mind.

Now there's a buzz in the newsroom about me. I overheard a few people saying that the "new guy" Cutler is making all of this up—that I never talked to Franco's agent and that I'm not getting the scoop. WOW!!!

I got the scoop all right. Franco was great. I let him talk. Shortly after that, Franco is released from the team...and is on his way to Seattle.

Within a few days, Jim Hefner, the news director who hired me, came to my desk and said I'm on the next plane to Seattle. OK—no time to get clothing, and I have twenty dollars in my pocket. They literally passed a hat around in the newsroom to give me cash. I kid you not—I'm getting cash put in a hat, and they are taking names and noting how much everyone put in. It quickly accumulated to over two hundred dollars. I'm told to go find Franco. No one knows where he is. There were no cell phones back then. And if I need to buy clothing—do it, but don't go crazy spending money. The plane ticket was waiting for me at the airport, and they got me to the airport with very little time to spare.

I went to the CBS-TV station in Seattle, called the Seahawks' PR department, the local newspaper, and the radio station that carried the Seahawk games. I heard a rumor Franco was eating dinner with some of the Seahawk players at a restaurant in Tacoma, Washington. Seemed like a long shot, but I had nothing else.

I walked into the restaurant in Tacoma and was so happy to be looking at Franco. I go up to him, and he shakes his head and starts laughing. He said, "Cutler, I just met you, and you tracked me down. How did you find me?"

When I tell Franco about the hat being passed around the newsroom to get me some cash and getting on the next plane, I think it's what helped me get another interview with him.

I got lucky again.

That's my start at KDKA.

44

How I Became a Big-League Announcer

In 1986, I was the only color commentator on a Major League Baseball TV broadcast who was not a former player. I had won the job on a tryout. I was shocked they asked me to try out. I went to St. Louis to do a game. I met Al Hrabosky, one of the great relief pitchers of the 1970s who's been part of the St. Louis Cardinals broadcasting team for more than three decades. I knew Al liked cigars, so I went out and bought him a couple of expensive cigars which I put on my expense report. I told KDKA's money man what I did. He laughed and said that was a good idea…KDKA paid for the cigars.

I gave Al a cigar. He took it and smelled it, stuck it in his mouth and said, "Who are you?" I told him I was trying to win the job as the color guy for the Pittsburgh Pirates and that I had never played the game, but I loved baseball, and I was a little crazy. He looked at me like I was crazy. I told him I had spent hours and hours of preparation reading about the Cardinals from a large book the St. Louis Cardinals' PR staff had put together since the start of spring training, and I was hoping we could share some information. We spent about a half hour together, and he gave me some really good nuggets about the team. He was really open and probably told me some things that he was even reluctant to say himself on TV.

We get on the air, and I have some terrific stories. John Sanders even let me talk. At times, he looked miserable when I was talking. BUT, I GOT THE JOB!

In the Pirates media guide, the new broadcasting team has a picture. There was Steve Blass, the former star Pirate pitcher who was also hired to be a color commentator in 1986—along with John Sanders, the play-by-play man—and me. I still have that media guide somewhere. I just wish I were that skinny again.

What *ticks* me off to this day if I think about it is that I was in the broadcast booth for four hours before my tryout when Sanders eventually walked in and sat down next to me. I said, "Hello," and he never said a word to me until we got on the air. It was well over an hour that we sat right next to each other without ever speaking.

I didn't have to put on my Sherlock Holmes hat to realize John Sanders didn't want me to get the job.

This part of my contract is tough to believe. I was *forced* to take a new five-year contract when they gave me the Pirates Baseball gig and wouldn't give me extra money for doing the Pirates. *Forced?* When I told them I didn't want a new contract, they said I couldn't do the Pirates without the new deal. I got *NO* extra money for doing the Pirates.

Without knowing if this was true, when I walked out of the news director's office with this new deal, I said to myself that I might be the only idiot to agree to do Major League Baseball for nothing because that's how much I wanted to do it.

When they don't pay you anything, they don't respect you, and you are much more expendable. The bottom line was, I knew I was on a short leash.

They promised me if the Pirate gig worked out, they would give me another new contract the following year. I didn't believe them. Would you? Plus, if there was a change in management, they would never honor the verbal agreement.

45

Harry Caray and Tim McCarver

The day before our first game, which was against the Chicago Cubs, our new broadcasting crew had a meeting at Wrigley Field. It was cold and windy—a typical April day in Chicago. Sitting by himself in the visitor's dugout was the legendary Cubs' announcer Harry Caray. He yells, "Hey kid, come here." I went over and sat down next to the living legend, and he started asking me about myself as he's talking about the Cubs. After about ten minutes, he slaps my shoulder and says, "Good luck kid." Then he gets up and leaves.

I was always convinced Caray knew I was a rookie and was there just to see if I was okay. It was a lovely gesture by a superstar to a rookie.

Tim McCarver, also one of the great baseball broadcasters—after enjoying a great career as a catcher for St. Louis—in his own way did the same thing. When things were falling apart for me with the Pirates, he came up to me before a game, put his arm around me and said, "Kid, hang in there." Then he says, "I'm Tim McCarver." He knew I was in trouble with my Pirates' gig.

It's important to mention that what Caray and McCarver did for me, I'm sure they have done for so many other broadcasters. It's like a club—taking care of each other in the business. I have deep regret that I wasn't part of that club for thirty years.

46

My Triumphant Return to Shea Stadium

I was flying to New York for a Pirates/Mets series at Shea Stadium. I brought Judy and my daughter, Jenna, on the trip. She's still a beautiful baby who is learning how to talk. She would try to say, "ship," and it would come out "shit." Little kids get hung up on words, and that was just a word she liked. People around us on the plane were laughing. I tried to explain, but no one bought it. Plus, I was already sweating because the air conditioning wasn't very good.

When J.J. was about the same age, he had trouble with the word *truck*. You probably already figured that one out.

We're close to landing, and Jenna sticks her arms out and wants to come to daddy. I'm thrilled. Judy's happy because she has been holding Jenna the entire flight. She passes Jenna to me with a big smile on her face.

Now count with me—five... four... three... two... one—MY DAUGHTER PROJECTILE VOMITS ONTO MY CHEST! It wasn't just a little bit, but as Judy will tell you—*BUCKETS!* It ran down my shirt, my pants, and all the way down to the seat behind us. *IT SMELLS!* People were yelling at me, and there were people yelling at the people who were yelling at me. Judy just thought it was really funny.

I was soaked. As soon as Jenna was done throwing up on me, like clockwork, she put her arms out towards Judy—and with a smile on her face, went back to her. The look on my wife's face was priceless. Plus, she's relieved that she didn't get thrown up on. Meanwhile, I stood up as people were yelling at me and took my shirt off—it was that drenched. Thank goodness back then, I was 185 pounds.

When the plane landed, everybody got out of my way so I could get off first. My brother, who has a dry sense of humor, was picking us up.

We're brothers, opposite as night and day in certain things, but I love him and would do anything for him. I walk up to him and he says with a straight face, "So, where's Judy and the baby…and why are you not wearing a shirt?" That was my triumphant return home to do TV against the Mets at Shea Stadium.

It's the first game of the series, and my two best friends were there. I was doing an interview behind home plate for the pregame show, and all of a sudden I hear my name being chanted from the stands. Come on, who's going to chant my name from the stands? I recognize my buddies Bobby Everett and Mitch Feldschuh, and they're in there just screaming like crazy. It was fun.

It wasn't long after that I lost my job doing Pirates Baseball. Tony Pena—the all-star catcher who had a cannon for an arm and was the most popular player on the team—opened up to me. More than once when I was around Tony before a game, he'd try to spit tobacco juice on my sneakers. The bad news for me was that he had a really good long-distance shot. Lots of practice. That was his way of saying he liked me.

The Pirates were terrible, both on and off the field. They were trying to get past a drug scandal that was national news. It included the FBI being involved, and they were getting rid of players.

Tony Pena tells me that he's going to get traded to St. Louis for not one, not two, but three players. When I got the Pirates' job, the TV station *told* me to "be a reporter." If I wanted to report on something, I should just do it. They encouraged me to be myself because the team stunk, and they thought the broadcasting was boring.

With a story like Pena, you don't just blurt it out. I told John Sanders, who does the play-by-play, and the executive producer that I had the Pena trade story, and this is what I'm going with, and does anybody have a problem with it? John says, "Alan, I'll even lead you into it." I did the story. It was a big story.

Syd Thrift, the Pirates general manager, goes CRAZY. The next time I see him, it's after a home game. I went into the Pirate bar, and Syd came up to me and started raising his voice. I told him that if he didn't like what I did with the Pena story, that's fine—but I told him not to raise his voice. He starts yelling and screaming that my comments weren't what he wanted on the Pirates TV network. I told him I was about to lose my cool, and if he didn't calm down, we were going to have a problem. He kept on screaming stuff like, "You're not a reporter—what are you doing? I don't want a reporter in the booth." He went crazy on me. If this were today, it would have been captured on a cellphone, the video would have gone viral, and Syd Thrift would have been in big trouble. He went NUTS! He was like a manager who had just been thrown out of a game, and he's going nuts on the umpire who tossed him.

I took a while until I finally told him to get out of my face. Then, I wasn't very nice about it. He was trying to show everyone that he was the boss. He was Syd Thrift, and he was walking around like he was the guy who invented baseball.

I'll bet you already guessed this. A few days later, Tony Pena was traded for not one, not two, but three players. And guess who he was traded to? The St. Louis Cardinals.

Thrift went to KDKA's management, and management said that if I had a comment I wanted to make on TV, I needed to check with them first. They cut me off. I told them to just fire me because I knew they weren't going to have me back next year. I didn't want to go on the road with the team and basically do nothing. Besides, they weren't paying me any extra money to do the games. I was dumb to agree to the deal, but I couldn't say no to doing Big League Baseball. TV management told me they would be embarrassed if I just walked away. For all practical purposes, my stint as a color commentator for Major League Baseball was over. No one had to tell me after the season that I wouldn't be back, but how I found out about it sucked. I read it in the newspaper. *Nice* communication.

Here's what should have happened. The right thing to do was for KDKA and the Pirates to give this three-man broadcasting booth more of a chance. The right thing to do was for KDKA management to stand up to the Pirates and say that not only did they know what I was going to say about Tony Pena, but they were the ones who told me to be a reporter. Instead, management crumpled like one of my cheap suits. Management admitted to me that they were worried about their next contract with the Pirates.

I have no problem admitting, however, that it was not a good broadcast. There was *NO* chemistry.

When I became host of the Cincinnati Bengals Radio Network, I thought I *sucked* for the first season. I asked my boss, Darryl Parks, why he had me back for year two. I wouldn't have blamed him if he had made another change. He said I got a lot better. I told him, "So you're telling me I sucked less by the end of the year?" He laughed. I had a long terrific run doing the Bengals.

I was dumb enough to think I could have had fun with Blass and just ignored Sanders, which is what I should have done from the beginning, and was just starting to do. The few times I did it up to then, it worked. Blass—who just finished a wonderful career broadcasting the Pirates—is a really good guy. But he had no clue at that time how to do TV—which he admitted.

Bottom line? I *sucked*. I got ripped in the Pittsburgh media. And they were right, but they either were clueless as to what was really going on or they chose to ignore it.

Ironically, Bill Currie told me more than once that if the Pirates and KDKA were smart enough just to put the two of us together in the booth, somehow the play-by-play would have evolved, and it might have even been *great TV*. Currie was convinced we'd be much better than the team, which at that point meant the bar was set pretty low.

47

Playing Doubles with John McEnroe

I never played tennis. Plus, I'm not an athlete. It's a bad combination.

When things were going well in Pittsburgh for me, my news director called me into the office and told me I was going to play a doubles match with Vitas Gerulaitis at the Civic Arena against John McEnroe and his girlfriend at the time, Tatum O'Neal. I looked at him like he was crazy. I told him I couldn't play tennis, and he acted like he didn't hear a word of what I said. He said it would be great publicity for me and the station. I then told him I didn't have any tennis gear. He tells me to go buy it, expense it to the station, and not to worry about it.

Just when I thought the sports department couldn't get any colder to me—they did. Why choose Cutler to do this, and not one of them?

The night of the match, I met Vitas—known as a friendly, free-spirit, who was a great friend of McEnroe. We introduce ourselves, and he asks me if I can play? "Not a lick," I answered. He starts laughing and assures me he'll cover for me. "No, you don't understand," I clarified. "I don't play tennis—*ever!*"

Vitas and I are just talking on the court, waiting for McEnroe to come out, when Vitas says to me, "McEnroe's going to be in a bad mood, so when he comes over and you say 'hi' to him, and he doesn't say 'hi' back, don't take it the wrong way. He and Tatum had a fight last night. I don't think he got laid, so he's going to be grumpy." We laughed. Forget that McEnroe is a superstar. He's just like everyone else. Vitas talks the way I do, and we shared a wonderful laugh in front of thousands who came to watch McEnroe. When we were laughing, we both knew people were watching, and Vitas saw that I didn't care—and he liked that.

Sure enough, McEnroe—winner of four U.S. Opens and three Wimbledons—walks over, and I stick my hand out to greet him. "Hey John, I'm Alan Cutler," I say. He just grunts. I look over at Vitas and wink. He winks back, and we both have a big smile on our mugs. McEnroe looked at the two of us and must have thought what the heck was that all about.

I swung at a few balls that night. I think I actually hit one of them over the net. They opened up the roof of the Civic Arena—which they rarely did—it was a beautiful summer night, and we ran the highlights on the 11 pm sports. Believe it or not, the tape of this match wound up on the BBC. I'm guessing the BBC was more interested in McEnroe's girlfriend than a no-name sportscaster in Pittsburgh. Ha!

Vitas was fun. He told me I was the kind of guy it would be fun to have a beer with. My boss was right—the entire evening was fun, and it was good publicity.

48

Why Dan Marino Wanted to Beat Me Up

There was a time when Dan Marino wanted to beat me up. He was already a Pittsburgh legend—an All-American who starred for his hometown university from 1979-82. On January 30, 1985, it just so happened that the Hall of Fame NFL quarterback who played seventeen seasons for the Miami Dolphins was getting married across the street from where he grew up. It's a very tight and narrow street. Dan made everyone aware that NO MEDIA was to come into the church where the wedding was to take place.

All the TV stations were camped out for the big event. I have no idea how we all fit in that narrow street with all the live trucks and equipment. When Dan went from his house to the church across the street, he literally ran. He knew he was going to get photographed, and he didn't want any part of the media at all.

Here's one of the *strangest* things to have happened in my career. One of my bosses made a deal with the photographer to get the wedding footage and then give it to me when it was done. I couldn't believe the photographer agreed to it. When the wedding was over, I felt uncomfortable because there was no one quietly coming up to me to give me a tape. My instinct was to go to the back of the church and see what was going on. My instincts have saved me countless times for over forty years in the business.

I went to the back of the church, and there was a producer from another TV station who I'd never seen before. He takes out a roll of bills and starts counting out money to give to the photographer who's holding the tape. I walk up and scream, "WHOA! What's going on here? We have a deal. You're going to give me that tape, and you're going to give me that tape NOW, and you're going to be lucky if I don't go on the radio and talk about how another TV station tried to buy the tape! Who buys stories? We don't do that for a living. You ought to be ashamed of yourself. GET THE *BLANK* OUT OF HERE!" I was loud!!

So the other TV guy left, and the photographer who I just yelled at isn't sure now if he wants to give me the tape. I said, "We have a deal. You're going to give me the tape." He still hedges a bit, so I just grabbed it from him. In reality, I was freaking out because I didn't want to see this tape on another station or tell my boss that I failed on this mission. But I wasn't going to show how stressed out I was. It's the only time I've *ever seen* anything like this. I couldn't go back to the station without that tape.

We got back to the station, and it's a great tape. The photographer did a decent job shooting the wedding. Because of unions in Pittsburgh, you can't edit your own story—you have to have editors do it. However, you *can* direct how it's going to be done. We went "*natural sound up*" when the Marinos were reciting their vows. It was beautiful. I did a *stand-up in* and a *stand-up out,* and in between, we just played the video. This is Dan Marino getting married, and NO ONE HAS THIS FOOTAGE but us. This isn't just a sports story, we led with it in our newscast. They played that story through the entire next day. That almost never happens.

Marino found out, and he assumed that I'm the one who put the deal together to get the tape. Word gets back to me that the next time Dan Marino sees me, he's going to beat me up. I laughed. Fortunately, I never ended up meeting Dan Marino.

Someone once asked me if I had any qualms about broadcasting someone's wedding vows publicly. My answer was NO. Dan was a huge star and a popular public figure. I wasn't there to make friends. I was there to do the best job that I could, as honestly as I could do it. I'm a very aggressive person. That bothers some people.

49

Did Someone Say Lou Carnesecca?

Lou Carnesecca, who coached St. John's University to 526 wins over twenty-four seasons, is coaching a game against the University of Pittsburgh. John Calipari was the assistant coach at Pitt at the time. St. John's wins the game, and "Little Looie" is all fired up in the postgame press conference.

I ask the colorful Hall of Fame coach the first question, and he answers me this way. "Young man," he responds. "My hearing aid was turned off. Can you ask me the question again?"

The place went crazy.

50

Too Tall Cutler

In 1985, I got a call from Steve Poricelli, my agent, who asked me what I thought about professional wrestling.

"What do you mean?" I asked him.

He told me that I was a finalist for a job as a ring announcer. They would fly me in from Pittsburgh to New York City on Saturday morning. I'd do two shows for a national wrestling organization and get paid a thousand dollars for the weekend. They'd put me up in a really nice hotel with all expenses paid. They had no problem with me staying overnight so I could see my family and friends whenever I wanted to.

I figured that if I did this forty weekends a year, I would make more than I was making at my regular job at KDKA. I went to my news director about the deal, and he started laughing. He tells me that if they're going to pay me a thousand dollars for a Saturday and that I'd be back by Monday, then I needed to go for it. He believed it would be good for me in Pittsburgh.

When I called my agent back to let him know my boss had approved, he mentioned that the final decision came down to me and another guy. He didn't make any promises, but he told me my tape was No. 1—they liked me better, and unless I blew the tryout, I had the job. Blow the tryout? I'd be challenging the wrestlers. This gig was made for me. I also knew it would lead to something bigger.

Steve calls me back in a couple of days. I'm sitting at my desk, and I remember it like it was yesterday.

"I got good news and bad news," he tells me.

I told him to give me the bad news first.

"You didn't get the job," he informs me.

I then asked him what the good news was.

"They liked you better," he says. "There was a problem with you,

161

though. You're too tall. The guy they hired is at least six inches shorter than you."

It turns out that they hired a guy who wasn't as good as me simply because he was short…so that all the wrestlers would look taller.

At 6'2", I was way too tall.

51

KDKA Radio—Fun with Bill Currie

KDKA-TV and Radio were both owned by Westinghouse. The TV and radio people didn't get along. They were both No. 1 in the market, but there was a lot of jealousy between them. I thought it was stupid. The talent at KDKA-TV and Radio was as good as any place in the country. They didn't want to share talent even though the resources in that building were unbelievable. I never understood it. If I were the boss at Westinghouse, I would have taken both general managers, sat their butts down, and told them to either figure it out, or I would.

Management decided to bridge the gap between the two stations by putting me on the radio. That really upset some of the people in the TV sports department.

I met with two people from KDKA Radio. One was the general manager—Rick Starr, and the other was the program director named...Chris Cross. Cross has his own chapter later.

They hooked me up with a guy named Bill Currie—not the football coach. He was the craziest guy I ever worked with. On TV, he wore weird jackets with a flower and quoted Shakespeare. He and I got along great. I learned so much from him. He was really successful at KDKA-TV before they moved him to KYW in Philadelphia. He went on the air the first night there and started talking about how sports really aren't that big a deal. To put it mildly, it didn't go over well. Needless to say, he didn't last long there.

Bill was one of the smartest people I ever met in the business. He hated management in both radio and TV. His rants during commercial breaks were about the personalities and managers he didn't like. They were really funny. At times he'd try to make sure I'd still be laughing when the commercial break was over, and he would push me to try and say what I was laughing about—knowing I would never betray our trust. He had me, and he knew it. All in good fun. Our radio show was very popular. He was the driving force, not me. We never said a bad word to each other. We never had a personal disagreement or argument.

Currie was gay. I didn't care about that. It bothered a lot of people, though. Remember, this was the 1980s. If it bothered me, he would have figured it out in seconds. The fun we had doing that show was off the charts.

It was a weekend show, so I was working seven days a week.

Bruno Sammartino was the top wrestler at the time. He was very popular. I did a TV story with him. He was old school Italian. The respect he had for his wife and how he treated her was wonderful. He had a tiny workout room with a bench and two fifty-pound dumbbells. He could toss them around for an hour like I might handle ten-pound weights.

Bruno had "retired" but was making a comeback with his son. I got permission to sit ringside for the event. The problem was, I sat in the wrong seat. Bruno's opponent jumps out of the ring to get the chair that I'm sitting in. Thank goodness he stops, winks at me, and takes the chair next to me to hit Bruno. My heart was racing. After Bruno and his son won, the wrestler winked at me again. I laughed big time.

I told Bill Currie that I had asked Bruno to do our talk show for fifteen minutes. Bruno stayed on for three hours. Every single phone line was full the entire three hours. Bruno Sammartino made our show. From that point on, our weekend show was very popular. However, there was the typical BS from KDKA—they wouldn't give us a raise. They paid us the minimum allowed by the union even though they were making money. And they knew the show was popular. I threatened to quit. They told me to go ahead, but I kept on doing the show. They won that game of chicken.

My grandfather was really smart. For some reason, I remember being five years old and staying in my grandparents' apartment. He would watch wrestling while sitting at the edge of the bed, and he would twitch and react to the fake hits. The man was a scholar who came here from Russia. Because my grandparents couldn't get into America initially, my mother was born in Romania and my uncle was born in Canada. My aunt ended up being the only sibling born in America. My grandfather, who I loved with all my heart, thought wrestling was real. I never figured that one out.

52

Get Me Out of Pittsburgh

Finally in 1987, I got a call late one night while I'm in bed from John Duvall, the assistant general manager at LEX18. It was the first time I had talked to him since I left LEX18. He was desperate and wanted me back in Lexington. The ratings *just happened* to skyrocket when I was there before. In the time I was gone, they had seriously dropped.

He knew I wasn't happy in Pittsburgh and offered to make it worth my while to come back. I told him I would consider coming back to Lexington if the money was right...and if they would put in writing that I could do radio or anything else I wanted as long as it didn't interfere with my job.

Bruce Keidan, the brilliant sports columnist for the Pittsburgh Post-Gazette, wrote a piece about me leaving KDKA-TV and returning to LEX18. It didn't take a brain surgeon to figure out KDKA-TV wasn't going to like what he wrote. Keidan was also doing a sports talk show and would have been a natural to get hired by KDKA Radio. I read the piece and called him and told him he was crazy to write the column because after what he wrote about me, he'd never get hired by KDKA. Their management had thin skin. He just said it was the right thing to do. Bruce and I weren't friends. He was just writing a column, and I really respected him for saying what he did.

I walked into Sue McInerney's office to tell her that I was leaving. Sue was in management when I got to KDKA and moved up to become news director. She came over and gave me a big hug, said she was sorry, and wished me luck. I still had three and a half years left on my contract. I broke the contract. I didn't even ask if I could break it. I just left.

When I came back to Lexington that year, I gave up my dream of ever working in a big market like New York. Had I been single, I would have never come back. Do I regret coming back to Lexington? No. And that's really important for you to know that. I think Lexington is a great place to raise a family. Did I think I was going to spend most of my life here? No. If you had told me as a teenager that I would have spent most of my life in Lexington, I would have laughed at you. Lexington is a terrific city. That's as honest as I can be with you.

Part 5 (1985-1989)

Cutler's Back!

53

The Cutler Rule

When I came back to Lexington in 1987, I was supposed to start work on a Monday. Three wonderful stories were part of my Saturday before I was officially back.

UK Football was playing Saturday night, so I asked Norm Kelly, our chief photographer, to shoot for me. Norm is one of my all-time favorites. A lot of laughs. He always seems to know the right moment to put me in my place. Plus, he's a big-time photographer.

Just don't ask Norm to tell you the story about a sportscaster driving the wrong way in Atlanta on purpose because we had one of those freak-out deadlines that we made with about two minutes to spare after a Kentucky game. We'd miss the deadline if we were *just* driving fast.

There was a *big* deal being made about me returning to Lexington. Norm and I were walking the sidelines during the UK football game. All of a sudden, the stadium starts chanting and cheering my name. I'm getting chills, so Norm pops my balloon by saying, "What? Am I standing next to a rock star?" We had a great laugh.

I had a way of finding out when recruits were coming into town. Before the UK football game, I went to the airport. Getting out of a brand new, beautiful white Mercedes is UK assistant basketball coach Dwane Casey. Guess who he's there to pick up? Chris Mills—THE Chris Mills—the same Chris Mills who was coming in on a recruiting visit who ended up being a *HUGE* part of the NCAA mess that turned into one of the darkest moments for UK Athletics.

I asked Dwane if it would be OK to do an interview with Chris. He told me he can't officially set it up, but if Chris wanted to do it, I was on my own.

I did the interview with Chris Mills. It was about two minutes long. Casey could have just said no, so I knew I had to be quick. When the interview was done, I sat on it. I didn't tell anyone. My photographer was sworn to secrecy. I was so cocky, I knew I could hold it until Monday.

So here I am...my first show back...Monday at 6 pm...and I'm running an exclusive interview with Chris Mills. *CUTLER'S BACK! THE EXCLUSIVE STORIES ARE BACK! CHRIS MILLS WILL BE ONE OF THE BIGGEST RECRUITS THAT EDDIE SUTTON IS GOING TO GET, AND I TALKED TO HIM ONE-ON-ONE. BOOM!*

The NCAA had a recruiting rule that someone inside UK started calling the "Cutler Rule" from that Saturday on. If a recruit comes to Lexington, the school not only can't publicize anything about the visit, but they must attempt to "discourage" any media doing an interview or even taking a picture of them and using that.

The NCAA says it can be a recruiting advantage. I had a long talk with the NCAA about the rule. They were very nice on the phone, but their argument literally made *NO* sense. I'm not allowed to go up and talk to the recruit even if we don't do an interview. Even if I just took a picture of a player visiting UK for a basketball game, it would be considered an NCAA violation which gets the school in trouble.

UK could get in trouble with the NCAA—not serious trouble—but as one UK official told me, it's just a pain in the *blank*. UK was just doing their job.

UK then started putting out a letter telling the media that they couldn't talk to recruits on their visit. If they did, they could lose their credentials. Someone—I believe it was UK—told the NCAA about what I did. Self-reporting a minor violation is done all the time. I had to stop talking to recruits—all because of the "Cutler Rule."

The rule is really against freedom of the press. I was never mad at UK. They're stuck because of the NCAA. I was ready to challenge the rule and see what would happen. But LEX18 didn't want to make an enemy with UK, and they were concerned about the lawyer fees.

That's BS! We should have done it. We would have gotten national publicity, and it would have been terrific for ratings with all the updates we could put on TV. The newspapers, both locally and nationally, would be covering our story.

I believe to this day, it would have been great publicity for LEX18. And don't forget what was most important to me—it would be the right thing to do.

My thinking has always been much more aggressive than management's. I was told we could probably win, but it could be a long and drawn out process which could include losing my credentials and going to court to get my credentials back. I was told I'd probably get my credentials back. But, I had to back off.

I was ready for the battle. I wanted the battle. I'm not ripping LEX18, but they often *didn't or couldn't see the big picture.*

LEX18 *blew a great opportunity* to be a leader.

54

No Hall of Fame for Eddie Sutton

I t's complicated. It's crazy how much thought I've put into this chapter.

In the end, I'm going with my gut, which is what I always *try* to do.

I get it—to many, this chapter might not be popular.

Eddie Sutton was great.

Eddie Sutton was awful.

Both happened at Kentucky.

Plus, you could make a case that even when Sutton battled the bottle when he wasn't at Kentucky—he was great.

It's complicated!!!!!

Take out the scandal at Kentucky, and it's easy to remember Sutton was the first to take four different schools to the NCAA Tournament—and he was AP Coach of the Year two times.

I'm sympathetic that he was battling a disease. *But you can't forget that he was battling a disease.* His battle with a disease *ruined* the best career opportunity of his life.

I'm happy for Eddie Sutton finding out before he died that he was going into the Naismith Memorial Basketball Hall of Fame. I'm happy for his family and the many players over the years that he made better people and players.

There is a reason Sutton was a finalist for the Hall of Fame *seven times*. Without his battle with the bottle, he would have—or should have—been elected to the Naismith Memorial Basketball Hall of Fame on his first try. 806 *wins!*

But...*Eddie Sutton DOES NOT belong in the Naismith Memorial Basketball Hall of Fame.* Here's why.

After thirteen seasons as the head basketball coach at the University of Kentucky, Joe B. Hall retired in 1985. Eddie Sutton wasn't the first choice to replace Joe B. Please don't take that as a negative comment towards Sutton. It's not.

UK Athletics Director C.M. Newton once asked his good friend, Duke's Coach Mike Krzyzewski, if he'd be interested in taking the job. It's a smart thing to do. I asked C.M. Newton about it one time. He just smiled, paused, and changed the topic. He ended up hiring a coach who was leading the New York Knicks.

I'd love to know all the calls John Calipari has gotten over the last fifteen or twenty years about coaching jobs. I'm sure it's also a lot more than will ever get reported. I've looked at hundreds of coaching job searches, and almost never do you end up hiring your No. 1 candidate.

When UK hired Rich Brooks, I'd bet money that he wasn't even in the first three choices. He turned out to be a wonderful coach. Sometimes you might be lucky *NOT* to get your first choice.

Coaches at the top of your wish list normally are very secure in their existing jobs—but you make the phone call anyway. You never know if someone has an itch to move on—or if $$ creates an itch to move on.

Back to Joe B. Hall. Kentucky was having a hard time finding someone to replace him. You think finding a basketball coach at the University of Kentucky would be an easy thing to do. Wrong—it's *NOT* easy! Many *want* to coach here, but so what?

Someone you might be close to hiring changes their mind at the last minute because they get a new contract at their current job. Or, they get cold feet, or something in their family makes them change their mind. There can be many reasons why deals fall apart at the end.

Anyone remember Arizona's Lute Olson? There are some at UK who believed he was coming. He said "yes" to Kentucky, ESPN reported it, but he never signed the contract. He stayed at Arizona and beat UK for the NCAA championship in 1997—a game Pitino *never* should have lost. You think Olsen got more money for staying in the desert?

As you know, Kentucky ended up hiring Eddie Sutton as Joe B.'s replacement.

The first time I met Eddie Sutton was at the Red Lion—a hotel in Boise, Idaho. I'm the sports director at KBCI-TV in Boise, and I get a tip that he's in town for a coaching clinic. Sutton, who had taken Arkansas to the Final Four, started the basketball program at the College of Southern Idaho—and did a great job. It was a fun, positive interview by the pool.

I'll never forget the second time I met Eddie Sutton. It was at a UK basketball practice. That same Saturday, I interviewed Chris Mills after he got off the plane in Lexington on his recruiting trip, and I covered the UK football game that night. What a day! That was two days before I officially started my second tour of duty at LEX18.

Eddie was warm, kind, and friendly. He was also wearing a very expensive white sweat suit that looked absolutely ridiculous. I won't even put in the book what I thought he looked like. I've never forgotten that outfit, nor have I seen any other coach wearing anything like it.

Eddie Sutton was a great defensive coach—but I wouldn't put him in the Hall of Fame.

First of all, I would never put a coach in the Naismith Memorial Basketball Hall of Fame until their career is over. Give it five years, and if you end up going back after five years, I'm good with it.

By my rule, Pitino wouldn't be in either. It doesn't matter that he won NCAA championships at Kentucky and Louisville—and he should have won more than one at Kentucky. I believe Pitino is without a doubt one of the greatest coaches of all time. But, Pitino was kicked out of college basketball in October of 2017 for the ugly NCAA mess that happened on his watch at Louisville, and he was exiled to Greece to continue coaching.

Pitino spent his time in the NCAA *jail* as far as I'm concerned. I agreed with Iona hiring him in 2020. Forget the twenty-five million plus he lost during that time—and the tens of millions he might have made at Louisville if he coached into his mid-70s there. I think he's suffered enough.

Understand, I've had my share of battles with Pitino. At one point we were close. But these thoughts have nothing to do with the relationship I had or don't have with him.

I have tremendous respect for the job Sutton did at Arkansas. But when you consider the problems he had at Kentucky—a disgusting NCAA scandal and a horrendous drinking problem—he doesn't belong in the Naismith Memorial Basketball Hall of Fame. To be fair, there are others in the Hall of Fame that I don't think deserve to be there either.

Showing up to any game and practices when your disease gets to you—is a problem.

In 1987, Sutton went to the Betty Ford Clinic. *But, that wasn't the first time he received help while at Kentucky*—although many believe otherwise. And, let's just say his arm was twisted to get help.

173

When Sutton got in the Naismith Memorial Basketball Hall of Fame, Rex Chapman said he was happy for Eddie. There is no doubt that Rex's addiction, and the way he's been so open and honest about his problems, made him a lot more understanding of what Eddie went through. But, the former UK great *hated* playing for Eddie. We're not saying that Rex hated playing for Eddie all the time. But he hated playing for Eddie for a number of reasons. More on that later.

I respect that Eddie was battling a disease. LEX18's anchor Mike Barry and weatherman Brian Collins taught me that, but you can be a great coach and not belong in the Naismith Memorial Basketball Hall of Fame.

On March 19, 1989, after Kentucky finished the season 13-19 with its first losing record in sixty-one years, Eddie Sutton resigned—before he was fired—as the UK head basketball coach.

Please let that soak in, 13-19–*THIS IS KENTUCKY BASKETBALL. LOOK AT THE NUMBERS AND THE HISTORY.* Go back and look at the last one hundred years of basketball and try and find a season like that. And, there was plenty of talent. *PLEASE!!!!*

In 1926, with almost no time to prepare for the season, Basil Hayden—who lived to be a hundred and three and was the first UK Basketball All-American in 1921—was asked to coach the team. They were 3-13 in his only season as the coach. Hayden once said he was handed a team of "scrubs."

Bottom line is that 13-19 at Kentucky isn't like at any other place.

Kentucky was facing eighteen formal NCAA charges ranging from recruiting violations, to academic fraud, and a lack of proper institutional control over the basketball program. When you are dealing with the NCAA—when they use the term "institutional control"—it is a big deal. That means you're in trouble.

Sutton's downfall at Kentucky started with his disease. It then took another level in the spring of 1988 when rumors began surfacing of improper recruiting with the now infamous "Emery package" which allegedly contained a thousand dollars to the father of UK recruit Chris Mills. Coupled with the academic scandal which surrounded Eric Manuel in 1989, Sutton was toast.

One, I never believed UK assistant coach Dwane Casey put the money in the Emery package. Yes, his name was on it, but his name was on many things for recruits. Casey wasn't even in Lexington when the package was sent.

Casey sued Emery Worldwide Freight Services for $6.9 million. Before the suit, Casey was kicked out of college basketball for at least five years, so he went to Japan to coach. After the lawsuit was settled, the NCAA lifted his ban.

The damage to Casey's reputation was so bad, I never thought he'd be allowed to be successful in coaching. Fortunately for Casey, the NBA didn't care. Casey worked his way from being a very successful assistant to one of the better head coaches in the NBA. With Toronto in 2018, Casey was the NBA Coach of the Year. They fired him two days later.

Kentucky went on probation for three years and was banned from postseason play for two years for the recruiting and academic violations. The NCAA said there was enough evidence to shut down UK from playing during the regular season—or, in other words, to give UK the "death penalty."

I always thought the threat of shutting down Kentucky's program was nonsense and an idle threat that made the NCAA look powerful. The TV networks don't want the Kentuckys and North Carolinas and Dukes of the world not playing basketball.

Chris Mills was told he could never play at Kentucky.

Eric Manuel, who sat out the season because of questions about his college entrance exam, was barred from playing in an NCAA school—ever again. The NCAA said that Manuel "committed academic fraud by cheating" on a college entrance exam.

In addition, Kentucky could add only three scholarship players for each of the next two seasons—so if anyone left, they could not be replaced by another scholarship player. That could have been a *huge* disaster. The NCAA said they would have been tougher on UK if they didn't cooperate. UK President Dr. David Roselle made sure there was plenty of cooperation.

After all of that, you might think I'm against Eddie Sutton. Nothing could be farther from the truth.

What's crazy is, I had a *very* tiny role in that next step in Sutton's coaching career.

A year later, Sutton returns to become head coach at his alma mater, Oklahoma State. Prior to his being hired, Oklahoma State Athletics Director Myron Roderick called me around 11 pm one night. I'm getting ready to do my evening TV sportscast, so I tell him to call back after it's over and I'd be glad to talk to him for as long as he wants.

Roderick, who won 13 NCAA championships as Oklahoma State's wrestling coach, called back at 11:45 pm. We talked on the phone for close to *TWO HOURS*. It was obvious that hiring Eddie Sutton wasn't his choice. He was scared. I understood his fears.

Roderick was late in his career, and he didn't want his legacy to include a big mistake. I found out he was calling me because he knew I had broken the story on Eddie offering up his assistant coaches in order to save his own job—which I'll tell you about later. Roderick said he was told that I was tough but fair, and that I was one of the names he had been "instructed" to call. I'd love to talk to the person who put me on that list. I'd love to know the list of media types Roderick was told he had to talk to.

Roderick asked me point blank toward the end of our conversation whether or not I would hire Eddie Sutton. I told him, "If Eddie had cleaned his act up and wasn't drinking, I'd hire him in two seconds." He then asked me *if* Eddie had cleaned his act up. How should I know? I told him I had no idea, nor would I guess, but I hoped he would stay clean for the rest of his life. I got the strong feeling he was looking for reasons to tell his athletics board why they *shouldn't* hire Eddie.

Eddie got hired, and he did a great job at Oklahoma State from 1990-2006. I was happy he got another chance.

Do as I say, not as I do. As a coach, Eddie was old school and a bigtime disciplinarian. In his life, that wasn't the case.

I've seen too many coaches who live their lives "do as I say, not as I do."

I always felt sorry for his son, Sean. Playing basketball for your father is not an easy thing to do. Playing basketball for your father—when a great program is falling apart—has to be a nightmare.

Sean loved his father as much as, if not more than, anyone else in his family. There were plenty of times that Eddie's battle with the bottle had him saying terrible things to Sean.

Eddie didn't handle his son the right way. There were other point guards ranked higher than Sean who didn't want to play at Kentucky because Sean was here. I said it on TV at the time that if Sean were the 6th man—with his heart, hustle, and ability to pass—many will think I'm crazy, but I always thought he could have been popular. Plus, he would have been more relaxed on the court. Fans were mean to Sean partly because they knew there were more talented point guards who would have come here if Sean was the 6th man.

Before the end of the 1989 season, everyone knew that Eddie Sutton was going to be history. The question was when, not if.

I get a phone call from a great source that I'd trust with my wallet telling me that Eddie had offered to fire all his assistant coaches in order to keep his job. I went on TV with that.

Less than ninety minutes after the story runs, Harry Barfield, the general manager at LEX18, comes to the back of the newsroom looking for me. He didn't come to the back very often. "Cutler, I just got a call from Eddie Sutton," he said. "He was yelling and screaming, and I couldn't understand part of his screaming. He wants a retraction and is going crazy. Just tell me one thing. Was what you said true?" I told him it was true. Harry waves, tells me to have a good night, turns around and walks away.

Harry trusted me. Trust is a big thing with me. I'm old school. That meant the world to me. I could have told Harry at that moment that I loved him. I probably should have.

Right after Harry leaves, Sutton calls and goes crazy on me. He never said the story wasn't true, and I asked him a number of times to tell me my story was wrong. I was tired of Eddie yelling at me, so I joined in—*yelling as loud at him as he was to me...* "*Eddie, tell me I'm wrong.*" He kept on pushing me to tell him who I spoke to—even though he knew I wasn't going to say. And I still won't say. I've never told anyone. And I won't.

Eddie Sutton never told me my story was wrong, but that didn't stop him from using a *ton* of words we can't use on TV. I was never upset at Eddie's language. His career was falling apart, and I've said tons of things that can't go in any book.

Sources talk for all kinds or reasons. Sometimes it's because of a problem, or they are mad at someone, and they really trust you to help. You can't buy trust. Sometimes a person can love a place but is so fed up when someone else is doing it harm—so, when they may *never* normally tell you something, they actually volunteer to tell you because they trust you.

What's even crazier is that person never even had to say, "Don't tell anyone I told you, or don't use my name." They knew I'd protect them. Don't blow off this paragraph. It's helped me a number of times.

As luck would have it, I had a vacation scheduled right when all this was happening. We rented a cabin down in Tennessee for some vacation time with Judy's family. My boss told me I could go, but if the story broke, I'd have to come back.

I got to Tennessee, and I was so exhausted from months and months of dealing with this story and the worst college basketball season I've ever been around. All I wanted to do was say hello to the family, have a couple of beers, and sleep. That wasn't going to happen. I had to come back—because Eddie Sutton decided to resign *before* he got fired.

Eddie Sutton didn't resign because of my story. But I had a source inside UK who told me my story pushed up the timing of what was going to happen.

The next time I did basketball interviews, Sean Sutton didn't want to talk to me. I get it. I did a less-than-flattering story about his dad. I went over to Sean and said, "You can hate me, and I'm OK with that, but we should talk this out." He asked me why I did the story as he was fighting back tears. I told him because the story was true. He said, "OK, I'm OK," and turned around and walked away with tears in his eyes. I'll never forget that.

If it's possible to feel terrible, but feel good about the story you did, when Sean walked away—that was me.

The next time I saw Sean, we talked like we had always talked in the past.

I always rooted for Sean partly because UK fans were way too tough on him. No one played harder for UK during the time Sean wore Kentucky across his chest. The public doesn't know or understand the garbage Sean took. It's that line I keep on using. Try walking a mile in his shoes. Trust me, you wouldn't like it.

When Eddie died, I read many stories about his life and career. Only one had a term he used all the time—"Big Valentine." That was Eddie's way of saying a player had a big heart.

"I heard that one many times in 1985-86," star UK forward Kenny Walker told me. "Despite the way it ended for Coach Sutton at Kentucky, he was still an awesome coach."

When Eddie Sutton showed up, Roger Harden—a high school All-American—had lost his confidence. He became a great player under Sutton.

"He believed in me when I didn't, and it changed my life," the point guard said after Sutton died. "Grateful to God that I got to call him a coach and life-long friend. Being a part of his first year at Kentucky and going 32-4 was the joy of a lifetime. Thanks Coach, and I will cherish the many warm memories you gave me until we meet again."

UK lost that season in the NCAA Tournament 59-57 to LSU. UK was trying to beat LSU for the fourth time that year to get to the Final Four. It's crazy having to play one team four times. To this day, that loss upsets Roger Harden. UK believed they were good enough to win the NCAA Tournament, which Louisville ended up winning that year. UK beat U of L earlier that season.

I will always believe that if Sutton didn't have the *disease*, he would have won an NCAA championship at Kentucky.

"I agree one hundred percent," Kenny Walker told me.

I'm still not picking Eddie Sutton for the Hall of Fame.

55

King Rex Crying

The worst kept secret during Rex Chapman's sophomore year at Kentucky was that he would be leaving after the season was over. No one could report it because you couldn't prove it.

The truth was that Rex couldn't stand playing for Eddie Sutton, and he was already good enough to go to the NBA. As much as Rex loved Kentucky, it was claustrophobic for him—a superstar that felt boxed in. He told me on TV when he played for UK that it got to the point that he couldn't be a normal teenager—that he couldn't even go to a mall because he'd be mobbed.

I'll repeat it—Rex couldn't stand playing for Sutton. Eddie Sutton wanted seven passes before a shot while Rex and Ed Davender wanted to run and gun. *Seven passes?* They were about as oil and water as oil and water could be.

It was always *ridiculous to me* that with Chapman and Davender in the backcourt, UK was 61st nationally in scoring.

My opinion? Sutton was stupid. As great as he was as a coach, with Ed Davender and Rex Chapman, if he only would have let them run at every opportunity. WOW, this could have been a great UK team. Sutton didn't see what he had. It really bothered me, so you know it bothered Ed and Rex a lot more. That's coaching.

I'm on my soapbox. I really liked Ed Davender. He and Rex were tight. What a backcourt. Davender and I were both from Brooklyn. He would challenge me during and after interviews. It was fun.

I was convinced back then, had Eddie Sutton let Rex and Ed go, Davender's skills would have been on display more...and I will always believe he would have made it in the NBA with a different style of playing ball. Davender had no problem playing second fiddle to Rex

180

because they were so close, but if Sutton took the shackles off them, Davender's skills would have shined a lot more.

Davender's story is really sad. He was convicted of a basketball ticket scam, sentenced to eight years in prison, and died way too young of a heart attack at the age of forty-nine.

Davender called me one time to borrow money. I wouldn't have given it to him even if I had it. I had an idea what was going on. Plus, I figured if Ed called me, how many others were in front of me. Sad—really sad because I liked him.

In the 1987-88 season—at Rex's last game of his UK career—I was sitting right behind UK's bench in their third game of the NCAA Tournament against Villanova. At that time, I was surprised to see that the players weren't paying much attention to Eddie Sutton. The players didn't look happy to be there. This is the NCAA Tournament for crying out loud!!!

Sometimes inside of you, there's a dichotomy—you want to win, but you're so tired of the season, and so sick of the nonsense, you just want it over with. To me, that was that team. It's like a bowl game where a football team gets upset because their season didn't turn out the way they expected, and they didn't want to be in that bowl in the first place.

I promise you sitting behind the Kentucky bench that day, I kept on saying to myself that a lot of the players wanted the season to be over.

After Kentucky lost the game 80-74, King Rex—who scored 30 points—was crying. There's a big gang of media people about ten yards away in the locker room. We were all on a tight deadline. Rex was the story because everybody wanted to ask him about his reaction to the season being over and if this was his last game at Kentucky—plus he was the star.

Rex was crying in the locker room. I remember looking at Rob Bromley of WKYT and saying, "Rob, we have a tight deadline." He answers, "Yeah, I know," so I walk up to Rex and whisper in his ear. "Rex, do you trust me?" I ask him. He nodded his head, yes. "Can I make a suggestion?" He nodded his head, yes again. "It's better for you—forget that we're on a tight deadline—it's better for you if you talk to us, get it over with, and this is what I'm going to do for you," I told him.

His eyes got big, and he looked at me. I then said, "If you will talk, I will bring everybody over, and in three or four questions I will cut it off so you don't have to stand here and keep answering the same question over and over again. It's your call."

That's word for word what happened.

In between sniffling, Rex quietly said, "Let's do it." So instead of being a hog, which I probably could have been—but it wasn't the right thing to do—I called everybody in the media over. Whoosh—everybody hustled to King Rex. After three or four questions, I said, "That's it. Rex is done." Some people looked at me funny, but I held my ground. "He's done," I said again. Everyone was cool, everyone stopped, and everyone walked away. We left Rex alone, and we all got the story. As I'm walking away, Rex nodded at me.

I always felt sorry for Rex. I always believed that if his body—with his skinny legs—didn't break down—he might have had a spectacular twelve-year career in the NBA. Rex averaged nearly 15 points a game—but he didn't have close to the career I know he could have had if he stayed healthy.

Back in 1994, as he was having his best season in the NBA—leading Washington in scoring—Rex is named to his only All-Star team. He broke his ankle and never played in the game.

How bad was the break? Mitchell Butler, one of three who helped Rex to the locker room told the Washington Post, "I've never seen anything like it. The foot was bent completely back when they took the shoe off. He couldn't talk. He was kind of in shock."

Rex had ten surgical procedures which led him to abuse drugs—prescription opioids.

Rex was prescribed OxyContin after being hospitalized for an emergency appendectomy. At one point, he told *Sports Illustrated* that he was taking close to fifty pills a day.

Anyone who is a True Blue fan and who's been around for a long time will remember the dunk Rex had against Louisville. He also had 26 points in that game as a freshman.

When he played at UK, he was friends with some of the players at Louisville. We did a story on it one time and the phone calls I received really *ticked me off.* There were plenty of fans who thought Rex shouldn't be friends with the arch rival. To me, that has always been *ridiculous.*

Players don't think like fans, and fans often get mad when a player doesn't think like them. Selfish?

You get some strange phone calls at any TV station. One time a caller was upset with Rex. He was furious that he heard a rumor that Rex's girlfriend was an African American. I had a one-word response.

"So?" The caller got *really angry* at me. I wasn't very nice in return. That caller wanted me to do a story and call the UK Basketball office.

Who didn't want to be able to play like Rex?—but walking a mile in his shoes at times wasn't easy.

I hope Rex is proud of everything he accomplished on the court, but it's only natural to think—what if he stayed healthy—what if he never got hooked on pills—what if he never played for Eddie Sutton?

If Rex played for John Calipari or Rick Pitino or Denny Crum—who he said at one point he was going to play for—he would have had a ton of fun. But, Rex is really proud that he wore Kentucky across his chest.

It's complicated.

Unfortunately, Rex played for Eddie Sutton, and the two did not mix. Eddie was the boss—and as great as he was—at times he didn't do a good job of adjusting to his talent. Eddie believed the talent had to adjust to him.

I have always believed that great coaches have a system, but in reality they will adjust their system to fit the talent they have recruited. How many times have you heard John Calipari talk about trying to figure out the best way for his team to play?

If there's one failure of Eddie Sutton's on the court at Kentucky, it's that he didn't look at the talent that he had with Rex and Eddie Davender. He had thoroughbreds working as Clydesdales pulling the Budweiser wagon. It didn't make any sense to me. He should have had his team playing like thoroughbreds on offense and then demand they play defense the way he wanted.

It makes me sad that Rex was not happy for a large part of his career here. He should have had it all.

Rex grew up in an era where "tough love" was the parenting style.

Wayne, his father, went to Kentucky to play basketball and then transferred to Western Kentucky University to help out his family. Wayne averaged 20 points a game as a senior. He coached Kentucky Wesleyan from 1985-90 and won two Division II national championships.

When Rex was growing up, he had the feeling that no matter what he did, it wasn't good enough for his father. "Tough love" can be good and bad. Because Rex was sensitive, I think it hurt him.

I think the world of Rex, and I like his father. I didn't walk in Rex's shoes or deal with his pain, but I do know that I'm scared of those pills. After my second shoulder operation, I refused pain pills. I had heard so many stories about athletes getting hooked on them that I decided I would just rather deal with the pain. After my first shoulder surgery, I quit taking pain pills after one day. That doesn't make me any better or worse than Rex.

Rex is very smart in speaking openly about his addiction. He's a powerful voice who can help others. He's always been a very opinionated person. I think he could do a really good daily radio talk show. The fact that Rex wants to talk to people and help them doesn't surprise me. Deep down, he's a teddy bear.

I really hope Rex stays clean.

56

Kenny "Sky" Walker

Kenny Walker was Mr. Basketball in the state of Georgia, a member of the Georgia Sports Hall of Fame, a two-time SEC Player of the Year, and a two-time All-American at UK. He was picked fifth in the first round by the New York Knicks in the 1986 NBA draft. He grew up in Roberta, Georgia—a tiny town of about a thousand people. His brother, Lewis, is the sheriff in Roberta.

When you talk about sports being a small world, future UK coach Tubby Smith went to Kenny's house to recruit him—for Virginia Commonwealth. Another assistant coach, former UK guard Reggie Warford, was recruiting him for Pittsburgh.

Not only did Kenny love playing for UK, but he's proud that he "helped open the door for other Blacks to play at UK."

Why couldn't Todd May, a Kentucky boy from Pike County, a 6'8" forward who could shoot with either hand make it at Kentucky? How many men that tall do you know that could shoot with either hand? Todd May could really shoot.

May was part of a great recruiting class with two McDonald All-Americans—Kenny Walker and Roger Harden. May should have been a star at UK.

Why was Kenny Walker, from a little town in Georgia with two traffic lights, able to handle Lexington and Todd May couldn't?

In 1982, Todd May was Mr. Basketball—winner of an award that goes to the best high school player in Kentucky. From Virgie—a very small town, he was part of five games before getting homesick and going back home.

May, and the great future star for the Chicago Bulls, Scottie Pippen, were repeat selections on the All-NAIA team in 1987. May led the NAIA in scoring at 40 points per game and was second in rebounds with 15. I mean no disrespect to the competition he faced at Pikeville compared to what he would have faced at a Kentucky practice or in games playing for UK, but being triple teamed at Pikeville wasn't unusual.

Oh my gosh, I wish I had May's talent. I would have made the NBA. I'm not knocking Todd. As someone from that neck of the woods told me, "Todd is country...and Cutler you don't understand." I hope Todd's happy and hasn't lived his life in the world of "what if." I don't think it's possible not to have "what if" as part of your thoughts.

Walker admits that Todd May was ahead of him when it came to basketball, but Kenny was a much better athlete. Patience and some time in the weight room was all Todd May needed. But he was shy, and there were people back home who were angry that he left Kentucky.

But you can't forget that "as a freshman, I was painfully shy," says Kenny Walker.

What bothers me even more is that both Walker and May were not only big-time scorers, but neither was selfish, and I believe they would have eventually become good friends while sharing the spotlight.

May had a lot more in common with Walker than I think he realized because he was so unhappy. Plus, May's father wasn't happy that Walker played ahead of him.

I can't imagine "Sky" Walker going from Roberta, Georgia to Lexington where 23,000 people are cheering and yelling at you every game. The jump from Roberta to Lexington to New York City and playing for the Knicks is huge. Kenny adjusted with that huge move and enjoys spending time in New York after playing there.

There is a reason he's "Sky" Walker. I don't think I've ever seen a Kentucky basketball player who was able to get off his feet so quickly. Not only could he jump super high, but Kenny was such a quick jumper. He was also one of the most efficient UK basketball players that I've ever seen.

I was in Seattle for the Final Four when Kenny and UK got destroyed by Georgetown in the semifinals. Kentucky shot 9% in the second half—*9% for crying out loud*—and ended up losing 53-40 to the Hoyas. Kenny was saddled with severe back spasms. Everyone will say that it wouldn't have made a difference even if Kenny had been healthy, but I'm not so sure about that. I think one player can make a difference and change the flow of the game. Kenny's back was so bad he couldn't run or jump. Had he been healthy, he could have created a mismatch problem for Georgetown.

Georgetown had a player named Michael Graham, who literally beat up Kentucky. Graham should have been in the NBA forever as a power forward who played defense, grabbed rebounds, and was an enforcer. Michael Graham—not Patrick Ewing—won that game for Georgetown.

There haven't been a whole lot of big games I've covered where one person—who wasn't great offensively and didn't start—changed a game the way Michael Graham did that day. Kentucky was intimidated. That's why they shot 3-33 in the second half. Afterwards, the Kentucky locker room was one of the saddest I've ever walked into—and I've seen a lot of crying through the years when you lose your last game in the NCAA Tournament.

What's forgotten is that not only was UK up by seven at the half, but they held the great Patrick Ewing to 8 points and 9 rebounds for the game.

John Thompson, the Georgetown coach, was an intimidating man who taught intimidation. He won the NCAA championship in 1984. I thought he'd win more than one.

During the Final Four in Seattle, I went to the hotel where Georgetown was supposed to be staying. The team never showed up. I did a story going to four hotels where the Hoyas might be staying. "Where's Georgetown?" I jokingly asked. They purposely didn't show up in town because John Thompson wanted his team to be secluded—away from everyone.

Intimidation can be a large part of sports and is a bigger factor than is often talked about. There's no question that Georgetown intimidated people. They played in the Big East. At that time, many thought it was the best and most physical conference in the country.

I was sad that Kenny Walker never played that game a hundred percent healthy.

Even though Kenny was a huge star at Kentucky, he has his share of "what ifs"?

"What if Sam Bowie didn't break his leg again?" says Kenny.

Think about this quote—"He [Sam Bowie] was the most athletic center I've ever seen."

In Joe B. Hall's last year, the team didn't think they'd make the NCAA Tournament. Kenny didn't even watch the NCAA selection show. While he was playing pool, someone ran in to say UK was in.

Kenny never saw Joe B. Hall so loose and relaxed as he was that year. There was no pressure on Kentucky. In their third NCAA game, they ran into St. John's. Their star, Chris Mullin, who had 30 points, 7 assists, and 10 rebounds hit Kenny in his right eye. Even with the pain, and his eye being swollen, Kenny hit 10 of 14 shots for 23 points and 8 rebounds. St. John's, however, knocks out UK 86-70 on their way to the Final Four.

After the game, it seemed like the team was on the bus for a long time. All of a sudden, someone who was with the team comes on the bus and says that Joe B. Hall had just retired. Although there were rumors that Joe B. might be retiring, it still was shocking.

Kenny started thinking about the NBA because he wasn't happy about changing coaches for one year. His parents let Kenny make the decision. He's glad he came back to UK for his senior season.

Kenny is still upset about losing to LSU 59-57. That loss kept UK from getting to the Final Four in his senior season under Eddie Sutton. UK, who finished at 32-4, was ranked No. 3. LSU wasn't ranked. UK was trying to beat LSU for the fourth time that season. Kenny believes if UK would have beaten LSU, they had a great chance at winning the national championship because they already beat Louisville, the eventual champs, earlier that year. It also really bothers Kenny because he still believes Kentucky was the better team.

Kenny also played an important role in convincing Rick Pitino, his coach with the New York Knicks, to take the head coaching job at Kentucky.

During the job search, UK athletics director C.M. Newton called Kenny and asked him to speak to his NBA coach. C.M. asked Kenny to keep this away from the media. So, Kenny went into Pitino's office to talk. At first, Pitino was flattered but wasn't interested. He was excited about his future with his New York Knicks—his dream job.

Shortly thereafter, Knicks general manager Al Bianchi made a few trades that upset Pitino. So, Pitino went to Kenny and wanted to know if Kentucky would still be interested. By then, C.M. Newton was in serious talks with P.J. Carlesimo who ended up taking Seton Hall to the Final Four and won 554 games in the NBA as a head coach. P.J. passed on Kentucky.

Pitino wanted Kenny to help convince Joanne, Pitino's wife, about moving to Lexington. Kenny was smart—when they went to breakfast, he pushed for how Lexington was a great place to raise kids. Kenny says that Joanne was not an easy sell for the big move.

Kenny has a perspective that no one else can have. He played for Joe B. Hall, Eddie Sutton, and Rick Pitino with the New York Knicks.

Kenny says that Sutton might be the best coach, that Pitino was the most fun to play for, and he believes that Joe B. Hall is "underrated and under-appreciated and doesn't get enough credit."

Coaches are people. They have bad years. Kenny agrees with me about Sutton's rule of making seven passes before shooting was ridiculous—"I never understood that," says Kenny. He also agrees with me that if Sutton let his good friends, guards Rex Chapman and Eddie Davender run all day after he left, UK would have been much better—and a lot more fun to watch.

There are many examples of athletes doing something special with a heavy heart. Three days after his father died, in 1989, Kenny won the NBA slam dunk contest.

I always liked how Kenny treats people. He is polite, kind, and happy to sign autographs. "Sky" has told me more than once that fans have been so good to him, so why shouldn't he be really good back to them?

The University of Kentucky is lucky to have an ambassador and former great like Kenny "Sky" Walker.

57

Jenna is Scared of Her Dad

In 1987–our daughter, Jenna, was two, and Judy and I had one of those weird experiences parents can have.

We had the Children's Miracle Network telethon on LEX18, so I decided to try a bluff. I figured no one would call me on it, but if they did, I was screwed.

I like my mustache—so much so that since I graduated college in 1975, I had only shaved it once. I went on TV during the telethon and said if anyone will give me five hundred dollars in the next fifteen minutes, I will shave my 'stash on TV. I figured NO WAY I'm in any jeopardy with this.

As luck would have it, fifteen hundred dollars was offered. Fifteen hundred dollars!! I had to shave my 'stash on TV!! It got some laughs and was good publicity for a great cause.

Here is the problem. When I got home, Jenna ran to the door to greet me like many times before. However, this time when she looked at me, she screamed like a monster had just walked through the door. She ran to Judy, clutching and shaking. Judy and I freaked for a moment. We sat on the floor while she was holding onto Judy's leg, and she had to listen to my voice for a good three to four minutes before she would calm down.

Where was this in the book of being a parent?

Eventually she came over and finally gave me a hug. It was crazy.

The next day Jenna came up to me and said, "Don't ever shave your mustache again." A number of times over the next six months, out of nowhere, Jenna would come up to me and say, "Don't EVER shave your mustache again!"

58

J.J. Completes Our Family

How lucky can we be? Jenna was perfect, and then there was J.J.

Dr. Glenn Moore delivers our son, puts him on the inside part of his forearm, then holds him up with one hand—and the first time we see J.J. in this world, he's wearing a *MUSTACHE.*

The doctor made a fake mustache, put scotch tape on the back, put it in his pocket—and before he held J.J. up, he slapped the mustache on him. Dr. Moore said, "I just wish I had a camera on you both when you saw him!"

We're laughing and crying at the same time.

The nurses were having a great time, and they took pictures with J.J. and his "stash."

When things calmed down, I asked Dr. Moore why he did it. He said he watched me on TV enough to know I had a sense of humor.

That night, my sports photographer, Robin Lynch, came to the hospital. I held J.J. up, and we put the mustache back on him for the 11 pm news. The videotape of that segment remained at the TV station for many years. I promised J.J. that I would show it to him one of these days.

That day finally arrived when J.J. was six. He and I went down to the station on a Saturday morning because we were dropping off Judy and Jenna for a trip to Cincinnati—and the TV station was close to where we dropped them off.

I showed him the tape of him being born. I play the tape, and J.J. was just staring and staring and staring at the image on the screen. I'm expecting a big reaction. Nothing. He sees the mustache and doesn't say a word. I thought he'd be laughing hysterically. The tape ends—and nothing—no reaction.

"Dad," he finally says. "I never knew you were skinny."

At that point, I was laughing and chasing him around the newsroom. Forget about the mustache, my son had never seen me skinny—because for most of his life, I was fat.

59

J.J. and Grandpa Roy Williams

I used to do a lot of interviews with visiting coaches when they came into town to play Kentucky. Almost all of the time, I was the only reporter trying to do this. It was a really good way of getting a scoop and a fresh story.

It was a Saturday, and Roy Williams came into town as the head coach of the Kansas Jayhawks. Judy, my wife, had something to do that day and was very insistent that I take J.J., my son who was two at the time, to do the interview. I didn't want to take J.J., but what choice did I have?

I met my photographer at Rupp Arena. As we're setting up, the sports information director of Kansas walks over, and I immediately apologize for bringing my son to the interview. He was very nice and told me not to worry about it.

Meanwhile, Kansas is shooting free throws—it's a very relaxed atmosphere—when Roy Williams comes over. He says, "Hi" to J.J. and was really warm and gracious during the two or three-minute interview. During the time that we're talking, J.J. takes off, and I didn't realize it. I thought he was right beside me. When we finished the interview, I said, "Where's J.J.?" Roy starts looking around, and I shout out even louder, "Where's J.J.?"

Everybody, including the players on the court, stop and look around. We can't find him. Not only is Roy Williams helping me look for my son, but the players on his team are spreading out at Rupp Arena looking for J.J. I'm still screaming, "J.J.! J.J.!"

J.J. was crawling up the steps on the other side of the court. He had this big grin on his face—*"Haha, I got away, come get me."* I went over and got him. He laughed and thought it was so funny. Roy Williams and the team got a good laugh as well.

I told Coach that I was sorry, and he said, "Are you kidding? I've got kids. It's all good. Hey, put your son down. I love little kids." He sits down, grabs a basketball, and starts rolling it back and forth to J.J. on the court. I wish I had footage of it.

I told Roy he didn't have to do this, and he answers me by saying, "What am I doing? I'm not coaching. This is fun for me." So he sat there on the floor for about five minutes rolling a basketball up and back to J.J. His time with J.J. was longer than our interview.

This is ROY WILLIAMS, one of the GREATEST COACHES OF ALL TIME—two-time AP Coach of the Year, three-time National Champion, he's in the Basketball Hall of Fame—sitting on the court at Rupp Arena rolling a basketball with my son. I loved it.

I told my viewers that night that if Roy Williams coached at UK, True Blue fans would love him. But for many, that's impossible to do because he represents the wrong color of blue. It doesn't matter that Roy Williams coaches at North Carolina, I will always think he's a really good dude.

60

Pete Rose Loves UK Basketball

Pete Rose never forgets a name. He has an amazing memory. The all-time hit king in baseball can tell you what the pitch was on a three-two count in a big game in 1968. Forget for a minute about the gambling that got him tossed out of his main love—baseball. Rose was a huge fan of King Rex.

Rex Chapman was playing for UK at the time. Rose comes to Lexington with the annual stop of the Cincinnati Reds Caravan. We did a live shot with the Reds' skipper downstairs in the lobby of the Campbell House Inn. Instead of asking him about the Reds, we talk UK Basketball.

Pete goes on and on and on about King Rex. The stuff he knew about Kentucky Basketball was mind boggling. It's like he watched every single game and was a freak about it.

We finish up by saying a few things about the Reds. I thank him, and he gets up and walks away. I start my lead in for the Kentucky highlights from the night before. Suddenly, Pete walks back into my live shot, grabs my copy, and yells, "Hey Cutler, you think you're so good? Try doing the rest of the sportscast without your copy." He walks away holding my script, waving it, and laughing. But he remains a few feet from my camera so he can watch me mess up. I said on TV that Pete just took my script.

Pete didn't know that I had cut the highlights. I knew everything on the tape, so I nailed the rest of the sportscast. Pete was standing there laughing. When I was done, I said on TV, "Thank you Pete Rose. Did I pass your test?" He laughed again.

"Yeah, you know your stuff," he answers, chuckling as he walks away. That was the Pete Rose I'll always remember.

61

I'm Number One

For television stations, Frank N. Magid Associates was the top research company in the 1980s. LEX18 paid a bunch of money for them to do research on our station and the market.

At the time, WKYT Channel-27 was the dominant No. 1 TV station in Lexington. We were No. 2, and WTVQ-36 was a deep No. 3. But when it came to sports and the best sportscaster, I had thirty percent of the vote, compared to fifteen percent for WKYT-27 and ten percent at WTVQ-36. In other words, more people liked me than the sportscasters at the other two stations combined—and then some. I'm proud of that.

All of a sudden, I was the first on the news open. Back then, they did news opens with the male news anchor first, the female news anchor second, the weather guy or gal, followed by the sports. I thought it was pretty cool that I was first.

Research showed that I was the top sportscaster in Lexington. I still have a copy of the research. One of the few things I saved.

In 1983, I got a call from David Crane, my agent at the time. He asked me what I thought about going to New York. He knows that's my dream. My heart starts beating quickly. He mentions the possibility of becoming the sports director of a New York station—WWOR—that's just starting a newscast. By now, I'm salivating.

My agent told me the news director at the station really liked me, and that he had a really good shot of getting me the sports job. They just hadn't decided yet if they wanted a sports guy with a crazy personality like myself. What stations often do is they look for a particular style.

The station had already hired a crazy weatherman—Lloyd Lindsay

Young.

I got a call from the station news director. He really liked my tape. It's down to three people, and I'm one of the three. But he didn't offer to fly me in for an interview. Until they give you the salary structure or offer to fly you in—to me—it's hot air. Until they're talking money, they're not really serious. The news director says he'll call me in a couple of weeks.

I haven't heard from him in a couple of weeks—which I'm guessing is bad news—but I call anyway. If it's bad, I'd rather know and move on. He says, "I've got good news and bad news. The good news is that you had the best tape." *So at that point, I know I'm toast.* "The bad news is that I *can't* hire you. My main anchor is Irish and male, my female anchor is Jewish, I have a crazy weather person, and I can't put two Jewish people in my top four because I need to hire an African American."

I'm speechless.

In today's world, no news director would be crazy enough to tell you that—because of lawsuits—even though those things still happen. I told the news director I appreciated his honesty. But, when I hung up the phone, I was really upset.

They ended up hiring a guy that wasn't very good. If you're going to hire someone—I don't care who you hire—just be sure they're good. If you say that you're going to have to hire an African American, I know I could have found someone who was much better. The guy they hired didn't last very long. When the job came open again, I thought I had another shot.

It turns out I had no shot at all. WWOR hired the Albert brothers. Marv Albert is the most famous of the Albert brothers—all of whom were big-time sportscasters. They hired his brothers, Steve and Al. They wanted one of them to be at the station every night. Both of them were popular, so I get why they weren't going to even talk to Alan Cutler from Lexington. I would have done the same thing. It was a really good hire for them. Doesn't mean it didn't hurt.

I also understand why they told me they needed to have a diversified news team. I hope no one goes crazy over this, but these are decisions that happen a lot more than anyone realizes. I'm not mad at anybody, I'm just telling you the truth.

Here's what else happens when you try to get a job in television. It's not unusual for a station to get two hundred tapes for one sports opening. A busy news director is not going to sit through all those tapes in their entirety. Normally you have about ten seconds to impress the news director. At times, you don't even get ten seconds. They might see something they don't like within ten seconds—and BOOM—your tape is rejected. If they don't like how you look—*BOOM*—you're history.

I've never liked the process. There are so many people who can't get a job because they're rejected that quickly. Many tapes start with a montage of stand-ups or funny things that you've done. If you don't grab the attention of the news director right off the bat, you're finished.

I once hired a young man who had one of the worst tapes I've ever seen. He's now a star in Alabama. He's been a really good sportscaster for a long time.

Back then, I called Jim Dunaway after looking at his tape. "Jim, you have one of the worst tapes I've ever seen," I told him. There was a pause on the phone, and I wasn't going to talk anymore. I wanted to hear his reaction. Jim then asks, "Then why are you calling me?" I told him I kept on watching his tape because, "it's so bad that I couldn't believe it. I finally saw your stand-up. Your stand-up was really good."

I've never seen anyone with such bad tape that had a stand-up that good. I can't teach anyone camera presence.

We hired Jim. We had one edit booth for sports. The rule was that if you're in there at two o'clock, you better get out because Cutler needs to get in. It's twelve-thirty in the afternoon...one o'clock...one-thirty...it's two o'clock...it's two-thirty, and Jim's still in there doing his first story. It's a simple story that down the road he probably edited in about a half hour.

He's stressing like crazy over his first story to make it look good. I told him he had five minutes to finish and get out of the edit booth. We had two shows to do. He asked me to look at his story. He plays it, I look at it, I take the tape, I flip it against the wall, I tell him it sucks, tell him why I thought it sucked, and to fix it in another edit booth. He was *terrified*—but he fixed it and we ran the story.

Jim really needed tough love. That was obvious the first time we were face to face. The truth also was that in this case, I was a *jerk*.

Jim and I had some fun working together. I remember he watched how hard I hustled, and it gave me great joy to see how hard he started working. He used to watch me hustling on the phone with all my stories, and he ended up doing the same thing after he moved on.

Jim left us and went home to Alabama. It was a nice step up to Birmingham as the No. 2 sportscaster. Jim gives me credit for helping him become good. I was tough on him. We had our share of ups and downs. When he left, he was mad at me—really mad. The next time I saw him at the SEC basketball tournament, he walked right by me and didn't say hello. Even though I knew he was mad, I was shocked.

The following year at the SEC tournament, he walks over to me, sticks out his hand, and says he's sorry. We then sit down and have a great conversation.

"I wouldn't change a thing about my life or my time with you," Jim said in a text after I told him he was going to be in the book. "I had lived my entire life in one area. I was a naive kid who didn't understand myself or others."

To this day, I still don't know why I kept on watching his tape.

To this day, I don't think he knows how proud I am of him.

Jim changed and grew a lot in the time we spent together, and he did a really good job. Going back to 1975 when I started in broadcasting, I can't remember anyone else I worked with—or worked for me— that grew more as a person than Jim did during our time together.

Who do I credit for the growth and change? One hundred percent it was all Jim.

It sounds corny, but it will always be true. Hard work still pays off.

62

He's Definitely The Boss—
George Steinbrenner

For thirty-seven years, George Steinbrenner was the most controversial, most vocal, most demanding owner in all of sports. For the thirty-seven years that he owned the New York Yankees, George Steinbrenner won seven World Series. He was nicknamed "The Boss," and he drove everyone crazy. But, he could also be very generous. This is a story about my relationship with him. As you'll see, it was crazy.

The first time I met George Steinbrenner was in the 1980s. I get a call from a source who tells me that Steinbrenner is in town buying horses at The Red Mile—and would I like to interview him? *WOULD I LIKE TO INTERVIEW GEORGE STEINBRENNER? WHAT? OF COURSE!*

I rush down to The Red Mile, a harness track near downtown Lexington. I'm escorted to a table where Steinbrenner is sitting.

"Nice to meet you, kid," he says to me. "Have a seat."

I tell him that I grew up a Yankees fan. Then John Cashman—Brian Cashman's father (Brian is the general manager of the Yankees)—comes over, and George greets him like an old friend. George then asks John which horses he should bid on.

John, who is in Harness Racing's Hall of Fame, ran The Red Mile and Castleton Farm—one of the top harness racing farms in the world that was established in 1793. John picks up the thick sales book and marks out five horses, bends the pages back, and tells George the suggested price range to buy these horses.

After Cashman takes off, I ask George for an interview. Remember, this was George Steinbrenner, and he was in a good mood. It was a nice local scoop.

Fast forward a year or two later, and George is back in town to buy some more horses. I went out to meet with him again for an exclusive interview. Did he remember my name? Of course not. But it was the same thing—we talked about the Yankees, and he talked about Kentucky Basketball. Once again, it was good stuff. This is George Steinbrenner, and he's giving me an exclusive—I'm happy.

A year or two later, I get a call again—"George is here. You want to talk to him?"

Again, I get an exclusive interview. But here's what was strange. They had a race that day. George had a horse in a race running against a world-class Swedish horse that was the heavy favorite.

We're watching the Swedish horse leading the small field by twelve or thirteen lengths. At about a mile, the strangest thing happened. The Swedish horse stops running. George's horse starts running like a bat out of *BLANK*. George starts going crazy as his horse comes back and wins. Interviewing George after a win like that...was beautiful.

George was good friends with Paul Hornung, the Hall of Fame running back who won four NFL titles and the first Super Bowl. The Heisman Trophy winner from Notre Dame was also the MVP of the NFL in 1961. The former Green Bay Packer star had a TV show in Louisville. George told me he'd been a guest on the show every year. So not only was George here for his horse, he was also here to do the TV show with Hornung.

I'm sitting with George, who is eating a small bowl of ice cream. The table also includes his two pilots who were wearing white shirts and ties. George turns to me and asks if there's any way he can get to the show in fifteen minutes. I tell him that I've lived here for years, and there's *ABSOLUTELY NO WAY* with the drive time to and from the airports, with flying, to get to Hornung's studio in fifteen minutes.

"Boys, did you hear that?" George says to his pilots. "Did you hear what this kid said? He lives here. He's a sportscaster, and he's saying you can't get to Louisville in fifteen minutes. HOW AM I GOING TO GET THERE, AND YOU BETTER FIGURE THIS OUT?!"

George is LOUD! It was like something you would watch on Seinfeld—only I'm watching George be George right in front of my eyes. It was incredible. I wanted to laugh. There's no way he made it to Louisville in time, but I'm sure Paul Hornung was very happy to see him when he got there.

Because of John Cashman and his relationship with George—as a favor—Brian Cashman got a job as an intern with the New York Yankees in 1986. During the day, he ran errands. At night, he was a security guard—at 160 pounds—who dealt with drunks in the stands.

Brian Cashman later took the Yankees' farm system and computerized it. Once this was done, the farm director didn't have to take nightly calls from every single minor league team manager with a rundown of what happened anymore. You've got six to eight teams and you're on the phone for hours. Cashman's computer skills moved him up in the Yankees' chain.

Cashman eventually became the second youngest general manager ever in Major League Baseball.

Brian attended Lexington Catholic High School. He told me he watched me on TV as a kid. He gave me his personal number and told me to give him a call if I were ever in New York and needed anything.

Later on, I had Brian on my talk shows in Cincinnati and in Lexington. He was really good.

A few years later, in 2001, I'm visiting my family in New York. I'm thinking of taking my brother's kids and J.J. to a Yankees game. I call Brian's private number, and his secretary answers. She places me on hold, and then I get the perfect answer.

"This is a little strange," she tells me. "I don't know who you are, but Brian told me to not only take care of you for however many tickets you want, but he'd like to see you in his office if you have time before the game."

If I have time?

So we all went, kids and all, to Brian Cashman's office. His office was very, very tiny. Remember, this was the general manager of the New York Yankees. I was envisioning this HUGE office down the hall. His office was located close to the elevator in the middle of the hallway. We're led in there, and my mouth is wide open. There was almost nothing on the walls. His office was as spartan as spartan could be. The desk is small, old, and not special.

This is the general manager of the New York Yankees' office?

Brian comes out from behind his desk and gives me a big "Hello." I introduce him to Ian and Justin, my brother's kids, and my son J.J.

"Yeah, I've seen that look before," Brian says, referring to my surprised look. "You're wondering why this is my office. Here's the deal. I didn't want to take the general manager's office down the hall. It's linked to George's office. If George needs me, he knows where to find me. At least this way, he doesn't walk into my office all the time."

I shook my head smiling.

Cashman then took out a World Series ring. He tells me it's real—not a replica. He asks me if I want it. I'm thinking there's no way I can take it. It's crazy. Ian and Justin are huge Yankees fans. They were almost drooling as they tried on the ring.

Cashman respected George Steinbrenner and appreciated Steinbrenner's trust in him, but in the end, George Steinbrenner is his boss—they aren't friends. He's "on call" every day. He's gotten calls from George on Christmas Day.

I asked Brian how often he gets back to Lexington. He told me that the last time was when he went back to see Willie Blair—a right-handed pitcher from Paintsville, Kentucky. Steinbrenner had heard that Willie was a free agent, knew he was from Cashman's "neck of the woods" and asked Brian to go check him out.

Cashman said, prior to that, he hadn't been home for a couple of years. But—since it was "The Boss" making the suggestion—Lexington here we come.

Part 6 (1989-1997)

The Pitino Years

63

C.M. Newton Saves UK

C.M. Newton was a great man—a mentor to so many—and perhaps the man who changed the South more than any other coach when it came to race. He was the SEC Coach of the Year six times. He's also in the Naismith Memorial Basketball Hall of Fame and the College Basketball Hall of Fame.

C.M. recruited the first Black players at Alabama (he was threatened by Klansmen), had the first all Black starting lineup in the SEC, and hired the first Black men's and women's basketball coaches at Kentucky—among his many changes.

Newton came to Kentucky in 1948—when Harry Truman was president—to play both baseball and basketball. He sat on the bench when the Kentucky basketball team won the national championship in 1951.

In 1989, UK's athletics director C.M. Newton saved UK Basketball when he hired Rick Pitino. After cleaning up a *HUGE* NCAA mess, can you imagine what would have happened to UK Basketball if he hired someone like Billy Gillispie?

If C.M. had hired the wrong coach instead of Rick Pitino, Kentucky would have been in big trouble. Likewise, if Mitch Barnhart had made another bad hire after firing Billy Gillispie, he could have set the UK program back a long, long time. Hiring the right coach is often more important than people realize, and athletics directors sometimes really screw it up. C.M. didn't screw it up when he hired Rick.

C.M. Newton was color blind—he understood the big picture of life and applied that to sports. He could have been a great governor or senator.

One of the obvious problems we have in politics—and this isn't new—is people not knowing how to work with others when they don't agree with you. Do you think there weren't powerful politicians who didn't agree in the 1800s? We could use more statesmen like Henry Clay, who was in the Senate and House for Kentucky. His nickname? The "Great Compromiser."

Somehow, C.M. crossed barriers that most wouldn't dare touch—he did it and kept friends on all sides.

Try to visualize what life was like for an African American athlete in Alabama in the 1960s. Bear Bryant, the great college football coach, ruled the state. When C.M. Newton interviewed to be the basketball coach at Alabama, he asked for and received permission from Bear Bryant to be able to recruit African Americans. If Bear hadn't said yes, C.M. would *not* have taken the job.

C.M. Newton recruited Wendell Hudson, an African American, who in 1969 became the first and only African American athlete on the Alabama campus. Imagine what it was like for Wendell Hudson when the Alabama team traveled all over the South for their basketball games. C.M. tells the story of how one time Wendell Hudson asked the team bus driver to pull over so he could kiss the ground because he was so happy to be back in the state of Alabama.

C.M. built Alabama into an SEC power. The Crimson Tide won the conference championships in 1974, 1975, and 1976. Prior to his stint at Alabama, while coaching at Transylvania University in Lexington, C.M. also broke the color barrier at that school. Although many won't admit it, recruiting the first African American basketball player wasn't the most popular decision in the state at the time.

C.M. Newton zeroed in on Rick Pitino to save UK's program, but Rick—who loved being romanced—turned him down the first time. There was also some luck involved at the time, as Pitino—who was the head coach of the New York Knicks (his dream job)—wasn't getting along with Al Bianchi, the Knicks' general manager. If they had a happy marriage, Rick Pitino *never* would have come to Kentucky. It's my belief that C.M. would have hired himself to be the head coach at Kentucky had he not been able to hire Rick.

The thing I respected about C.M. was that he would always listen to you. He would tell you if he disagreed, and he would tell you if he thought you were wrong. Even if he thought you were wrong, he never held a grudge. He really had media savvy and was way ahead of his time. You talk about someone living a full life. My goodness, C.M. Newton lived a full life.

Outside of former SEC Commissioner Roy Kramer—who secured some unbelievable TV contracts for the SEC—I'm not sure there has been a more powerful and influential figure than C.M. in the South-eastern Conference.

Power is one thing, but when it comes to helping, influencing, and becoming an ear for so many athletes, coaches, and administrators, C.M. Newton will always be at the top of the list.

64

Rick Pitino I—Camelot

The first time I saw Rick Pitino, he was playing for UMass. I was sitting in the second to the last row of the old Madison Square Garden. A few rows in front of us were some crazy gamblers with plenty at stake. Listening to their complaining was perhaps more entertaining than the game itself.

Pitino, a backup guard for the Minutemen from 1971-74, averaged 4 points a game. Even though I'm sitting in the second to last row of the old Madison Square Garden, I'm watching him closely because he's also from Long Island. I told my buddy, Bobby Everett, "That guy is cocky." I laugh thinking about it. Little did I know that I would later spend so many years with Rick Pitino.

The second time I saw Rick Pitino, it was the summer of 1986, at the Howard Garfinkel Five-Star Camp—which was, at that time, the best basketball camp in the country.

Garfinkel was a power broker in basketball. The first coach he hired to speak at his camp was Bobby Knight at fifty dollars a day. At least seventeen Hall of Fame head coaches worked that camp over the years. That list included Pitino and John Calipari.

Garfinkel told me I should interview Pitino because he was going to be a superstar. I interviewed Pitino at his coaching station where he was going crazy. I just watched him for a while waiting to get the interview thinking, *"This guy is out of his mind!"*

The third time I saw Rick Pitino was when he was coaching at Providence. They were playing Pittsburgh—where John Calipari was an assistant coach. Providence's star player was Billy Donovan. Pitt physically beat the crap out of Billy who was the Big East Player of the Year, leading that '87 team to a Cinderella Final Four.

Fast forward to when Billy Donovan became an assistant at Kentucky from 1989-1994. Billy and his dad—who was a terrific player for Boston College in the 1960s—are two of my favorites. I think Billy Donovan is one of the class acts in sports.

During the last year Billy was coaching at Florida, I called the sports information director to request an interview. He told me that Billy doesn't do interviews at shootarounds the day before the game. That made me mad. I told him I'd known Billy forever, and I'm sure that Billy will be happy to see me. I hung up the phone as steam came pouring out of my ears.

I didn't listen to the Florida official and showed up to Rupp Arena for Florida's practice. The SID sees me, and starts walking over, and he's mad. Then Billy comes out and yells across the court at me, "Hey Alan, how are you?" The SID stopped dead in his tracks, and I got a dirty look. I threw him one of those "I told you so" smiles.

Billy and I had a terrific talk. I don't want to make it out as if I'm really close to Billy, but there was a bond from the glory days of Pitino at UK.

Before I left that day, I went over to the Florida SID—and with a big smile I said, "Thanks for your help." He apologized.

Billy has been the head coach at Oklahoma City in the NBA since 2015. It always bothers me how fans can be. This isn't a shot at True Blue Fans but fans in general. It's the kind of thing that happens everywhere. When Billy decided not to become the Kentucky coach, people were ripping him. His father told me years before he went to the NBA that Billy always wanted to coach in the NBA.

It always bothers me when fans act out when they don't get what they want—when they feel like they're shunned—they then lash out at that person. The average Kentucky fan doesn't know Billy Donovan.

For whatever reason, Billy decided Kentucky wasn't for him. If he thought it wasn't for him, he was smart for not taking the job. I believe if he wasn't happy at Florida, he would have become the Kentucky coach.

To win two national championships at a football school like Florida in 2006 and 2007 is one of the great coaching feats in the last fifty years of college basketball. Winning one championship at a school like Florida is crazy. Winning it twice—really? Do I think Billy Donovan could have won a national championship at Kentucky? Yes, I do. But life in a fishbowl like Lexington can be difficult, and Billy built a wonderful life for his family in Florida.

Here's one of my craziest Rick Pitino stories.

This is without a doubt one of my wildest days on TV that covered parts of five decades.

Just before Rick Pitino became the coach of Kentucky in 1989, I got a call from Jay Picciano. He was what's called a catch driver at The Red Mile harness racing track in Lexington. He's from New Jersey and we became friends. As a driver and trainer, he won over a thousand races.

Jay told me a *wild* Rick Pitino story. This was when UK athletics director C.M. Newton was trying to hire Rick. It was after Rick had already turned down UK but was now seriously interested again.

Rick Pitino had dinner with a bunch of buddies a couple of years earlier in New York. They all chipped in and bought a horse who ended up having a bad throat. The horse didn't race for a long time and then all of a sudden showed up in Lexington at The Red Mile. Picciano told me that Pitino owned part of this horse, and that he probably doesn't even know the horse is alive. Picciano just happens to be on the horse that night.

Hang on, we haven't even gotten to the *crazy* part of the story yet.

I told Jay I'm on my way, slammed the phone down and screamed, "I NEED A PHOTOGRAPHER RIGHT NOW!" I rushed out to The Red Mile to talk to Jay Picciano about Pitino's horse racing that night, and I had to get there quickly because of the timing of the race. I get the story, and it turns out even better than I'd hoped. I'm on a tight deadline, and it's crazy.

It's 10:30 pm, and who calls me but *Rick Pitino*. I tell him quickly about the horse. He laughs and tells me he didn't even know the horse was alive. And I quickly tell him I'm swamped...I can't talk to him until after the eleven o'clock news—and if he wants to call me back afterwards, he can. I hang up on him.

The three or four people in the newsroom who heard my conversation can't believe I just hung up on Rick Pitino. Every reporter in Kentucky would love to talk to him, and I hang up on him. Trust me—this wasn't strategy on my part. My script for the sportscast wasn't written, and the deadline had already passed. The story on Pitino's horse wasn't edited. I can't repeat to you what a photographer there said to me at the time...something about me being out of my *blankety-blank* mind for hanging up on Pitino. HA!

Guess who calls me back at 11:35? Rick Pitino. He says, "I was told that you're the guy in Lexington." I didn't know if he was buttering me up or not, but he told me he always has one guy in town that he goes to for stories. "I was told that you would tell me the truth," he says.

"You're from back East. I'm from back East."

I told him the story about when I watched him play for UMass, the gamblers sitting in front of us, and he laughed. I told him the Billy Donovan playing against Pitt story, and he of course remembered the game. So we hit it off quickly.

I answered his questions very directly. Some answers he didn't like, but I told him all about the lay of the land and how the fans were. We talked for almost two hours on the phone.

Before we hung up, I said to him, "Look, if you're going to take the job, I know you have some in the New York media you need to take care of—but I want to break the story if you're going to be the next Kentucky coach." He found a way to tip me off, and that's how I broke the story that he was going to be the Kentucky coach.

Before I broke the story about Pitino coming to Lexington, I called WNBC in New York to talk to Len Berman, a really good TV sportscaster. When he said he didn't have a crew to get an interview with Pitino—who was coaching an NBA game that night—I started *yelling* at him, which I still can't believe I did. I told him that I was planning to break the story that Pitino was coming to Kentucky and that I would help him out with the story—but he had to get the interview with Rick for both of us. We both knew Pitino wouldn't say anything yet, but I had to have something for the story. Berman sent a crew, got the interview, and I called him back after his producer sent me the tape. I apologized for screaming, and he thanked me for being so aggressive because it was also a good story for him. And yes, I called him back when I got the scoop. He thanked me a second time.

What I never forgot about Len Berman was that when I needed help from him, he went out of his way to take care of me. We ended up going to New York to cover Pitino's team when they played at Madison Square Garden. Berman made sure we had our own edit booth and an editor to take care of us for the few days we were in New York.

Every Kentucky fan remembers Rick Pitino taking over and "Kentucky's Shame" being on the cover of *Sports Illustrated* because of the NCAA mess—which is how Pitino got hired.

What you may not remember is that Pitino's strength coach at the time was Ray "Rock" Oliver. Rock and Calipari both worked on Pitt's staff when I was in Pittsburgh. Rock is close to both Pitino and Cal. Think of the book he could write about those two. He never would, though. Rock is as loyal as anyone I've met in the business.

I don't know if there was a better trainer in the country than Rock.

He killed those players on Pitino's first team. I smile as I say that. The stories are famous about what he did to the team. The first day, he takes out a picture of his children. He says, "See these kids. I love them more than anything else in the whole world. If you don't get in shape, I'm going to get fired and won't be able to feed my children. You're going to go through hell." The players show up for the workout, and there are big garbage buckets at the other end of the court for them to throw up in. A number of players on the team told me when they saw the garbage cans, they were scared.

Can you blame them?

The TV story I did with Rock was fun, as he was holding up the small picture of his kids he showed the team. Not only that, but Rock can be *very* intimidating. The other side of Rock is that he's helped so many athletes at UK—and never gotten enough credit for it—and he doesn't care.

In the beginning the players hated Rock, but they eventually became very close to him. They ended up loving him because they had fun, they trusted him, and the players knew he always had their back. They also got in spectacular shape because of him. The players told me they never thought they could get into this kind of shape.

Pitino and I would talk on the phone every now and then. That's not something that happens much with coaches anymore. I knew his players were in unbelievable shape. *Pitino Ball* with the three-point shot would have helped Rick Pitino the player. He was a slow guard from Long Island who could shoot but couldn't create his own shot off the dribble. Rick Pitino was ahead of his time in spreading the court out. If you ran up and down the court, and players went to certain spots, the defense was going to get tired of doing all that running. Or if they weren't hustling enough, Pitino's players would be open to hit three-point shots. Smart!

C.M. Newton, when he recruited Pitino, told him he might win three or four games the first year.

I remember going on TV and saying that Kentucky, under Pitino, was going to win half their games the first year. I took heat for that—until they went 14-14. People said I was lucky, but I knew what great shape the players were in. I knew they'd wear their opponents down.

The game of the year that first year was *so loud*. You couldn't hear the person next to you on press row. It wasn't just that UK beat No. 12 LSU 100-95. But LSU had Shaquille O'Neal, Chris Jackson—who could hit from anywhere—and a second seven-footer named Stanley

Roberts. Deron Feldhaus had 24 points for UK. He was past amazing that night.

Pitino's Bombinos took almost 30 three-pointers per game in his first season. They made 281 for the year and gave up only 167. They ran and ran and ran. I remember going on TV talking about how Adolph Rupp would have loved their hustle, defense, and fast break.

Here's another time my job was on the line.

When Pitino was recruiting Gimel Martinez, a 6'8" blue-chip forward out of Miami High in 1990, I remember getting the exclusive pictures of Pitino sitting in Miami watching Martinez play. Shortly after that, I did a story and said, "A *source* tells me that Kentucky is having trouble recruiting some of the top players in the country because Kentucky won't cheat."

I was shocked when *Sports Illustrated* ripped me for that comment. I'm just a big-mouth TV sportscaster in Lexington. I was shocked I was even in *Sports Illustrated.*

Because I made *Sports Illustrated,* and it was so negative, the president of our company—Harry Barfield—called me into his office. "Cutler, I need to see you," he said. Now you have to understand, Harry never did that. He didn't ask to see me five times over my entire career. Plus, he had a tone of voice that day that I wasn't used to...it was bad.

When I got to his office, Harry was a lot angrier than I anticipated. He started questioning my ability to do the job. I had always used "*sources*" on television a lot back then. If the source trusts you, and you have a good relationship, the odds of you getting a good story are really big. There can be a lot of obvious reasons a source can't have his or her name on TV—especially if they don't want their boss finding out they were talking to me.

I got a lot of stories that way, and what ticked me off to no end was that it would get back to me that some others in the media made fun of how I used "*sources.*" But I didn't care. I was beating them to stories—and that made me want to beat them even more.

A little later, I had a second conversation with Harry, and he was still fuming over my story. I remember telling Harry that he had to either trust me or not trust me. Harry said he trusted me, but we couldn't have mistakes in stories like this.

I got really mad. "Harry, I didn't make a mistake," I replied back to him. I can still picture him looking at me and saying, "And you're not going to tell me your source, are you? I'm not so sure about your future here."

I left Harry's office really upset. I then called my source and told him my problem. The source then asks me what I wanted him to do. I assured him that I would never go on TV and reveal who he was. I had given him my word. I suggested, though, that he pick up the phone and call the president of the company himself. I hated having to ask him to do this because I knew he would think I owed him one. And, as a reporter, I can't have that. He told me not to worry, and that I owed him nothing. The source said he would be happy to make the call.

The "source" was Rick Pitino.

I get a call from Harry shortly after Pitino called him. "Cutler, why didn't you tell me it was Pitino?" he asked. I told him that I had never told him my sources, and I didn't want to get in a habit of telling him my sources. "And...Harry," I said. "I'm pissed off you didn't trust me." My tone of voice to Harry was as bad as his had been to me. I was really hurt by his reaction. Harry said he was sorry and that he wouldn't do it again. That's a "wow!" Harry is the general manager, and I respected him a great deal. He was the kind of man who if he gave you his word, you believed it. That wasn't always true with many of the bosses I dealt with.

Back to Pitino.

I told Rick that someday I wanted to tell this story publicly. "Not while I'm coaching at Kentucky," he replied.

When Pitino went to Louisville, he didn't win as much as I expected. Four times in his first six years, he lost at least ten games. He only lost more than ten games one time while at UK—in his first year when he lost fourteen. He didn't play *Pitino Ball* in Louisville. It made no sense to me. And for the first four years, Louisville played in an easy conference. I was convinced at the time—said it on TV—questioning why he went away from what had previously worked.

Pitino won 74% of his games at Louisville and 81% at Kentucky. I thought Pitino would have fewer seasons with ten losses at Louisville.

As successful as he was at Louisville winning a national championship, I've always been convinced that he should have kept that running, three-point shooting style he used at Providence and Kentucky. That's what he was great at. He should have made everyone adjust to him like he did when he was at UK.

Here was Rick Pitino's biggest problem.

Rick Pitino was his own worst enemy. I'll always believe that leaving UK for the Boston Celtics was a *dumb* decision. I thought that at the time. If Pitino had stayed at Kentucky, he might have won many more

NCAA championships.

Pitino failed in Boston. A big reason was that he didn't adjust. NBA players don't want to be yelled at in the same way Pitino got away with it as a college coach. Players are millionaires. The stars make more than the coach. Plus, Pitino picking players wasn't nearly as good as Pitino the coach.

I always believed that John Calipari would have the same problem if he went back to the NBA—if he didn't change. Do you really think that a huge star in the NBA like John Wall would take Calipari's yelling today?

John Wall is not the same person he was in college. Now, if Cal changed, he could be very successful in the league. I could be wrong, but I don't think Cal would be able to change if he went back to the NBA. And I don't think he's going back—something I've believed for the last six or seven years.

It's OK if your style doesn't fit the NBA. That's not a negative comment to either Pitino or Calipari.

Pitino was not a Lexington guy. What's wrong with that? If those of you from Kentucky had to move to New York City, you probably wouldn't like it. That's not saying anything negative about anyone in Kentucky or New York.

He's a New York guy who liked to go to places like the Carnegie Deli after the Knicks won and hold court until three o'clock in the morning. He started his Lexington restaurant, *Bravo Pitino*, so he could have someplace to go late at night.

I told Pitino that he needed to get out of Lexington as soon as the season was over. He should come back for his camps, but otherwise— spend his time where he's most comfortable. That way, it'll be more likely that he'll want to be at Kentucky for a longer period of time. He could then build a legacy that would be unbelievable. As long as you win, people won't care whether you spend your time in Lexington or not in the offseason. That's the advice I gave to Rick Pitino. He told me he couldn't do it that way. He told me I was wrong. *He was wrong.*

As great of a coach as Pitino was at UK, I always thought he was very insecure. I've seen people use this problem as motivation for their success. I've known a news anchor or two and some successful radio personalities that were the same way. I believe that insecurity pushed them professionally to get to where they landed. I've kept this opinion of Pitino to myself for all these years.

Brooks Downing—then the sports information director for UK

Basketball—would call me and a few others up and say, "Don't ask Pitino about a certain topic because he doesn't want to talk about it."

Sometimes Pitino would just start talking about that issue. The funny looks on Brooks Downing's face were priceless.

Sometimes Jerry Tipton of the *Lexington Herald-Leader* or I asked about that subject anyway, and Pitino would sometimes go on and on about it. You just don't make that the first question during the press conference.

65

Rick Pitino II—The Breakup

It was February 19, 1994, and Kentucky was playing Vanderbilt at Memorial Gym in Nashville. During the game, Kentucky guard Travis Ford put the wrong guy at the free throw line on purpose. To me, it's pretty obvious what he was doing, but no one wanted to freely admit it at the time because Kentucky players caught cheating would obviously make the program look bad. Kentucky eventually wins the game 77-69.

How did Vanderbilt not see it? How come Vandy fans weren't yelling and screaming?

Here's exactly what happened that night. It was like the hidden ball trick in baseball.

Kentucky is leading 57-47 with 6:23 to go in the game. Andre Riddick—who's shooting less than 35% from the free throw line—is fouled.

So, how did Walter McCarty get to the free throw line instead of Andre Riddick?

This is from my TV script:

> "Yeah it didn't take too many brains to figure it out," said a smiling Travis Ford after the game.

> Ford told Walter McCarty to take the free throws.

> "I saw the referee run to the table, and he had no idea who was fouled, so I told Walter to get to the free throw line, and it turned out fine," said UK's point guard to me exclusively after the game.

Don Rutledge, one of the best referees in college basketball, missed the switch.

"Yeah, I didn't think anybody caught that," said a smiling McCarty, who hit both free throws.

Then I said to Walter, "Great con job."

"Yeah thanks," the smiling UK forward said.

Pitino—being Pitino—during his post-game press conference said he's trying not to play Riddick and Prickett together.

"It's very painful to watch them together," said Pitino.

UK led 62-55, Jared Prickett was fouled. Not only was he 0-for-6 in the game, but the last one was an air ball from the free throw line. He missed by a lot.

For our TV story, we slowed down that horrible miss.

Travis Ford told Gimel Martinez, who was shooting 80% from the free throw line, to take Prickett's place."

Cool hand Travis?

"I don't know. I don't know if I will try that again. Next time I will probably put myself up there," said Ford with a big smile. Ford remains one of the best free throw shooters in UK history.

"Did we do that?" asked a smiling UK forward Jeff Brassow. "I won't admit it."

Back then at Vandy, I sat upstairs in their press box. After the game, when I got to the court, I asked Robin Lynch, my photographer, "Did you get it? You sure you got it? This is big." Robin assured me that he had gotten it all. This is another example of where a big-time photographer is worth their weight in gold.

I was never going to ask Pitino in his press conference about what happened with the free throws. At the time, I didn't know who knew about it, and if others didn't know about it, why give this story away?

All I was trying to do for this post game was to get my story while staying away from Rob Bromley of WKYT-TV and Jerry Tipton of the *Herald-Leader*. I wasn't sure if they knew. And, if they didn't, I wanted the exclusive. You can never be cocky and assume that you're the only one who knows in a situation like that.

I remember Bromley and Tipton came over a couple of times while I was talking to somebody about the free throws, and I quickly changed the subject. Or I would just quickly break away and go someplace else if I saw them coming over. That didn't really cause a red flag because that's normal when you have a limited time to get a lot of interviews. I would quickly move around the locker room to do as many interviews as I needed.

Although this story really upset True Blue Fans—and perhaps I shouldn't say this—it was a great story. I said at the time, and I'll stand by it today, that *it's the best story I ever did covering a game.* Catching someone on the court cheating is a big deal. I still can't believe so many in the media missed it. But the interviews we had were crazy good. That would *never happen today.* I remember purposely getting up early the next morning to see if the *Herald-Leader* had anything about the story. They didn't.

Pitino was eventually told about my story. *HE GOES CRAZY!* I've now painted him in a corner, and he has to do something. He ends up suspending Travis Ford, Jared Prickett, and Gimel Martinez for the upcoming Tennessee game. How Andre Riddick and Walter McCarty didn't also get suspended is absolutely baffling. I was so excited because I thought five players were going to be suspended.

People wanted *ME* out of town. They were saying how dare I expose Kentucky, *da da da da da.* I was also doing a sports talk show then. Every single call was against me. Phone lines were lit up from the time I went on the air until the show was over. I took every call and let everyone vent. I told them as long as the language is clean and it's not personal, I'm good.

Despite playing only eight players, including little-used guard Chris Harrison getting his first career start, Kentucky rallied from 14 points down to beat Tennessee 77-73 in Knoxville.

Can you imagine how I was feeling when UK was down? All of a sudden, they hit a few shots and were flying around the court. It didn't hurt that this wasn't a good Tennessee team.

Thank God Kentucky won the game. If they lost, I was going to be blamed. People quickly forgot about it because Kentucky won.

I always want Kentucky to win, but a story is a story. I cheered harder for Kentucky that night than ever before. I never cheered at that level even covering the national championship games.

Here's where the divorce from Pitino is signed, sealed, and delivered.

I get a call from UK's sports information director Brooks Downing telling me that Pitino wants to see me. I went down to Memorial Coliseum, and Pitino met me just outside the upstairs' doors. It happened fast, but Pitino started screaming at me like Earl Weaver, the former Baltimore Orioles manager who had some famous shouting battles with umpires. He told me that I had *NO* right to put that story on the air. At that moment, my thought was he thinks I owe him for helping me with the *Sports Illustrated* mess.

When he told me that, I got really loud back.

There are a lot of things that Pitino has told me over the years that I've never revealed because they were off the record—and I believe in off the record. *None of THAT will be in this book!!!* There are things about Rick that I know—and they're not necessarily bad—that just aren't going to be for TV. Our relationship was close enough at that time that he would tell me things that I couldn't put on TV. I knew what I could and couldn't say. He trusted me. People trusted me. There's very little trust today between coaches and the media.

I said to him, "Hey Rick, I have never put a word on TV about all those things you told me off the record, but on the court—I own you!" I pointed my finger at him as I said it for emphasis. It wasn't the *smartest* thing to say or do, but he was already loud and strong with his own comments. It's true—whatever happens on the court, I could care less what a coach thinks. Perhaps my method of communicating could have been a lot better.

After that, Rick went *berserk* on me. I started yelling right back at him. This went on for quite a while. It wasn't just for five seconds. We were screaming at each other for a couple of minutes. If this were today, with cell phone cameras—oh my gosh—it would have gone viral. We've never been the same since. Our relationship ended right there. Rick never called me again.

I had some people tell me this one story wasn't worth it because Pitino *never shared* anything again.

I said it then, and I haven't changed my tone.

I would do the story the same way. I wouldn't change a thing.

Would I change how we talked outside of Memorial Coliseum? Sure—we both were wrong. I've made plenty of mistakes.

When I went back to the station, I told my boss what happened. He said I shouldn't have yelled back at Pitino. I then told my boss that if he ever yelled at me like Pitino did, I'd get in his face too. I then turned around and walked out. Believe it or not, I don't regret saying that to my boss. I actually really enjoyed saying it.

Two years later, Rick Pitino won Kentucky's 6th NCAA Championship.

The toughest game in the Final Four in 1996 was against some team coached by John Calipari. Kentucky beat UMass 81-74. UK was in control, up 15 points with 18 minutes left, but UMass cut it to 73-70 with 1:03 to go.

Any UK fan who says they weren't worried in the final five minutes isn't telling the truth.

Making free throws has been a bigger story in the Final Four than is often reported. UK missed free throws which cost them winning the national championship three years in a row. In 1997, they lost to Arizona in overtime 84-79. UK hit only 9-of-17 free throws. Arizona lived at the free throw line hitting 34-of-41. Arizona shot twenty-four more free throws and missed one less than Kentucky.

Nazr Mohammed missed all six of his free throws. He also had 12 points, 11 rebounds, and 3 blocks off the bench. UK had tired legs that night—otherwise Arizona never would have gone to the free throw line a ridiculous twenty-four more times. Four UK players fouled out. FOUR—that's crazy. That's also a UK NCAA championship game record.

Back to their win against UMass—UK hit their last eight free throws.

Marcus Camby had 25 points, 8 rebounds, and 6 blocks for UMass. I thought before the game started that whoever won this game would win the NCAA championship. Not only was UMass ranked No. 1 in the AP, with Kentucky being No. 2, but UMass handed UK one of its two losses earlier that season 92-82 when Marcus Camby had 32 points. Do I think that Kentucky loss has bothered Calipari more than he admits? *Absolutely*!!!

UK had a great team.

UMass had a great team.

Tony Delk led UK with 20 points against the Minutemen.

Delk did it again against Syracuse two nights later for the NCAA championship. He scored 24 points to lead Kentucky to a 74-67 win.

He tied a championship game record with 7 three-pointers. I can still picture the one when he was falling out of bounds. I never thought Kentucky would lose this game. I wasn't sure about the UMass game.

After the game, I walk over to congratulate Pitino. He grabs my hand and says, "Alan, I'm so tired."

A year later, Pitino is headed to Boston.

In 1997, when Pitino was introduced as the head coach and president of the Boston Celtics, my big-time photographer, Greg "Punk" Gorham, and I went up to Boston to cover it. I was surprised that we were the only Lexington TV station there. The dog and pony ceremony show the Celtics put out for Pitino was big time. It was a wonderful press conference, and the euphoria for Pitino was crazy. It was more like a coronation.

The problem was that we were on a very tight deadline. We had to drive across town in Boston rush-hour traffic, get to a TV station, and edit the footage. Punk is great in putting things together quickly, but he was only going to have ten or fifteen minutes if we got there really fast.

Punk never liked me driving—especially after that day. I insisted on driving because of the fast-approaching deadline. I ended up doing a U-turn in the middle of rush hour in notoriously crazy Boston traffic—crossing six lanes in order to get to our destination. Punk was fearful for his life. He still brings it up every time *Boston* is mentioned. I'm not even sure I should be telling you this, but if a cop saw how I drove that day, I probably would have ended up in jail.

The thing is that I never missed a deadline. Sometimes deadlines are not in your control. When we got to the station, I was numb. Adrenaline was flowing. Punk started editing as fast as humanly possible. His hands were shaking. I don't remember his hands ever shaking on any other deadline like that. It was one of the worst deadlines we'd ever had. But we made it!

Rick Pitino will always believe that had Boston won the NBA draft lottery, and been able to get Hall of Famer Tim Duncan, he would have had a great coaching career being the boss of the Celtics. I know his odds would have been tons better had he gotten Duncan. Unfortunately for Rick, things didn't quite work out.

I get why Pitino took the Louisville job, and I defended him even though I thought it was stupid at the time. There weren't many big-time jobs out there at the time. I thought it would have been better for him to sit out a year, do some TV, and chill out. He could have had the pick of any of the better jobs coming up the next year.

I disagreed with fans who hated Pitino for taking the Louisville job. You can try to beat his butt every year, but the hate and the venom he got for coaching at Louisville—I thought fans were *way* too rough on him. The man saved Kentucky Basketball.

One year there was a golf gathering in Lexington that was a reunion with Pitino's players from Kentucky while he was coaching at Louisville. He didn't want to go because he didn't like coming back to Lexington. Sad—really sad.

Fans are great, but there's a reason why the word fan is short for fanatic. My thought was always for Kentucky to try to beat Pitino every single year, but when Louisville is playing someone other than Kentucky, True Blue Fans should root for Louisville. I remember saying that once on TV, and it didn't go over very well.

But that's how my mindset is. I grew up in New York with the Mets and the Yankees. I was one of the few people who liked them both. I'm a much bigger Yankees fan, but I like the Mets too. In New York, you either pick one or the other. I liked both the Giants and Jets. I liked the Giants better, but my uncles took me to Jets games where I got to see Joe Willie Namath a number of times play quarterback the year they won the Super Bowl. I'm thinking why can't you pick both?

If Pitino stayed at Kentucky and kept clean, he might have won as many or more national championships than Duke coach Mike Krzyzewski. That may not sit well with Duke fans, but I thought that back then, and I think that now. No one will do what John Wooden did—ten national championships in twelve years—but I think it could have been the best run since UCLA. I think it could have been a better run than what Adolph Rupp had over his glory years. This is *not* negative towards Rupp, but the competition is much tougher today. There are more great coaches today, more great players today, much better training—and all races are finally welcome to play anywhere.

Rick Pitino's biggest enemy is Rick Pitino. I think what happened to him is sad. Tragedy may be too strong a description, but it's pretty close. This is a guy who should have gone down in history as one of the greatest basketball coaches of all time. Although that's true, it's not what many will remember him for. He brought a lot of it on himself. Rick Pitino has nobody to blame but Rick Pitino.

In 2009, Rick admitted to having an affair with Karen Sypher—the wife of the team's equipment manager—and he allegedly paid for her subsequent abortion. Sypher then tried to get millions from Pitino and was convicted for her attempt at extortion.

Then there was the scandal of strippers and prostitutes in 2015 in the dorm named after his best friend and brother-in-law, Billy Minardi—who died while working in the World Trade Center on 9/11 when the planes hit. Pitino still claims that he knew nothing about what went on in Minardi Hall—the on-campus dorm he helped raise money to build.

Ironically, I'm one of the few that believe Pitino didn't know what was going on during those infamous parties. Those that ripped Pitino have no idea how close he and Minardi were. He wouldn't allow that to happen in a dorm named in honor of Billy. I've been ripped for believing this.

If you think I'm just a Pitino defender, I'm laughing. I think it drove him crazy that John Calipari got the best of him when he was at Louisville.

I've always also laughed at those who say Calipari is just a recruiter.

Then in 2017, Louisville fired Rick after the program was implicated in a federal bribery and fraud investigation. The board of Louisville's athletic association voted unanimously to fire him with "just cause."

A high-ranking Louisville official told me that if there was no Karen Sypher, Pitino might have survived.

The man lost Daniel, his son, in 1987 from congenital heart failure. He lost his brother-in-law and best friend in 9/11. Don Vogt, another brother-in-law, was killed when he was hit by a New York City cab. And Pitino told CBS Sports Network that his grandson has a form of epilepsy.

Forget all the money Pitino has made, his hand-made Italian suits, and the games he's won. The bottom line is, I feel sorry for him.

Did Pitino bring a ton of his problems on himself? *YES!!*

This won't be popular with UK Fans, but I had a great time covering Pitino's teams in Lexington. It was a ton of fun. You could get to know the players much better back then. There were so many really exciting games. And, I know there are a lot of you who can't stand Pitino today even though you loved watching his teams play.

I don't see Pitino ever coming back to Rupp Arena and receiving a standing ovation. But, time can do funny things.

66

Rick Pitino III—The Unforgettables

I'm guessing that the overwhelming majority of people reading this book don't like Rick Pitino. I have a pet peeve—I can't stand it when anybody decides to rewrite history. If you want to rip the guy for a lot of faults, so be it. But give the man credit for what he did. When I look at the great teams that I've covered at Kentucky— and I'm using the word "great" on purpose—that Pitino team that went 14-14 in his first season was one of the best teams I've covered.

Before you say I've lost my mind, it's really very simple. When it comes to potential—and squeezing every drop of juice out of a lemon—you tell me what team squeezed more juice out of their potential than that team. Think of the National Championship teams and the Final Four teams. Think of teams that lost big games. That 14-14 team personified the word "overachieving" if there is such a thing. Perhaps when a team overachieves, it's because we didn't see its potential. That was a great team.

As dark as it was before Rick Pitino showed up, that 14-14 team— laced with beautiful Kentucky kids—brought joy back to the Commonwealth. As much love as they've gotten, I still think they've been overlooked today because of the hate for Rick Pitino. I don't think it's fair to those players or Pitino. You can dislike Rick Pitino for what he did in his personal life, but respect Pitino for what he accomplished at Kentucky as a coach. I've always been able to dissect the two. It has always driven me crazy when someone decides to hate someone, after they used to like them, and no longer appreciate what they accomplished. Rick made mistakes. I've made plenty of them too. So have you. Rick's mistakes are in the public eye. If you've never been a public person, it'll be hard for you to understand.

That 1989-90 Kentucky team was a great team. People will always say how unathletic they were. The truth was that team was quick—not fast. They were smart, they knew what they were doing, and they knew where they were going. The players on that team had wonderful basketball minds. They had a great teacher. They were true basketball players and embodied the true concept of team. They were far better collectively than individually. Isn't that the true meaning of a team? I can remember it like it was yesterday. You knew that Camelot had returned with Kentucky Basketball.

The end of Rick Pitino's career, by contrast, was more like a Greek tragedy. Both Camelot and the scandals at Louisville are part of his legacy. We shouldn't forget either one.

Nor should we forget the players on that team. They were truly unforgettable. Richie Farmer, Deron Feldhaus, John Pelphrey and Sean Woods—the senior class. On April 7, 1992, after losing the heartbreaker to Christian Laettner and Duke 104-103 in overtime, in the NCAA Tournament, the team was honored at Rupp.

Athletics Director C.M. Newton, who had three of the four seniors turn him down when he was the Vanderbilt coach, told the players to look to the rafters. Their jerseys were retired. Wow!!

Sean Woods

Sean Woods is like a little brother who I've tried to watch over. He won't like that comment, but he knows it's the truth. He refused to listen to me over the years. I always thought he could make it in the NBA. He quit too soon. I told Sean to go back and try out for the NBA or to play minor league basketball for a year or two if he had to. If he ever made it back to the NBA as a backup, he would have probably played in the league forever. We'll never know, but I think he could have made it.

Years later, he told me I was right.

Sean considered himself a Kentuckian, even though he played basketball in Indianapolis. Sean was tough, he was smarter than people gave him credit for, and he played defense. He didn't have a very good shot, but he had terrific shot selection. I compared him to Avery Johnson, who was the point guard for the San Antonio Spurs when they won the championship in 1999. Avery bounced around before he finally got his chance, and it took a really smart coach to appreciate his skills. Avery Johnson wasn't drafted by the NBA. Neither was Sean Woods.

I will always believe Sean was better. And Avery ended up having a wonderful NBA career.

Sean Woods was the head coach at Morehead State from 2012-2016. During that stint, he had problems with his temper. One summer, I told him he needed anger management. I also told him he needed to change the way he coached. He yelled back at me that I was wrong, that he was old school, and that he knew what he was doing. We actually had that talk at LEX18, where Sean was a salesman before he got into coaching.

The next season, Morehead State played Kentucky, and he embarrassed himself when he yelled and screamed so much at one of his players that everyone courtside was embarrassed for Sean Woods. That wasn't his only problem at Morehead State. There's no question that his lack of self-control had everything to do with why he was pushed out the door.

Sean Woods cares. He should have been a head coach at a major school. Sean Woods' biggest enemy is Sean Woods. I hope he changes. I'll do anything for Sean if he calls. I'm far from perfect, but Sean has driven me crazy because I know he has so much potential.

If you want to ask what is the greatest shot in UK history that isn't remembered the way it should be—I'll vote for Sean's. That running hook from about fourteen feet against Duke with 2.1 seconds to go in overtime that should have beaten the Blue Devils is now an afterthought because of Christian Laettner's shot at the buzzer.

Richie Farmer

If Rick Pitino's life turned out to be a Greek tragedy, Richie's was worse.

Richie Farmer could have been governor of Kentucky. All he had to do was keep on the straight path. He couldn't do it. After your eligibility is used up, there are always some players who feel they're still on scholarship—that was Richie Farmer. Richie Farmer felt like he was entitled.

I will never forget going up to Clay County for the special we did for television about Richie's high school team. That 1987 Clay County team beat Ballard High School 76-73 in overtime to become the first eastern Kentucky school to win the state championship since Carr Creek in 1956. The movie "Hoosiers" has been personified, rightly so, as being one of the great places for high school sports. There's no doubt in my mind that when it comes to the purity of sports—when it comes to the joy given out by a high school gym— Clay County, Kentucky equals Hoosiers.

Their great coach Bobby Keith, Richie, and their teammates had no business being as good as they were. It was all about the team. One of the great joys in sports is when you're watching something, and you recognize how special it is.

I hadn't talked to Richie's coach, Bobby Keith, in decades. Bobby won an amazing 767 games with a winning percentage of 86% at Clay County, where he also played ball. Did you know he was also valedictorian at two colleges?

Bobby Keith is one of my favorite characters I've covered in sports. Sadly, he died of a heart attack in October of 2016.

Before Bobby passed, James Phillips—now retired as the circuit court clerk from Clay County—called when Bobby wasn't doing well and asked me to give him a call. He thought that just hearing from me would lift Bobby's spirits. I was happy to do it. I call Bobby up and say, "Coach, I just wanted to tell you that I know you're not doing well. I'm praying for you, and I'm glad I'm getting the opportunity to tell you the respect I had for you as a coach and what you built in Clay County. It's one of the greatest things I'll ever see in my life in sports."

We talked for about fifteen minutes as we both fought back tears.

James Phillips called the next day and told me that I changed Bobby's spirits. This is not about me. But when you're in my position, lifting others up is something that you ought to do. I did it a bunch in my career, but I regret not doing it a lot more. Anytime you can uplift people's spirits like that, it's a blessing. I probably got as much out of the conversation as Bobby Keith did because I could feel his energy and adrenaline.

Months later, my friend asked me to call Bobby again because they thought they were about to lose him. I called—"Coach, I'm coming up to Clay County, and you and I are going to do some jogging." He just laughs and says he'd love to see me, but he wasn't going to do the jogging part. He passed away shortly after that.

Even in Bobby Keith's condition, he probably would have outlasted me.

One of the things you learn in this business is that your sports stars, your heroes, and the people you look up to—they're just regular people. They have the same problems we all have, and when their shot clock is up, their shot clock is up. I had a ton of respect for Bobby

Keith. I loved his team's discipline. I never told him that when I was covering Richie Farmer. I'm glad I was able to tell him that while he was still alive.

Another one of my pet peeves in sports is not honoring sports figures while they are still alive. Ron Santo, the great third baseman for the Chicago Cubs, didn't make the Hall of Fame until after he passed. He was a great broadcaster and cheerleader for the Cubs. He loved the Cubs as much as anybody. His statistics didn't change over time. Why shouldn't he have gotten the joy of being put in the Hall of Fame while he was alive? It drives me *crazy*. When I can say something nice about someone and put a smile on their face like I did with Bobby Keith—it's one of the great parts of the job.

The pride that Richie Farmer gave to the people in the mountains— and I didn't understand it when I first moved to Kentucky, but I do now—was second to none. He led Clay County to the state championship in 1987. In 1988, Clay County lost in the Sweet Sixteen, but Richie scored 51 points. Richie went on and had a good career at Kentucky.

Later in his life, while working in state government, Richie was charged with forty-two counts of violating state ethics laws. He spent twenty-seven months in federal prison.

I'll always have a soft spot in my heart for Richie. Richie Farmer's worst enemy was Richie Farmer. Richie Farmer should have retired with millions in his bank account. Instead, Richie Farmer ended up in jail. It's sad.

If Richie walked up to me today, I'd give him a hug and would love to have a beer with him. Deep down, I think he's a good guy who at times was just misguided.

John Pelphrey

There are few Kentucky basketball players who baffled me more than John Pelphrey. John Pelphrey was really smart on the court. He was Mr. Basketball in Kentucky in 1987. He knew what he could and couldn't do, and he knew how to share the ball. He couldn't run, or jump, but—man—he could play. Whenever you interviewed John, he had a terrific, sarcastic sense of humor. I thought he would end up as a big-time college coach.

He was and he wasn't. Pelphrey was fired at Arkansas in 2011 after four years coaching the Razorbacks. He had just put together his best recruiting class, and they still got rid of him. He had a taste of the big time.

I'm not saying I thought Pelphrey was going to be in the Hall of Fame, but I did envision John Pelphrey winning five or six hundred games as a college coach.

I'm happy he's got another shot to be a head coach at Tennessee Tech.

Deron Feldhaus

Deron Feldhaus was like the movie icon, John Wayne. *TOUGH!* He didn't like to talk. If he's reading this, I think he'll just smile. The way Feldhaus played basketball was like everything you admired about John Wayne the actor.

Deron Feldhaus comes from a great family. Deron's dad, Allen Feldhaus, Sr., was a tough guy, a Hall of Fame coach—who played basketball at Kentucky for Adolph Rupp from 1958-62—and a terrific catcher on UK's baseball team. His brother, Allen Feldhaus, Jr., won a state championship as head coach of Madison Central High School—with future Kentucky guard Dominique Hawkins—in 2013. I've called some Madison Central games on the radio after I retired. When you get to see a coach up close like I did, it's way different from just putting together some highlights on TV. Allen Feldhaus Jr. would be a wonderful college coach. He's demanding, smart, and he can make adjustments on the fly.

A few years ago, Allen Sr. passed away. It was a Saturday, and I was running the story down for the TV station. I called Allen Jr., asked him if it were true about his dad, and told him I was really sorry. Their family owns a golf course, and they were going to go out to the course, bring a bunch of beer, and just celebrate their father's life. I thought it was the perfect way to celebrate who they were, because that golf course was such a huge part of their family.

To this day, Allen Jr. misses talking to his dad after his games. I'm so jealous. I wish I felt the same way about my father.

Reggie Hanson

Reggie Hanson, the 6'7" star for Pulaski County, played for Kentucky from 1987-91. I called him "the man with the million-dollar smile." Reggie, coached by Dave Fraley, was a wonderful high school player. I've always believed the high school coaching in the state of

Kentucky is much better than many realize. Farmer, Pelphrey, Feldhaus, and Hanson all received great high school coaching—with fundamentals pounded in their heads.

As much credit as Rick Pitino deserves, and he does deserve a ton of credit, these players came to Kentucky better prepared than most Kentucky fans realized. All four of the Kentucky players had wonderful high school coaches.

They all had one thing in common. In the beginning, they all hated Rick Pitino. *They hated him.* He drove them to the brink. They hated him, but they respected him. Richie Farmer told me that was a big bond for the team after Pitino took over—how much they all hated him. That hate changed when they started to win. And they kept on winning, and the fun was *huge*—and those early feelings obviously disappeared.

For Reggie to play center at a major college is a credit to him. He was 6'7", and he looked like he was generously listed at 195 pounds. I interviewed him many times one-on-one, and it was amazing how many times we ended up laughing. I would just let his laughs go on camera. Having Reggie's laugh on TV was much more important than mine.

Reggie bragged one time about how he dunked over the great center Shaquille O'Neal. There's a yes and no to that. The truth is he did dunk on Shaq, who just happened to be in the paint. However, when I pulled the tape out and slowed it down, the LSU center was looking the other way, so Reggie didn't actually dunk *over* him. Reggie was mad, but he just laughed. That was the give and take I had with him. You could kid those guys, and they would give it to you right back.

Jamal Mashburn

Jamal Mashburn, the "Monster Mash," really needed Rick Pitino—and Pitino really needed him. His father was a nationally ranked heavyweight boxer who lost to heavyweight champs Larry Holmes and Ken Norton, and who was also a sparring partner for Muhammad Ali.

Helen, Jamal's mother, was a sprinter in high school—and a very strong and polite professional woman. After meeting her, it was easy to see how Mashburn was so grounded.

In the first interview I did with Jamal Mashburn, I remember him talking about playing in the NBA. That part isn't unusual. Then he made a stronger pitch about becoming a very successful businessman—which he is today.

When I think about all the hundreds of UK athletes I've talked to through the years, never have I talked to anyone who, right off the bat, talked about being a successful businessman. NEVER! He wanted to prove that he was much more than just a basketball player.

Here's why Jamal Mashburn needed Rick Pitino. The book on Mashburn before he came here was that he had a lot of potential, but that he was a little pudgy, a little slow, and that he wasn't the hardest worker in town. He got in shape, though. He understood Rick Pitino as well as anyone because they're both from New York.

UK lost two heartbreaking overtime games two years in a row in Mashburn's final two seasons.

In 1992—the Duke game where UK lost 104-103 on Christian Laettner's shot—Mashburn had 28 points and 10 rebounds. I will always believe if he didn't foul out, UK wins the game and might have won the NCAA championship.

In 1993–against Michigan in the Final Four when UK lost 81-78—Mashburn had 26 points and 6 rebounds. I will always believe if he didn't foul out, Kentucky not only wins—but might have won the NCAA Championship.

Mashburn left UK as a consensus All-American averaging 21 points a game.

Mashburn retired from the NBA averaging 19 points for 12 seasons.

67

Calipari Versus Pitino

L ike it or not, John Calipari and Rick Pitino were joined at the hip. However, if you ask either one of them how Calipari got the UMass job in 1988, they'll tell you different stories. Did Pitino really help? Or was that all just hot air? The fact that their stories are so different speaks volumes about their relationship.

Losing to Calipari so much since Cal moved to Kentucky has driven Pitino crazy—*really crazy*. Pitino believes he's a better coach than Cal, and his *HUGE* ego can't handle how many times Calipari has beaten him.

Overall, Calipari is not only 8-2 against Pitino when he coached at Louisville, two were NCAA wins, including the 69-61 victory in the 2012 Final Four.

Pitino hates it. He really *hates* losing to Kentucky for every reason you can dream of.

Calipari confirmed a rumor years ago about a story I did on LEX18. The story came from a great source, and it went like this. Cal had told Dick Vitale that he had an out of bounds play that he was going to use at the right moment against Pitino. Vitale then went and told Pitino. Pitino, so I'm told, went back and looked at a lot of tape just to try and figure out the play. The truth, according to Cal, was that this out of bounds play never existed. Calipari got a good laugh out of it.

The bottom line is that if Calipari retires with only one NCAA championship, there will be True Blue fans who believe he failed because it's easier to win it all at Kentucky than it is at other places like Florida.

Pitino won a lot of games at Louisville, but you could easily make a case he was more successful at Kentucky. So was it being at Kentucky that made him a bigger winner, or did Pitino slip as a coach after he left?

When you pay people like John Calipari and Rick Pitino all that money, you expect a lot.

Kentucky was smart to hire Rick Pitino.

Kentucky was smart to hire John Calipari.

68

How I Recruited Travis Ford

I put the deal together for Travis Ford getting a scholarship at Kentucky. When Travis was leaving Missouri after the 1989-90 season, I had a private conversation with his father. "Eddie, I can get Rick [Pitino] to look at Travis," I said to him. "You're going to have to let me know if you want it."

Eddie gets all emotional and asks me if I could really do that.

I told Eddie, "I'm close enough to Pitino that I can get to him and tell him that Travis would immediately consider transferring to Kentucky because that's where he always wanted to play."

While at one of his summer camps, I tell Pitino that Travis wanted to come to Kentucky if he were interested. Pitino tells me that Travis would have to contact him if he were interested in transferring *after* the release papers were completed. He doesn't want to mess with anybody unless they're released from their scholarship—but if Missouri released Travis, then *of course* he would be interested.

I relay all that to Eddie, and he doesn't believe me. After he realizes I'm not messing with him, he tells me that coming to Kentucky would be the greatest thing that could ever happen to his son. He always wanted Travis to play for UK and was upset that Travis wasn't recruited by Kentucky initially.

As you know, Travis ended up coming to Kentucky. He sat out the 1990–91 season due to the NCAA transfer rule. After playing sparingly his sophomore year, he became a starter during his junior and senior years and set school records in single-game assists with 15, single-season three-point field goals with 101, and consecutive free throws made at 50. Travis was named to the All-SEC team his junior and senior years and was recognized as the Southeast Region's Most Outstanding Player in the 1993 NCAA Tournament.

Pitino ended up quietly thanking me. I can't tell you that Travis wouldn't have come to Kentucky if I hadn't done what I did. I have no idea. Who knows, it could have happened anyway. But in the end, Pitino and Eddie both got what they wanted, so I told Eddie he better make darn sure that I got the scoop first. And that's the truth. I got the story.

Later on, Travis and I would again cross paths. After his college career ended in 1994, Travis tried his hand at professional ball. It didn't work out, so he decided to become an actor. He was doing a movie called "The Sixth Man."

During that time, Dr. Kenneth Winters—the president of Campbellsville University—contacted me. We met at a country store about forty-five minutes outside of Lexington where they sold some of the best southern fried chicken I've ever eaten. We sat in the corner and talked about me potentially becoming the next athletics director at Campbellsville. To me, that was wild and crazy. Did I really want to leave TV, leave Lexington, and move to a small town?

We talked about my philosophy on education and how I would change the athletics department. I had a plan that would be good for the university that would also make it enticing to recruit very tall smart students from Africa to play basketball. I was going to run summer camps for many sports. It could generate money for the school, coaches, and the athletics director. And I wanted to build the best facilities on that level of college athletics. Dr. Winters liked my plan.

Then he told me that Campbellsville was going to be looking for a basketball coach, and I immediately told Dr. Winters that the first guy I would call would be Travis Ford. Dr. Winters loved that idea.

I found Travis up in Canada—while he was involved with the movie. I always thought he would make a big-time basketball coach, so I asked him what he thought about taking the head coaching job at Campbellsville. After his initial shock subsided, he told me he was absolutely interested.

I met with Dr. Winters again. By then, he was looking for me to give him an answer—the athletics director position was mine if I wanted-ed. He even invited my family to come up for a visit, and we did, but I was still torn.

Just a short while later, while I was still thinking about the major career change, I was surprised to learn that Campbellsville didn't want me after all. As part of my interview, I was asked if I would go to church on Sunday. I'm Jewish—so I told them, "No—that's not what I do. If my wife wants to go, that's up to her, but I'm not going to church on Sunday." I'm Jewish, and I don't even go to temple on Saturday."

I was later told that someone on the board at Campbellsville—who was evidently very powerful—didn't like my answer...and they were no longer interested in me.

Travis became the head basketball coach of Campbellsville University beginning in 1997. He won 7 games the first year and 28 games his second year. Travis has also been the head coach at Eastern Kentucky University, UMass, Oklahoma State, and St. Louis.

So I started the recruiting to get Travis to play ball at Kentucky, and I was responsible for starting his college coaching career.

And I never even got a thank you from Campbellsville University, who admitted they never dreamed of Travis being their coach until I brought it up.

69

Kentucky Versus Duke 1992

I'm ashamed to say I didn't cover the famous Kentucky versus Duke game in the NCAA East Regional Final in Philadelphia. Duke beat Kentucky 104-103 in overtime on Christian Laettner's famous shot in what some consider to be the greatest college basketball game of all time. We were probably the only camera in the state NOT there. If I put a top-10 list of things that ticked me off about LEX18, that would definitely be up there. They'll probably get mad at me for saying all this, but it's the truth.

Due to serious budget cuts, we didn't cover the NCAA Tournament at all in 1992. I understood what was happening, and I still thought it was a ridiculous move. The first round was held in Worcester, Massachusetts. I offered to drive to save money. My photographer, Robin Lynch, wasn't too thrilled at my offer because he knew he would end up driving while I slept in the car, drank coffee, or read sports magazines.

I had a terrific habit of easily falling asleep while going on the road covering UK Football and Basketball. I've been told I've sometimes fallen asleep before the car even left Fayette County, but I don't think that's true. The truth is that I put in a lot of long hours, and these long road trips provided a good time to sleep. Do you think my photographers in all those decades had any sympathy for my lack of sleep?

Since the station decided not to cover the tournament, I told Judy that I wasn't going to be seen in public during the time the team was away. I wasn't going to leave the house when Kentucky played. I wasn't going to go to the grocery store. Just going for a workout was awful because so many people came up to me and asked, "Alan, why aren't you with the team?" I was too embarrassed to be seen in public. The TV station would be furious with me if I explained the real reason why we didn't go. I didn't want to lie, so I didn't want to be seen in public. I also received calls at the TV station after many shows with folks asking what I was doing in the studio.

When the Duke game came on, I was so upset that I wouldn't even watch the game with my family. I went up to our bedroom, shut the door, and turned the radio on to listen to legendary Kentucky broadcaster Cawood Ledford call his last game while I watched on TV. As the game started, I had this really eerie feeling about how good the game was. This game was *really good*. As the game went on, I realized I was watching something I knew I wasn't going to see very often in my career.

I'm convinced that, as silly as it sounds, if Kentucky had won the game in overtime—due to the wild shot Sean Woods hit with 2.1 seconds to go—Sean's odds of making it in the NBA would have increased. There's a perception, whether you like it or not, of an athlete when he goes into an NBA camp. I remember thinking it was a desperation shot as the ball left his hands. I've watched or covered every one of Sean's games, and I never saw him take a shot like that. When I told Sean that I thought it was a desperation shot, he tore my head off. We ended up laughing.

Seriously, to make that shot, under that pressure, from that distance—it's one of the greatest clutch shots I've ever seen.

And then Laettner hits THE SHOT. The 15-footer, a turnaround that capped off a perfect game. Remember, he missed nothing from the field or free throw line that game.

I'll never understand how Rick Pitino didn't put center Andre Riddick on Grant Hill to guard the inbounds pass. I'll always believe had Rick Pitino done that, Kentucky would have won the game. Andre Riddick would have done something to alter the way Grant Hill was going to throw the ball. I can't put in the book the words I used at that moment—when I saw Pitino was not putting a tall man with long arms in front of Hill who made a perfect long pass to set up the winning shot. Riddick was 6'9" with long arms. Pitino didn't trust Riddick. That was the biggest coaching mistake of Rick Pitino's career in Lexington. There's not even a number two.

Had Pitino put a man on the ball, it could have started the second best run of NCAA championships ever.

Would they have gone on to win the national championship that year? I think their odds of winning the national championship would have been pretty good. It definitely would have been one of the greatest stories in the history of collegiate sports—winning an NCAA championship that soon after going through their NCAA mess. Shortly after the game ended, Bob Ryan of the Boston Globe wrote "Best Game Ever?" on the back of his scorecard and showed it to Cawood, who nodded in agreement.

When Laettner's shot was halfway in the air, I remember going, "Oh *blank,* it's going in!" Kentucky lost their aggressiveness on that last play because of Rick Pitino. I'll bet that out of bounds play bothers Pitino to this day. One of the things I've learned about coaches is that they remember the losses more than the wins.

I listened to the postgame afterwards. I know a lot of people in Kentucky don't like Mike Krzyzewski, but he did one of the classiest things I've seen or heard in sports. He came over to Cawood Ledford and congratulated him on the air for his unbelievable career. He should have been celebrating with his team. It's easy to be gracious when you win—I get that—but that doesn't mean everybody always does that. I'm telling you—I had tears in my eyes listening to that. You can go ahead and hate Mike Krzyzewski, but if he were the Kentucky coach, you would have loved him.

About five or six years ago, Kentucky traveled to Atlanta. Laettner was there, and I was surprised that we were the only TV camera at this promotion. Laettner allowed a UK fan who won a raffle to stomp on his chest, just like Laettner did to Kentucky forward Aminu Timberlake during that '92 game when the refs swallowed their whistle and didn't kick Laettner out of the game when they should have. He had a great sense of humor about the whole thing. It didn't make me like Christian Laettner, but it was a fun story for TV that no one else got.

At Duke, Laettner ran everything. He was a jerk to his teammates, especially to Bobby Hurley, their great guard. Players in the NBA weren't going to take that garbage from him. Michael Jordan? Yes. Christian Laettner? No way.

Laettner played 13 seasons in the NBA for six different teams—averaging 13 points a game. He was an NBA All-Star. That's nothing compared to being the Player of the Year in College Basketball, induction into the College Basketball Hall of Fame, and being the leader of a team that won back-to-back NCAA championships in 1991 and 1992.

To be successful in life, you have to be comfortable in your own skin. Laettner was perfect in college...but the NBA was a different world.

70

The Forgotten Concussion

The 1993 Final Four game between Michigan and Kentucky—with 64,000 plus in the Superdome in New Orleans—is deemed one of *THE* great games.

Picture this—at the end of the game, three of Kentucky's five starters were on the bench—a combination of injuries and fouling out. And the fourth starter played the most minutes of anyone on either team—and he was playing with a concussion. That was Travis Ford.

It was surprising how I broke an exclusive story. When the team was running off the practice floor the day before, Travis was the last to leave. I literally ran up to him. Since I had a good relationship with Travis, I asked him directly, "Hey Trav, is it true you have a concussion?"

"Yeah, I bumped my head," he acknowledged. "But I'll be fine."

I then asked him if he was going to play the next day. He looked at me like I was out of my mind. Had to ask—but I respect Travis for *not liking* the question.

We blew that story up like crazy. I'm surprised it didn't become a bigger story. First of all, you're playing in the game of your life. But I always wonder how Travis would have played if he didn't have that concussion. It was a big part of the game, but Travis would never make it an excuse.

With 3:23 to go in the overtime, Kentucky led 76-72. Consensus All-American and SEC Player of Year, Jamal Mashburn—who had 26 points—fouled out. Kentucky was never the same. Jared Prickett, who led the team in rebounding with seven, had also fouled out.

Next to Travis' concussion, the biggest story of the game might have been Dale Brown. The Kentucky guard played a wonderful game. He had 16 points and he played terrific defense, but with a little over six minutes to go in regulation, he hurt his shoulder. I remember the scream when it happened. I knew he was done.

It's easy to say that if Travis didn't have a concussion, if Dale Brown didn't get hurt, if Jamal Mashburn didn't foul out, would Kentucky have won the game? YES!

But that's part of sports. In overtime, Michigan came back to beat Kentucky 81-78. Travis Ford played 45 minutes—longer than anyone else—with a concussion. He did have 12 points, 6 assists, 3 steals, and 2 turnovers.

The bottom line is that Michigan's Fab Five, according to their leader Jalen Rose, claimed it was their greatest win EVER. The Fab Five were tremendously controversial. A lot of people didn't like them. They were loud. They were boisterous. They bragged a lot. But they were really good.

There was a headline after the game that said, "Michigan's Villains Nip Kentucky in Overtime." Jalen Rose relished in the fact that people thought they were the villains of college basketball. That was his way of saying, "BLANK YOU!"

It seems to me over the course of time that when you lose, certain things are overlooked. Sean Woods' shot, which would have beaten Duke had it not been for a guy named Christian Laettner, is often forgotten. Travis Ford, playing with a concussion in a Final Four against Michigan was overlooked and forgotten. Dale Brown, with a serious injury to his shoulder and couldn't play, was out and forgotten.

It's not difficult to remember the plays when you win, but it's even easier to forget what happened when you lose.

71

Relaxing with Evelyn Newton

Right before Bill Curry came in to be interviewed for the vacant Kentucky head football coaching position in 1990, I was on my way to the Hyatt Regency in downtown Lexington. I had a tip that Curry was going to be there. As I walk in, Evelyn Newton—wife of UK athletics director C.M. Newton—is sitting at a table in the bar sipping a glass of wine. "Hi Alan, how are you?" she calls out to me as soon as she spots me. My eyes got really big. I don't know who the last person I'd expect to see be so friendly when I'm trying to get a scoop would be—but she would be high on the list.

"Oh, it's OK," says Evelyn. "They haven't landed yet [referencing the plane carrying the Alabama coach coming in for an interview]. "Why don't you come over and have a drink with me?"

Evelyn's a real sweetheart, but at that time we really didn't know each other that well. She's enjoying her drink and seems really relaxed. "Sit down," she tells me. "I'll tell you when you need to get your camera ready. Relax. How are you? How's the family?" Looking back on it, it was a really crazy conversation. I had a great source for that story, and Evelyn saw that I wanted to be sneaky—to be on the side—so that no one would see me and alert another TV station that Alan Cutler was there with a camera.

About ten or fifteen minutes later she says to me, "Hey Alan, you might want to get your camera guy ready." Now remember, there were no cell phones back then. I had no idea how she knew that Bill Curry was fast approaching. She then puts her hand on my forearm and says, "Alan, nice to see you. I really enjoy seeing you on TV."

I thanked her, got up, took my photographer out toward the side—and in less than five minutes—Bill Curry walks in, and I do an exclusive interview with him. He was kind, gracious, and cool, but you always want to look at people's facial expressions to see how they're really feeling. I'll never forget that when Bill Curry first saw my camera, his eyebrows went really high—as if saying, "There's a TV camera here."

After I introduce myself, I say to him, "Coach, I know why you're here. Even though you can't say much, would you mind answering a few obvious questions?" He then responded in a way I'll never forget. "Absolutely," he says. "Ask me anything you want."

Once again, I got the exclusive. Some people will say that I got lucky again with my source. Why was I the only media person there that day? Why was I the only one there when Mike Shanahan was interviewed? Why was I the guy who broke the story of Rick Pitino coming to Kentucky? Why did I beat Channel 27 by about five minutes on the John Calipari story?...And so many other stories?

I've been very lucky, but I also made *a lot* of phone calls to *a lot* of people. You have to spend *a lot* of time perfecting your work, and I spent *a lot* of time securing my sources.

What I remember most about that day is that right before I left, I stuck my head into the bar, smiled at Evelyn Newton, and nodded. She lifted her glass in response. It was a great day.

72

Why Bill Curry Flopped

Kentucky football coach Jerry Claiborne was on a recruiting trip when he suddenly decided that he didn't want to recruit anymore—he was done. Jerry was so honest that he would never cheat anyone—especially the university he loved.

It was kind of like the way I retired. It just hit me that I was done. One moment, *bang!!* And it's decided. More on that later.

Jerry ended up as the AP Southeastern Conference Coach of the Year in 1983. The Kentucky program was a mess when he took over in 1982, and I thought he did a good job. Claiborne retired eight seasons later with two bowl victories and a record of 41-46-3. He was an easy man to respect. He stood for all the right things—discipline and hard work.

Kentucky went hard for the next coach. They had their eyes on a great choice, Mike Shanahan.

I just happened to be inside the Hyatt in downtown Lexington with a camera when Mike Shanahan walked in for his job interview. I got an exclusive interview with him, but he wasn't happy seeing a TV camera in the hotel—but he was a pro, and I kept it short.

Shanahan spent time with C.M. Newton, UK President Dr. David Roselle, and the UK Athletics Board.

Shanahan didn't take the job. At the time he was an assistant coach with the Denver Broncos. The Kentucky Athletics Board was scheduled to meet, which you do when you are hiring a coach, but they canceled it when Shanahan picked the NFL over Kentucky.

"It was a tough decision," Shanahan said in a news conference in Denver. "Kentucky's a great university, but I'm really happy to be here with the Denver Broncos. It was best for me and my future just to stay right here."

C.M. Newton really wanted Mike Shanahan.

I've often wondered what would have happened to Kentucky Football had he accepted. Shanahan should already be in the NFL Hall of Fame after being 2-0 in the Super Bowl with Denver and winning 170 games as head coach.

Kentucky's search then led them to Bill Curry. Curry was the coach at Alabama from 1987-1990, but for many reasons, he was oil to their water for Crimson Tide fans.

As an outsider, the hate or dislike Alabama fans had for Curry baffled me back then. I had a few Alabama fans tell me I couldn't understand because I'm not from Alabama. Crazy!!

Alabama hadn't won the SEC since 1981, and Curry got them a share of it. Curry leaves Alabama, and the team he left then wins the national championship. You think he hasn't thought about that a thousand times?

It was similar to the relationship between Rex Chapman and Eddie Sutton. They just didn't mix.

I'll never forget the time Kentucky played Alabama on October 1, 1988, when Curry was the Tide head coach. Kentucky makes a great comeback in the fourth quarter at Commonwealth Stadium, and the stands are going absolutely crazy. Alabama takes the ball and marches down the field. They still need a touchdown to win with less than twenty seconds to go and the clock running.

Alabama quarterback Vince Sutton ends up throwing a 3-yard touchdown pass with ten seconds left on the clock to Gene Newberry, a fifth-year walk-on tight end who had never caught a touchdown pass. Alabama wins 31-27. It was a great football game—another one of those games that Kentucky played their hearts out and lost at the end.

That winning touchdown pass turned out to be the best stand-up I ever did on TV—at least that was my thought at the time. With a little over 20 seconds left in the game and the clock moving—and you can't hear because it's so loud—I scream at Robin Lynch, my photographer, to shoot me. I'm going to do a stand-up and then pan over to the center. *Robin SCREAMS he won't do it. I scream back at him again, and he does it.*

I can't screw up. I can't talk too long. There is a clock in my head. I nail the stand-up. Robin nails the shot—getting to the center at the exact moment to record the touchdown pass. Robin is now retired from local TV sports. He said he's only shot one other stand-up in his career, while he worked at WTHR in Indianapolis, that was better.

The news director for the Alabama station who came with his sports staff to cover the game was editing on a tight deadline. He made them stop to watch the stand-up—said it's the best stand-up he's seen covering a game.

What a rush...but, my heart was heavy for the players wearing blue.

Afterwards, inside the Kentucky locker room, I'll never forget how many guys were fighting back tears. Others were openly crying because they lost to Alabama, and they were so close to winning. Beating the Crimson Tide that day might have changed the fortunes of the Kentucky program. Instead, many just said it was the "same old Kentucky."

That seemed to be the mantra for Kentucky Football for such a long time—these kids would give everything they had and just come up short. My theory for that was that they didn't have enough depth—they got worn down. I believed that Kentucky's first team on offense and defense was often better than people realized. But, the confidence just wasn't there.

Kentucky football coaches always lamented that they had no depth, but that's the job of the coach—to play young players to develop depth. Or, *recruit* better. And it's the coaches' job to recruit. I always put that back on the coach. That's why you pay them the big bucks.

I have always believed that if the top two assistant coaches that Curry said he wanted to bring to Lexington actually came here with him, Bill Curry's tenure as Kentucky's head football coach could have been totally different. Homer Jones was a smart offensive coach, and Dale Lindsey was a terrific defensive coordinator.

I'll say it again—Bill Curry was more of a leader who needed great coordinators like Lindsey and Jones. That's not knocking Bill Curry, but had both those guys come, Bill Curry may have retired here a very successful coach. Instead, his winning percentage—when you only win 26 of 78 games—was just awful. He couldn't even beat Vandy, a bad football program, and that's one of the many reasons why he got fired in 1996 after seven seasons.

Bill Curry is a great man—stood for all the right things, but it always baffled me why he wasn't a better recruiter. I thought recruiting would be a huge strength which is what Kentucky desperately needed. I saw him going into homes and winning over the mothers of so many recruits.

Curry is such a powerful speaker. When he coached at UK, many times during press conferences, he would talk about the Black athlete and equality, and how he learned so many life lessons playing football with Black athletes. There weren't many—if any—coaches back then talking about that, and how playing football with Black athletes was a great life lesson. I thought that would be an additional help recruiting more great Black athletes to Lexington. Black, white, blue, or any color, Curry failed miserably in recruiting them all. Sometimes in life, you just don't figure something out. I was never able to figure out why Bill Curry wasn't a better recruiter.

In all my years of doing TV in Lexington, thinking that Curry was going to elevate the Kentucky program is the biggest mistake I made when it came to judging people.

A former player of Curry who is very respected had another theory to Curry's failure.

Curry wanted his Kentucky teams to lose weight. This player said it made some of the offensive linemen too weak, and that many football players were "crazy" in how they lost weight, and that wasn't a good thing. Not being big and strong enough in the best football conference in America dooms you to failure. It gets worse when you don't have enough talent.

According to this player, that was like putting the nail in the coffin—Kentucky's coffin.

When Curry played in the NFL for ten years as a twentieth-rounder in the 1964 draft—which is really beating the odds—he was very light for an offensive lineman. And yet, Curry was the starting center on the first Super Bowl team with Green Bay. He was an All-Pro, was in three Super Bowls, and two Pro Bowls.

Curry also won two different national coaching awards in two different seasons in college, was the SEC Coach of the Year twice, and the ACC Coach of the Year.

Curry recently came to Lexington for a speech. It was great seeing him. He's a powerful motivational speaker and a wonderful person who I believe can help a lot of people if they listen to his message.

But that doesn't change the fact that he *flopped* at Kentucky.

Bottom line is that Bill Curry is one of the great winners of his generation, but that didn't translate to his time in Lexington, Kentucky.

My first love, radio play-by-play. Grand Junction, Colorado. Mid 1970s. Ninety-five degrees. Paul Molitor, who made the Hall of Fame, was on the Grand Junction Eagles. Great times.

The night before Judy and I got married in 1982—watching my friend, the great Gene Harris—with my brother Joel.

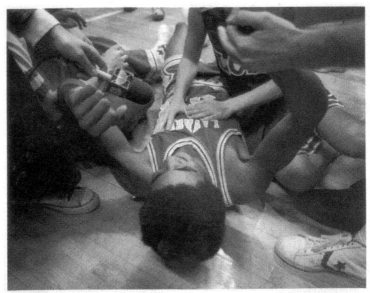

Interviewing Laurel Co. star Paul Andrews right after he hit a shot past half court to win the State Championship in 1982.
Credit Charles Bertram/Lexington Herald-Leader

At my desk in the early 1980s. Pretty typical—can't seem to find my buttons, and I'm using a typewriter. A typewriter!!
Credit Frank Anderson/Lexington Herald-Leader

1984–my going away party from Lexington to Pittsburgh. Torrence Mulder and Norm Kelly, two LEX18 photographers from the 1980s who are like brothers.

Great leader. Great quarterback for Kentucky. Derrick Ramsey.

John McEnroe, Tatum O'Neal, Vitus Gerulaitis, and me playing in the Civic Arena in Pittsburgh.

This made the Today Show and the Tonight Show. UK wins the 1995 SEC Championship. I'm doing my stand-up, and I didn't see Chris Harrison and Jared Prickett sneak up to me and start messing with my ears and hair. I had no idea what I said. It was loud. Fun stand-up.

Lost a great man and a roommate from college—Ken Van Auken on 9/11. Matt and Sarah grew up without their father. Lorie lost her husband. I still think about him all the time.

I pushed my friend, Chip Cosby, who was covering UK Football for the Lexington Herald-Leader, to run the 40-yard dash in front of the team. It made national news. Chip wrote his story for the book.
Credit David Perry/Lexington Herald-Leader

With LEX18 sports anchor Mary Jo Perino and photographer Zach Tucker after UK won the NCAA Championship in 2102. A terrific team!

1959—Five members of UK's staff went on to become head coaches in the NFL, including Don Shula, who had the perfect season with the Miami Dolphins. Left to Right: Ed Rutledge, Howard Schnellenberger, Ermal Allen, Blanton Collier, Don Shula, John North, Bob Cummings, and Bill Arnsparger.

For some reason I shaved my head. UK Sports Information Director
Tony Neely got me.

Larry Vaught from Vaught's Views. A Kentucky gem.

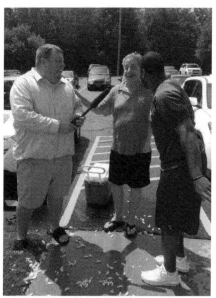

Two of my all-time favorites. Quarterbacks who competed for playing time, but remained great friends. Jared Lorenzen and Shane Boyd—got me with the ALS bucket challenge.

Kenny Rice and I were chasing the same story on Derby Day.

Parts of four decades doing live shots on TV before UK played basketball.

Keith Farmer, Jonathan Dunn, and Kyle Scott. Fun sports team.

Andrew's first game at Rupp Arena.

Family Christmas 2018. Me, Judy, Eliza, Jenna (Cutler) Bickett, Andrew Bickett, Jonathan Bickett, JJ Cutler, Marissa Kinsley.

I have a ton of respect for former UK coach Joe B. Hall.
Credit Your Frame of Mind Galleries

With former Bengals great Bill Berger hosting the Bengals Radio Network.

After Vandy upsets Kentucky, their fans go crazy. You get one shot at doing this stand-up.

Calipari sticks his finger in my ear during stand-up. I don't know he's there until my ear feels funny. Turned into a terrific stand-up.

Rob Bromley, who I competed against for decades, Dr. John Huang, and me.

Bill Curry—a great person and former UK Football coach.

Greg "Punk" Gorham, Ryan "before he fixed his hair" Lemond, Mary Jo Perino, and Keith Farmer. What a crazy sports team!

Judy—the rock for our family. Thank you for being you.

Super tough former jockey P.J. Cooksey. This was my last day on TV—Kentucky Derby 2018.

UK Football coach Mark Stoops shows me how much he will miss me at the big-time retirement party LEX18 gave me.

Part 7 (1997-2001)

Mumme

73

Hal Mumme I—
The Untold Story of His Rise and Fall

In 1996, UK Athletics Director C.M. Newton was looking to do something different with UK Football because the program was in shambles. Bill Curry—a classy man who did a terrible job—was fired.

C.M., with a great deal of help from Tony Franklin, then a high school coach at Mercer County High, discovered Hal Mumme—the coach at Valdosta State in Georgia from 1992-96, who ran a fun, wide open offense that has since been copied all across college football.

Franklin wasn't trying to get hired by Kentucky. He admits to not having set the world on fire at Mercer County, but he has since become one of the better offensive minds in college football.

Franklin was watching UK lose 65-0 to Florida that year. Kentucky somehow has Tim Couch, the future All-American quarterback, *running* the ball in his first start—one of the *dumbest* things I've ever seen in sports.

Franklin tells his wife Laura he thinks he can get Hal Mumme the Kentucky job.

"I was crazy enough to believe I could do it," Tony tells me. That's Tony!

Franklin gets seven high school coaches to sign a letter that he sends FedEx to C.M. Newton. He asks for five minutes of C.M.'s time to talk about his frustration—and his peers' frustration—with the state of Kentucky Football.

Franklin thought it was ridiculous that UK Football was that bad. Plus, he really wanted Kentucky to win. To this day, Franklin believes Mumme was a really good hire even though it didn't have a happy ending. That includes both Mumme's career at UK and his and Mumme's relationship. To put it mildly, Franklin and Mumme aren't close to being friends today.

Different things are often tried when things are that bad. If I were to say to C.M. Newton—if he were still alive—that he was desperate back then, trust me, he'd be mad at me. But I believe UK was desperate when they hired Mumme.

After he sent the letter to C.M., Franklin then called Hal Mumme and asked him if he'd like to be the Kentucky coach. Pretty crazy? He wasn't close to Mumme, who by then had moved up to be the coach of Valdosta State. Franklin knew Mumme because he brought a few of his players to Iowa Wesleyan—while Mumme was coaching there from 1989 through 1991—on recruiting trips when Franklin was the head coach at Calloway County High School. A friend of Tony's in Texas told him that Mumme would take anyone, so he went to Iowa Wesleyan two years in a row to help his players find a place to play college football.

Franklin asked Mumme if he knew of anyone who knew C.M. Newton who could call on his behalf. That person was Carl Parker, a very good wideout at Vanderbilt when C.M. Newton was their basketball coach. Parker, who played for the Cincinnati Bengals when they went to the Super Bowl in 1988, called C.M.

It just so happens that the day after Parker's call, C.M. Newton agrees to a meeting with Franklin. C.M. hears Franklin's pitch and says it's ironic that he just received a call from Carl Parker praising Hal Mumme and his offense. To this day, Franklin is convinced that C.M. *did not know* this was a setup.

C.M. Newton and his right-hand man—assistant UK Athletics Director Larry Ivy—go see Mumme.

By the way, Franklin is surprised when Mumme makes him his running backs coach at Kentucky. That career move changed Tony's life.

I called Mumme and asked him if he knew how he got hired? Mumme laughed and said, "I think so, but tell me what you know." Our phone call lasted exactly a hundred minutes. It took me to places I never expected. I wish I taped the conversation. It would make for a great podcast!

This is Mumme's *take* on what happened. I felt no emotion or anger from him as he explained what happened to the best professional opportunity of his life.

I started by asking Mumme if he knew that C.M. Newton recommended *two* names to UK President Dr. Charles Wethington as finalists to become the next UK football coach. That in itself was part of C.M.'s chess game to get what he wanted.

C.M. had gone down to Mumme's house in Valdosta to interview him. As part of the interview process, he asked Hal what he asked everyone else who he interviewed. "We have a quarterback problem," C.M. began. "You have Billy Jack Haskins from Paducah in western Kentucky, and you have Tim Couch, one of the greatest—if not THE greatest—high school football players in Kentucky history from eastern Kentucky. It's going to be controversial and a battle. What would you do?"

Hal knew Billy Jack Haskins' dad from recruiting. Billy Jack, who won the Mr. Football award in 1992 as the best high school player in Kentucky and finished his high school career as the No. 1 passer in Kentucky history, was a great kid—and his dad was a very successful high school coach.

How Mumme came to know about Tim Couch, who broke Billy Jack's records and set national records as the star for Leslie County— and was also Mr. Football in 1995—was a little more unusual.

Mike Leach, Hal's top assistant at Valdosta (and later at Kentucky)—walks into Hal's office and tells him that there's this kid they have to have from Kentucky named Tim Couch. He shows Hal the press clippings, and Hal's thinking to himself that there's no way they can get this kid. This is Tim Couch, a USA Today High School All-American in 1995 who might end up being the National Player of the Year. Why were they wasting their time recruiting him?

Mike Leach is different from most other coaches. Mumme believes he's the BEST college football coach. So Mumme looks at the Couch article, smiles to himself, and tells Leach to "go for it." Leach calls Couch a couple of times. His pitch was that Couch would throw more passes than anybody else in the history of college football, Valdosta was going to score a million points, and Couch would become famous through the Valdosta offense. It's crazy—but that's Mike Leach.

So, when C.M. asked Mumme about the two quarterbacks, Mumme knew something about both of them. "Are they both good kids?" Mumme asks. When C.M. answers affirmatively, Mumme responds, "Well, it's pretty simple. Couch will be my quarterback, and I'll make Billy Jack Haskins the slot receiver." He then explained to C.M. that in his offense, the slot receiver is a very important position because of how quickly the quarterback is getting rid of the ball.

C.M. Newton later told Mumme that he was the only coach he interviewed who immediately made the decision of what to do with the two quarterbacks. He liked that Hal was decisive.

Decision time. C.M. Newton was an athletics director with a ton of power—all deserved. But, it's not his call. C.M. brings two names to UK President Dr. Charles Wethington—one was Mike Gottfried, the other was Hal Mumme.

I've known Mike Gottfried for a long time. I stood in the rain and lightning outside the University of Pittsburgh football offices and broke the exclusive story on a live shot for KDKA-TV that Mike Gottfried was going to be the next Pitt football coach in 1986.

Mike was a very good football coach. Mike had some off-the-field difficulties from Pittsburgh that haunted him—and got him fired after his fourth season there when he was 7-3-1.

There were a number of occasions, when Mike was up for a job or about to get a job, that those off-the-field difficulties *sacked* him. More than once, Mike was either a finalist or about to get hired when a phone call to that particular school ended that possibility.

I had called Mike and told him that he needed to make peace with some people from Pittsburgh or else he was never going to get a head coaching job. Mike did not like my comment, and our phone conversation did not end pleasantly. Typical me—I'm trying to help somebody, it's a very sensitive issue that I won't duck if I care enough about that person to tell them, but sometimes people don't want to hear the truth. Mike eventually heeded my advice and cleared up the situation—but it was *after* he couldn't get the job at Kentucky.

Rick Pitino was pushing for Mike to be the UK football coach. He had pushed Mike the last time UK was looking for a coach, but he didn't have a lot of juice at that time. He had just arrived, so his push didn't get very far. But this time, Pitino had a lot of juice. By now, Pitino was king in Lexington.

C.M. Newton knew that Dr. Wethington was going to find out about Gottfried's off-the-field difficulties, so he brought in Mike Gottfried's name knowing Wethington would say "no" to it.

Mumme is convinced that had David Cutcliffe's name been brought in instead of Gottfried, Cutcliffe would have gotten the job. Cutcliffe was an assistant head coach, offensive coordinator at Tennessee, Peyton Manning's coach, and later was 44-29 as the Ole Miss head coach when he was fired in 2004 for not winning enough. Cutcliffe, who has also had a terrific career as the head football coach at Duke, is considered a big-time offensive mind.

When you look at David Cutcliffe's career and his temperament, it's not a stretch to think that if C.M. Newton hired him—he might still be the Kentucky coach.

Mumme said that C.M. purposely didn't bring Cutcliffe's name in. That's how Mumme got the job.

No one in the Commonwealth knew who Hal Mumme was before his name popped up as Bill Curry's replacement at UK. I thought it was crazy. I like Hal. I think he would tell you we are friends. My number one question at the time wasn't whether he could coach—if you can coach, you can coach—but whether he would have enough help running the program. Coaching football is only part of what a head coach does. There are so many other things involved.

I was convinced that Mumme's offensive system, or "Air Raid," was that good, and he could get his players to listen to him. When I met him, I liked his personality and saw how college kids could relate to him. I knew, especially since he had Tim Couch, that he was going to put a lot of points on the board.

After Mumme got hired, Pitino showed up to his office and told Mumme, "Be yourself. Do your thing. Do what got you here." He wanted to give Mumme his support even though Gottfried wasn't hired.

Pitino then tells Mumme the story of when he first became the Kentucky coach in 1989, and how they went out to Kansas and got destroyed 150-95 by the Jayhawks. Pitino said it was so bad that at halftime he was thinking of running the four-corners offense just to run the clock down to get out of there. But that would have been heresy, so he changed his mind and decided to play the way Kentucky usually did. His players were ultimately going to have to learn to play his style. The next year, Kentucky came back and defeated Kansas 88-71 in what was Pitino's biggest victory up to that point in his time at UK. Pitino was encouraging Mumme to keep playing his style.

Mumme did all these great things by bringing fun and excitement back to Kentucky Football. In 1997, he beat Alabama 40-34 in overtime, in his third home game. Mumme could have retired on the spot and become our next governor.

I can picture it like it was yesterday. Couch to Craig Yeast for the 26-yard touchdown pass. Not only was it the first time UK beat Alabama in seventy-five years, but Turner Gregg—then ninety-eight years old—the quarterback who led UK to that win in 1922, was at Commonwealth Stadium. They tore the goalposts down during the celebration. I was on the field for one of the greatest moments in UK Football history.

But in 1999, Mumme's third year at Kentucky, he got blown out by Louisville 56-28 at home. The next day, UK President Charles Wethington showed up to the UK football office to watch tape with the coaches. It was the only time he ever showed up to watch tape—as if to say, "This is a dark day, but I'm here for you." Hal Mumme has not forgotten about it to this day.

Then it all starts falling apart.

It began with Mumme's big quarterback decision.

In 1999, Dusty Bonner led the SEC in passing efficiency, total offense, and passing yards per game. He led UK to wins over LSU and Arkansas, but UK lost to Syracuse in the Music City Bowl 20-13. All-American tight end Jimmy Whalen had a ridiculous 79 yards receiving on 4 catches in the first quarter when UK's top threat dislocated his elbow.

After the game Mumme said, "When we lost him, it took a lot of the wind out of our sails."

For the 2000 season, no one questioned that Bonner was by far the best quarterback in spring football. But in the summer, Mumme inexplicably decided to go with Jared Lorenzen. The big lefty ended up having a great career at UK, but not only was he *not* ready to be the starting quarterback, the team knew that Bonner had beaten him out fair and square. Bonner was very popular with his teammates. Many were really upset Mumme chose Lorenzen over Bonner.

Bonner ironically transferred to Mumme's former place of employment, Valdosta State, where his former quarterback coach at Kentucky, Chris Hatcher, had gone back to his alma mater and was a big star, and was about to become the head coach. Bonner goes on to win the Harmon Hill Trophy two years in a row. That trophy goes to the best Division II player in America. He also threw 107 touchdowns at Valdosta State for those two seasons. *Yes—107!!!*

I thought as good as Dusty Bonner was in 1999 for UK, that he would be even better in 2000. Dusty didn't have a great arm—but so what. Jared Lorenzen had a great arm and ended up having a wonderful career at Kentucky, but he still never should have been the quarterback in 2000.

I always thought Dusty was one of the classiest players ever at Kentucky. He kept his mouth shut and didn't rip Kentucky for the way he felt he was treated—and he easily could have.

Kentucky went from going to two bowl games in two years for only the second time since 1951 to a 2-9 record the next year. There is *no way* UK is that bad if Dusty Bonner is the quarterback. *No way!!*

I will always believe UK would have gone to three bowl games in a row if Dusty was the quarterback.

That decision by Mumme, who brought so much excitement to a football program that was soon to be on life support, really hurt his program.

74

Hal Mumme II—The Set Up?

Hal Mumme resigned in early 2001 because of an NCAA investigation. Mumme told me he never did anything wrong, but since it's his program, he's responsible for it. Mumme also believes that part of what happened was a set up.

Claude Bassett, Kentucky's recruiting coordinator under Mumme, was accused of sending money orders totaling fourteen hundred dollars to a Memphis high school football coach. Claude has *never* denied doing it, but he told me there was a plausible explanation for why he did it.

C.M. Newton had retired on June 30, 2000, and his handpicked successor, Larry Ivy, took over as athletics director.

Mumme wrote a letter of recommendation for Ivy to become Newton's successor—because Newton wanted him to get the job. Ironically, Mumme didn't want to write the letter because he didn't like how Ivy *wasn't* helping the football program. But he had so much respect for C.M., who had given him the break of his career, he couldn't say no.

Rob Manchester is Larry Ivy's stepson. Ivy went to Mumme and told him that Rob needed a job. Mumme says that Ivy suggested that Rob replace Mike Leach, Mumme's former offensive coordinator, who had left Kentucky for a similar position at Oklahoma. Mumme says he had to control himself not to laugh in Ivy's face.

Manchester got his master's degree at Kentucky and has had a very successful career in coaching. Manchester, who made the SEC academic honor roll three years in a row at Kentucky, has done a terrific job as the long-time defensive coordinator at Georgia Military College.

But being the offensive coordinator at Kentucky was a whole different ball game, so Mumme offered Rob a graduate assistant job running the summer camps instead—which was a lot of work. But that was a very good way to step into the world of coaching, where a lot of graduate assistants start. Mumme thought he was doing Ivy a favor.

Mumme said that Rob Manchester and UK recruiting coordinator Claude Bassett didn't get along. Bassett was the one responsible for bringing a group from Memphis into UK's summer camp. Manchester was then supposed to pay the coaches of that group.

Manchester, according to Mumme, refused to pay because he didn't set it up with the Memphis group in the first place. Bassett didn't want to stiff the coaches that he brought in, so he told me he decided to pay them himself and didn't tell anybody about it. It was a really dumb thing for Bassett to do.

Bassett later told Mumme that he was planning to wait until the end of the season to tell him because he didn't think it was that big of a deal. Again, that makes no sense because he and Mumme talked all the time. Bassett never denied paying it, though.

The problem was that Bassett kept a photocopy of the money orders used for payment in his desk. Mumme says that what he calls "an office assistant in the football office" got a hold of the copy and sent it to Ivy.

Mumme believes that this person was there to spy on the UK football program. Having someone in a football or basketball office spying on coaches is something that happens more than many fans realize. And we're not just talking about the University of Kentucky.

After the last game of the year against Tennessee, Ivy calls Mumme and says, "We have to meet—and it's serious." Ivy lists four things under Mumme that he thinks are NCAA violations. Mumme disagrees. Ivy may not like any of the actions, but none of them are violations in Mumme's mind. Then Ivy shows Mumme the photocopy from Bassett's desk, and Hal knew he was in trouble.

Mumme called Bassett, and Bassett admits to giving out the money. He explains why he did it. He also tells Mumme that UK isn't after him (Bassett), but that they're trying to get Mumme instead. Bassett was forced to resign in November of 2000 over numerous NCAA violations and was slapped with an eight-year show-cause penalty by the NCAA in 2002. That basically means he's done coaching college football.

He later sued the University of Kentucky Athletics Association, the SEC, and the NCAA for fifty million dollars—a suit that was ultimately dismissed in 2008. To this day, Mumme still calls Bassett a friend.

Mumme described Bassett as less than perfect, but he still feels that there was no reason to do an investigation. Regardless, in January of 2002, the NCAA would put UK on a three-year probation, cutting the number of football scholarships, and banning them from bowl eligibility that season.

Ironically, I can see Ivy's point of view, and Mumme's also. Ivy was a veteran at UK going back to the late 1960s. After what happened to UK Basketball in the 1980s under Sutton, UK still had a hangover and needed to be very upfront about their problems.

But I can also see Mumme's point of view because not only did it ruin his career, the crimes committed under his watch weren't serious. But there were plenty of rules that were broken.

"If you think about it, they took our program down," Mumme told me. "There were thirty-three violations which—when added up—totaled seven thousand dollars. Were they mistakes? Yes. Are they big deals? No. Should this have ruined the program? Absolutely not."

Mumme had already resigned by the time he showed up to the NCAA hearing, which he described as *"the inquisition."* He called it that many times. When he arrived at NCAA headquarters in Indianapolis for the hearing with his lawyer—Travis Bryan, of Bryan, Texas fame—Mumme kept his mouth shut while his lawyer refuted the accusations.

When Mumme was riding on the bus with his Jackson State team, he sent me an email adding to his thoughts on the hearing.

"The investigation was totally run by [Larry] Ivy and Sandy Bell [UK compliance director]. UK had such a great reputation with the NCAA [thanks to C.M. Newton] that they allowed UK to have its own investigation, unfettered by NCAA watch dogs. All the evidence that went into the report was done by those two [Ivy and Bell].

I was under a gag order by Bell not to speak to media, but near the end, my friend, [former Kentucky governor] John Y. Brown, told me I should anyway—and he was right. The SEC sent a retired FBI guy to ask some questions, but he didn't do much."

It's no coincidence that when Mumme goes to the bathroom during a break in *"the inquisition,"* he just happens to run into SEC Commissioner Roy Kramer—in my opinion the most powerful man in college sports at that time. Kramer says to him, "Tell your bulldog lawyer to back off. They're not after you. They're not going to get you. Tell him to calm down, and let's get this over with. Nobody's going to say that it's your fault."

In other words, Roy Kramer already knew what the outcome was going to be before the hearing even began. That should tell you that with these hearings, they've often already decided how they're going to do things. Nothing will change because the committee has already decided the outcome.

Mumme continues in his email to me.

"In the end, I believe the NCAA saw through what was happening. UK got the bowl ban for turning in a false report. After the dramatic question to Bell concerning her hand written notes about her conversation with Mike Leach—in which her NCAA report was proved false—the head of the NCAA committee told my lawyer and I that we could go. He then looked at [new UK president] Dr. [Lee] Todd, Ivy, and Bell and said, "After this break, we will discuss lack of institutional control." C.M. looked at me and smiled. We both knew what Kramer said in the restroom was true."

75

Hal Mumme III—
The Day UK Had Two Head Coaches

February 6, 2001 will go down in UK Football history as the day there were officially two head football coaches.

Hal Mumme knew he was out of a job by then, but his sources told him that his offensive line coach—Guy Morriss—had just been hired to replace him and that UK was planning a press conference to announce it.

This is Mumme's take on a wild day where he officially parted ways with UK.

UK Athletics Director Larry Ivy called Mumme and told him they needed to move forward. Mumme told him that his lawyer just happens to be in Lexington and invited Ivy to bring his lawyer over to Mumme's house.

With their lawyers present, Ivy offers Mumme $200,000. Mumme's lawyer—who's doing all the talking—says that there's no way he's going to accept that number. "You think we just fell off a turnip truck?" Mumme said he asked.

When Mumme's lawyer turns down this first offer from Ivy, Ivy counters by saying he had a statement from assistant coach Mike Leach stating that Mumme knew about the cheating. Mumme's lawyer then says, "Let's call Leach right now because we talked to Leach, who says he not only never said that, but if you claim that he did, he will call a press conference to say Sandy Bell [UK compliance director] is a liar." On top of that, Mumme said that Leach said he ended every staff meeting by saying, "Don't break any rules."

It turns out that when C.M. Newton had drawn up Mumme's initial contract, he had written it by hand on a legal pad. In it, he had put in a clause that he told Mumme was "going away" money. If it didn't work out for Mumme at Kentucky, not only would C.M. help him get another job, but he would also give him $150,000. C.M. was generous with Mumme. Soon after Mumme beat Alabama in the wild overtime game, C.M. walked up to Mumme in practice and said, "Hey Hal, I don't want to disturb you during practice, but I just wanted to let you know I gave you a $150,000 raise." By the end of his contract, the "going away" money was up to $2 million.

Mumme told me he had a six-year contract paying him $800,000 a year. That's $4.8 million. Forget the $200,000 offer by Ivy, or the $2 million "going away" money—his lawyer said they'd take the entire $4.8 million—because UK never proved that Hal did anything wrong, and neither did the NCAA, so the settlement amount had to be much larger than the "going away" money clause. Ivy—who Mumme said was obviously shaken—went outside to call Dr. Wethington. Mumme thought Ivy was going to have a heart attack in his house. He felt his lawyer was killing it.

Mumme knew he wasn't going to get the $4.8 million, but he also knew he wasn't settling for $200,000 either. He ended up getting $1.66 million. Mumme was good with that. He agreed to the payments being around $300,000 a couple of times a year.

Mumme thinks the reason the payments were split up like that was partly because of the budget, but also because UK didn't want the media to find out how much they had to pay Mumme. If the media found out Mumme was getting $1.66 million, it would be easy to figure out that UK is paying money to get rid of him, knowing he didn't do anything wrong.

Mumme gets the first check right on time. He then waited and waited and waited for the second one, but it didn't come. Mumme believes they didn't want to pay the rest of the money. It got to the point that Mumme had to threaten to go to the media. He wanted to show everyone that he didn't do anything wrong, and to show that UK had no proof he did anything wrong—which would make UK look bad.

UK paid him the rest of the money.

Hal Mumme was convinced that Larry Ivy didn't want to pay a lot of money for a head coach. He wanted to bring somebody in and pay them less than a million dollars.

Ironically, Mumme saw Ivy at C.M. Newton's funeral in June of 2018. Ivy hugged Mumme. At the age of sixty-eight, Mumme hasn't forgotten, but he has forgiven Ivy and moved on.

Just because of the circumstances involved, that shouldn't detract from Ivy's outstanding career. In 1969, he was the director of student housing and, by 2000, had moved up to athletics director of a major university. That's a remarkable accomplishment by anyone's standards, and Ivy should be commended for that.

I attempted to reach Larry Ivy, Sandy Bell, and Dr. Charles Wethington—but I received no response. I respect all three, but I never expected any of them to talk to me. Lots of people like history to stay history. At least we now have Mumme's side of what happened to his career.

This is the kind of thing that drives me crazy. Why didn't Hal Mumme get to run the offense at a big-time school after his problems at UK? No disrespect to Jackson State, where he ran the offense, but it makes no sense.

And why didn't Mumme get much better head coaching opportunities after Kentucky? No, you wouldn't expect him to get another head coaching job in the SEC, but if I'm an athletics director in many other conferences a notch below the SEC, and I see there is a coach who brought excitement to a dead program and filled seats, wouldn't you want to talk to Mumme and see how much he learned from the experience at Kentucky?

Mumme should have had better head coaching jobs than Southeastern Louisiana, New Mexico State, McMurray, and Belhaven.

76

Hal Mumme Gives Billy Gillispie
His Big Break

In 1987, Hal Mumme was the head football coach and athletics director at Copperas Cove High School in Texas. He needed a basketball coach. His principal gave him a list of some very prominent high school coaches and asked him to try to get one of them. The problem was that they were already very successful in their current locations—bigger schools, better programs, and more money. Mumme made the phone calls anyway. No one was interested in coming.

While that was going on, Misty Gillispie, Billy Gillispie's wife—who worked at Copperas Cove High School—brought in Billy's resume and asked Mumme to consider her husband for the head basketball coaching position.

Billy, at the time, was an assistant high school basketball coach and the JV coach at nearby Killeen High School. Mumme went to Killeen to watch the varsity and the JV games. He liked what he saw, went back to Copperas Cove, and asked Misty if Billy would like to come and talk to him.

Billy showed up right away, Hal hired him, and the rest—as they say—is history. Billy and Hal are friends to this day. Mumme says they still talk three or four times a year. In high school, there can at times be jealousy between a football and basketball coach as to who gets what athlete. Billy and Hal shared the athletes. The basketball players played football and the football players played basketball. Billy and Hal got along great.

"Anytime Billy took a job, he would always call me before," Hal told me. "He didn't call me about getting the job at Kentucky until after he accepted the job." Mumme would have advised him not to take the

Kentucky job. Billy was a really good basketball coach, but Mumme knew the hugeness of the Kentucky program would have been a bad fit.

Are you thinking what I'm thinking? Billy G didn't call Hal Mumme before taking the Kentucky job because he didn't want to hear what Mumme was going to tell him.

77

My Visit to See Claude Bassett

TV stations like LEX18 don't often get on airplanes to do stories. It's just not in the budget. I went to my boss, Bruce Carter, and asked him if Claude Bassett would talk to me, would he fly me down to Texas? Bruce stopped me in mid-sentence and told me he'd fly me anywhere I needed to fly. It was that big of a story.

To get to Claude, I had a number of conversations with his lawyer, Bob Furnier. Bob was a good guy. We had a number of long talks as he was trying to make sure he knew where I was coming from. Bob talked to Claude, and the agreement for the story was on.

Claude had agreed to speak with me about his role in the NCAA allegations against Kentucky while he was Hal Mumme's recruiting coordinator. I was anxious to get that story from his perspective. Getting Bassett to open up for the first time in years was a big story.

Brian Gilbert, my photographer, and I flew down to Robstown, Texas. It's a very poor community. As we're driving toward the town, we pass by something I had always heard about—one of these big Texas high school football stadiums. It was spectacular! I've always heard these stories of how some of these players in high schools in Texas are taken better care of than at small colleges. I've also heard stories about how some of these Texas high school football coaches are making a lot of money. Even a coordinator at a big high school can make a lot of money.

When we get to Robstown—it's pretty obvious—there is no money there. They don't have a lot of athletes, and trying to win there is a very difficult thing to do. That's where Claude Bassett ended up. He takes a job that nobody wanted just to get back into coaching. His office was really tiny, and he's a huge man who loved to talk. You think I talk a lot?

In the process of setting up the interview, I told Bob Furnier—and then Claude—it was no holds barred. I could ask anything I wanted. I wasn't looking to come down and ruin anybody's life. I was looking to come down and be fair and tell Claude's side of the story. I wasn't going to sugarcoat anything either. I had no agenda. That's the way I've always done things. Because Claude and I had a good relationship, he agreed to the interview.

As you'll see in the transcripts of the tapes to follow, Claude didn't hesitate to say he broke NCAA rules, or that cheating was going on all over college football. At the time the story broke—and I remember it like it was yesterday in a conversation I had with Claude—he told me he wasn't innocent, but he was accused of things that he not only didn't do, but also that he didn't know anything about. To me that was really powerful.

I believed him.

Hal Mumme told me the same thing—that Claude wasn't innocent, but that he was accused of some things that Hal believes he didn't do. That part gets overlooked and it shouldn't. Hal believes that Claude was honest with him.

Claude talked about how Kentucky was cheating before he got there. That's a part of this story that people either overlooked or *didn't* want to hear.

I also don't believe that paying players will stop cheating. That's such a silly argument that it's not even funny. Will paying players help some young people who are poor? Absolutely. But if you think paying players will stop them from taking money if someone offers them a bunch of money, that is ridiculous. It's no sillier than if you asked someone whether they would take a big raise across town to another TV station. Paying players is not going to solve the cheating problem. I've literally laughed at some of the people who have made that ridiculous comment.

Plus, there are some boosters that I call jock sniffers, who have a lot of money and who want to be close to the athletes. If they can give some cash, which means little to them, to a star athlete to get to know them better—why not?

Claude Bassett is the person deemed responsible for taking the Kentucky football program down. According to Hal Mumme, Claude Bassett had a legitimate reason for paying the Memphis coaches. He just should have reported it right away. If they did, I don't believe Mumme would have gotten fired. Slapped on the wrist? Yes!!

Not reporting it was Claude Bassett's biggest mistake. It was a *DUMB* mistake. Once the NCAA opened Pandora's box of cheating, they were bound to find other things.

People didn't believe Claude's explanation of why he did what he did because they didn't want to believe him. If you don't like somebody, you're likely not going to believe what they say.

Claude Bassett's quotes should be taken seriously, but I know there are people who won't give Claude the proper time of day. Claude Bassett was loud and bombastic. I think his weight and his appearance helped create an image that some people didn't like. It never bothered me. I spent my career dealing with all kinds of characters, which only made my job more interesting.

One other part of Claude that was huge to me—his son Jed, who played for UK, was a great kid and a great student. For a son to be that good made me pause, stop, and take a deep breath. Jed's parents had to have done a lot of things the right way. I always remember that, and I don't believe many who knew about Jed took that into consideration about their feelings towards Bassett.

This is worth reading slowly. If you believe Bassett—cheating in college football is part of a big business.

Part I of my story:

Bassett: It was evident that there were players that were being taken care of.

Cutler Narration: There's a big part of Claude that will always love Kentucky. When he first arrived and didn't even know most of the names of the players, it was sort of culture shock. Some of the players started coming into his office and asking for...certain things.

Bassett: Here comes one of the better players. "Coach, listen, I gotta have seven or eight hundred dollars to fix my car."

Cutler Narration: Claude at first was confused, since he knew Kentucky was paying players.

Bassett: Heavens to mercy. Then why are they not doing well?

Cutler Narration: By the time Kentucky was getting ready to play Louisville for the first game under Hal Mumme, Claude understood why Kentucky was cheating and not winning.

Bassett: By that time it was evident to me that we were a speck on the road compared to the intricate organizations that were operating—that I can look you in the eye and swear to—for SEC schools.

Cutler Narration: He's called the most hated man in UK Football history. Today, Bassett has tried to build a winner at Robstown High. The Cotton Pickers didn't win a game for years before Bassett returned to Texas.

Bassett: I needed to drop out of sight. You gotta want to get to Robstown, Texas.

Cutler Narration: Bassett has never denied breaking NCAA rules, but for the first time, he's trying to set the record straight. Kentucky failed to recruit some of the best high school players in the Commonwealth during Claude's first couple of years. He says other schools were "better cheaters."

Bassett: We lost five football players to out of state schools for things that were scandalous at best.

Cutler Narration: Bassett admits that he had no other choice if Kentucky was going to win.

Cutler: So did you end up paying players?

Bassett: Yes I did.

Cutler Narration: Bassett believes that if C.M. Newton had not retired as athletics director, Bassett still would have resigned due to the NCAA violations. But, Hal Mumme would still be the head coach at Kentucky.

Bassett: What you have in twenty-five words or less is a coup d'état. They used me to get Hal Mumme out as the head football coach at the University of Kentucky.

Cutler Narration: Larry Ivy replaced C.M. Newton as athletics director. Bassett believes Ivy knew how UK Football was being run.

Cutler: Did Larry Ivy know?

Bassett: I would think so.

Cutler: What would you say to Larry Ivy if you could get in a room with him?

Bassett: That's not a proper question for me to answer.

Cutler: Alan Cutler, LEX18 sports.

Part II of my story:

Bassett: Now let's get this understood. I think this is something that's going to come out real clear. Claude Bassett did not put anybody on probation. The reason I resigned on that Sunday was to make absolutely sure that nothing like that would happen. And there were many different guarantees given on that day that no such thing would happen.

Cutler Narration: Bassett believes others above him at Kentucky knew you had to cheat to win. He quickly discovered that Kentucky was cheating before he moved to the Bluegrass.

Bassett: It was evident that there were players who were being taken care of.

Cutler Narration: This also shocked Bassett. One of the Commonwealth's most famous and powerful men walked into his office and offered some help in getting recruits.

Bassett: What are we going to do about this young man? What are we going to do to get him? What kind of package do we have to put together?

Cutler Narration: Which of course is against NCAA rules. Bassett won't say who this powerful person is. Bassett believes Kentucky wasn't going after him, but his friend—the head coach—Hal Mumme.

Bassett: I believe the University of Kentucky had an agenda. And I believe the NCAA rubber stamped some things they probably shouldn't have.

Cutler Narration: That agenda according to Bassett was to get him at any cost. He claims that a Southeastern Conference investigator went to a home of a UK football player and threatened the family to give up information about Kentucky's recruiting coordinator.

Bassett: And that if they didn't show him to his satisfaction, their son was going to lose his scholarship.

Cutler Narration: Before Bassett agreed to sit down with Kentucky's investigators, Bassett says he was promised a copy of the interview. To this day, Bassett says there is no tape. In his lawsuit, Bassett will charge Kentucky with breaking the Kentucky Open Records Act, which Bassett says kept information from getting to the public.

Bassett: You couldn't kick a kid out of Robstown High School with the due process I was given at Kentucky.

Cutler Narration: There were over three dozen NCAA violations. This was the big one, which Bassett says he didn't do. A money order from Bassett for fourteen hundred dollars was sent to Tim Thompson, a high school coach from Memphis. Thompson was about to be hired as an assistant football coach at Kentucky. Thompson and two other coaches worked Kentucky's football camp. Bassett claims that the money was not given to buy players.

Bassett: That did not happen. I gave Tim Thompson fourteen

hundred dollars in money orders to pay two assistant coaches that in my opinion had been poorly paid at one of our football camps. Used my own money to do it.
Cutler Narration: Bassett has never denied breaking rules.

Cutler: So did you end up paying players?

Bassett: Yes I did.

Cutler Narration: Alan Cutler, LEX18 sports.

78

Kentucky Football Through the Years

It's embarrassing how few bowl games UK has gone to since 1952.
Fifteen—ONLY FIFTEEN!!
There are great football fans in the Commonwealth. They deserve better. I think it's nonsense to say that you can't win here. For a long time, I seemed to be in the minority with that opinion.

Remember that Kentucky Football was *dead* when Hal Mumme arrived on campus. Athletics Director C.M. Newton had the guts to go outside the box when he tabbed Mumme, and UK Football suddenly became fun. It's sad how things quickly got out of control.

I've traveled all over the South, and I was surprised how bad UK's facilities were compared to the other SEC powers. UK has made so much money from TV through the SEC, it's a shame they didn't build facilities years before they recently did. And, I don't want to hear any excuses from UK's administration. Alabama did it. Tennessee did it. Georgia did it...etc...UK chose *NOT* to do it for way too long.

Kentucky should have hired Howard Schnellenberger who—based on his track record—I believe would have put UK Football on another level.

If Fran Curci didn't get in trouble, he also had Kentucky to the point where the winning could have continued.

I've wondered, and so has Rich Brooks, what would have happened for him if UK built the facilities he wanted while he was here? He was tired of not getting what he asked for. Rich went to four bowls in his last four years.

This has always been a pet peeve. *EVERY Kentucky* coach I've covered—everyone—complained in their first year that there was a lack of "team speed." Jerry Claiborne, Bill Curry, Hal Mumme, Guy Morriss,

Rich Brooks, Joker Phillips, and Mark Stoops all said that. Whose job is it to bring in more speed?

I believe that if Paul Bear Bryant would have stayed at Kentucky, and not ended up at Alabama where he won six national championships, Kentucky would have been—perhaps—as respected in football as they are in basketball.

UK Men's Basketball, UK Women's Basketball, and UK Football should have been the best ever! UK BLEW IT. More on that later.

I don't know if Mark Stoops is going to be here twenty years from now. Would it shock me if he were here fifteen years from now? It would not—if he continues to be successful. And, the foundation he's built after six years is the best I've seen since 1981.

There have been a lot of times in the past when athletics directors hired the wrong coach. You think that if Nick Saban came to Kentucky instead of going to Alabama, he wouldn't have won big? No—not as big as Alabama where he's won five national championships since 2007, but *much much much* bigger than UK's record since that time.

You almost can't pay a coach like Nick Saban too much. People look at big salaries the wrong way. Football is a big business. Recently, football programs in the SEC have paid over fifty million dollars to coaches who were fired, who had existing contracts. That's an unbelievable figure. The reason they're trying to pay these coaches off is that they're trying to catch Alabama. They want the next Nick Saban.

The right coach can be cheap.

A bad coach can be very expensive.

79

The Great Tim Couch

Most of the time with a great sports hype, it ends up being not true. Not in the case of Tim Couch from Leslie County, Kentucky. He was like the *Paul Bunyan* of quarterbacks. He could do nothing wrong.

Tim Couch shows up to Lexington on a Friday night to play at Tates Creek High School, and it's the largest crowd I've ever seen pack that stadium. People were everywhere. Just watching him warm up was an "oh my gosh" experience. He had a charisma about him that was shocking for a high school kid.

I can't think of another player during my time covering Kentucky that changed the program more than Tim Couch. John Wall or Jamal Mashburn in basketball? Maybe? I'm OK with that. But who else would there be? The beautiful part with Tim Couch was they finally found him the right coach. Hal Mumme was perfect for Tim Couch.

Unlike Elliot Uzelac, the offensive coordinator during Bill Curry's last year when Tim was a freshman, Mumme played to Tim's strengths. Uzelac started Tim Couch at Florida for his very first game. Powerful Florida—who shut UK out. Uzelac had Tim Couch run the option. Uzelac should have been *fired* the next day.

What Kentucky did to Tim during his freshman season was almost as *dumb* as what the Browns did for Tim's career in Cleveland.

Coaches might know sports better than I do, but coaches can still do really *DUMB* things. I'll always believe that Elliot Uzelac was upset that he didn't become the head coach at Colorado. From there it spiraled down. I always thought that when Elliot Uzelac was at Kentucky, he was a bitter, angry man. There were a few times after I talked to him when I left thinking, "This dude is mad at the world."

I never said Uzelac couldn't coach. He was a very good coach who was the head coach at Western Michigan and Navy. He ran the offense at Ohio State, at Colorado when they were special, and at many other places including Kentucky. But running Tim Couch might be the most ridiculous coaching move I've seen at Kentucky.

When your career in any business lasts a long time, you have years that aren't so good—I can give Uzelac a pass for what he did at Kentucky—but I'll bet Couch's father never felt that way.

Uzelac came out of retirement to coach at Benton Harbor High, which had no winning seasons since 1989. He showed up in 2015, and they won every year for three seasons. I was happy for him. He still had a lot to offer. He quit over a disagreement with the school board.

Tim Couch brought hope back to the Kentucky football program. When Bill Curry couldn't beat Vandy, there was no such thing as hope. Kentucky lost five in a row to Vanderbilt during his tenure.

I remember the 1998 game against Louisville. Tim completes 29 of 39 passes for 498 yards and 7 touchdowns as Kentucky beats the Cardinals 68-34. He couldn't miss. Tim had a quick release, he was very accurate, and he could make quick decisions. The system was perfect for him.

I will always believe that the Cleveland Browns, who drafted Couch with the first pick in the 1999 NFL Draft, would qualify as the *dumbest* franchise in sports during that particular time period. Athletes are commodities. The Browns made a huge investment in Tim. Don't you want to protect your investment?

In two of the five drafts when Tim was there, Cleveland drafted *NO OFFENSIVE LINEMEN. Go ahead and look it up.* Until 2003, which was his last season there, the highest draft pick for an offensive lineman on a *BAD OFFENSIVE LINE* was a sixth rounder. That's crazy dumb. In his last season, the Browns drafted offensive linemen in the first and fifth round.

One of my favorite lines is "common sense is king." I don't think I took that from anyone—so I'll claim it. I LOVE THAT EXPRESSION. Where were the Browns when it came to common sense?

Tim could have sued his offensive line for a lack of support. But in reality, it's not all their fault. They tried. They just needed better players.

It seems like the first thing you would do if you were the Cleveland Browns would be to make sure your quarterback, who determines the fate and fortune of your franchise, is protected. And, when it's a *huge investment,* it's even more important.

Tim Couch was much tougher than people realized, but he got the *crap* beat out of him in the NFL. Quarterbacks get beat up all the time, but Cleveland's offensive line ruined Tim Couch's shoulder. Back when Couch played, the quarterbacks weren't protected by officials like they are now. Huge hits after you threw the pass were celebrated back then—but are penalties now.

As a rookie, Couch was sacked 56 times, which was tops in the NFL.

Two years later, it was 51, second in the NFL.

Despite the sacks, Couch was fearless in the way he stood in the pocket.

Ironically, Tim's last game in the NFL was December 28, 2003. The Browns beat the Cincinnati Bengals 22-14. I was host of the Cincinnati Bengals Radio Network. When I was doing sports talk radio on WLW in Cincinnati, I would defend Couch. I was labeled as a Kentucky backer. That really bothered me. I was right, but I got labeled. Nonsense.

I said it then, and my opinion hasn't changed. It gets me angry when anyone calls Couch a "bust." He hears that a lot less now than when he played. Awful opinion!

Couch was only twenty-six when he was done...it makes me sad.

The Chicago Bears were one of the many teams who were interested in Tim after his time in Cleveland. I know they wanted to sign him. Couch got a shot in his shoulder before he went to Chicago just so he could throw when he got there. The Bears just wanted to see if he could throw the ball. If he could, then the contract was his.

The next day Tim couldn't lift his arm.

Ryan Leaf was a bust.

Jamarcus Russell was a bust.

Akili Smith was a bust.

Tim Couch took an expansion team to the playoffs. Tim Couch was *NO* bust.

If anything, he's owed an apology for the dumb management that didn't bring in enough talented offensive linemen.

It always bothered Couch that he didn't deliver a championship to Cleveland. Plus, he will always believe that he was *never* able to show Browns fans what he was capable of doing.

Couch should have been a big star in the NFL.

As the big man on campus, he could have gotten away with anything. Instead, Tim Couch was always friendly, respectful, polite, and he never big-timed me when I dealt with him at Kentucky.

He was just a good kid from the mountains of Kentucky who just happened to be ridiculously talented.

Part 8 (1997-2009)

Rolling With Tubby and Rich

80

The Significance of Tubby Smith

One of the most important Americans in the 20th century was Jackie Robinson.

When Jackie Robinson took the field in 1947, the U.S. military was still segregated, despite so many African Americans giving their lives in World War II.

In the 20th century, Jackie changed the culture and the mindset of people in America as much as anyone else I can think of—including Martin Luther King Jr. I'm good if you don't agree. We all need to learn how to disagree more. I also believe some people that won't agree don't fully understand the history of Jackie Robinson and what was going on in America at the time.

Jackie Robinson was picked to be the first African American to play in the Major Leagues, not just because of his playing abilities, but more so for his temperament. There were better African American baseball players at that time—and he was really special on the field. But Robinson was selected because of his ability to handle all the garbage and threats that were sure to come his way. He was picked because he understood that he wasn't allowed to answer back when confronted and criticized.

Tubby Smith is not Jackie Robinson. But, Tubby had more to do with helping other African Americans succeed than he's ever been given credit for.

In 1999, I asked Tubby why he didn't grow his mustache back. I told him his mustache was cool.

Tubby smiled and said, "I can't because I'm at Kentucky."

That spoke volumes to me about what Tubby felt deep inside his heart and soul about his responsibilities as an African American. This was about Tubby—a classy man—always believing that he had to look and act a certain way in order to help other African Americans get future head coaching opportunities.

It's easier to win a national championship at Kentucky than at most places—five different coaches have done it. It's a record that might never be broken, but there's also more pressure to win a championship at Kentucky. When is Georgia going to win the national championship in basketball? Don't hold your breath. What Georgia coach has ever been under intense scrutiny for not getting to the Final Four like Tubby was at Kentucky—even though he had already won a national championship?

C.M. Newton—one of the most powerful men ever in the SEC—hired Tubby Smith. He did it partly because he thought Tubby would be a really good coach. But more importantly, C.M. Newton—who was a trailblazer for African Americans for his entire career as a coach and administrator—wanted to be a pioneer at his school, the University of Kentucky, because of the history and reputation.

Tubby Smith had to keep his mouth shut while coaching at Kentucky. He knew that if he lashed out at all the people who criticized him and were against him because he was an African American coach at the University of Kentucky, it would make it more difficult for other African Americans to become head coaches at other big-time colleges and universities.

Tubby's son Saul was adopted (I broke that story on TV). He played point guard for his father. No one—no human being—should take the garbage that Saul Smith took from fans.

When playing for your father—forget the color of your skin—you have to be tough.

The legendary coach Al McGuire, who built Marquette into one of the best basketball programs, had his son as the point guard. When he was asked about Allie—one tough point guard—he said, "Of course he'll start, he's my son." *Coach Al's boy* is how *Sports Illustrated* labeled him.

It didn't help Saul that there were other highly ranked point guards who didn't want to come to Kentucky because even if they were better, they believed Saul was going to play. That made it worse.

"Daddy's boy, Daddy's girl, Saul you suck, Saul's a woman," could be heard from the stands. I heard it covering UK games on the road. Fans held up signs making fun of him. Even Kentucky fans were unfailingly critical and unbelievably cruel to him. Yet, Saul persevered. Saul played as hard as anyone at Kentucky during his tenure here. Saul

Smith had thick skin—he had to in order to survive.

Tubby was famous for his hard stare. I once asked Tubby off camera why he doesn't lash out against those that are so unfair to Saul. Not a word—but I got that stare. That was my answer—loud and clear. I nodded and smiled at Tubby.

Tubby had thick skin. Coaching at Tulsa or Georgia is nothing like coaching at Kentucky. It's nothing like being the first African American head basketball coach at the University of Kentucky.

Tubby Smith was only one of five coaches to win 365 games in 15 years or less. His record speaks for itself. But I will always believe—I've believed this forever—that Tubby as a coach became more conservative at Kentucky than he would have been had he stayed at Tulsa or Georgia.

Forget about the color of Tubby's skin. Replacing Rick Pitino wasn't going to be easy for anyone.

It'll go down in history that Tubby Smith won the National Championship at Kentucky in 1998. Tubby will make the Hall of Fame.

But what Tubby did as a man—acting with class—might be as significant as anything he ever did on the basketball court.

81

Keith Bogans' Injury
was the Tip of the Iceberg

Keith Bogans, a first-team Parade and McDonald's All-American, was a star recruit for Tubby Smith's recruiting class in 1999.

I will never forget the first interview I did with him. When he opened his mouth, he sounded like an old-time Motown disc jockey. My first impression was—wow, he's got a great set of pipes. The second thing I noticed about Keith was that he's about as modest as I am. I asked him how long he was going to be at Kentucky. "One year," he answered.

From that moment, I decided to like Keith Bogans.

So many players today are counseled and coached to say that they're not going to be one-and-done when you know they're either going to be or really want to be one-and-done. The standard answer is to say, "Well, we'll see how the year goes. I'm here now. I'll worry about that later." Almost everyone who gives you that answer usually already has a foot out the door. I interviewed Keith countless times over four years. One time after an interview I said, "Keith you're as modest as I am." We both had a big laugh.

Keith Bogans was open and honest—and very secure in his own skin. He had a great career at Kentucky. He was a four-year starter and both the SEC Player of the Year and an All-American in 2003.

Keith got drafted in the second round of the NBA draft. I've always given Keith a lot of credit for a couple of reasons. One, he swallowed his ego, worked on his game, and became a good defensive player. Secondly, he was a good teammate. Otherwise you wouldn't play for nine different NBA teams and thrive for twelve years as a role player.

After he left, Keith didn't come back to Lexington for a long time.

Off camera, when he came back, I asked him why he didn't come back more often. Although something obviously kept him from coming back, Keith told me that he *was* going to come back more. He was surprised how well he was received by UK fans. I told him I wasn't surprised at all.

Keith's a good guy—one of the UK players that adjusted about as much as anyone. He went from a huge star with a big ego to a role player in the NBA. He made a lot of money, and he never would have made so much money if he didn't change. I was always happy for his success.

One of the things that will bother UK fans and Keith forever is his last college game. Kentucky was upset by Marquette 83-69 in the 2003 NCAA Midwest Finals in Minneapolis. That was future NBA great Dwayne Wade's coming out party. Wade had 29 points, 11 rebounds, and 11 assists. Keith scored 15, as the No. 1-seeded Wildcats finished their season with a 32-4 record.

Keith had a really bad ankle that game. He couldn't run. I don't know if Kentucky would have won, but I do know they would have had a much better shot of beating Dwayne Wade if Keith had been healthy. Keith's ankle was so bad that he couldn't guard anyone. Kentucky had to compensate, they missed some open shots, and subsequently saw their title hopes evaporate. I'm sure Tubby Smith and Keith Bogans both feel that with a healthy Keith Bogans, the outcome of that season could have been totally different. That team was undefeated in SEC play and won the SEC Tournament.

I can't think of another school in the history of the NCAA that has *potentially* lost more championships due to injuries than the University of Kentucky. Keith Bogans is just one of many.

The person everyone forgets about is Mike Casey. As the 1966 Mr. Basketball in the state of Kentucky, Casey led Shelbyville to the state championship. During his career at UK, he was a three-time All-SEC player. Adolph Rupp called Casey his best money player.

In the 1969-70 season, Kentucky was ranked No. 1 in the country. They finished the season 26-2. It was Rupp's best chance at his 5th NCAA championship before they retired him. The problem was that Mike Casey suffered a severely broken leg in an accident when the tire on his new Camaro blew out, and he missed the entire season.

In spite of that, Kentucky still made it to the Regional Finals where they lost to Jacksonville 106-100. I remember watching that game as a kid. Dan Issel led Kentucky with 28 points. Tom Parker had 21. Terry

Mills—Cameron Mills' father—had 18. Mike Pratt—one of the most underrated Kentucky players—had 14 points and 13 rebounds.

Jacksonville, on the other hand, had the twin towers. Pembrook Burrows—who ended up becoming a Florida state trooper, and 7'2" Artis Gilmore—who made the Naismith Memorial Basketball Hall of Fame and became good friends with Dan Issel when they dominated with the Kentucky Colonels. It was a great game. Kentucky hung in there and had a chance to win it in the end.

Four UK players fouled out. Kentucky was playing on fumes when Issel fouled out on a controversial charging call with ten minutes to go in the game—a call that both Rupp and Issel said was bogus. Kentucky was behind, but they made a valiant comeback. In addition to Issel— Pratt, Mills, and Larry Steele all fouled out. It was incredible.

Ironically, what is often forgotten is that when that recruiting class came in, they had eleven players. Some say it was the greatest Kentucky recruiting class of all time. I don't know if it was the greatest, but it certainly was one of the best. Casey, Issel, Pratt, and Mills all included in that class. Wow—it was unbelievable.

Mike Casey never made it in the NBA or ABA because he lost his quickness due to the broken leg. I always thought he would have been a starting guard forever in the NBA had he not had that car accident.

Casey was only sixty years old when his heart gave out on him. He loved the game as much as anyone who wore Kentucky across their chest. He grew up spending countless hours shooting at a hoop that was on the side of his family's barn.

John Stewart was another UK player that many have forgotten about. John Stewart? A great seven-footer, from a wonderful family in Indianapolis, who Tubby will always believe could have helped Kentucky win another NCAA championship. Stewart, who was so excited to play for Tubby, had a rare heart condition that they didn't know about.

You can't forget the video from the game. It's upsetting writing this. If you ask Tubby about it today, he still gets emotional. Stewart had 22 of his team's 33 points in a regional championship game in March 1999 when he collapsed on the court and died.

It's easy to say today, but if Stewart had the career Tubby expected, I don't think Tubby leaves to coach Minnesota in 2007.

Sam Bowie was another player whose injury probably also cost Kentucky a national championship. Bowie was just a shadow of his former self after his leg injuries. I was at the Final Four in 1984 when Kentucky lost to Georgetown 53-40. Kentucky was up by seven at halftime before shooting an incredible 3-33 during the second half. I believe Sam was the only player to be a two-time first-team All-American who didn't play either season.

In 1997, after Derek Anderson rips his knee, Kentucky ends up losing the national championship to Arizona. Anderson thought he was healthy, and he wanted to play. Rick Pitino didn't let Anderson play because he was concerned about Anderson's future. With everything that has gone on with Rick Pitino, the fact that he might have cost himself a national championship by not playing Derek Anderson is pretty interesting to say the least. I can't imagine Arizona beating Kentucky with a healthy Derek Anderson.

Casey, Bowie, Anderson, Stewart, and Bogans. That's five national championships Kentucky might have missed out on due to injuries to key players.

82

A Fun Day Spent
with Pat Summitt and Chris Lofton

I'd heard a rumor that Pat Summitt was going to be the Kentucky Women's head basketball coach before she became the Tennessee coach—and the only reason that didn't happen was because Kentucky didn't want to pay her moving expenses. I always thought that seemed to be too crazy to be true. I heard it in a number of different places, but the truth also is that Lexington, at times, can be a gossipy town. I'm not trying to be nasty, but a lot of sports towns are gossipy.

When Kentucky's Mr. Basketball, Chris Lofton, went to Tennessee, I never understood why Kentucky coach Tubby Smith didn't want him. It made no sense to me. Chris Lofton had nine three-pointers—which tied legendary Clay County guard Richie Farmer's record—to carry Mason County to the state championship in 2003. He was the world's greatest kid and a really good football wide receiver.

Lofton ended up not only on the cover of *Sports Illustrated*, but he was first-team All-SEC three times and the SEC Player of the Year.

I did a story with him in high school when he opened up his locker and recruiting letters started falling out all over the place. The letters weren't opened, and he wasn't going to open them. Chris said he had more in other places. He's getting offers from all over the country to play basketball, but Kentucky still doesn't want him. I think Tubby thought his feet were too slow. Nothing else made any sense.

This kid could get a shot off on anybody—and he was a great shooter. The two-time All-American was better off going to the Vols because I don't think he would have ever gotten a fair shot at Kentucky.

Chris went down to Tennessee, and he had a great season right

302

away as a freshman. I did something I had never done in my career. I went down to Tennessee to do a story with Chris before he played Kentucky. I called Tennessee ahead of time. They were terrific helping me out. They even let us shoot practice, which you couldn't do at Kentucky anymore.

In the process of going down to Knoxville, it just so happened that Mickie DeMoss was the Kentucky women's basketball coach. She was going to play Tennessee later that year against her old boss and dear friend, Pat Summitt. So I arranged for Pat to do a sit down and do a one-on-one interview with me.

Pat was really smart, tough, warm, funny, and gracious. What a wonderful woman. She was "on" for the TV camera, and I understand what that is because this is what I do. She was GREAT!

She was great to talk to, you could feel who she was, you could feel her intensity, and you can see why she built one of the greatest programs in the history of college sports. Notice I didn't say women's sports—she built one of the greatest programs in college athletics. She doesn't get the credit. She's called one of the greatest *women's* basketball coaches. I think that's a bunch of baloney. She's better than that. She is one of the greatest coaches—period!"

Pat's record speaks for itself. As the Tennessee Lady Vols head basketball coach from 1974-2012, she won 1,098 career games, the most in college basketball history when she retired. She won eight NCAA championships and coached the USA women's basketball team to a gold medal in the 1984 Olympics. She was named the Naismith Basketball Coach of the Century in 2000. In 2012, Pat was awarded the Presidential Medal of Freedom by President Barack Obama, and she also received the Arthur Ashe Courage Award at the ESPYs that year.

I can picture her smile like it was yesterday. "Pat, I have to ask you this question," I say to her. She tells me she knows exactly what I'm going to ask. "It's true," she answers. She starts telling me that she was offered the head coaching job at Kentucky. I don't remember what the salary was, but it was very very little. Female coaches back then got absolutely nothing. I don't think it was over ten thousand dollars a year. Pat asked for moving expenses of five hundred dollars to move to Lexington. She was turned down.

Pat Summitt would have become the Kentucky coach. Now she hedged it later on because she's a Tennessee gal forever, but had Kentucky paid for moving expenses, she would have become the Kentucky coach.

Pat's players loved her. She was a very stern taskmaster on the court, but there were other sides of Pat that you may not have seen because it was off the floor. She was tough and amazingly demanding—but when you show that you really care, and you're smart, then you can be demanding. That was Pat.

When I first heard that she had Alzheimer's, I couldn't believe it. There are certain people that you think are indestructible. To me, Pat Summitt was this indestructible giant of a woman. This couldn't be happening to someone like Pat. She's too young.

The last time she coached against Kentucky in Memorial Coliseum on January 12, 2012. I was staring at her like I think a lot of people were. She wasn't the same on the sidelines. Kentucky upset the sixth-ranked Vols 61-60, but I was sad watching her. She wasn't really coaching her team.

I'll say it again. Pat Summitt was one of the greatest coaches in the history of college sports. UK made a huge mistake with not hiring her. Saving five hundred dollars or whatever on a move cost them millions and many national championships.

Think about this. UK once had football coach Bear Bryant. Bear leaving also cost UK millions and probably many national championships. If UK could have had Bear Bryant, Pat Summitt, and Adolph Rupp for their entire careers, you could make a case for them having had the greatest football coach of his time, the greatest women's basketball coach of her time, and the greatest basketball coach of his time.

By the way, I believe the entire story about why Bear Bryant left UK has never been told.

Bear died twenty-eight days after he retired. He won five AP national championships at Alabama and when he retired, he was No. 1 with 323 wins.

People in power—athletics directors—get paid to project the future. Those mistakes off the court hurt Kentucky big time.

83

Nolan Richardson's Cowboy Boots

Nolan Richardson—the head basketball coach at the University of Arkansas from 1985-2002—and I had a bond. We both wore cowboy boots. Back then, I wore cowboy boots all the time. My problem was, Nolan's boots were tons nicer and much more expensive than mine. I was jealous.

Before the first game of his that I covered, I said, "Hey, nice boots, Coach." Nolan looked down at my boots, smiled and said, "Thanks, nice boots too." I'm convinced my boots were the reason he always remembered me.

In 1994—the year Arkansas won the NCAA championship—Nolan gave me a great one-on-one interview after Arkansas was knocked out of the SEC Tournament. I wasn't sure he'd do the interview. A lot of coaches would blow you off under those circumstances because it wasn't a press conference.

No kidding—at the time I thought the reason he granted me the interview was because I also wore cowboy boots.

Nolan was down and sad that day. He knew how good his team was.

"Maybe now my team will listen to me on Monday," Nolan told me. *WOW—great line.* At times, a loss can help you. When your head gets too big, what a coach says might go in one ear and out the other.

I liked Nolan. I had tremendous respect for him. I'll never understand the amount of racism he faced as a child, and how he had to work his way up from coaching junior college to Tulsa, and finally to winning the NCAA championship with Arkansas in 1994. I don't think we get it, I don't think people in New York get it, and I'm not sure white people in Kentucky get it. I don't get it. I never walked a mile in his shoes.

Nolan, who took Arkansas to three Final Fours, created his "40 Minutes of Hell." He was going to run and press...

I don't understand why more teams don't play the way Nolan did.

I don't understand why more teams don't play the way Pitino did in the 1990s at Kentucky.

Basketball should be played with teams running *all* the time. Let me emphasize this again. On offense you run *all* the time. If players get tired, then just play more players. You gave them a scholarship. If a scholarship player sits on the bench for four years, odds are the coach did a bad job both in developing the player and/or judging that player's talent. Coaches make mistakes. Coaches make a lot of mistakes.

Nolan's style was brilliant—absolutely brilliant.

Nolan's teams were *intimidating.*

His teams were greater than the sum of their individual parts. It's a true testament to great coaching. Nolan also strongly believed that African Americans didn't get the coaching opportunities that they deserved. He was right.

Before Nolan Richardson coached his last game in Lexington on February 23, 2002, I got credit for a story that I have always attributed to my photographer, Greg Gorham—who I call "Punk." This is Punk's story, and it's a big story, and he deserves one hundred percent of the credit for it.

I'm in the Rupp Arena media area before UK plays Arkansas when Punk comes up to me after he had been taking some shots on the court. He whispers that he thinks he got one of the best pieces of tape he's ever going to get.

Nolan and Tubby were talking on the court. Because Punk has the video of the conversation, I knew exactly what Nolan said to Tubby. After the game, I did the obvious. I asked Nolan what he said to Tubby.

I was shocked that Nolan didn't do what just about every other coach breathing would have done—downplay what he said.

"If they go ahead and pay me my money, they can take this job tomorrow," said Nolan.

Let's just say how Nolan put it to Tubby before the game was *much, much* stronger. He said it with emphasis, and he said it with anger.

Days after that, Nolan was fired. There was a clause in his contract that said Arkansas could fire him "at the convenience of the university." It surprised me that this sentence was in his contract and that Nolan didn't ask to have it taken out before he signed it.

Nolan sued for eight million dollars. The case was dismissed. As part of the lawsuit, the University of Arkansas called me to get a copy of the tape. TV stations and a few newspapers from Arkansas also called. I was told the University of Arkansas might want me to testify in court. I thought—*wait a second*—outside of the tape and me asking the obvious question at the press conference, I knew nothing. I didn't want to be part of the story, and there was no reason for me to be part of it. I talked my way out of it.

When Arkansas came into the Southeastern Conference, the competitiveness within the conference changed.

The mutual respect between Nolan and Rick Pitino was terrific. Coaches throw you hot air all the time about how they respect the other coach or program. Sometimes it's true.

Kentucky coach Tubby Smith and Nolan were friends. Nolan, with his very strong personality, acted like a godfather to other African American coaches.

It is so sad how Nolan's career ended. It all ended with the conversation Punk recorded. To be fair, Nolan and Arkansas were probably on their way to a divorce whether or not my photographer got that valuable piece of tape.

If you're on the court, a photographer can shoot anything. Nolan never should have had that conversation with Tubby on the court. *NEVER!* Find another place to have it—on the phone, whatever. I asked Nolan the first question in the postgame press conference about what he said to Tubby, and all hell broke loose.

Nolan should have known that anything on the court is open season for photographers. I think he flat out didn't care because he was *that* angry at some people at the University of Arkansas. LEX18's tape was the explosion.

After Nolan was fired, he became really bitter and angry. The truth is, growing up the way he did, a *HUGE* part of his life was being bitter and angry. I don't blame him. It's sad.

Nolan Richardson should have coached the Arkansas Razorbacks into his seventies. He's one of the greatest coaches of all time. He's the winningest basketball coach in Arkansas history, compiling a 389-169 (.697) record in 17 seasons. He's in the National Collegiate Basketball Hall of Fame and was inducted into the Naismith Memorial Basketball Hall of Fame in 2014.

Nolan is the only head coach to win a Junior College National Championship (1980), the NIT Championship (1981), and the NCAA

Championship (1994). He's also among an elite group including Roy Williams, Denny Crum, Jim Boeheim, and Tubby Smith as the only head coaches to win 365 games in 15 seasons or less.

Ask yourself this question. If Nolan were white, would he have gotten another chance to coach at a big-time school? All he did was win. Maybe I'm naive, but I thought he wouldn't be out of work for more than a year.

If I would pick out five people who I respect and trust the most covering college athletics, Mike DeCourcy has been high on that list for decades.

The columnist for the Sporting News, who's also on the Big Ten Network and Fox Sports and is in the United States Basketball Writers Hall of Fame, is sensitive to the obvious—that Nolan's "circumstance was impacted by race."

But in life, timing is everything.

The job market was different.

"Back then, when a coach in their sixties was going after a recruit, age was often used against them by a rival recruiter," says DeCourcy. "The obvious question? Will that coach be there for the four years of your career? It was common for coaches at that age to have a 'successor-in-waiting' appointed to help defuse that question."

"Athletes no longer worry about having a coach for four years because they didn't plan on being there four years," says DeCourcy.

DeCourcy wanted to see Nolan have another chapter in his career. "He was one of the greatest coaches I covered. The game was diminished because of his absence."

I was really happy to see that Nolan is no longer the angry person he once was. He's much calmer now, as he enjoys retired life on the golf course and on his farm in Arkansas. It's a far cry from his previous life on the basketball court.

An African American coaching at the University of Arkansas in the mid-eighties was a big deal. Not only did Nolan Richardson coach, but he also won a lot of basketball games.

As I looked at a recent picture of him standing by all his basketball trophies, one thing stood out. He wasn't wearing his cowboy boots.

I call it having equity in the bank. Nolan had a ton of it when he was fired at Arkansas.

Cooler heads should have prevailed.

It was in the best interest of everyone if Nolan had kept on coaching. It's sad they couldn't have figured it out.

Both sides should have been calmer and cooler.

But, those that stood up to Nolan, never had to walk a mile in his shoes.

84

Dick Enberg's Socks

On the Monday after Grindstone won the Kentucky Derby in 1996, I was invited to owner W.T. Young's farm. For nearly thirty years, I lived right behind W.T.'s Overbrook Farm, one of the most beautiful farms in the world.

W.T. Young made a fortune with "Big Top" peanut butter. When he sold it to Procter & Gamble in 1955, it became "Jif Peanut Butter," and W.T. eventually got into the thoroughbred business.

His best horse, Storm Cat, was much better in the breeding shed. Storm Cat at one point was commanding a five-hundred-thousand-dollar stud fee as the No. 1 stud in the world. Try and grasp at Storm Cat's value. If he was bred to a hundred mares in a year, that's fifty million dollars—in one year!

In 1996, W. T. Young wins the Kentucky Derby with Grindstone.

Our backyard for thirty years was next to part of W.T. Young's Overbrook Farm. It's one of those beautiful places. After W.T. died, his son—Bill Jr.—wasn't interested in horses. The sale for their horses topped thirty-eight million dollars.

I was the only media invited to W.T. Young's house on that Monday following the Derby. One of the few things I've saved over the years is a handwritten thank you note I got from him for the stories I had done on Grindstone. It was written on the thickest paper I have ever felt in my life.

His secretary had called and asked me if I wanted to interview W.T. Young. I quickly answered, "What time do you want me there?" Remember, this is W.T. Young, who gave away a ton of money during his life and made fortunes in many businesses.

There was another part about W.T. Young that was really easy to like. He seemed just like a regular person.

When I showed up at W.T. Young's house, his trainer, the great D. Wayne Lukas, and Dick Enberg were both there.

Dick Enberg was one of the greatest sportscasters of all time—a real gentleman. Over his nearly sixty-year career, he provided play-by-play of numerous sports for ESPN, CBS, and NBC. He was well known for his signature on-air catch phrases such as *"Oh, My!"* whenever he witnessed an outstanding or poignant athletic moment.

The day before Kentucky was to play Kansas in the 1990s, I went to Rupp Arena to do an interview with Dick after practice. After we finished, we stood around talking when Dick picked up a basketball. He goes out on the court—and here's Dick Enberg who's not six feet tall—and he starts shooting hook shots. I also notice that Dick Enberg took his shoes off. He's in his socks, and there's nobody else there. There's an old saying that says "do the right thing, even when nobody's watching."

Dick continues to make a number of hook shots in a row from five or six feet with pretty good form. I say to him, "Dick, when did you learn how to shoot a hook shot?" He starts laughing and says, "Alan, as short as I am, I was a center on my high school basketball team." I started laughing and asked him why he took his shoes off. He said, "This is Rupp Arena. I respect Rupp Arena. I'm not walking on this court with shoes on."

Wow! This is Dick Enberg—one of the greatest announcers in the history of sports—who is just being respectful because that's how he was brought up. It's times like these that you really get to know what someone is really like.

85

No One Said Life is Fair

If Tennessee could throw out their hero, football coach Johnny Majors (I talked about that earlier in the book), what happened to me is nothing. Let's just say at the time I was mad. Nah—mad isn't strong enough.

I always found it comical that TV stations want their news department to get the dirt—the scoop on others making mistakes—but these same TV stations can often be very, very thin-skinned if the arrow is pointed at them. If you stay at a place long enough, there is often plenty of dirt to go around.

I'm not angry at anyone anymore. That ship sailed a long time ago, but there was a time I was past furious. You may be surprised too when you find out how I got fired from my role as the sports anchor at LEX18. I *loved* anchoring the sports at LEX18. I was wild, crazy, and made strong comments. And they fired me.

In the early 90s, management was upset with the quality of our news product. The ratings had slipped. Our competition at Channel 27 was boring to me—but to their credit, they were consistent in their approach to news.

Mike Taylor, our assignment manager, reminded me that John Duvall—who was running our station—ripped our own news department in an article in the *Lexington Herald-Leader* newspaper. Morale in the newsroom was bad before that. This only made it worse.

In 1994, not that long after I was asked if I wanted a new three-year contract (not once but twice), I suddenly lost my job as sports anchor.

They hired Jill Carlson. It was a package deal with her boyfriend, Paul Kelly—a news anchor. I was told that Kelly wasn't coming without Carlson. And they really wanted Kelly who was the key to this deal. I walk into the station, and out of nowhere management tells me Jill

312

Carson would anchor the 6 and 11 pm sportscasts from now on. That was the first time I heard Jill's name. That's it—I'm done. Just like that.

TV management tells me my salary is still good—that they won't mess with it. They still want me to cover Kentucky—AND they value my presence.

Much to my surprise, I ended up liking my new situation much better. I was tired of doing the eleven o'clock news. I had gone to management within the last couple of years before all this happened and asked if someone else could do the eleven o'clock news. I was working too much already. On a normal day, I was at the station before noon Monday through Friday. It was around twelve to thirteen hours a day—I didn't go home for dinner—didn't see my kids—plus I covered games on Saturday. There was one year covering the SEC and NCAA tournaments where I worked thirty-one out of thirty-two days.

During this period in the mid-90s, many believed I was the No. 1 television personality in Lexington.

Earlier, in 1992, LEX18 got rid of popular weatherman Brian Collins, a dear friend. The station took a lot of heat about that move. I was convinced they were now trying to get me to quit or leave for another job so they wouldn't have to take the criticism like they did for Collins. Only with me, the criticism would have been much worse.

One day our news director had an impromptu meeting. There was yelling and screaming while standing on a desk. The AP wire machine happened to be out of paper. And we are told that the next person who didn't put paper in—*will be fired.*

It gets worse.

One night, this news director came into the TV station with a "spiritual person." This news director and a psychic friend burned incense in various parts of the TV station. The goal was to ward off evil spirits and remove the negative energy on site. This news director got security to open three different offices, including the general manager's office. Several employees got sick from the burning incense.

That news director was fired.

I don't want people to get the opinion that this book is sour grapes—because that's not true.

If you stay in any job long enough, odds are you're going to have ups and downs. Plus, there is plenty of emotion in a newsroom because of how things have to get done on deadlines—sometimes very tight deadlines.

As angry as I was about losing my anchor job, I felt bad for Jill Carlson. Jill was a nice kid, knew sports, knew nothing about Kentucky, and was good on TV. I immediately thought she was headed for a better job somewhere else. She was good, but she frequently froze—and it wasn't her fault.

There were many times I caught her staring at the typewriter at four-thirty in the afternoon. I offered to help her many times, and unless it was time to panic because of the deadline, she always refused. She was put in an absolutely horrible situation by management. After she left Lexington, she got a job in Chicago—where she's from—working for a cable TV station. She then moved up to one of the main stations and has had a very good career.

Jill and I never said a bad word to each other, but at times it was as cold as ice. I never blamed Jill. None of what happened to me was her fault.

After she left, I went up to cover opening day in Cincinnati. The Reds happened to be playing the Chicago Cubs, and I wondered whether Jill would be there. I'll never forget this. She was sitting in the Cubs dugout. I start walking over when she sees me and smiles. I had no idea how she would react to me.

She quickly comes out of the dugout, gives me a hug, and tells me she's sorry. I say to her, "I'm sorry too, but I never thought I did anything wrong, nor did I ever think you did anything wrong. You were put in a horrible situation." We had a terrific talk. I haven't seen or talked to her since, but I've always felt that management didn't do her any favors. Under different circumstances, I think we would have been friends.

I was always happy for Jill's success in Chicago, and I wasn't surprised by it.

During this time, I pulled off one of my great coups in my career. The power of Channel 27 with UK Athletics couldn't be overstated at that time. They were partners—which makes this a big deal.

C.M. Newton was the UK athletics director, and Channel 27 had the contracts for the UK coaches shows—and a number of UK football and basketball games. Because of that, they got all kinds of favors. It was my job to beat their butt to the story, and it was my job to make sure they didn't get extra benefits.

I had a huge disadvantage—but kept on winning.

I complained that Channel 27 was able to fly with the team. I believe I stopped that for a while. I complained that UK was a public institution, and that Channel 27 couldn't do that. They were with the team and got to see things I didn't get to see. I even threatened to go on TV and talk about it and to go crazy on a certain administrator. All of a sudden, Channel 27 couldn't be on the team plane anymore.

I then convinced C.M. Newton to have a year-end basketball banquet on the floor of Rupp Arena, to sell tickets, and LEX18 will do a TV live show. I told C.M. that this was my idea, and if this idea goes to Channel 27, I would go absolutely crazy. I wanted LEX18 to own the rights to it for at least one year. I would have loved to do it forever, but I knew that Channel 27 would complain, put it in their contract, and find a way to take it away.

Believe it or not, I hadn't yet said a word to my management or anyone else about any of this during the negotiations.

The deal was done *before* I told LEX18.

The main reason I didn't tell anyone was trust. I didn't trust anyone, especially since there were times I was able to find out things from inside our competition. Media types love to gossip.

I walked into John Duvall's office and told him about making this big commitment for the station without talking first to him. The look on his face was priceless. John got a big smile on his face, laughed, and asked me how I pulled it off. Remember, John's the same guy who approved pulling my anchoring job from me. John is also the same person who called me in Pittsburgh one night in 1987 about nine-thirty when I was in bed and asked me to come back to Lexington.

We ended up doing the banquet for one year. I would have loved to have been a fly on the wall at Channel 27 when they found out what I hustled.

C.M. thanked me after the show.

Meanwhile, things were so different back at home after losing my anchoring job. I used to miss being at home Monday through Friday. Now I was home much more frequently. But guess what—I discovered that my kids had their own lives, so it wasn't like they started hanging out with Dad. There was an adjustment to me being home more, and I had to incorporate myself into my family's life. At first I was *really hurt*. But that was all my fault for being a workaholic.

Although I still had freedom at work and more time at home, this change in my duties at the TV station still felt like a huge demotion. There are people who will tell you I owned Lexington before they took my anchoring duties away from me.

What made everything worse was that I couldn't tell anyone why they took my anchoring job away. For the next year, everywhere I went, people would ask me why I wasn't anchoring.

My friend, Doug Flynn, was a great defensive second baseman and a former Major League Gold Glove winner. He's an even better person, and we once shared a microphone on a terrific local sports talk show. He called and asked, "Did you do something wrong?" Doug was getting asked in church and many other places about why I wasn't anchoring because they thought he would know.

For him to ask me if I did something wrong meant a lot of people were thinking the same thing. Nobody could figure out why they took my anchoring job away. They thought I must have messed up somehow. That really, really, really hurt me. I remember hanging up the phone call with Doug and fighting back tears—I literally walked out of the station for a few minutes because I was that upset.

I didn't tell Doug what happened. For a guy with a big mouth, I kept it shut.

I know of a local high school football coach who ripped me to his team, using me as an example of what happens to someone when they mess up. I was told this is what he said by someone who was there and was a fan. "Look guys. See what happens to you when you don't do things the right way. Look what happened to Alan Cutler." That really hurt because what he said wasn't true!

It took a lot of discipline on my part not to call this coach up and rip him like crazy.

I had plenty of chances to leave the station. Until I was forty, the phone rang a lot. After forty, it was like my phone number was unlisted.

Another news director left the station for the same job in San Antonio, Texas. He called me up and offered me a job as his sports director and main anchor. He had already sold me to the general manager. I quickly turned him down.

We didn't get along at all during his time at LEX18. He drove me out of my mind nit-picking like crazy. Ironically in that phone call, he told me he thought we were friends. I hated being around him and had no desire to move to San Antonio. I didn't even stretch the phone call out to find out what he would have paid. Didn't care!

If I had gone to San Antonio, I would have been covering the Spurs—a class organization. Think about all the championships that they've won. I think I would have become HUGE in San Antonio. And a fresh start might have been wonderful.

Do I regret not going? NO. Things happen for reasons that I'm not smart enough to understand. If I had gone to San Antonio, my daughter Jenna and my son-in-law Jonathan never would have met. I can't dream of having a better son-in-law in our family.

If I never made it back to a major TV market and my daughter was happy—was it worth it? *YES.*

Things happen for a reason. God has a plan. And I'm certainly not smart enough to understand it.

So, I'm making the same money just covering UK sports as I did anchoring. One day, I'm called to carpet row (management), then I'm told by the same person who said my salary would never be cut that I was going to take a severe cut.

THEY CUT MY SALARY BY MORE THAN SIXTY PERCENT!!

And I was told I was now part-time. I wasn't sure how we would pay our bills.

They also decided things I could and couldn't do. For example, if I were doing a stand-up for a story, it had to be in an arena where people were around to create the right atmosphere. How was that going to work when I did my stand-ups at a basketball practice on a Tuesday afternoon? *EVERYONE IN TV DOES THOSE KINDS OF STAND-UPS.*

At this point, it didn't take a genius to figure out they wanted me to leave—but didn't want to take the heat for pulling the plug.

I don't even know if I have health insurance because I'm only part-time.

I walk into Sandy Byron's office—Sandy's the No. 2 person in the company—and I'm fighting back tears. I couldn't live on what I was making, and now I didn't think I was going to have health insurance. Sandy apologized for what had happened to me, said she had nothing to do with it, and she promised me that I would have health insurance. Before I retired, I thanked Sandy again for helping me out when things were really bad.

The day I hit rock bottom?

I had five bucks in my wallet and a pair of Michael Jordan sneakers—originals. The plan was to keep them as long as I could (I still wear my Kentucky sweatshirt that UK equipment man Bill Keightley gave me in 1984 as a going away present). I thought I'd still be wearing those original Michael Jordan sneakers today.

I ended up selling them just to get seventy dollars. That was the low point. But, when I was driving home, I literally screamed out loud—

and that was it. I decided to stop feeling sorry for myself—when you look at everything I had, I was a very lucky man with a great family. I went back to thinking how lucky I was. And...I wasn't going to let those bastards win.

That drive home was *huge* for me.

Everyone gets knocked down. It's what you do when you get back up. On the way home after selling my Jordan sneakers, I quickly bounced back.

One of my favorite pictures was given to me by a man from England a few weeks before I retired. He just dropped it off at the TV station. I would have loved to have met him to say thank you. It was a picture of Henry Cooper, who knocked down the greatest—Muhammad Ali—in 1963. It's what you do after you get knocked down that counts. Ali fought Cooper twice and won both times. Cooper was known for being a bleeder, and bleeding stopped both fights.

As difficult as it was during that period in my life, I stayed with LEX18. It wasn't easy. Money was extremely tight, but somehow we managed. After a couple of years—all of a sudden, things changed. I even got an apology—and my salary started to slowly go back up.

Many people think it's so cool to be working at a TV station. The truth is, working in TV is no different than working at any other company—there are good times and bad times.

In spite of the stories I told you in this chapter, for most of the time I worked at LEX18, I loved what I did. Hopefully you realize by now that I never did the show or a story to please management. I did all those stories specifically for you, the viewer—and for me...doing it the right way and not caring what anyone else thought.

86

CUTLER and Cross

I did a very successful talk show on KDKA Radio with Bill Currie that we talked about in the Pittsburgh section. Before I met with Currie, management wanted to talk to me.

I'm sitting in the room with two people telling me about the job. One of them was the general manager of KDKA Radio, Rick Starr—and the other was the program director...Chris Cross.

Fast forward to the 1990s. I'm in Lexington, driving around and flipping stations. I accidentally tuned the radio to 1300AM, which was doing a network financial news show. Nobody was listening to it. All of a sudden, I hear Chris Cross's voice. *Are you kidding me?* I knew he had been in Chicago doing pregame and postgame shows on radio with the Chicago Bulls, but we didn't keep in contact after Pittsburgh.

Unless it's because of family, going from Chicago to an AM station in Lexington that no one is listening to has a bad twist to it. Cross needed a job.

A consultant had recommended Cross to Lynn Martin—who owned 1300 and a number of other stations. Cross had just recently come to Lexington for his job interview. About a week or so later, he calls me up. "Cutler, Cross here," he says. "What are you doing tomorrow? Can you meet me for a cup of coffee before work?"

Cross was going to do a sports talk radio show, and he wanted me to do it with him. Our secret place to meet was a Waffle House by the TV station.

They weren't going to pay me much for doing the show, but Cross kept telling me how he was going to make all this money on the side. He was quickly making a lot more money doing live commercials than I was making for doing the entire show. The deal was that he was going to split the live reads with me fifty-fifty. Plus, he was going to get me

319

some additional commercial work. He laid everything out on a napkin at the Waffle House. Most of my money was going to come on the side, and he told me I could never tell Lynn Martin because he would get really mad.

We started doing the show, and it's very successful. It's funny and fun. We're bantering up and back, and the listeners are loving it. It was a really good radio show.

Less than six months into the show, Cross and I start having problems. He's doing all the live reads, and I'm not getting any. It started getting really contentious. It was nasty. He was getting a lot of money on the side. Half of it was supposed to go to me, but I wasn't seeing any of it.

I found out from a salesman at the station that the reason sales people weren't getting me any live reads was because they thought I wasn't *allowed* to do live reads or commercials because of my TV gig. Cross was in charge of the sales staff.

I WENT NUTS! Before we went on the air that day, I was screaming at Cross in the studio. As far as I'm concerned, he stole my money. That's the way I looked at it—stole my money—and I told him that. From then on, our relationship was done. Whenever he said something stupid on the air, I would often put him down. There's a difference between attacking and bantering, and this was not bantering. He was tired of me attacking him.

The ironic thing was that the show was popular. It was interesting. The ratings book came out, and we more than doubled WVLK—which had previously been No. 1 in that time slot forever. It only took us one book to become No. 1 on AM radio.

I had told Lynn Martin before I started, that when—*not if*—we got ratings, that he would either have to pay me or I was going to quit. That's exactly what ended up happening. But getting to that point was fun, just sometimes painful.

By this time, Cross and I were barely talking. This went from a fun show that we both looked forward to doing—to this. I kept on attacking Cross at every opportunity. I remember there was a feature article in the newspaper about a UK tight end. I knew Cross often didn't read the sports page, so I purposely quizzed him about it on the air. I understand that he had a lot on his plate and didn't know Lexington—but I told him he needed to become more knowledgeable about what we were talking about on the air.

Cross got mad and insisted that I worked for him. I told him I would *never* work for him. Either this was a partnership or he could go kiss my butt. All I was asking him to do was to read the paper every day. Then when I said something, he could react off of it and look good. The whole point was to make each other look good. I was good at spitting things out, and he was really good at reacting to it. For a while, that worked really well. At this point, our relationship had really deteriorated.

When I knew Cross hadn't read the story, I went on a five-minute rant. I went crazy on him on the air. During the commercial break, he started yelling at me, and I got up and started walking out. "Do your *bleeping* homework," I yelled at him as I walked out the door. He followed me, and we were screaming at each other outside. When we came back in, we sat down and turned the mic on. I told him to do his homework next time, and we went into it again.

Shortly after, I met with Lynn Martin after the rating book came out. I reminded him what I had told him before we started the show. He suddenly changed his mind and wanted to see a few more rating books before paying me a decent salary for my time.

I asked Chris to meet me in a parking lot. He pulled up and I said, "Chris, it's pretty simple. *Bleep* you, I quit!" I rolled up the window and drove away.

Funny how the ratings dropped like a stock market crash after I left.

For at least a year, Chris and I wouldn't say a word to each other. We'd walk by each other at Rupp Arena, and he would turn his head. A little over a year goes by, and I finally call him up. I told him this was really stupid. I knew we couldn't be friends like before, but it's stupid that we can't say "hi" when we see each other at a game. I suggested we talk it out.

We agreed to have coffee at Starbucks. I tell him to go first, which surprises him—because I always liked to talk first. I tell him that he can say anything he wants, and I'll just sit there and take it. Then I tell him that when he's finished, he's going to "shut the *bleep* up and listen to me."

He started telling me all the things he didn't like about me. He went on for quite a while. I actually agreed with most of what he said. But, when it was my turn to talk, I told him he was missing the whole point of *why* I was the way I was. I went through the whole thing about him drawing on napkins and me not making all the money he said I was supposed to be making. I reminded him of how I went to him two or three times to nicely voice my concerns about what was going on. I knew I wasn't going to get rich doing this, but just doubling what I was making doing the show wouldn't have taken a lot of effort on his part. I mean, sometimes the guy was making over fifty dollars an hour on the side doing a local radio show. It was a three-hour show. I was happy he was making a lot of money, as long as he split it with me fifty-fifty. I would have been happy with close to 50/50.

After I went on and on and on about the whole thing, he apologized. I told him I wasn't going to apologize for acting the way I did because it was all his fault. "It *was* my fault," he agreed. I told him that we probably wouldn't be having coffee together, but next time I see him at the game, I'm going to say "hi." We shook hands and buried the hatchet. Chris and I have been fine ever since.

After all of that, *money* isn't why I told Cross, *"Bleep you, I quit,"* which for a few minutes felt great. Notice I said for a few minutes. After that rush wore off, I was actually quite sad.

I had stopped trusting people in the business long before Cross. But with him, I let my guard down. The truth was that I was mad at myself for trusting Cross.

There was a time period that *Cutler and Cross* or *Cross and Cutler* was really good—and we both knew it. Forget Lexington, it could have been a really good talk show in lots of big markets.

That radio show could have ended up being syndicated in every market where Kentucky Football and Basketball had radio outlets—and we talked about that. The show was that good, and if we were smart, we both could have made a lot more money and had a great time doing it.

After I retired, Chris said I was the best partner he'd ever had. I was speechless.

87

Shane and Jared—Joined at the Hip

They are two of my favorite people in Lexington—Shane Boyd and Jared Lorenzen.

At age thirty-seven, Shane was still playing pro football. I teased him about being way too old to be playing. We bust each other all the time. He responded by ranting back about how he was different than others, about how tough he was, and about how much he still loved the game. All true!

I will always believe that Shane Boyd made a mistake coming to Kentucky. Should I tell you I told him that while he was still the star quarterback for Henry Clay High? I told him I didn't think he'd get a chance because Jared Lorenzen was ahead of him, and that's a battle at times you can't win.

That's not meant to be negative towards anyone.

Shane Boyd, like all quarterbacks, needed snaps. He needed to play more. I believe that if he went to a school in which he could have started for three or four years, he would have played in the NFL. He was smart, and he was super tough. He was a leader. He had a rocket of an arm that wasn't as accurate as he thought it was. I always thought he threw the ball too hard. Even back then, I wondered if he changed his motion like Mike Leach's quarterbacks do—with a tighter throwing motion to be more accurate—it could have changed everything for him.

Jared Lorenzen deserved to start. He threw some of the best passes I've ever seen at Commonwealth Stadium. His arm was one of the best I've seen. That's not just college, but I watched warmups in the NFL for fourteen years hosting the Bengals Radio Network. That's a lot of quarterbacks, and not just the starters.

Jared's game against Georgia where he threw for a record 528 yards is one of the most amazing performances I've ever seen. Wouldn't surprise me if his record of 10,354 yards passing at Kentucky stands for fifty years.

The starting quarterback for an NFL team doesn't always have the best arm on the team. Back in 1980, Seattle Seahawks starting quarterback Jim Zorn came to Boise, Idaho for a clinic. He not only told me that he had the worst arm of the three quarterbacks on the team, but as a little kid, he wanted to be a fireman—there was no thought about playing football. Zorn threw for over 21,000 yards in the NFL.

At UK, Jared threw some passes that looked like rainbow punts that hit wideouts in stride. Too much of Jared was based upon his weight versus his talent. Jared was never going to be skinny, but if he didn't have a weight problem, I think he would have been drafted and would have played in the NFL forever.

I remember watching Jared play basketball in the Sweet Sixteen, the wonderful Kentucky state championship tournament in high school. It was great because he was a role player. Derek Smith, who wound up playing tight end at Kentucky, was the star.

Jared was not only willing to take a secondary role, he embraced it. That's all I needed to see to know he was all about the team. This was before he got really heavy. He would sprint down the court and pass and get rebounds as a role player.

Derek Smith was really good. If I put a short list together of players who should have made it big but didn't for whatever reason, Derek Smith would definitely be in the top five. I thought Derek was going to be a starting tight end playing on Sundays for a long time. That's not negative towards Derek, who was always terrific to interview and talk to.

Basketball forward Richard Madison would also be up there when it came to having potential that made you scratch your head.

Richard Madison was one of the great athletes I have seen come to the University of Kentucky. At 6'6" and 215 pounds, the "Master Blaster" was a Parade All-American and a McDonald's All-American who averaged less than six points a game at Kentucky. He could throw a fastball in the nineties and run like a deer. He was strong, and he could jump. He was the kind of athlete a lot of guys have looked at and said, "If I had his body, I would have made it in the NBA with my work ethic." I thought that myself.

That opinion of Richard Madison goes back to when he played at UK. When I was finishing up the book, Kenny "Sky" Walker talked about Madison.

"Could have been the best forward ever at Kentucky, if he would have applied himself and stayed focused," said Kenny. "Sky" wasn't being mean, he was just being matter of fact. There are more athletes like Madison that most of us remember. Not everyone loves the game. Not everyone wants to work as hard as you need to do to make it big.

Remember how good Kenny already was when Madison showed up to Kentucky. When Kenny saw his potential, he was concerned about Madison taking some of his playing time—which never happened. Eddie Sutton used to get on Madison and tell him how good he could be if he worked as hard as Kenny "Sky" Walker and Winston Bennett.

Potential is a funny thing. When the New York Giants cut Jared Lorenzen, they did it because of his weight. Tom Coughlin, the New York Giants coach, really liked Jared. Eli Manning, their starting quarterback, really liked Jared. They told him to lose weight, and he didn't.

When Jared died—way too early at the age of thirty-eight—Eli Manning came to Kentucky to say good-bye. Due to his weight, which at one point topped five hundred pounds, Jared developed kidney and heart issues, as well as an infection.

Jared was funny, and he was sensitive.

I always think of Jared and Shane as joined at the hip.

Remember that Shane could also throw a baseball over ninety miles-per-hour, and that he played minor league baseball. Had he just played baseball, he might have made the Big Leagues. And I'll say it again—I think if he'd just played quarterback at a school where he would have been able to start for years, I think he would have made it to the NFL. That's not a rip on Hal Mumme. That's not a rip on Shane. That's just the circumstances surrounding the situation. I thought at the time that Shane needed to find a place to *play*. That's partly because he's one of my favorites to wear Kentucky across his chest, and partly because I thought he had that much potential. Practice can only get you so far. You need to have the reps in a game to grow and develop.

There is a reason why so many talented quarterbacks who aren't the starter transfer today. And many have not only made it in the NFL, but probably *never* would have if they didn't find another school. I'm amazed this trend didn't start a long time ago.

Shane is tough, kind, caring, and a natural leader. When they had the "ice bucket challenge" a few years back promoting awareness for ALS, both Shane and Jared got me. They ganged up on me and pounded me about stories I did with them. They were prepared for how they were going to pick on me, and it ended up being really funny. The fact that both of them got along as well as they did based upon how they competed directly against each other speaks volumes about their character.

It's not easy to compete so hard on the field and leave it all there when you walk off. I don't know how athletes do that. It's a credit to anyone who is able to do it. It's a credit to both Shane and Jared. It shows you what kind of people they are.

After all this time, I'm still in pain writing this. On July 3, 2019, we lost Jared Lorenzen.

Shane Boyd was crushed when Lorenzen died. He put this on Facebook.

> "Today I lay my brother Jared Lorenzen to rest in Northern Ky. Love & surely miss you. I'll remember all the great times we had, adversity we fought through together & all the fun we experienced. With a world that tried to drive a stake between us, we remained 1 unit. You're not gone, God just moved you to paradise. Set up the garbage cans so we can do a football toss w/ The Messiah in Heaven to see who wins milk & cookies."

In 2017, Jared sent this to Shane.

> "What's up my brother. Man, just reaching out to you and letting you know I love you. Always been my brother and we grew stronger and closer together with what we went through as QB's at UK & to let you know I'm riding with you on this journey. Anyway you need me or want me to be part of it I'm down for you. Always lifting you up in prayer and thinking of you."

I'm not ashamed to admit that I cried after reading this—just as I did when we lost Jared.

88

Dennis Johnson

Dennis Johnson from Harrodsburg High School, who was National Player of the Year for many media outlets—and will always be one of the greatest high school football players in Kentucky—also had a wonderful career at the University of Kentucky. In 2001, he led the SEC in tackles for loss, sacks, and forced fumbles.

As far as pro football, Dennis was picked in the third round of the 2002 NFL draft by the Arizona Cardinals. He played two full seasons and ended his career with 57 tackles and 3 sacks in 29 games. I'll always believe the NFL quit on the defensive end way too soon.

Dennis Johnson: My most memorable story on Alan Cutler was when he interviewed my father, my mother, and myself during my freshman year at UK. I was struggling rushing the passer, and Alan asked my dad what I needed to do to get better. I'm mid interview/sentence—and my dad began using my mom as an offensive lineman to demonstrate what moves I needed to work on. I wasn't shocked, but I can remember Alan laughing and having a good time with the rest of the interview.

I told Alan that this is just how we roll.

Alan started my TV career by calling me the biggest second grader in the country. I was already 5'7" and 135 pounds in second grade. I had no idea at the time how much press we would receive. He put me on the map.

When it comes to athletes and families, in the history of the state of Kentucky, the Johnsons are high on any list.

89

Favorite UK Athlete I've Ever Covered

W hen I was a kid in broadcasting, I would occasionally ask coaches who their best or favorite player was. They would always tell me they couldn't answer my question because they might slight someone else or hurt someone's feelings. Way back then, over forty years ago, their lack of an answer used to bother me. I was like, "COME ON, TELL ME WHO YOU LIKE THE BEST!" I'm now going to be partly guilty of answering like them—but here's my answer.

If I had to pick an athlete who was the smartest, most caring, and most logical of anybody I've covered in my entire career—going all the way back to Farmington, New Mexico—I'm not sure I could find anyone better, more rounded as an individual and as an athlete, than Jacob Tamme.

Forget the fact that he was All-SEC a couple of times, that he played nine years in the NFL, and was on one of the greatest high school teams Kentucky will ever have—winning four straight state championships at Boyle County. Forget the fact that he's Kentucky's all-time top pass-catching tight end with 133 catches for 1,417 yards— Jacob Tamme was also really smart. He should run for governor.

Jacob is a farmer on land that has been in his family for a long time, and he's also in the horse business. Five years ago, I went out to Machmer Hall, owned by friends, Craig and Carrie Brogden. They've built a beautiful horse farm. I was talking to Carrie Brogden about an upcoming Derby, and she told me one of her new clients is Jacob Tamme. Jacob now works a farm that has been in his family going all the way back to his great grandfather.

Before he retired from the NFL, I asked Jacob, "Would you rather catch the winning touchdown in the Super Bowl or win the Kentucky

Derby?" Jacob never ducked anything, and I'll never forget the laugh on his face when he answered. "Don't make me make that choice," he answered.

The resurgence of Kentucky Football under Coach Rich Brooks, who coached at UK from 2003 through 2009, happened a lot because of Rich Brooks obviously—but also because of Tamme, Keenon Burton, Wesley Woodyard, and Andre Woodson. They were leaders. They were all great people who took control of the locker room. They all cared. They literally willed this program to change. They all respected Rich Brooks—tough, old school—but they were good with that because they knew Brooks was fair. The other thing about those four was the respect they had for each other. I NEVER detected an ounce of jealousy between them, and I did so many interviews with them.

Rich Brooks said the players lifted him up. They trusted Rich—and accepted that UK would be a physical team. That never happens without those four players getting behind their coach. I know I'm leaving out a lot of other players who you could add to that list.

One of the things that happens as sports society moves forward is that you can still be tough, but being fair is more important. Back in the fifties and sixties, if you were mean and tough—but not fair—you often got away with it because of the power that coaches had. It's a lot more difficult to get away with that meanness today because players are more independent—and they should be. That's one of the reasons there are more transfers now than ever before.

What Jacob Tamme has done with his *Swings for Soldiers* charity is one of the greatest things I've seen. Jacob is a man of faith. He told me one time, "God has blessed us [he and his wife Allison] in many ways, and part of that blessing was to share it." He's raised so much money for that charity and donated more money himself than he's ever going to tell me. He's helped out so many vets who come home and have lost an arm or a leg or have some other physical impairment. He and his charity have built homes for these men and women. It's beautiful. It started with a golf tournament and auction. It has grown into one of the purest events I've ever seen when it comes to what an athlete is doing.

I just couldn't do this book without including Jacob Tamme. There are so many athletes I could do stories on that we're not putting in the book because the book would be seven hundred pages. But I'd be remiss if I didn't devote a chapter to Jacob. I think he's one of the most special human beings I've met—who just happened to be a clutch tight end.

Winning might be Tamme's middle name. He was part of four state championship teams at Boyle County High. Even back then, his coach—Chuck Smith—called Tamme a "great leader."

Shortly after I retired, Judy and I took one of those lifetime vacations to Spain with my roommate from college, Jimmy Slevin, and his lovely wife Pam. We were on a train, about to get off, and I needed a bathroom. I had to go to the next car because the one in our car was occupied.

I walk into the next car, and there is Keenan Burton with family and friends. We're in Spain yelling at each other. We both looked at each other totally amazed.

When it comes to doing the right thing for the right reasons, Tamme, Burton, Wesley Woodyard, and Andre Woodson were as good as it gets.

90

Fired from WLAP

Out of nowhere in 2007, WVLK and WLAP—two of the top AM radio stations in Lexington—are on me like crazy to do sports talk. I can't remember who approached me first, but they asked that I not say a word to anyone. I told them I would tell my wife, and if the talks got serious, I would tell my boss at LEX18. You don't want to surprise your boss and have him find out from somebody else that you're doing radio.

There's so much gossip in radio and TV that it's ridiculous. The other station somehow found out that the first station had already come to me—and at that point, I hadn't even told my boss.

It then became intense. You would think it would be great for two stations fighting for my services—but it was an awful experience. I was brutally honest in my negotiations, which really ticked some people off. Sales people from different stations all talk. There are very few secrets. The entire process was very uncomfortable.

"Here's the deal," I finally told both of them. "You have twenty-four hours to come up with your best offer. I'm not dragging this on. I'm OK with working at either station."

That made both stations mad, as they both thought I should only want to come to work for them. That's silly. The whole situation was ridiculous.

It was an even tougher decision because I had a fear that if I went to WLAP, they wouldn't allow me to be me because WLAP had the UK game broadcasts and the coaches shows. They'd be afraid of anyone saying anything that would tick off the UK brass, who I knew could be sensitive. WVLK had previously had those rights forever. WLAP went out of their way to tell me not to worry about it, but I was never really comfortable with their assurances. I made a mistake going with WLAP.

I should have taken the WVLK job.

When I agreed to the WLAP offer, WVLK called me a couple of minutes later with a much better offer. I had given WLAP my word, so I wasn't going to back out. Nevertheless, WLAP rushed over a contract within thirty minutes for me to read and sign. It was nuts.

I was an instant success. AM sports talk is rarely No. 1 in the entire market. Guess what? I was No. 1. I still have the ratings book. I brought in a lot of former athletes to do the show with me. It was fun, it was funny, and it was informative. The show was a big hit, and I was proud of what I had done.

Well, there was a problem. It had nothing to do with me or with local management within WLAP. It was solely a corporate decision from higher up. Radio and TV politics essentially got me and two others fired.

The UK Basketball and Football broadcasting contract had recently gone from WVLK Cumulus Media to WLAP Clear Channel Communications. That changed everything. My radio show was on Clear Channel. Our TV competitor, Channel 27—was doing the news and weather for Clear Channel, and they didn't want anybody from LEX18 to be on the station which was doing the UK games—so they did their best to get rid of me. They also fired Lee Cruse from our TV station on the same day. Farrah Wellman, who worked with LEX18 during elections, also got fired that same day.

I have never held a grudge against the local management of WLAP. Michael Jordan, the operations manager at the time, told me he was ordered to fire me. He told me he didn't want to fire me and had nothing to do with the decision. I believed him.

The other problem in all of this was that I didn't trust my gut. Almost every time I don't trust my gut, the situation comes back to bite me.

WLAP tried hard to convince me that I could say anything I wanted—even if it involved something negative about UK. I don't do personal attacks, but I told WLAP there would be times I was going to criticize UK. I still wanted UK to do well, but I felt like I could still be impartial and fair in my commentary along the way—because that's how I've always been.

You should be able to talk about UK missing a bunch of free throws versus Arizona in 1997 which cost them the national championship. Why don't people bring that up more? You can tell the truth and still want the team to win. I've always been able to do that, and I've always laughed at old time newspaper guys who claimed that you couldn't.

I did a rant once on something against the team, and UK called to complain. They wanted me out. What UK didn't know was that since I was also working in Cincinnati at the time, I had sources at Clear Channel who knew what was going on. I had a wonderful source tell me that UK didn't want me around because UK considered Clear Channel as *their station.*

I promise you that if anyone on WLAP radio goes on the air today and starts ripping UK basketball coach John Calipari like crazy, some-body from UK is going to call and tell them to chill out. Somebody's job might be in jeopardy. That's the part of this business that not many people know about. I've talked to people on the UK network who love the university. There were times when the football team wasn't doing well, and they felt like they were broadcasting with a chastity belt on. They simply couldn't say what they really felt when UK was playing poorly. They have to couch it, make up excuses, and sugarcoat the poor play.

I interviewed a guy on my show who wrote an article ripping UK. After he explained his position, I counterbalanced it with some opin-ions of my own. UK calls and complains. I was called into the station manager's office. They weren't happy to say the least. It was obvious that I got called in because UK called them.

I then got called into the program director's office again and was told that I was actually fair with how I presented the segment with the guy criticizing UK—and UK goes crazy.

I got into a heavy argument with UK Athletics Director Mitch Barnhart at Rupp Arena over the episode. He said some things I didn't like, so I said some things he didn't like. It got loud. I went back and told my boss about it because I didn't want him hearing it from any-body else. He told me I couldn't be like that. I told him that nobody talks to me like Mitch did. I didn't start it.

If somebody wants to tell me that they didn't like what I did on the radio, that's fine. If the athletics director wants to tell me why, I have no problem with that. But I'm not going to be talked to like that by anybody.

There are a lot of things about Mitch Barnhart that the average fan doesn't know. He's human. There are a lot of different sides to him that may surprise you. I know he complained about me. He kept talk-ing about how WLAP was *his radio station.* On one hand, I'll never forget that, but on the other hand, you have to put yourself in his shoes. He's the athletics director and has a relationship with the radio station covering the team. The UK contract was worth a fortune. Although my show was top rated, I was a little pawn to WLAP. The amount of money I generated for WLAP was *nothing* compared to the UK contract. I was expendable.

I should have never taken the WLAP job.

It was a *dumb* move on my part.

How would you feel about being No. 1 in the market when the ratings come out, and you got fired? And not surprisingly, the ratings dropped the very next book. It was a big drop after I left.

91

Don Shula's My Old Kentucky Home

This is one of my favorite stories. In 1957, Blanton Collier's Kentucky Wildcats had a ridiculous number of assistant coaches who went on to become head coaches in the NFL. Don Shula—together with Chuck Knox, Howard Schnellenberger, Ed Rutledge, Ermal Allen, John North, Bob Cummings, and Bill Arnsparger—comprised one of the greatest college coaching staffs of all time and yet, Kentucky wasn't a great football team that year. Although they finished the year only 3-7, that doesn't mean they didn't get the most out of the talent they had.

Don Shula retired as the winningest coach in the history of the NFL with 347 career wins and two Super Bowl trophies. He's famous for guiding his 1972 Miami Dolphins team to an undefeated season—something I'm not sure anyone will ever be able to do again.

I'm covering the Kentucky Derby. My live shot that year was on the fifth floor of the clubhouse at Churchill Downs. A guy who's an executive of a healthcare company comes up to me and says, "Alan, why don't you come up to our box and have a drink?" I tell him I can't do that because I'm still working, so he asks me to come by later and watch the Derby with him after I'm off the air. I thought, "Sure, why not?"

We got off the air at four o'clock, and I went into their suite. We got to talking, and suddenly he said, "Let me introduce you to Coach." I turn around and Don Shula is in his box. He introduces me to Shula, and we go through the perfunctory introductions and greetings. We talk for about a minute and then head out to watch the Derby.

There are 140,000 people standing up when they play *My Old Kentucky Home,* and Don Shula is right in front of me. I can tell you that Don Shula not only knew every single word of *My Old Kentucky Home,* but he was belting it out and singing it louder than anyone else in the private box. Two or three words in, and I was freaking out and staring at him. It didn't take very long for the forty or so people in his box to start staring at him also.

This is Don Shula, one of the greatest NFL coaches of all time, an assistant at Kentucky in the 1950s, belting out the words to *My Old Kentucky Home* louder than anybody. After that, comes the national anthem. As soon as that was done, I grabbed his arm and said, "Coach, I can't believe that not only did you remember the song, but you knew every word." He then grabbed *my* arm and said, "You have no idea how special my time was at the University of Kentucky."

I then told him about a picture I saw of him in 1957 with all the UK assistant coaches that made it to the NFL. He immediately grabs my arm really hard—like I'm one of his players—and asks me if I could get a copy to him. He writes his address on a sheet of paper and makes me *promise* that I'll send it to him.

I called Tony Neely, Assistant AD for Athletics Communications and Public Relations, to ask for the picture—and he's as excited as I am that Don Shula wanted it. I write a nice little note and mail it to Don Shula.

Besides his singing, I can still picture the huge smile on Shula's face when he talked about how much he loved coaching at Kentucky and how close that coaching staff was. It was a beautiful thing.

Head Coach Blanton Collier—from Paris, Kentucky—would soon be pushed out, which I still think was stupid—and he became head coach of the Cleveland Browns in 1963. He would go on to win an NFL Championship that season while coaching Jimmy Brown, who I consider the greatest football player of all time.

92

9/11

Every American is affected by 9/11. I lost one of my college roommates on that fateful Tuesday morning in 2001. My best friend thought he lost his cousin who was a captain at the fire station right by the World Trade Center.

I think everyone remembers where they were and what they were doing during 9/11. I was at Memorial Coliseum where Adolph Rupp's teams used to play. From there, like a lot of other Americans, everything was a blur. I got to a TV set as quick as I could. Considering what happened, I have no idea how we got a sportscast together that day. I'm not even sure if we had a sportscast. Like I said, that whole day was a blur.

My former college roommate, Kenneth Van Auken, worked at the World Trade Center in New York. Jimmy Slevin and I were just at Kenny's house the month before, eating steak, drinking too much beer, and telling old college stories, and acting stupid—which we were good at.

Kenny had one of the great laughs, a great smile, and we would sing Frank Sinatra with Jimmy Slevin, also a college roommate who I'm still close to. Back then, I would sometimes play Sinatra on radio. That wasn't the normal thing for a college kid in the 1970s.

I'm watching the 9/11 coverage about people surviving and getting out of the twin towers, and I'm trying to be positive about Kenny's fate. I got a call that night from another college friend telling me that they couldn't find Kenny. I then called Kenny's wife, Lorie, but she didn't pick up. I finally got a hold of her the next day. She's crying and says—they can't find Kenny. They never did.

Kenny worked at Cantor Fitzgerald. The financial services firm lost over six hundred and fifty of its employees in the terrorist attack that morning. You may have heard the stories of people calling home and leaving messages to their loved ones right before they died.

Oprah did a story about Kenny and filmed it exactly where Kenny, Jimmy Slevin, and I were sitting just a month earlier. Oprah had the recording of Kenny calling and telling Lorie that he loved her and assuring her that he would be fine. That was the last time Lorie heard from him.

My wife, Judy, taped the story for me. About halfway through, I walked out of the house crying. I never watched the rest of the story.

Kenny and Lorie's kids were the same ages as mine. I can't imagine how hard it was for both of them to have lost their father at such a young and impressionable age.

Lorie went on to become one of the four *Jersey Girls*, a very vocal group of survivors and family members of the victims advocating for the formation of an independent commission to investigate the attacks. They went everywhere, calling on everyone, and petitioning for a thorough and credible investigation into the tragedy.

Lorie and I didn't really keep in touch—but four years ago, Lorie surprisingly showed up when we invited her over to Jimmy's house for our annual get-together. As we sat around the kitchen table, I politely asked her what she really thought happened with 9/11.

Lorie and her activist group believe that 9/11 *was* a conspiracy. They concluded that it was impossible for a structure like the World Trade Center to have collapsed the way it did as people have previously speculated. They didn't make that conclusion—they had experts look at the structure. The group strongly believes that the truth has been purposely hidden from the American people.

Unless you google *Jersey Girls* and start doing some reading, it's tough to understand how much work and sacrifice they put into attempting to find out the truth, which I'm convinced we don't know.

We've recently started keeping in better contact. Being grandparents, there is the joy of sharing pictures a few times a year. I can't see a picture of her and her beautiful family without thinking of Kenny.

I've been back to the World Trade Center now four times after 9/11. I always make it a point to stare at Kenny's name on the memorial grounds. It's always an emotional time for me. If you're ever in New York, you should go and experience it.

You cannot visit the World Trade Center and not cry. When you see the humongous chucks of steel and how it's been sliced apart like heating up butter and putting a knife to it—it's just unbelievable. When the

9/11 museum opened, Mark Nussenfeld—another dear friend and college roommate of mine—spent hours and hours just walking around the grounds with red eyes. You can't help it.

The fourth time I visited, my brother drove us with our kids. The new World Trade Center was going up at the time, and Jenna and J.J. had never seen it. This was at night. With the skyline, it was absolutely spectacular.

Bobby Everett and I have been laughing for about fifty-five years. After his battle with skin cancer, which scared me, we will often now say "love you" before we hang up. His younger cousin, George Mayer, who I knew when we were kids, became a captain for the Fire Department of New York City. There's a fire station around the block from the World Trade Center. George was a captain for that station during 9/11.

George gets a call before 9/11 from a friend in the fire station asking him to switch shifts. George should have been part of the first responders. But, because of the switch, he was off duty. George was listed as being dead because of what happened to the rest of his normal shift.

We should never forget what happened that day.

Part 9

My Time in Cincinnati

93

WLW in Cincinnati

W LW Radio in Cincinnati was a frat house. During my time there, they had some great talent. It's amazing how many Marconi Awards—which goes to the best talent in America—they had.

I was hired in 2002. They had three Marconi Award winners then. Ironically, two of the most talented people—Jim Scott in the morning and Gary Burbank in the afternoon—were also two of the nicest guys.

Gary was one of greatest disc jockeys of all time. He created many characters—like Earl Pitts—who were syndicated all over America. When I first met Gary, I remember this little dude, wearing old jeans and an old shirt, walking in with a briefcase. In the briefcase was a putter and a couple of golf balls. That's it. He seemed quiet when you started talking to him. Open the microphone...and WOW!

The few times I was in his studio doing sports updates, I would watch Gary putt. I was honored to be a part of a station with this level of talent. I was doing weekend SportsTalk and some fill-ins during the week, besides being the host of the Cincinnati Bengals Radio Network. I was doing all of this while I was still doing TV full time in Lexington.

When I was hired, Darryl Parks—the program director who taught me so much—asked, "Cut Man, who are you talking to?" I froze, because honestly I wasn't sure. Darryl said, "You're talking to the forty-year-old white guy. That's our audience."

This wasn't a racial comment. What he was saying was that if women want to listen to us—great! If African Americans want to listen to us—great! But you have to program to your audience. The forty-year-old white guy was our audience. One of the mistakes that radio and TV stations make is that they don't always know who their audience is.

Just before I was hired, Darryl, Dave Armbruster—known as Yid, who was in charge of sports—and I were sitting having lunch at an outdoor café a few blocks from the station. I thought I was there for the job interview, but Darryl later told me that he had already decided to hire me. "We just wanted to see if you could fit in with all the crazy people here," he tells me. "You'll fit in just fine." That's how I found out I was hired.

I'll never forget the first phone call from Darryl. He said, "How would you like to be the host of the Cincinnati Bengals Radio Network?" My response was far from brilliant, but typical me. "No sh*t?" I said. He laughed and said, "THAT'S why I'm calling you." In my world, I will always owe Darryl and Yid.

Just before my second year doing the Bengals Radio Network, Darryl said to me, "Cut Man, don't you want to know why I hired you?"

It turns out that on his job interview to come back to Cincinnati for a large promotion, Darryl was driving around town and listening to different stations. I just happened to be on the radio at a small station that was doing sports. He heard me and said to himself, "Someday I'm going to hire this guy."…Crazy, how things turned out.

WLW left you alone to do what you wanted. It was amazing some of the dumb things that people said about other people on that radio station.

Darryl Parks only showed up to the studio twice in all the years that I did either SportsTalk or the Bengals. The first time was about thirty seconds before I was about to go on the air for the first Bengals game. "Cut Man, you OK?" he asks. "Yeah, get out of here," I answered back jokingly.

The second time was a Saturday. I was doing SportsTalk in the afternoon before doing the pregame show for Reds Baseball. After the Reds game was over, I would do SportsTalk until midnight. It was a routine I had done countless times. Darryl walked into the studio about a minute before I was to go on the air. "Cut Man, what are you talking about today?" he asks. I can remember it like it was yesterday. I knew something was up because he never asked me what I was talking about.

Marty Brennaman, the Hall of Fame radio voice of the Reds, had just signed a three-year contract. His broadcasting partner, "The" Joe Nuxhall (Nuxy), just signed a two-year contract. I was planning to start yelling about how the Reds were trying to get rid of Nuxy—because why wouldn't you give Nuxy a three-year contract just like you did Marty? They were great together. The love they had for each other was real. I was going to let it rip. I was going to go nuts and have a lot of fun with it.

"Cut Man, you can't say that," Darryl tells me. "It's the truth, but you just can't say it." He was telling me I couldn't say what I wanted because the Reds on radio had been on WLW for decades and decades, and the station needed that relationship to continue. That relationship was tons more important than a part-time sports talk show host. I couldn't talk about Nuxy, one of the most beloved and popular guys in the history of Cincinnati, and if he was really wanted by the Reds. I couldn't question the obvious. Did they think he was getting too old?

Now what was I going to talk about? "Ahh, you'll figure something out—by the way, you're right—have a good show," Darryl says as he turns around and walks out.

For a second or two, I froze—and then said something out loud after Darryl left that I can't put in the book. I just trusted myself— I had no idea what I was going to say—but when the light went on, I started rambling about something else.

What was even crazier was that Darryl apologized for doing this to me. He didn't have to do that. In that crazy moment, as much as I respected him, my respect went up another notch. For Darryl to tell me I couldn't talk about something was unheard of. He was the boss, so I was going to listen to him. When Nuxy's contract was brought up a couple of times during the show, I just danced around it.

With all the ripping and nasty comments that were made at that station, that was the only time I was told not to talk about something.

At the time I was getting hired, Andy Furman—nicknamed "Furball,"—was doing sports talk at night on WLW. Andy was very good on the air, but I don't know how much of the time he believed in some of the crap he said.

Andy got in trouble for something he said about Cincinnati Bengals owner Mike Brown. He told me that he thought he said that Mike Brown was "sperm lucky." Mike's father, Paul—for my money—did more to change modern football than anyone. Paul Brown was brilliant and way ahead of his time.

Darryl and Yid asked me about this during the hiring process. I told them that I'd rip people, but I'm never going to make it personal—it's not my personality. I remember sitting there and seeing Darryl and Yid kind of nod at each other. That was the last piece of the puzzle. They just wanted to make sure I wasn't going to say things similar to what Andy had said because it became a huge problem for them.

There's a point where a radio host can make it uncomfortable for listeners on the air. I know at times I have done that, but I wasn't trying to. What I don't like are people who make stuff up just to get people to listen to them. *DRIVES ME OUT OF MY MIND!*

There's enough out there to talk about if you really believe in sports and have strong opinions. There are some people on national radio right now who I'm convinced don't always believe what they're talking about. Just because you can debate it, doesn't mean that you believe it.

I was even asked multiple times by WLW management to take a side whether I believed it or not and make a controversial argument on radio. I told them I wouldn't do it because my credibility meant the world to me. I was on TV in Lexington, and doing that just wasn't smart.

94

Snakebit in Cincinnati

I don't know who's the most snakebit organization in the NFL, but the Cincinnati Bengals have to be up there. They haven't won a playoff game in forever—since 1990—it's the longest streak in the NFL. Marvin Lewis was the Bengals head coach from 2003 through 2018. There is no other NFL team that would keep a coach that long without winning a playoff game. They're snakebit.

I'm convinced that the Bengals lost Super Bowl XXIII in 1988 partly because of their starting fullback, Stanley Wilson—who had already been suspended for two seasons by the NFL in 1985 and 1987 for violating the league's drug policy.

The night before the Super Bowl, Wilson lost his battle with cocaine again. That was strike three—he was kicked out of the NFL forever.

Wilson was a tough blocker, and an underrated runner, who scored two touchdowns in the first two playoff games to help get the Bengals to the Super Bowl.

Because of the condition of the field, Bengals coach Sam Wyche, a brilliant offensive mind, believed Wilson could have had a big day running the ball. But, the night before the game when Wilson didn't show up to a meeting, the Bengals sent running backs coach Jim Anderson to his room.

"They found him in the bathtub naked, coked out of his mind," Bengals offensive coordinator Bruce Coslet said to the Cincinnati Enquirer. "So they got him dressed, called the paramedics, and were taking him to the hospital when he ran away. He literally ran down the steps of the hotel and was gone before they could get him in the ambulance. I never saw him again. They didn't find him for three or four days, I guess."

Or, what about Tim Krumrie? Pound for pound—for my money, in his prime—Tim Krumrie might have been the best defensive lineman in the NFL. What nose guard makes 152 tackles in a season? Only 270 pounds, he missed only four games in his twelve-year career, but what happened in Super Bowl XXIII dearly cost the Bengals. Krumrie shattered his left tibia, fibula, and ankle on January 22, 1989.

It was one of those replays when someone shouts—Don't look! It was the 13th play of the game.

For Bengals fans, that Super Bowl loss was painful. Joe Montana, the 49ers' quarterback, played in four Super Bowls and won them all. One of the clutch quarterbacks of all time, he never threw an interception in any of those Super Bowls. Montana drove the 49ers ninety-two yards with a little over three minutes to go in that game. He hit wideout John Taylor with the winning touchdown pass from the 10-yard line with 34 seconds left to beat the Bengals 20-16. It was Taylor's only catch of the game.

In 1981, the Bengals also lost the Super Bowl to San Francisco 26-21. The Bengals led the NFL in fewest turnovers during that season. They had four on Super Sunday alone. Had the Bengals won, I'm sure that quarterback Kenny Anderson would be in the Hall of Fame. I guarantee that if Kenny played in New York instead of Cincinnati, he'd already be in.

Here's another instance of being snakebit. How about the time when Kimo Von Oelhoffen, a former Bengal playing defensive line for the Pittsburgh Steelers, ripped Carson Palmer's knee on the second play from scrimmage in the 2005 wildcard playoff game. That hit by Von Oelhoffen sucked the air not only from Paul Brown Stadium, but also from our broadcast booth. We believed the Bengals had a better team, but they ended up losing to Pittsburgh 31-17. I know the Bengals thought they had a shot at winning the Super Bowl that year.

There has been so much negativity around the franchise because of the losing seasons. You have to wonder what if Stanley Wilson didn't have a drug problem, what if Tim Krumrie didn't break his leg, and what if Carson Palmer didn't rip his knee? The Bengals probably win at least one Super Bowl...and everything would be different.

So with all those years and years of negativity, I always thought they were snakebit.

Despite all the negativity that was there before I started as host of the Cincinnati Bengals Radio Network (remember that from 1991 until 2005, the Bengals never had a winning season), there were plenty of fun moments after Marvin Lewis showed up.

I remember a couple of Monday Night Football games—plus the home playoff games—where just before you went on the air, you could feel the electricity in the broadcast booth. It doesn't happen very often, and it's not one of those things I can easily describe—but you remember those times when Paul Brown Stadium is electric, and the crowd is going crazy.

And then there are some games like the fourth game of the preseason against the Colts, when it seems like there are twelve people in the stands. You're asking yourself why the NFL even does this. Why can't the NFL figure out a better way to make money than to have preseason games where the stars are not going to play? It's sheer stupidity. Coaches like to say they are still evaluating talent before cutting the roster before the season starts. Nonsense! Coaches have seen these players enough. They can decide without that last preseason game.

You have to have the TV dollars, but they need to find a better way. If the marquee players are not going to play, you're just sticking it to the fans who pay money for the tickets.

The wonderful fans of Paul Brown Stadium deserve better.

95

Carson Palmer's Deep Drop

I have this strong belief that if I'm smarter than the coach, then the coach is making a mistake. I'm never supposed to be smarter than any coach. Coaches know their sport, but when it comes to common sense, some of them make bad decisions.

Common sense should be king. That's the way it should be.

The Cincinnati Bengals were having their training camp in Georgetown, Kentucky in 2004. I was planning to do an interview with quarterback Carson Palmer, who the Bengals selected with the No. 1 overall pick a year earlier in the 2003 NFL draft.

I'll never forget this. Carson Palmer—who won the Heisman Trophy in 2002—was a big, strong, studly athlete from USC who worked on his game after practice. I was convinced he was going to be a secret weapon for the Bengals during the upcoming season. He would take these deep drops—really deep drops—and roll out to both the right and the left. He would then throw the ball downfield and hit his receivers perfectly in stride. He's not just throwing the ball 10 or 15 yards. He's throwing the ball 40-50 yards on a line, on down and outs.

Carson was dropping back so deep, no pass rush was going to be able to get to him. All the offensive line has to do is hold their block. By that time, Carson would be so deep in the backfield that he's going to be able to easily get rid of the ball.

I'm watching him drop back throw after throw, right and left. When you roll out, you're cutting off half the field. That's a problem, but if you're rolling out, it takes so much longer to release the ball that you're asking the defense to cover the wide receivers that much longer. That can be a huge problem for any defense. Carson was throwing these laser-like, tight spiral bullets with a perfect arc. I watched him and thought it was amazing. This is what the Bengals were going to do this year.

I talk about this during the next pregame show. *How can any opponent stop this?* I've never seen a quarterback roll that deep and throw the ball like that. Granted, there was no defense. Granted, there was no one rushing. But when you see someone that talented do it well, you knew they had to be planning to use it.

It turns out that I hardly ever saw Carson Palmer roll out much during that regular season. It was stupefying. It reminded me of when Kentucky offensive coordinator, Eliot Uzelac, had Tim Couch run the option during his freshman season. Why have a super talented passer like Tim Couch run the ball in his first start? It made no sense.

One of the things I got to do for years was watch opposing quarterbacks warm up. For a one o'clock pm game, I'm in the broadcast booth by nine-thirty in the morning. I'm watching what's going on down on the field. I've gotten to watch everybody warm up—from Peyton Manning to whocver. Anyone that the Bengals have played, I've watched them all warm up.

Carson played 15 seasons in the NFL, made three Pro Bowls, and was the NFL passing touchdowns leader in 2005. Yet, they seldom had him roll out. It makes you wonder.

There's a yes and no to criticizing coaches. I like to think that every coach I've ever talked about knows tons more than I do about their particular sport. I also know that I've studied sports, and I've got common sense. I've also seen coaches under pressure make bad decisions. I'm not saying roll out every time—that would be stupid. But why not make some tired defensive lineman have to chase Carson Palmer? They'll be sucking wind in the fourth quarter.

Bengals owner Mike Brown is smart, and at times, a stubborn guy. He's often been accused of being very cheap. At one point, the Bengals players didn't even have big enough towels to wrap themselves with when they got out of the shower—that's how bad it was. I respect Mike Brown. He wasn't someone you could easily push around. I just hope he wins a Super Bowl before his time is up. He certainly deserves one.

Carson Palmer was tired of the losing culture in Cincinnati under Mike Brown. It got to the point where he couldn't take it anymore, so he forced himself out of town. He ended up having a really good career. I'll always believe that if he didn't get hurt in that playoff game against the Steelers, his career and the Bengals' fortunes could have been totally different.

96

Fired and Rehired

In 2009—after hosting the Bengals Radio Network since 2002, doing SportsTalk on weekends on WLW Radio, along with some fill-ins during the week, and hosting a daily talk show on 1530 Homer—I got a call that I had expected for quite a while.

They fired me.

Two minutes before I got the call, my producer—a great kid—called me to tell me he got fired. He was crying.

In a matter of months, Clear Channel fired over 2,400 people. Yes, 2,400!!!

This might sound strange, but instead of being upset—I was OK with it because with everything I was doing, it was way too much. Unlike some, I still had another job. It was obvious that when it came to my health and my family, I was working way too much.

There were a lot of talented people who had already been fired nationally by Clear Channel before this 2,400 massive cut, so I figured it was going to happen to me and wasn't worried about it.

I was just about to quit the daily morning show anyway. I was doing six to nine o'clock am Monday through Friday before starting my TV day. It was past crazy. When the Bengals played, with TV, plus SportsTalk on weekends—there were weeks I topped a hundred hours a week. I'm not kidding or exaggerating.

It had to be one of the dumbest routines I've ever done. All I did back then was work and workout. The truth is—I knew the quality of my work was slipping. I don't see how it couldn't have. Talk about burnout. By the way, I've always wondered how good of a talk show I could have done if that's all I did five days a week.

LEX18 was great during all of this. Tim Gilbert, the best general manager I've ever worked for, had set me up nicely for the morning

351

show in Cincinnati. He asked me what I needed? I told him that I could do the show from the extra production booth that was never used during that time period. An engineer came down from Cincinnati to put in a call screen, so I knew who the callers were, and my producer was in my ear whenever I needed him. LEX18 went out of their way to help me out, and I never forgot that.

With all of that said, I wasn't upset getting fired. I had gone months and months working seven days a week. Plus, when the Reds played on the west coast, I obviously had to talk about it in the morning—so the word "sleep" was a four-letter word.

As much as I liked doing SportsTalk—with the ninety-minute drive each way and doing call in shows lots of times before and after games, and prepping for the show—that came to thirty hours on weekends. The pay wasn't very good either. Weekend talent got almost nothing compared to their stars during the week. I get that.

Fast forward two years. When their contract was up, the Bengals owned the radio rights to their games, and they decided to keep it in house. They called me to come back and host the Bengals Radio Network—which I did until I retired.

I had a lot of fun on WLW, and I really enjoyed doing the Cincinnati Bengals Radio Network. But for the last two years that I did it, the fun was going away.

Part 10 (2007-2009)

Chasing Billy Gillispie

97

Chasing Billy Gillispie I—A Really Bad Fit

"What the hell are they thinking? *THIS IS STUPID!*" That was exactly what I was thinking on the night of April 5, 2007. That night was a "freak out" for anybody in the media trying to run down and get confirmation that Billy Gillispie was going to be the next head basketball coach at the University of Kentucky. You can't work fast enough or hard enough on a night like that. I'm calling everybody I can think of all across the country—including reporters who I didn't even know—to get information about Billy. In three hours of me doing research on the phone, I found out enough about Billy G that I would *never* have hired him. *NEVER!*

One of the things I was told is that when Billy was at Texas A&M, there were only a few in the media covering him. Of the four or five people I spoke to in the state of Texas, none of them felt that he would be able to handle the large media contingent that covers Kentucky Basketball.

What baffled me was that Kentucky allegedly spent a lot of money with a coaching search firm, and yes, he was a really hot coach...but it seemed to me that there were *way* too many red flags. This was so obvious that you shouldn't need a coaching search firm to realize that Billy Gillispie was an awful fit. After all, *this is* Kentucky Basketball. Just because you can coach basketball doesn't mean you can coach *Kentucky Basketball.* How anybody could think that Billy G could handle this is beyond me. Mitch Barnhart, the UK director of athletics, has done some terrific things for this university. *That* was an egregious mistake.

Fast forward to the first time Billy G did a press conference in Memorial Coliseum. He's wringing his hands like crazy under the table while he's answering questions. I'm staring at his hands. I'm staring at him, and he's so uncomfortable.

Media shouldn't be the reason you hire a coach. That's silly. But if you can't handle the media, you shouldn't be in Lexington, Kentucky. Now if that eliminates some candidates, so be it. Handling the media and the fans in a proper manner is part of this job. If you can't do that, I don't care who you are as a coach. It just doesn't work. Billy never should have been here—*at all!*

I've wondered if Billy Gillispie was coaching in the 1950s, if none of this would have been a problem for him. There was no internet, no social media, and the regular media was soft compared to today. Coaches were also different in the fifties. Coaches were meaner, and tougher, and had too much power. Coaches weren't questioned by the fans and media like they are today. Today, coaches can get very thin skinned when criticized. That's partly because of their egos, their salaries, and their understanding that their critics don't know their sport like they do. Today's coaches believe their critics are often clueless.

Back in the 1950s, during summer camp practices under the brutally hot sun, coaches sometimes didn't give you water when you were on the football field. They wanted you to prove your "toughness." How do you not give a human being water when you're on the football field and it's close to a hundred degrees and you're sweating and dehydrated?

Everybody knows that Billy was a bad fit. Everybody knows that he was abusive to players. Telling someone they need to keep on running even after you know their feet are blistered and bleeding might be considered abusive.

Star forward Patrick Patterson once told Gillispie his feet were blistered, and there was blood coming out of his shoes...and he was told to keep on running. Tywanna Patterson, Patrick's mother, was really nice and really tough. I was waiting to hear that she literally decked Gillispie. I was disappointed she never did.

There's tough coaching—and there's going way too far and being a jerk.

Banishing a player to a toilet during halftime of a road game at Vanderbilt because he's not performing like you want, and then telling him to ride back to Lexington in the equipment van instead of with the team certainly qualifies as blatantly inappropriate. That's going too far and being a jerk.

Shortly after center Josh Harrellson went through that, I waited and waited until everyone else was finished talking to him during a media session. The shot clock on the media time was just about over. I asked

Josh point blank about the incident at Vandy. He lied. I don't remember catching anyone else with a lie when I asked them a direct question and me not being mad at them. I felt sorry for Josh that he had to lie. I was going to try and help him tell the story.

I've wondered if he would do it differently now. Just answer my question. I understand why he was scared, but being honest about what happened would have forced UK's administration to get immediately involved. I don't think he realized the power he could have had if he answered my question the right way.

Josh turned white when I asked the question.

With Josh denying it, even though I knew it was true, I couldn't put it on TV with the way LEX18's management was. If this were the 1980s or early 1990s, I would have done the story with "sources tell me" because I trusted my source.

Gillispie's actions with Josh crossed the line of any coach who considers himself a mentor and a teacher. Why action wasn't taken immediately when UK administrators found out about it is *baffling* and extremely disturbing to me.

Just after Billy got fired, did anyone think he wasn't going to be fired? Nobody thought he was going to survive. If they hadn't fired him, who was he going to recruit? He couldn't recruit anyone that was good enough to help Kentucky win championships. Plus, look at all the players who were obviously going to leave if he stayed.

Look, I'll stand by this—that if during Billy's last year they won thirty-two games and made it to the Final Four, he wouldn't have been fired. A lot of people would have praised him for keeping all the players in shape—and pushing them to the Final Four.

If that had happened, I bet UK's administration would have had some serious talks about Gillispie needing to change, but getting to the Final Four I believe would have saved him. Not making the NCAA Tournament for the first time since 1991 was ridiculous. That's what ultimately cost him his job.

When you don't win, and you can't recruit, and there's all kinds of rumors about you, and this is *Kentucky Basketball*—it was just a bad fit.

98

Chasing Billy Gillispie II—Fired!

Kentucky fired Billy after two years. His Wildcat coaching tenure ended with a 77-67 NIT loss to Notre Dame. It was the first time Kentucky missed the NCAA Tournament since 1991.

Joe B. Hall, Eddie Sutton (before he had drinking problems at UK), Rick Pitino, Tubby Smith, and John Calipari all would have made the NCAA Tournament with that team. Plus, home court regular season losses to unheralded and overmatched opponents like Gardner Webb and VMI certainly didn't help Billy keep his job either.

On April 27, 2009, the day they got rid of him, we had two cameras set up—which was most unusual. Live trucks and TV networks were there. It was a media circus.

Billy came out of Wildcat Lodge, where the players stay, which is right across the street from Memorial Coliseum. His cell phone is on his ear, but he's not moving his mouth, and all he's doing is nodding. The first thing I say is, "He's not on the phone." I said it right away, and a lot of people agreed with me. He's *NOT* on the phone. He walks to a vehicle and is driven away.

Now we have to figure out what to do. He's not going to come out of Wildcat Lodge again. I had no idea where he was going. I'm guessing he had to go back to his office. I could have guessed wrong, so we left one camera right where we were, and I went to the other side of Memorial Coliseum hoping—that he might try to sneak into his office another way.

I go to the other side, and much to my surprise, there are only a few media types there—which made it more interesting. There's still this huge throng of media on the other side of Memorial Coliseum.

If Billy shows up, I'm just going to ask him a question—just like I normally would do any other day.

My colleague, Ryan Lemond—during a loud rant on KSR radio—said it best. That I was just *doing my job*. Nothing more, nothing less. Ryan added that my getting ripped for chasing Billy Gillispie was *ridiculous*.

Sure enough, I got *really lucky* again as Billy showed up on the other side of Memorial Coliseum where I'm waiting with my TV camera. Once again, he's holding a cell phone to his ear as if *pretending* to have a conversation. Just like before, everyone thinks he's just faking the call and walking away just to avoid talking to us.

Walking and talking and doing an interview has never bothered me. I've walked backwards and done interviews many times. Having a good photographer is really important. Keeping the shot steady while you are walking backwards isn't easy.

I did it in my last TV interview as a reporter for LEX18. It was at the 2018 Kentucky Derby with Hall of Fame trainer Bob Baffert, who had just won the Derby with Justify, as he was walking off the track.

Despite all of that, the fact of the matter was that Billy simply didn't want to answer questions. All he had to do was say, "I just got fired. I'm really upset. I can't talk right now. Catch me some other time." That's all he had to do. I would have done a follow up question and that would have been it. But Billy was never very intelligent when it came to the media. He just wasn't. The funny thing is that he's not a stupid guy, but when it came to the media, he just wasn't very smart.

So you would think that even if you don't like the media, *master* it because it's part of your job. The fact that he hid from that, to me spoke more about him than it did about Kentucky Basketball.

What does any coach do when one of his players can't shoot a free throw? Tell him to practice. Coach up his form. Billy Gillispie didn't know how to deal with the media, and he never corrected his weakness. Do as I say and not as I do. Billy G was a hypocrite—*A BIG TIME HYPOCRITE!* You have a job to do. Get comfortable with the uncomfortable. Get comfortable with the media. Learn to be better at it. That doesn't mean you have to love it or like it.

I can't tell you how many times a basketball or football player came to Kentucky as a freshman, and they're not very good as an interview. Why should they be? If someone stuck a TV camera in my face when I was seventeen, I would have freaked out. As time goes on, most players get much more comfortable in front of the cameras. Plus, Kentucky puts them through media training.

I've been able to tell so many football and basketball players over the years how much better they've gotten in dealing with the media. It's usually a quick, quiet comment that, as an athlete, every single one of them has really appreciated. I can't tell you how many athletes have smiled back and thanked me because they don't usually get that type of feedback.

Starting in the 1980s, I got used to making strong, quick comments to players just to help them out—because even though they are very talented, they're just kids. There are a lot of these kids, who as seniors, ended up being wonderful interviews.

How much better did Billy G get from the time he arrived until the time he left? I don't think he got much better. That's on him.

But it's also on Mitch Barnhart to have made sure that Billy got enough instruction and training in order to improve his ability to deal with people. Maybe Mitch tried to do that, but the fact remains that Billy Gillispie couldn't handle the suffocating public relations demands associated with the Kentucky basketball program.

Kentucky Basketball is worth how many tens of millions of dollars every year? And the person who is representing your university is awful at publicity? *IT WAS EMBARRASSING!* If you're the president of a university, you should know that your basketball coach is awful with the media. You might not sit down with the basketball coach, but you at least sit down with the athletics director and tell him to clean up the problem. It was never cleaned up. Management was hiding and didn't want to take responsibility. *SHAME ON THEM!* I blame Billy G, I blame Mitch, and I blame Dr. Lee Todd, the president of the University of Kentucky at the time.

I attempted to get Mitch Barnhart to comment on Billy G specifically for this chapter. He respectfully declined.

I called Billy G too, but you can guess that he didn't answer the call.

Every executive makes bad decisions because they're human.

Tim Gilbert, former general manager at LEX18, once told me, "Cutler, if I've made eighty percent of my decisions correctly, then I'm doing a really good job." Although I think Dr. Todd did a good job during his tenure as president, and although I think Mitch Barnhart has done a good job overall with the athletics department, in this one particular case, they failed. Because I respect both of them, it's always been baffling to me why they screwed this up so badly.

If you read the entire book, I admit to plenty of bad decisions myself. It's called life.

Just so you understand that I'm not totally ripping Billy G—he had a wonderful record when he went back home to his school, Ranger Community College. I'm not surprised that he's donated money out of his own pocket to help their facilities. I'm not surprised that he's helping some of the young men who have played for him. I'm not surprised that there are many of his former players who never want to talk to him.

There's a lot of good things about Billy G that his players at Kentucky didn't see, but those things have been there at some of his other coaching stops. At Ranger Community College, there aren't hordes of media, there's not a lot of public attention, and Billy seemed comfortable in his own skin. In that setting, he can be a very good coach. It's just sad that he was exposed to something he wasn't *capable* of dealing with in Lexington, Kentucky. No one's perfect. Not Billy G. Not Alan Cutler.

You've probably seen the video of the infamous chase by now. I was just trying to get that interview with Billy Gillispie. There is nothing that happened in my career that gave me so much attention. The power of YouTube.

When Billy wouldn't answer me after he was fired, when he went into Memorial Coliseum, I started walking (and running) with him.

CUTLER: You're not really going to run away from me, are you?

GILLISPIE: You need to get in shape, don't you?

CUTLER: I can run all day with you.

GILLISPIE: (chuckles)

CUTLER: Your reaction, Billy?

GILLISPIE: Nope. Nope. Get him out.

LINDA CARMACK: Go out. Go out. Go out.

CUTLER: Please take your hands off me.

LINDA CARMACK: Alright.

CUTLER WALKS OUT.

When I tell Billy that I can run with him all day, that was just me trying to be funny. At that point, what are you going to do? Then, when I follow him into the basketball office, Billy tells Linda Carmack, the administrative support associate, to tell me to get out. Linda was put in a terrible situation. She told me to get out, so I got out.

To me, this entire episode honestly wasn't that big of a deal. Nobody else had the shot. The other media quit on the story—which shocked me. I'm not going to quit on trying to get an interview, and especially one *this* big. That's who I am. I'm trying to get a story. You don't know what somebody's going to say. I actually thought the odds were pretty good that if you kept on running with him, he'll tell you a couple of things while he's running. Never did I think he was going to stop and turn and do an interview. Remember, I'm trying to beat everybody. I'm trying to do what I always did.

I'm not mad or upset about always being linked to Billy Gillispie. Would I rather be known for something else? Yes. But it doesn't bother me, and I'm not losing sleep over it. I wasn't doing this to create a stir. I was doing this to get the best sound and the best video to do the best job I could with the story. I was just reacting to what I had been doing my whole career. *Nothing more. Nothing less.*

99

Chasing Billy Gillispie III—Fire Cutler??

When I get back to the TV station with my Billy G tape, I'm fired up. No one has what I have. Plus, the newsroom was buzzing with excitement…a few people in the newsroom were cheering and were clapping when I got back. That's something that never happens.

It quickly changed. We started getting a ton of "I hate Alan Cutler" emails. There were a few people who liked what I did, but the overwhelming majority of the emails were hateful—at least in the beginning.

It was crazy—we got over a thousand emails in a couple of hours. In those first thousand emails, people were furious at me. "How dare you. The guy just got fired. You should leave him alone," they wrote. I had never had anything like that happen in my career. Plus, I was called some pretty strong names.

The truth is, all I was trying to do was to get the best interview and the best sound to beat everybody. That's all it was—nothing more, nothing less. That's what management pays me to do. But, management changed their tune because of all the negative emails coming in.

There's something I refer to as the "CNN news cycle." When something bad happens to you, you've got forty-eight hours to live through it. If it's really bad and you can't survive forty-eight hours, you're in trouble. When the emails started pouring in, I knew it was going to be a rough forty-eight hours at the TV station. But I had no idea it would end up being as bad as it turned out to be.

I was so mad at *myself* and with management at LEX18 in the wake of this episode. I was good when asked to *respond* to all the angry emails flooding into the station. What angered me tremendously, however, was that I was told I needed to *apologize* to every single one of them. If

I had been twenty-five years old, I would have told management to go jump in a lake. Trust me, those weren't the words I would have used. But I was much older—with a family—and I was at a little different point in my life by then.

Nevertheless, I was so mad at *myself* for agreeing to apologize. I'm still mad at myself just thinking about it now.

At that time, and even today, *I STRONGLY BELIEVE THAT I DID NOTHING WRONG!* Why should I have to defend myself for doing my job? The truth is that management crumpled like one of my cheap suits. Had most of the emails congratulated me about trying to run down a big story, or had they lauded me for doing such a good job, management never would have interfered. But because so many people instantly wrote hateful emails about me to the TV station, they said I had to apologize.

I will never forgive myself for writing the following email. I'm not sorry I wrote an email, just the fact that I apologized for something I shouldn't have had to. I apologized for just doing my job. *I HAD NOTHING TO APOLOGIZE FOR!*

Dear WLEX Viewer,

Thanks for writing and for watching LEX 18 News. Your feedback is important to us.

You have written to our station to voice a complaint about the coverage that I did on Friday on the termination of UK basketball coach, Billy Gillispie. Your criticism of my story, and the criticism that I have received from many other viewers is appropriate and appreciated, and I want to apologize to you for putting that report on the air. I realize now, that in my zeal to aggressively report on a major story, that I crossed a boundary that I should not have crossed. Coach Gillispie deserved more respect than I provided and I regret my involvement in making a difficult time for him even more difficult.

I have been in contact with the UK Athletic Department and they have been kind enough to accept my apology. I am attempting to reach out to Coach Gillispie with the hopes that he too will be so kind. And I am reaching out to you, our viewers, to try and make amends for a situation that took on a life of its own, and that I enormously regret.

During the past 25 years of reporting on sports, I have tried to cover all stories fairly and factually. Unfortunately, in this particular case, I failed to live up to my own standards and those of WLEX-TV. I will try harder in the future, and I hope that you will continue to watch WLEX news and my reports, as I learn from this valuable lesson.

And, I have apologized on the air.

Sincerely,
Alan Cutler
Lex18 Sports Director

Every time I read this email I sent, I feel like I sold my soul. I feel like a wimp. Makes me want to throw up. I'm *really really* ticked off just proofreading it for the book.

It didn't take a genius to instantly know that if I didn't write an email with an apology, I was probably going to get fired. My first reaction was not to write it. I should have trusted my gut and lived with the consequences.

Bruce Carter, my news director, is the one who told me I had to write this email. And, before it was sent to anyone, he had to approve it. He made it clear that he was just doing what he was told.

Later on, a source confirmed that *I WAS* going to get fired—but things changed as the public changed their attitude about what I did. Plus, I was told that Bruce Carter wanted to save my job because of all the things I'd done for the TV station. When I found that out after the smoke had cleared, I walked into my boss's office with a big thank you.

The day after the station received over a thousand emails in a matter of hours, I got called into the general manager's office.

Pat Dalbey, the new president and general manager, started *yelling* at me. He started questioning me about whether I could do my job. He told me he didn't know if I could cover Kentucky sports anymore. He went on and on and on. For what seemed like a long time, I kept my mouth shut and took it.

To say I was furious at Pat is putting it mildly. I told him he was being ridiculous. At a certain point, I stand up, wave my finger at him, and I tell him to stop yelling at me and that he better not ever yell at me again—and if he keeps on yelling at me, he and I are going to have a personal problem. That's the truth.

Now there are just the two of us in the room. I yelled back at him and when I was done, I walked out, and I slammed the door on my way out. If you don't like what I do— fine. But I'm a grown man, so don't yell at me. I can't yell at the president of the company, so he shouldn't be able to yell at me. Why is the president of the company better than I am? He isn't.

One of the things that has always bothered me about management is that they claim talent like me has a big ego. I have a *HUGE* ego and I know it. But so many times in my career, I have seen management at so many stations have such *HUGE* egos themselves. But, they have the power—they can hire you and they can fire you.

The bottom line to me has always been that management often doesn't realize the egos they have.

I'm mad at myself for being such a chicken. Being a chicken is not normally part of my personality. Being a chicken is not who I am. By me getting out of my comfort zone, *that* bothered me even more. I never should have had to apologize. I should have told management to immediately go jump in a lake. I'm *much madder* at myself than I ever was at them.

A couple days after our heated discussion in his office over all the negative emails, Pat Dalbey who never came to my desk, walks over and sticks his hand out without saying a word. Something had definitely changed in his mind. I stared hard at him, waiting for him to say something, and purposely making him uncomfortable because I was so mad at him. He says, "Alan, I'm sorry."

I stuck out my hand to shake his and said, "Pat, if you're man enough to apologize, then I'm man enough to accept it." He said he was sorry a second time, and I told him that we were good. Now I had to decide what I would do next.

100

Chasing Billy Gillispie IV—The Aftermath

I t was right after General Manager Pat Dalbey apologized to me, that I started to make a *joke* of the whole Billy Gillispie episode. I had survived what I called the CNN bad news cycle. Not only that, but the president of the company had just apologized to me.

I give Pat Dalbey a lot of credit for that because in my forty-four years in radio and TV—rarely do you ever see or hear an executive apologize. It almost never happens. So from that point on, to me "the chase" was funny, and I started to make a joke of it. I also knew that if I didn't make a joke about it, it was going to haunt me forever. I thought about the Melvin Turpin story, which I told you about earlier. I also thought about Billy Buckner. Buckner saved me.

Billy Buckner had a great career as a first baseman. What people don't know about him is that Buckner was one of the fastest minor leaguers until he had an injury to his ankle that was so bad that many thought he would never play again. He couldn't run. Yet, he still had a quasi-hall of fame career.

In the World Series against the New York Mets, after a ground ball went through his legs, Billy Buckner began receiving death threats and subsequently had to move his family from Boston to a different part of the country. That ground ball which went through his legs—which didn't end up costing the Boston Red Sox the 1986 World Series against the New York Mets—ruined that man's life. He couldn't make a joke of it. I was not going to end up like Billy Buckner. I used that experience to help me with Billy G. Had I gotten tense and defensive, I think my career would have turned out totally different.

Making a *joke* out of chasing Billy Gillispie is one of the smartest things I did in my career.

So, when asked about Billy Gillispie, I'd make a joke. I'd be gassing up my car, and there'd be someone yelling at me from two rows over, "Hey Cutler, you should run faster." I'd respond back, "Hey man, I shouldn't have worn cowboy boots." What are you going to do? I mean it wasn't going anywhere. I can't tell you how many hundreds and hundreds of times in public since that time that I made a joke of what happened. I made a lot of people laugh in those short conversations. Almost all of these conversations were with strangers, but people think they know you because you are on TV.

For a long time, I couldn't go anywhere without someone bringing it up. And the funny part is that as time goes on, so many people have since told me it's the "greatest video" they've ever seen, or they've watched it "countless times," or it was funny, or that this video turned me into a "legend," or that I'll always be known for this.

An ironic twist to my apology is that I got hundreds of additional email responses back from viewers telling me that they had overreacted when they sent me their initial hateful email. Many apologized for the email they first sent me.

The truth is that when Billy G was fired, you had all these Kentucky basketball fans, *THAT LOVE THIS PROGRAM*, who were really ticked off at how far the program had fallen. They were embarrassed. A lot of people took that anger out at me. I understood that as it was going on. Management was clueless and they overreacted. But it was still crazy how many people ended up apologizing to me.

Here's a final thought. I've always respected management, and I've always believed that management is no different than you and me. They're just people. They're protected by their power, and they often don't use their power fairly.

I'll give Pat Dalbey even more credit. A couple of days before I retired, he came over to my desk again, thanked me for everything I've done at LEX18, made a joke about us surviving Billy Gillispie, and told me that I should call him personally if there was ever anything I wanted to do at the TV station.

He went on and on about how valuable I've been to LEX18. He walked all the way over to my desk to say that, and it made me feel really good. Everyone makes mistakes. I've made plenty of mistakes. Sometimes, you have to move on.

TV's been great to me, but this is the truth. They want reporters to find legitimate dirt in any story they're doing. But—oh, no—don't criticize the TV station. At times, we're all hypocritical. The hypocrisy with television can be ridiculous.

Here's something you should know. About a year ago, before LEX18 was sold, I met with Pat to talk about the book. I showed him what was in here. He not only told me he had no problem with the book, but he called our problem with the Billy Gillispie chase as "just business."

When our meeting was over, he wished me good luck and said he looked forward to reading about it. Pat couldn't have been any nicer about the entire mess. He also sent a positive email about our meeting. I appreciated it and thanked him.

I wanted to meet with Pat for two reasons. One, I wanted to clarify a clause in my contract. And two, I wanted Pat to know what I didn't think he knew—that I gave my heart and soul to the station. Although things happen in life that cause friction, I wanted Pat to know this book is about my life and career.

This book was not written to go after LEX18. I have some *great* memories of my time working for them. There are a lot of people at the TV station that I really care about. And, it's important to me that they want to continue to invite me to their Christmas parties.

Here's something else you might find interesting. Almost every year since Billy G left, I've tried to call him. I didn't call him this year because I knew he was undergoing a kidney transplant. I may have missed one other year during the stretch he's been gone. He's never returned my phone calls, but my message to him is always the same. "Hey Billy, Alan Cutler. It's been a long time since the chase. How about if we have some sort of fun run to raise money for charity? Give me a call."

I'm still waiting for him to respond.

The tide of public opinion turned so quickly after the chaos of Billy G. It didn't take long before people thought the whole episode was great. Over time, me chasing Billy Gillispie has taken on an entire life of its own. Now you finally know how it all really went down.

Part 11 (2010 and Beyond)

The Last Decade

101

Cal

I remember the moment I met John Calipari. Yes, as Cal says, I was wearing sneakers, jeans—with a tie and jacket. I was working in Pittsburgh covering a Pitt basketball game for KDKA-TV.

Cal, an assistant coach at Pitt, walks up to me in a bombastic way—which is comical because I'm accused of being bombastic—and says, "Alan Cutler...John Calipari...nice to meet you." It was right by the Pitt bench as his players were shooting around before the game.

I got to know Cal a little bit while I worked at KDKA-TV in Pittsburgh. My perception always was that he was going to be a big-time coach.

It's kind of interesting that the Pittsburgh coaching staff back then included John Calipari, former UK guard Reggie Warford—who was also an assistant—and Ray "Rock" Oliver. Reggie Warford should have become a big-time head coach, while Rock Oliver eventually became the strength coach for both Calipari and Rick Pitino. Rock's done a lot to help athletes. They trust him.

Imagine being great friends with both John Calipari and Rick Pitino. Rock Oliver could write a wonderful book.

Did I ever think at that time that Cal would end up at Kentucky? Of course not. I actually thought he'd end up as head coach at Pittsburgh because he's a Pittsburgh guy. When Judy and I moved to Pittsburgh, we rented an apartment in Oakdale, about fifteen minutes from where Cal grew up in Moon Township.

Remember that Kentucky was *desperate* when they finally hired John Calipari in 2009. Do I expect Kentucky to agree with that? Of course not.

When Calipari wanted the Kentucky job two years earlier, Billy Gillispie was hired instead. John Calipari is a *fixer*. If Kentucky had gone to the Final Four and Billy Gillispie left, and there were no NCAA problems or anything negative floating around, no way Calipari would get hired.

Cal will probably never admit this, but he wasn't happy when Billy G was hired instead. I know because I'm the one who told him. He was really upset. He got loud. I had to go down to our basement standing by our washer and dryer to finish the call. I got loud also—not at Cal, but because of the conversation.

When I went back upstairs, Judy quickly asked, "Who were you talking to, and why were you so loud?"

Think about how loud I had to be—because don't you think my wife already knew she married a big mouth?

To me, hiring Calipari instead of Billy Gillispie was a move as obvious as the nose on my face.

I even went on TV and said I'd hire Calipari before Billy Gillispie was in the picture. UK Athletics Director Mitch Barnhart should have hired me as a consultant. *I would have saved him a lot of pain and embarrassment.*

There were people inside UK who were afraid of hiring Cal because UMass and Memphis got in trouble with the NCAA while he was their coach. After those problems, Cal had some strong haters in the media. That didn't make it easier for him. Calipari to many was the bad man of college basketball.

Granted, UMass had their Final Four appearance in 1996 taken away because star center Marcus Camby took money from an agent. The NCAA said Cal had nothing to do with it, but it was still *his* program.

I've heard the inside story about what Marcus Camby did, and I don't believe Cal had anything to do with it. Camby made a mistake. He said he was sorry, gave $150,000 to UMass that they were forced to return, and eventually went back and got his degree in 2017. Camby was not only the Naismith College Player of the Year in 1995-96, but he also had a great seventeen-year-career in the NBA and is in the UMass Hall of Fame.

Superstar guard Derrick Rose led Memphis to its first national championship game in thirty-five years in 2008. The NCAA Clearinghouse approved Rose to play as a freshman. But it was later decided that Rose got into Memphis with a fraudulent SAT score, that someone had taken the test for him. However, the NCAA approved the score which is why Rose played for Memphis. So why punish Memphis?

Calipari, who was not personally implicated in either of the NCAA messes, is the only coach to have two Final Fours on his watch taken away.

Although Cal is a great people person and motivator, his greatest strength is that as he's gotten older and more mature as a person and coach, he still maintains his *VISION*. What Calipari does for college basketball reminds me of the famous Wayne Gretzky quote. The greatest hockey player of all time said, "I skate to where the puck is going to be, not to where it has been." Calipari has the vision to see what should happen, so he jumps on it. I believe Calipari would make a wonderful senator. He spots a trend early and goes for it.

The word pioneer might make you think of covered wagons going across America in the 19th century. Cal is a pioneer in college basketball.

He made the "one and-done" a thing, thanks to the NBA rules. Stay one year in college and then jump to the NBA for millions. Ironically, there are coaches who ripped him for doing it that are either copying it or perhaps are mad because they aren't good enough to copy it.

In his first season at Kentucky, five of his players went in the first round of the NBA draft, including John Wall going No. 1.

"We're a players-first program," Calipari said. "And we might have just had the biggest day in Kentucky Basketball history with a No. 1 pick and five first-round picks."

All high school stars who were thinking about the NBA had to take notice. That's the point. Calipari is always recruiting. He wasn't trying to negate the NCAA national championships won at Kentucky. He got ripped big time for that. Perhaps he could have worded it another way, but then he wouldn't be Calipari. I instantly knew what he was doing. The truth is I laughed when he said it. I thought it was really smart. And, I instantly knew he was going to take some heat.

Duke's Mike Krzyzewski wasn't for the one-and-done. Today he's all for it, and at times beating Cal at his own game. Because Coach K started doing it, it's become "Main Street."

Players like Calipari because of his no B.S. approach. In recruiting, there can be tons of B.S., so that makes Cal stick out. Plus, he's built the best track record of sending players to the NBA.

When I went to work for WLW Radio, the boss and program director Darryl Parks asked me if I knew who I'd be talking to. I didn't (we talked about this in the Cincinnati section). I was told it was the forty-year-old white male. That's not a racist comment by Parks—it's the reality of who was their audience which made the station No. 1.

Who is John Calipari and all the top basketball coaches talking to? Young African Americans. Many are from a tough neighborhood. Do you think all of these young men have had great experiences with older white men growing up?

Trust—Calipari says that African American families trust him with their sons.

Do you think Eric Bledsoe, who at one point was living in a car, and John Wall, who admits to having some trouble as a kid and now donates a lot of money to help kids out—do you think they had great relationships with older white men growing up? And ditto for DeMarcus Cousins? *PLEASE!*

Superstar big man Anthony Davis lived in a rough neighborhood in Chicago. He offered to meet Calipari somewhere else when he was recruiting him. Calipari came to his house and got out of his car like he owned the neighborhood. That was huge for Davis. So was Cal's *NO B.S.* approach. NOTHING ABOUT THIS APPROACH WORKS IF CALIPARI ISN'T REAL.

Another amazing thing Calipari does has me at times scratching my head. How does he do it? How does he get so many five-star recruits to sacrifice their individual games, give up minutes, and to swallow their ego to play as a team? Plus, Calipari does this even though he can be really tough on his players. But if you sincerely show players that you care, show players how to get where they want to go—the NBA, and you know what you're talking about, you can get away with being tough. Smart players want tough coaches. You can't fool players. Players know if you care or not.

There are times players who play for Cal don't like him. John Wall—first pick in the 2010 NBA draft—loves Cal. But if you don't think there were times he was really mad at his coach, you're kidding yourself. That's OK. It's part of the relationship.

If a player is doing an interview, do you think they're really going to say that they're mad or upset or don't like their coach? No! If they said what they were really feeling, their playing time could change—or at best, there would be an intense problem.

It's tough for the media to tell that story because players won't talk about it.

I remember so many players on the *Unforgettables* telling me well after the fact that their common bond in the beginning of being coached by Pitino was that they all hated Pitino. Yet Pitino ended up being their guy. They'd run through a brick wall for Pitino, they respected him, and they loved playing for him. As teenagers, athletes go through emotional periods that are often more amplified than the public will ever know.

There is a *GQ* article from 2018 that calls Calipari a "devil" many times—that he was the most hated man in college basketball. I was uncomfortable reading it. Devil? "The devil walked into church," is how Reid Forgrave started his long article for *GQ* magazine. While I was reading it, I was baffled by the writer's thought process. Is this writer that smart about Cal, or am I that dumb?

How could Forgrave possibly come to that conclusion? This piece really bothered me, and although I've been for the most part really good about ignoring those that don't like me, I wonder how Cal can push that aside. Saying that something doesn't bother you and living it can be two different things. You don't want to show you're bleeding and hurt.

I understand Cal because I'm a big mouth myself. He has a big mouth and a great ability to create attention for himself, his program, and his players. He's a smart marketer. If he went into private business and had a product to market, he'd be great at it. There are other coaches who are jealous of his ability.

The world of sports is full of rumors, innuendo, and backbiting. And believe me when I tell you, Cal doesn't like it when he's way ahead of the other coaches and doesn't get enough credit for being a trailblazer. I don't blame him.

Cal has always been sensitive—with good reason—that he hasn't gotten enough credit about how his players hit the books. He's taken many shots at the media about this. He's really proud of how his players have done in the classroom. And he should be proud.

Generally speaking, the media doesn't care about players' grades. It's not unusual for a coach and the media to have different agendas, and sometimes when that happens, neither side is wrong.

Cal pushes his guys to come back and get their education. His grandparents couldn't speak English when they came to America, and his daughter is a doctor. You know he values education. Cal even pushes former UK players who didn't play for him to come back and get their degrees. I think it's great.

There's a reason Cal's in the Naismith Memorial Basketball Hall of Fame. It's because he deserves to be in it.

102

Basketball Benny

C al likes to kid the media about how *stupid* they are about basketball. He likes to test the media at his press conferences—asking questions to what he calls the Basketball Bennies on press row. Somewhere in his kidding, he really believes the media knows nothing. There is some truth in the kidding.

Here's what I know about running a team. My theory goes back to the 1960s—when I started watching the NBA.

Basketball is a sport about running. I say run every time you get the ball in an effort to get easy buckets. If the defense stops you, then grind it out. But more motion is usually needed. Too many teams stand around on offense.

Play defense all over the court. If you need to play more players because this is more work—so be it. It's a great way to keep more players involved and happy.

This running style is a great way to wear down whoever you are playing because odds are they don't run as much as you do. Your team will be in better shape, which will get you some extra layups and dunks, because you're running as much as you can. If your point guard walks the ball up, or jogs the ball up, you take them out of the game because they're either mentally or physically tired, or both.

I would still shoot a lot of threes. But in my world of basketball, it's not all just about the three-pointer. The layups and dunks would give you more space to shoot even more three-point shots if you wanted to.

With this style of play, slower players can also get easy buckets just by running and going against a lazy defense, or a tired defense. Faster players have even more of an advantage.

Cal doesn't like his teams to shoot too many three-pointers, because if you are having a bad game in the NCAA Tournament, boom—your season could be over. I don't know how many times I've heard Cal talking about grinding it out in the NCAA Tournament because you are going to have to win six games against many different styles. My style would get Cal or anyone some extra dunks and layups. My style should get you more wide open three-pointers.

What is one of Calipari's strengths? He's not afraid to change.

But—you knew this was coming. Cal is all about getting his players ready for the NBA, so why doesn't he shoot more threes? Tell his one-and-done players that he will play like the modern NBA. The players will like that style even more. And as great of a job he and his staff have done in recruiting, playing that style will help him to recruit even better.

Back in 1968-69, there was no three-point shot and there was no shot clock. Somehow, UK still scored at least *a hundred points ten times. TEN!!!* Fans love to watch scoring, and players love to play in systems that score a lot. It's a win-win!

Adolph Rupp—at the end of his career—still wanted his players to run.

"If you mean transition baskets—every chance we could," said star UK forward Mike Pratt, who was also an academic All-American. "We were not a big team overall but good passers and bucket getters."

Dan Issel averaged 26 points a game. Mike Casey—who was All-SEC three times, who I still think would have been a key to winning the national championship the next year if he didn't get hurt—averaged 19 a game, and the underrated Mike Pratt was at 16.

With the athletes Kentucky had, I never understood why they didn't run more. I don't understand why Cal doesn't run more. I didn't understand why Tubby didn't run more. I thought Eddie Sutton and Joe B. Hall should have run more. I even thought Pitino could have run more. No need to comment on Billy Gillispie.

When Paul Westhead was coaching Loyola Marymount, I thought everyone would copy what he was doing. They led the nation for three years in scoring from 1988 through 1990—110, 112 and 122 points a game. That was a great way to recruit kids who normally wouldn't go to your school. The way they ran up and down the court was so much fun to watch. When they were playing the late game on ESPN, I always tried to stay up and watch.

To this day, I'll never figure it out why what Westhead did didn't take off. And I never understood why a blue blood program didn't go after him. Westhead put a no-name school on the map. That's not easy.

As a coach, Westhead won an NBA Championship with the Lakers in 1980 and a WNBA Championship.

I have believed for decades—and I could continue to be *wrong*—that everyone should play the way I suggest. I know I can be stubborn. I guarantee you that if Cal starts running more or playing more like Westhead in the NBA, other coaches will start copying him.

What Cal does with the UK Pro Day is brilliant. When he first came up with that idea, I thought, "Wow—why didn't I think of that? Why hasn't that been done before?" You're sitting in a kid's house, and you're able to tell them that many NBA scouts and executives are going to be coming to watch them practice. It's a show, and it's on ESPN. You think that doesn't help excite high school stars?

Cal was ahead of his time with the idea of pushing positionless players. Think about it. If you're 6'10" tall, and Cal is recruiting you, you'd love it because you don't want to be pigeonholed into playing low-post basketball. The first time I talked to star center Karl-Anthony Towns, he told me he wanted to be like Kevin Durant—shoot threes.

Now you're talking to a recruit and telling them you're going to run it at every opportunity. We're playing positionless basketball. We're playing like the NBA is playing right now. How do you think that sounds in the home of a five-star recruit?

Some True Blue fans feel that Cal doesn't focus enough on national championships and is only interested in getting his players to the NBA. To me, that's one of the *most ridiculous things ever said about Calipari*—and the list is long.

If you don't get a reputation of being able to put players in the league, you're not going to get a lot of these recruits. To anyone who thinks Cal doesn't want to win championships—that's *crazy*. He's just trying to get the best players.

When Cal is talking about putting players in the NBA and all the money on their contracts, he's using the press conference to recruit! Cal is just doing what all smart coaches do. If he says he has to win that next championship, he's putting unnecessary pressure on himself, pressure on his team, and pressure on his legacy.

When coaches tell you, "Well if it happens, it happens—I'm just going to try and do the best I can," that's the biggest bunch of crap. It's nonsense. I'm not calling Cal a liar. I'm calling every coach who ever said that a liar....

I'm smiling—what do you expect them to say? "I have to win a national championship, or my career won't be the same?" Fans want to hear more talk about a national championship than players going to the NBA—but that doesn't help Calipari recruit. Basketball is all about recruiting. As that old saying goes, you can't win the Kentucky Derby with a donkey.

The *truth is,* I don't blame coaches for saying what they say because you don't want to allow fans and/or the media to put more pressure on you and your job. Coaches have enough pressure on them already—but they get paid a lot of money to deal with the pressure.

Kentucky was *undefeated* when they played Wisconsin in the semis of the 2015 Final Four. I wondered if Cal second-guessed himself for not putting in Tyler Ulis and Devin Booker for the Harrison twins. With 6:36 to go, Kentucky didn't score again until there were fifty-six seconds left. Wisconsin went on an 8-0 run, and UK blew a game that will bother some of the players for the rest of their lives. They should have won the national championship.

Old-timers will tell you that Kentucky Basketball will always get great recruits. WRONG! A lot of True Blue fans don't want to believe that. If Billy Gillispie kept on coaching at Kentucky, who was going to come play for him?

Do you think John Wall would have come to Kentucky with the wrong coach? He *never* would have come to Lexington to play for Billy Gillispie. Do you think Boogie Cousins or Eric Bledsoe would have come here with the wrong coach? No and no.

Kentucky Basketball's tradition is as good as it gets anywhere in college basketball. I respect the tradition—it's a beautiful thing. But for people to automatically think that Kentucky will always get the best recruits is ludicrous. I don't think anybody should think that. It's arrogant.

It's my opinion that the first recruiting class Cal had at Kentucky is one of the greatest recruiting classes in the history of college basketball. Now before you go "Whooooooa," think about this. One of the many reasons Billy Gillispie was fired was that had he stayed, there would have been a mass exodus of players. Kentucky would not have won ten basketball games the next year. Kentucky would have been filling out their team with walk-ons and scholarship players who couldn't normally play at UK.

If Cal didn't pull off such a great recruiting class, Kentucky would have been very mediocre. The most amazing thing of all is that he had almost no time to put that class together. That's what makes it extra special. He was hired in April. Had this been a normal recruiting class that Cal had time to work on, it still would have been considered one of the best classes of the past fifteen years. But to do what he did right when he arrived—to get Wall and Cousins and Bledsoe to be included in that group—was absolutely phenomenal. I've looked back on recruiting classes, and I'm not being biased.

When UK won the NCAA championship in 2012, it took a gorilla off Calipari's back—even though he won't admit it. With all the great things Cal has done, if he retires from Kentucky and doesn't win another NCAA championship, there will be fans who will always think he didn't win enough because of all the talent he brought to Lexington.

Kentucky is a blue blood program. There are only a few of them. Credit Calipari for restoring that and being a pioneer in many ways for Kentucky Basketball—and college basketball overall.

103

A Great Hire in Mark Stoops

I remember when Mark Stoops had his press conference announcing that he was hired as the new head football coach at the University of Kentucky.

December 2, 2012 was a Sunday—and I had a Cincinnati Bengals game to do. I was the host of the Bengals Radio Network, so I called up Dave Armbruster, my boss for Bengals games at the radio station, and asked him what he wanted me to do with this conflict. In the past, there were a couple of times I had to drive back really fast from Cincinnati in order to make it on the air back in Lexington, but I had always been able to work things out between my TV and Bengals schedules.

I had to be at the press conference covering Stoops' announcement. I covered Kentucky and if I weren't there for that announcement, I wouldn't blame my boss at LEX18 if they told me I couldn't be the host of the Cincinnati Bengals anymore. On the other hand, I didn't want to stiff my Bengals bosses either.

Dave, or Yid as we call him, told me we could just tape the Bengals pregame show. As a pregame show host, I'm like a traffic cop—going in and out of stories. So we taped the show with all the ins and outs. I would never lie to my audience, so I never told them that I was live.

It actually worked pretty well. The problem was that I now had to watch the Bengals game in order to do the postgame show. The Stoops press conference, meanwhile, was going on at the exact same time.

Zach Tucker, my trusted photographer, had a TV set up with our live truck without me asking, so I could watch the Bengals game while I quickly wrote the Stoops story. The story is already in my head, so writing that quickly on a deadline is normal.

As soon as I finished putting the story together, I just left it with

Zach, and I took off to do the Bengals post game show at WLAP in Lexington, which thank goodness, was really close to the press conference.

I've had so many really good photographers. You really are a team. I'm nothing without pictures—and the way they hustled for me and for us has always been a *BIG* key to my success. I've often wondered why I got so lucky this way. Zach is part of a long list of photographers who not only could really shoot video—but they had my back.

Yid had arranged for me to do the postgame show from the WLAP studios in Lexington. Yes, the same WLAP that fired me with great ratings—because in their mind, I worked for the wrong TV station. Broadcasting is crazy. I've been back in the building for shows a number of times, and everyone there has always treated me with respect.

I drove like a bat out of you know where to get there. Shortly after I arrive, I'm on the air doing the postgame. My producer—for the only time I hosted the Bengals Radio Network—picked all the plays for me to use for my highlights, and I was able to get through everything just fine even though I only watched snippets of the game. In other words, I faked it. Since I was a guy who prepared like crazy, it was uncomfortable—but we made it work. I never want to do that again. I loved deadlines—I had a lot of fun that day—but this was too crazy.

The Stoops press conference was this big show held in the Nutter Field House. The place was packed for this rah-rah type pep rally to introduce the new coach. That day on TV I said, *"If he's any good, you'll have to give him five years."* That bothered some people.

FIVE YEARS? Patience and fans are two words that don't often mix.

UK Football was awful when Mark Stoops took over. They had very little talent. They had no depth. They didn't have the size and speed to compete in the Southeastern Conference.

I was always amazed that former Kentucky coach Joker Phillips didn't do a much better job recruiting. *AMAZED*—since he had the reputation of being a good recruiter *AND* he loved this place. I will never figure out why Joker was that bad.

Rich Brooks gave him a wonderful foundation that I thought he could actually improve. Was I wrong!! Joker may never talk to me again after this. And I like Joker. He was ready to be a head coach, but he failed, big time. I covered him during his playing days at UK.

A lot of coaches who take over losing programs—and UK was a losing program when Stoops took over—will generally say the program was in much worse shape than they thought it was going to be, in order to make themselves look better when and if they eventually turn the program around. It takes a little heat off them when they start out. I believe that Stoops really believed the program was in worse shape than even he expected when he took it over.

For people to think that Mark Stoops was going to come in here, and in two years take this team to a bowl game, is past silly. Since Kentucky was not beating out the Georgias and the Tennessees of the world for recruits, you can't expect Stoops' first two recruiting classes to all of a sudden bang heads with and beat them. *That thought is crazy.*

Stoops ended up winning only twelve of his first thirty-six games. That's really bad. I credit UK Athletics Director Mitch Barnhart for his patience. As dumb as the Billy Gillispie hire was by Barnhart—you have to be fair and give him a lot of credit for Stoops.

Stoops has gone to four consecutive bowl games since. A wonderful turnaround.

When Stoops first took over, most of the linemen Kentucky were getting needed to be redshirted. That meant that two years in, you're then expecting Mark Stoops to be winning football games with redshirt freshmen on both sides of the ball. *Not happening.*

The culture in Lexington was awful at the time. It was a losing culture. I can't tell you how many stories I did, starting in the 1980s, on how the culture around UK Football was awful. Rich Brooks, Hal Mumme, and Jerry Claiborne changed that for a while, but for most of the time in parts of four decades, there was a lack of belief that UK could beat the big boys in the SEC. Players, deep down, didn't think they could win. That's not knocking the players. That's based upon history repeating itself. What always bothered me was that there were so many players giving it everything they had—and they were good guys. I felt bad for them.

When Mark Stoops took over, Kentucky was a part of the best football conference—but their facilities were inferior, they had no reputation for recruiting, and they had no reputation for winning. Now you're going to expect a guy to come in and win in two years? *Really?* That's not a shot against Mark Stoops. Very few coaches not named Nick Saban could have come in here and turned this thing around quickly. And I don't even think Alabama's Saban could have turned the mess Stoops walked into around in two years. And, Nick Saban wasn't walking through that door anyway.

With Mark Stoops being Mark Stoops, and Vince Marrow being a great recruiter, and the rest of the staff doing a very good job, Kentucky started recruiting better athletes. They now are able to redshirt players that in Mark Stoops' first couple of years would have been forced to play.

Josh Allen is a wonderful NFL football player. He was very lightly recruited—going to Monmouth when Kentucky called. He never should have played that first year at Kentucky. He told me he barely weighed 190 pounds when he got here. And he's going to rush the passer?

If he came to Kentucky today, they would redshirt him. Josh Allen was fast, but he was skinny, light, and not strong enough. He had no business playing that first year, but UK was desperate. Josh Allen also had a huge heart, and he really wanted it. He's made himself into a great player, a leader, and made himself into a top ten pick in the NFL draft—with some really good coaching.

So, some fans weren't fair with Stoops. Along the way, he made some mistakes. All coaches do. Overall, I think he's done a terrific job.

Mark Stoops has built the Kentucky program brick by brick. That fits with his personality and how he grew up. Everybody knows that Stoops is from Youngstown, Ohio—a rough town. Stoops told me that in Youngstown, parents would take their cars, line up around the football field, and turn on their headlights so they could practice football at night.

Stoops was brought up the right way, with a father who was a successful high school defensive coordinator and who worked hard to make a living for his family.

That's reflected in the culture Mark Stoops has built at Kentucky.

104

Magic Johnson Does the "Y"

As an all-star point guard for the Los Angeles Lakers during his thirteen seasons in the NBA, Magic Johnson won five league championships, three league MVPs, and was selected as one of the fifty greatest players in NBA history. He also became a two-time inductee into the Basketball Hall of Fame—honored in 2002 for his individual career and again in 2010 as a member of the "Dream Team."

Magic Johnson came to a Kentucky game in 2010. He immediately went over to former UK coach Joe B. Hall, gave him a hug, and they had a lovely conversation. Many forget that in 1978, when Kentucky won the national championship under Joe B., their toughest game in the NCAA Tournament was against Magic's Michigan State team.

UK, led by Kyle Macy's eighteen points, won 52-49 that day to advance to the Final Four. Magic, one of the greatest players of all time, hit only two of ten shots for six points. He also had six turnovers.

Before the game, instead of me asking him about his great Laker teams or their championships, I asked Magic about "that" game with Kentucky. Magic is famous for his smile, but when he heard my question, his expression totally changed. He was upset. "Losing that game to Kentucky still bothers me to this day," said Magic. "We thought we had the best team in the country. Losing to Kentucky helped us win the national championship the next year. We were all so mad that we lost to Kentucky."

Without me asking, he started talking about how much he respected Joe B. Hall and that team. "They were tough and strong, but we were tough and strong too," he said. "They were just a little better than we were. That loss haunted me the entire off-season."

Great athletes, like Magic Johnson, often take a tough loss and use it as fuel to turn it into a positive.

Magic also did the "Y" in the famous Kentucky cheer. His million-dollar smile was definitely back for that.

105

Cory Johnson Talks About Poop

Every now and then, you'll come across a player who will just tell you things—you never know what's going to come out of their mouth.

The first time they brought Cory Johnson in front of the media—and I got him off to the side—I was quickly thinking that I hoped this guy could play at least a little because he was great copy. The first time I stuck a microphone in his face, my eyes lit up. That doesn't often happen.

Cory turned out to be a good defensive tackle. One of the highlights of the 2015 college football season for Kentucky was watching him return a fumble seventy-seven yards for a score.

One of the first interviews I did with Cory, he talked about how nobody in his family had graduated college, and that he came from such a small town that the big thing to do on a Saturday night was to drive to Walmart. But he did it in a comedic way. He was funny—naturally. If he had some direction, I'm convinced he could do stand-up comedy.

I was doing a normal interview that I would normally do in the spring. I tape a lot of these interviews for use later on in the summer when there typically may not be a lot of things going on. At LEX18, we had to put on a UK story every Monday through Friday, and it doesn't matter that there is no one around to talk to. So I bagged as many of these stories as I could to use during the slow summer months. Cory Johnson's video was intended to be one of these.

I'd like to say that I pulled the answer out of Cory. No—Cory just laid it on me.

Cutler: Corey Johnson, the junior college defensive tackle,

says his weight is—quote—flexible.

Cory Johnson: I'll be 290, and the next day, you know, I'll be 300...the next day I'll be 280. My weight's flexible. It goes on its own.

Cutler: So if you have like two steaks and two extra meals, you put on ten pounds?

Cory Johnson: I mean, I guess because I poop so much. I try to poop like five times a day, three times a day, so it's hard to keep weight when you got so much going out.

Cutler: I'm not sure I have a follow up question.

We laughed when I said that...I don't think I've ever said to an athlete that I didn't have a follow up question. It was hysterical.
Was I surprised that Cory said it? *Absolutely.*
Was I surprised that Cory Johnson would say something surprising? *Absolutely not.*
One of these days, a grandpa will bring his grandkids to Kroger Field and tell them all about the time Alan Cutler asked Cory Johnson a question—and his answer was all about poop.
Poop has become so big for C.J., who played in the Canadian Football League, that he wrote a book called "Poopy Stew"—which is all about entertaining your child as they learn how to potty-train. Amazing!

106

Huggy Bear

Lots of coaches have a nemesis. You can be in the Hall of Fame and still have trouble beating a certain coach. That kind of stuff has been going on forever. For John Calipari, his nemeses have always been Jim Calhoun, Bob Huggins, and Bruce Pearl.

When Bob Huggins coached at Cincinnati (1989-2005), I was also doing Sports Talk on 700WLW in Cincinnati—one of the most powerful stations in the Midwest—beginning at three o'clock in the afternoon on weekends. In addition, I would also do a call-in show that would lead into a UC basketball game. Afterwards, I would stay on until midnight and do more Sports Talk after either the UC, Xavier, or the Cincinnati Reds baseball game.

In the first UC game I did that they lost, the producer told me, "I'm going to put Hugs in cue, but you've got to promise me you won't use any of this on air (meaning we could listen to what Coach was saying in commercial breaks, but it wasn't going to be broadcast over the air)." At that time on WLW, everything was game—nothing was sacred. You could do anything you wanted, so I'm shocked a producer would say that to me.

Huggins sits down with Dan Hoard, the UC play-by-play announcer. For the next minute and a half, it seemed like every other word out of Hugs' mouth was a curse. I was laughing so hard I was trying not to cry. He was ripping into his team saying how they were lazy—this, that, and stupid—the whole thing. It was just absolutely hysterical. But that's who Hugs is.

We go back on the air and Dan says, "Tough night, Coach," and throws Hugs a real softball question. Hugs responds, "Yeah, we didn't get back on defense, da da da da da da." Now I'm laughing so hard I'm doubled over. Obviously he's not going to curse when we're on the air, but he's like a completely different person, with a totally different tone of voice than he was a minute ago off the air.

In the early 2000s, Cal was coaching at Memphis. I was doing a Memphis versus UC game, and my producer told me that "Huggins owns Cal." Now remember, I had known Cal since the 1980s, which my producer didn't know, so I asked my producer to tell me why he thought that was true. He then goes on and on about how Huggins has Cal's number. The record showed he was right.

Fast forward to John Wall's Kentucky team playing Huggins' West Virginia team in the 2010 NCAA Tournament. It's not the worst loss in Cal's career, but it's close (losing the national championship to Kansas in the last two minutes while he was coaching at Memphis has to be No. 1).

I'm watching Cal and I'm watching Huggins courtside. A lot of people don't know that Bob Huggins was an Academic All-American. He's smart. Great basketball coaches, who are smart, feel things—they feel the situation.

Coaches, on the other hand, can also at times make huge mistakes. One of the advantages of being a fan or part of the media is being able to second guess the coaches. *They hate that.*

I believe that Huggins could feel when Cal was losing it. I've always believed that—Hugs is smart. I'm not ripping Cal.

Cal was going crazy on the sidelines that day. In fact, I'm not sure I've seen a big game Cal has coached at Kentucky where he was going any crazier. I think Hugs knew it, he could see it, and he could feel it.

West Virginia never should have won that game. Cal will go to his grave thinking he should have won the national championship that year. John Wall believes the same thing.

West Virginia's best player was 6'8" and a second-round draft pick for the Lakers for crying out loud. On the other hand, Kentucky had five first-round NBA draft picks on their team. They never should have lost that game. They kept on passing the ball around in a horseshoe, and they could not get the ball inside to DeMarcus Cousins—who was stopped by someone 6-foot-8. Ridiculous!

It's as obvious as the nose on my face—Cal got out coached by Huggins. I'm not ripping Cal.

I watched Coach K of Duke get out coached by Tubby Smith. It happens.

I'm just telling you what happened. I could see it happen. A coach can go *too* crazy. A coach can get so crazy that it can actually affect his players. Sometimes when a coach goes crazy, it actually really helps players and can amplify the performance of the team. On that day, Cal hurt the team by going crazy. I absolutely believe that.

The friendship between Cal and Hugs is legit. I don't think Cal would go and visit Hugs—you know that story that's been told a million times about when Cal went to visit him when Hugs almost died—if their friendship wasn't real. That friendship won't change the fact that, on the basketball court, Bob Huggins has been a nemesis to John Calipari.

107

Blue Calipari Sneakers

C al loves to kid. When he was introduced as the coach at UK, at a huge press conference, he pointed me out for my running ability—obviously of which I have none.

Cutler: Hey Cal...over here. How are you, pal?

Calipari: Pittsburgh. I'm doing good. Did you chase that guy? Did I see you chasing somebody? (laughter) Let me ask you, do you have tennis shoes on right now?

Cutler: No, I still have cowboy boots.

Calipari: Alan, you're getting gray. Alan and I go way back to when I had holes in my shoes. And wait a minute. He had holes in his shoes back in Pittsburgh. And I know he's crazy. Folks, he will not bother me. Not at all. Just so you know that. I'm telling you right in front of everybody.

He got exactly what he expected—a good laugh from the large crowd. And he used me to relax a little bit. All good.

Before I retired, Cal made a terrific gesture after I covered my last home game at Rupp after thirty-four years. It was a special night for me, as he presented me with a pair of blue sneakers. UK beating Ole Miss 96-78 that night made it even better.

What many don't know is that the first time Cal tried giving me the blue sneakers, I *screwed* it up. At the press conference *before* the Ole Miss game, Cal started by saying it was my last time covering Kentucky. I quickly said, "No it's not. We still have a game." I didn't know what I had done at the time.

It was after midnight when I got back to the TV Station when LEX18 sports anchor Keith Farmer told me what really was going on at the press conference before the Ole Miss game. As the press conference was starting, the newsroom had stopped, especially the main news desk where a number of people were watching it live because they knew Cal was supposed to give me the sneakers. Eric Lindsey—who is in charge of publicity for the basketball program—had called Keith, and Keith had called Judy to get my sneaker size. Of course they kept it from me. But before I found that all out, I was wondering how Cal knew my shoe size…Ha!

So when I said, "No, we still have another game," a couple of the people at the desk were yelling, "NO CUTLER. YOU JUST RUINED THIS, CUTLER!" They were yelling *at ME*. Keith told me I really messed it up. Eric Lindsey told me I threw them for a loop. Cal had the sneakers there ready to give me at the moment, and I messed it up— which made it even funnier. Everyone was laughing about it.

When he finally gave me the sneakers AFTER the game, it was a really nice gesture on Cal's part.

Calipari: Last question. Since you've never chased me, I'm giving you a pair of shoes so that you can chase me at any point. I'll let you come to practice. There's no way you can run me down.

Me: First practice next year, I'll own you.

Calipari: You better train for a year, my man.

Me: A year might not be long enough. Thank you.

Calipari: You're welcome. Last question?

Me: (Silence)

Calipari: I've never seen this before. Put all the cameras on him, please. I mean, you don't have something to say?

Me: Nah, I'm not going to ask what I really want. It's all good. Thanks, man.

Like I said, it was a lovely moment thanks to Cal. It's actually kind of funny how many people who knew about Cal giving me the blue sneakers ask me if I'm wearing them or if I'm going to bronze them.

Of course I'm wearing them. They're a cool pair of sneakers.

Part 12

Other Random Encounters

108

Arnold Palmer's Grand Entrance

Arnold Palmer did more for the game of golf than anyone—
and that includes Tiger Woods. Unfortunately, it's amazing
how often people forget, or don't know athletes who lived
in the past.

If ESPN talks about the greatest quarterbacks of all time, they'll
never say Otto Graham's name. Very few people living remember Otto
Graham. He was the quarterback for the Cleveland Browns when they
won championships. Graham led them to the league championship
game ten times in ten seasons. The Browns won seven of those championship games between 1946 and 1955.

Many remember Arnold Palmer—not just for his seven Major
championships and sixty-two PGA Tour victories—but for his charisma, his energy, and his charm. He was loved by fans like very few athletes of any generation. Muhammed Ali is the greatest in my lifetime
when it came to fans loving an athlete. In his prime, Palmer was a superstar.

Arnie was playing in a Seniors PGA Tournament in Lexington. This
was a cool event that probably stayed in Lexington for longer than it
should have. Lexington could only pay so much and when the purses
started going up, the city couldn't compete with bigger cities, so the
tour had to move on.

I had set it up that Arnie would do a live shot with me. I went up to
him, and he told me to tell him the *exact* time I would need him. I told
him I would need him exactly at 6:20 pm. And he says—I'll never forget this—he says, "That's not five minutes before, right?" I told him I
needed him exactly at 6:20, and he assures me that he'll be out there.

"Now do this," Arnie says. "If it's one or two minutes before, come
inside and knock on the door. I have a business call I have to make to

Japan."

Two minutes before we're about to go on the air, I knock on the door. Arnie acknowledges me and nods, and I go back out. I told the news producer that Arnie told me he would do the live shot, but it might be tight.

I'm just off the practice putting green at the Griffin Gate Resort surrounded by a lot of people. This is like something out of a movie scene—just as I'm saying hello, I hear people starting to clap. The clapping gets louder and louder. It's pretty obvious—Arnie is coming out. As I turn around, it's like the parting of the Red Sea. People just walk to the side, and Arnie walks perfectly right into the shot. It couldn't have been any better had we tried to choreograph it.

Arnie had a smile on his face and he says, "See, I told you I'd be here on time." We did the interview on a golf cart. Arnie was spectacular. It was a great interview because Arnie is always a great interview.

The moral of the story was that in his life, Arnold Palmer never big-timed anybody.

I learned a great lesson about how he treated people. He was always kind, warm, and gracious. He tried to make you feel like you were special and that you were important. It is a wonderful trait—just like being on time. This was Arnold Palmer.

109

Gary Player and "Alex" Cutler

By the tender age of twenty-nine, Gary Player became only the third person in the history of professional golf to have won all four Major championships. His nine Major championships on the regular tour, his 165 tour victories on six continents over six decades, and his nine Senior tour victories places his career squarely into the elite category.

Gary Player loves Lexington because he loves horses. The native South African is also one of the greatest fitness freaks of all time. He's in unbelievable shape. With his push-ups, sit-ups, and his focus on fitness—his discipline is unbelievable. If he ends up breaking ninety when he's a hundred years old—I won't be surprised. Plus, he is one of the most positive human beings I've ever met.

Gary Player, for decades and decades, was known as the greatest "sand man" in golf. Once I asked him if he thought he was the best in the world in hitting shots out of sand traps. He told me to show up later that day to find out.

I came back after the 6 pm news and got there just before he started. It was around seven o'clock, and the sun hadn't started setting. It was perfect. He says, "Alex,"—he always called me Alex. I had interviewed him four or five years in a row—and he says "Alex, so great to see you." You know what? I didn't correct him. He's *GARY PLAYER*. Hey, I'm just glad he called me *anything*. At least he remembered *something* about me.

The respect I had for Gary Player was off the charts. He was kind to people, he was considerate, he smiled, he made you feel good, he shook your hand and looked you right in the eye. He's a superstar, and he treats people with grace and class. It's just a great lesson when you see somebody that you look up to treat you like you're an equal—treat you like you're special.

Gary's in the sand, and hitting shots out. He hit dozens of shots that evening. His routine was that he wouldn't leave the course until he knocked one in the cup. After he knocked one in the cup, he came over and did the interview with me. He said that at least once during a tournament, at the end of the day, he'll put a ball in the sand trap and not walk off the course until he knocks it in.

"Gary, what happens if it gets dark?" I asked him. He says, "Well, that's happened Alex. I keep on doing it. There were times my caddy had to literally bring a tux to the golf course so I could quickly change and show up to a speaking engagement or dinner. I would explain why I was late, and everybody would understand."

There were also times that Gary hit one in while his caddy was holding a flashlight.

Now eighty-four, his goal remains the same—shoot a round fifteen strokes less than his age. Gary Player still heads to the gym after playing for an hour-long workout.

"You can forget about guys hitting the ball ridiculous distances off the tee, as I've always believed the power of the mind, paired with a strong short game, are the key ingredients to win tournaments," says Gary on his website. "I was fortunate to have been born with the drive and focus to win. Coming from a humble background in South Africa, that fighting spirit gave me the strength of mind to win."

Here he is, a Hall of Famer—but Gary Player's discipline to succeed is unparalleled. To be special, you must work at it. That's the secret. You know what LeBron James does every year after his NBA season is over? He picks a weakness in his game, and he practices to improve it.

Magic Johnson became a great free throw shooter. Twice in his last four seasons before he was forced to retire, he topped ninety percent for the season. When asked why his free throw percentage went up, Magic answered, "Practice."

Practice! Great players become even greater with practice!

The superstars often make it look easy, so it can be easy to overlook the work they put in to get there.

110

Lee Trevino on Choking

Lee Trevino, a member of Golf's Hall of Fame, was one of the great clutch players of all time. In head-to-head matchups against Jack Nicklaus, the best golfer ever, Trevino won more than his share.

In 1968, in his second year on the PGA tour, Lee not only won the U.S. Open, but he beat Jack Nicklaus, the defending champ, by four strokes. In 1971, he won the U.S. Open again by defeating Nicklaus in an 18-hole playoff.

His grandfather Joe, a grave digger, helped raise Lee. When Lee was five, he was working in the cotton fields. School wasn't for him. At fourteen, he quit school to make thirty dollars a week as a caddy while shining shoes. Working at the golf course allowed him to practice golf for free, and Lee claims to have hit three hundred balls every single day.

The former machine gunner in the Marines in the 1950s was a ton of fun to hang around with. He also taught me one of the greatest lessons of my life.

It happened when Lee Trevino came to Lexington to play in a Senior event. We were doing an interview, and he just lays this on me all at once. He says, "The winner is the one who chokes the least. So when I win a tournament, I choke less than everyone else." When I heard that, I was literally dumbfounded.

I follow up by asking him how he handles choking when he wins. "I'm usually pretty calm," he answers. "Because I've done it before." WOW! *The winner is the one who chokes the least.* I've used that quote many times since while speaking to groups—and I always say it's from Trevino.

Everybody chokes. It's how you handle choking that's important.

Everybody misses shots. It's how you handle your choking that is often the difference between winning and losing.

I'm convinced that's one of the great life lessons.

111

My Fifteen Seconds of Fame

Technology today is amazing compared to back in the good old days. Back in the 1990s, after you edited your story, you had to get it up on satellite—and then people at the NBC hub in Charlotte could see any story you sent back to your TV station. They could pick your story and use it for their feed to all NBC stations. Today you edit on a computer, and you don't need to travel with editing gear which was a big pain. You hit a few buttons, you don't have to buy satellite time, and it's amazing how fast it gets back to any TV station.

After Kentucky won the SEC basketball championship over Arkansas 95-93 in overtime on March 12, 1995 in Atlanta, I was doing a stand-up as the postgame celebration was happening. Everybody was going crazy. There's jubilation everywhere around me.

In the stand-up, Kentucky forward Jared Prickett comes over to me and starts messing with my hair. Then, guard Chris Harrison sticks his finger in my ear while I'm talking. I don't know if you've ever tried to talk with someone sticking their finger in your ear, especially if you don't see it coming, and it's loud, and there's a lot of celebrating going on. Robin Lynch, my photographer, kept his poker face on while shooting the stand-up.

Robin is a smart photographer. We could both think in the moment. When you work with a photographer who can really think in the moment, there's a powerful chemistry I can't explain. It's wonderful. I've been fortunate to work with many photographers that were really good—not just in taking pictures—but they could think instantly in the moment.

I'm really good at thinking in the moment. If that sounds pompous, don't care. If I'm working with a photographer who can't think in the moment, it holds me back and drives me crazy. You develop a trust with your photographer if you work with them for a long time. It's an unspoken bond that's impossible to communicate, but you both know it. Robin and I had a great bond even though we had some battles. Greg "Punk" Gorham and I had a great bond. And they weren't the only ones I was lucky enough to work with. The truth is I owe a lot of my success to my photographers who did not get enough credit.

If you've seen the tape of that stand-up I'm talking about, you'll notice that I don't break during the segment. I quickly learned you just keep talking. You don't stop, no matter what. I've been trained not to stop and react. Some of the best stand-ups I've ever done happened because someone did something goofy, and we captured it on tape. Like the time when John Calipari walks up behind me. I don't see him, and he sticks his finger in my ear. I just keep on doing my stand-up.

The stand-up's over, and I want to do a second take, just in case this one didn't turn out. Robin tells me, "No," and runs off to shoot the team cutting down the nets. I don't ever remember him telling me "no" before, and me not winning that battle. So much for me being the boss (I'm smiling as I write this).

Anyway, I was not going to chase Robin down. How dumb would that look? So I just had to stand there fuming inside. I didn't want to have to do another stand-up later when the arena's quiet. That's bad TV.

When Robin comes back a few minutes later and the celebrating is over, he can see steam coming out of my ears. I want to break his neck while we're walking off the court, and he's just laughing at me. He tells me not to worry about it. I asked him if he knew what I said on camera. I didn't even know because there was chaos all around and a finger in my ear. Robin said he had no idea what I said because it was too loud during the celebration. When we finally looked at the tape, he told me, "See, it's the best stand-up you've ever done." And he laughed both with and at me.

That clip was obviously part of our postgame package. One of the network sports guys in Charlotte saw it, and they just picked it off.

I'm driving to work the next week, when I hear this lady honking her horn at me like crazy. When I roll down my window to see what she wants, she tells me that I was great on the Today Show. *What?* I had absolutely no idea what she was talking about.

When I get to the TV station—Mike Taylor, our assignment editor—tells me, sure enough, our clip ended up on the Today Show. *You think somebody might want to tell me about this?* They pull the tape out and show me.

The guy in Charlotte saw my stand-up and told Len Berman's producer. Berman was the local NBC sportscaster in New York and did some funny segments with bloopers. In addition to the Today Show, my fifteen seconds of fame got played on many stations all across the country. I had people from all over telling me that they saw it.

It eventually even found its way on to David Letterman. The exposure was terrific—all because I kept on talking with a finger stuck in my ear.

112

In Tipton We Trust

I was anchoring sports for LEX18 when John Calipari came to town. He was coaching UMass at the time.

Calipari was in Lexington the day before the game, and he calls me at two-thirty in the afternoon. He tells me that Rick Pitino wants to see him and asks me for a ride. He doesn't really need a ride. He obviously wants something.

I pick him up, and we're driving from the Hyatt to Memorial Coliseum—it's about a mile and a half.

"So, is it true about [Jerry] Tipton?" he asked. "Rick tells me you can't trust him. Is it true?" Tipton has covered Kentucky Basketball since 1981 for the *Lexington Herald-Leader* and is in the Kentucky Journalism Hall of Fame. He started on the UK beat at about the same time I did.

That question had more than one meaning. One, it spoke volumes of what Pitino thought about Tipton. Two, even though they were about to play each other, at that point in their up and down relationship, Pitino and Calipari were on good terms.

When Pitino came to town to be interviewed for the Kentucky job, Tipton dug up some NCAA rules that were broken by Pitino. It happened when Pitino was an assistant at Hawaii. It almost stopped Pitino from becoming the Kentucky coach.

My phone at the TV station was ringing off the hook back then because of UK fans calling and ripping Tipton to me.

I said two things. One, don't tell me—call Tipton. And two, it took "guts" to ask that question and do the story. No UK fan liked the "guts" comment on my part. Most fans don't want you to ask a tough question. I never ducked from that, and neither did Tipton. That part of Tipton I respected.

The truth is that Tipton was never going to be trusted by Pitino, who has at times incredibly thin skin. If it wasn't the Hawaii story, it would have been something else. And, Pitino never forgets.

Remember Pitino never forgave me for doing the story against Vanderbilt when UK put—not once, but twice—the wrong free throw shooter on the line. It was a really good, legitimate story. Pitino was *way out of line with me.*

But I'm not here to defend Tipton. We are not friends.

Without telling the whole story, I had one of my favorite sports photographers who literally wanted to knock Tipton out—and I talked him out of it. I did it because I really liked my photographer and didn't want him to get fired. Let's just say that my photographer had a right to be mad.

Oh, I never trusted Tipton...but I respected him.

113

The Legendary Cawood Ledford

Cawood Ledford was one of the great voices of all time, one of the classiest people I've ever met, and one of the great play-by-play people in broadcasting history...and he did it at Kentucky for close to forty years.

People loved Cawood. It was easier to love Cawood back then than it would be today. Back then, people would literally sit around the radio and listen to his play-by-play. How many people sit around the radio today? It's not the medium that it once was.

Here's something that really stuck out to me. Once, Adolph Rupp said something to Cawood on the bus after a Kentucky game. It's something that you can't imagine Calipari or Pitino or Krzyzewski or Roy Williams would ever say to their play-by-play broadcaster. Rupp told Cawood that he wanted him to be completely honest while calling the games. If the team stunk, he wanted Cawood to say that they stunk. Rupp's a really smart guy and had the ulterior motive of utilizing the power of radio to motivate his players. If the team stunk, he wanted the players to know about it—to get them upset.

Smart coaches use the media to get their message out. Pitino and Calipari are really good at this. Tubby Smith didn't do it as much. Rupp was able to use Cawood to get his message back to his players. To me, that was Rupp's way of telling Cawood to be honest about the product.

One of the best days I spent in all the years at LEX18 was the morning my photographer, Jim Robertson, and I went up to Cawood's house. Jim was a really good photographer. We left before four-thirty in the morning in order to arrive in time to see Cawood hanging out early with his miniature ponies just as the sun was coming up. It was a day of hoops heaven. I wish I had the tape of everything we talked about.

Cawood's home was magnificent. He bought the home he was born in, which at the time was tiny. Cawood, being very successful, built all kinds of extensions.

Cawood had one of the biggest collections of huge pictures of sports stars that I've ever seen. They were everywhere. I'm trying to remember the pictures he even had over his washer and dryer. They were pictures that people would have loved to have had in their living rooms.

Cawood told me he was kind of shy. He didn't like to do public speaking. He was so much against public speaking that he raised his fees tremendously so that no one would hire him. He told me he got more speeches after he raised his price.

I asked him if he started doing more speeches. "For the amount of money I was asking, I'm not that shy," he answered.

Here's the feature I did with Cawood.

Cawood: I grew up with horses. I always had a horse when I was growing up here—a riding horse. And then I rode in college. I rode in some shows. I've just always just enjoyed them.

Cutler Narration: The living legend, whose golden tones were the voice of the Wildcats for almost four decades, got involved with miniature horses at the end of his career—and has owned as many as eighty at a time.

Cawood: When you get a few birthdays in you, these little fellows are easy to handle, and I really enjoyed them. I fool with them a lot.

Cutler Narration: Cawood has retired with his lovely bride Frances in the home he grew up in, in Cawood, Kentucky. He broke in at UK under the legendary Adolph Rupp, who was way ahead of his time—wanting Cawood to tell it like it is.

Cawood: He called me up to sit by him on the front seat of the bus. He said, "What'd you say about us tonight?" I said, "Coach, you didn't play very well." He said, "Anytime you see one of my teams stinking up the place or doggin' it, by Gawd, burn 'em." He's just a great coach. I don't know what else you can say. I think Kentuckians owe him a great debt of gratitude for what he did for the program.

Cutler Narration: Cawood's last game as Voice of the Cats was more than forty minutes of hoop heaven. In 1992, the underdog Cats thought they had the defending champs from Duke knocked out of the NCAA.

Cawood: [After Sean Woods hit the shot to put Kentucky up by one in overtime] Bob Ryan with the Boston Globe, sitting in front of me—he turned around with just a piece of notebook paper and it was written on there, "Greatest game ever?"

Cutler Narration: Cawood's home was full of hundreds of pictures, memories, and awards from his tremendous career. But the one thing he cherishes the most isn't here in Harlan County...Cawood is now in Rupp [Arena] with so many of UK's greats.

Cawood: It [having his jersey hanging in Rupp's rafters] came as such a surprise.

Cutler Narration: [After former UK guard Richie Farmer called Cawood a hero] Cawood will always be a hero, not only to the people around the walls of his home in Harlan County, but to millions of sports fans everywhere.

Cawood: [Signing off his last Kentucky radio broadcast] For those of you who have gone down the glory road with me, my eternal thanks.

114

Dale Brown Tossed

Dale Brown was head coach at LSU for twenty-five years. He took the Tigers to two Final Fours. He always had a tremendous amount of respect for Kentucky and their huge success in basketball.

In all the years I was doing TV and radio, I would put Dale Brown at the top of any list when it comes to having concern for other human beings. He was very strong in his beliefs, but he was also one of the kindest, caring people I've ever met. Crazy yes—but I'm good with that.

Brown, who grew up poor, has always fought for the average person. To this day, even in his eighties, he's fighting for all of us to be better to each other.

In an email to me, Dale wrote, "Kindness sees no color, ethnicity, age, gender, status, wealth, or religion. However, it does see another person of God. Kindness is a language the deaf can hear and the blind can see. With one small gesture you can change a person's life for better or for worse."

At the end of his career at LSU, it was pretty obvious that Dale was going to retire. When he came to Kentucky for his last game, he didn't have a very good team. Because LSU quickly fell behind, he purposely got himself thrown out of the game. He didn't want to be there, and the officials did him a favor by tossing him.

I've been friends with Dale for a long time, so I did something you could never get away with today. This was a late nine o'clock game, so I went into the locker room where he was sitting and asked him if he would come out and do the eleven o'clock sports segment with me live. He looks at me like I'm crazy, but says, "Sure, why not?"

I then tell him that we'll have to sneak him back into Rupp Arena—

because remember—if you're thrown out of a game, you can't go back into the arena. So, about five minutes before we go on the air, I sneak him underneath the stands. As soon as people spotted us, they started chanting Dale's name. It was crazy.

As soon as we're done with the live segment, one of the ESPN photographers runs towards us with his camera. Unfortunately for him, he missed it by that much. You talk about bad timing.

We finished up, and Dale gave me a really nice handshake. Think about this. The last game Dale Brown ever coached at Kentucky, he gets thrown out on purpose...and I'm doing a live interview with him while the game's still in progress...and he's not even supposed to be in the arena.

During his career, Dale Brown went through an NCAA investigation where he always claimed he was innocent. For decades, he has said the NCAA—the ruling organization of college sports— needs to go.

"The counterfeit ineffective NCAA should be dismantled and [be replaced by] a new and refreshing organization that does not legislate against human dignity, practice monumental hypocrisy, profit from athletes while restricting them from earning a profit, and give preferential treatment to some of the elite schools. This is the truth and can no longer be tolerated."

For what it's worth, I know a Kentucky Basketball coach who feels the same way. He's no fan of the NCAA, partly because of what he perceives is the unfair treatment of the student-athletes.

115

Advice for Dick Vitale

Dick Vitale, whether you like him or not, is one of the all-time great broadcasters. He was also a power broker and liked to tell everybody what to do.

I've known Vitale since he wasn't Dick Vitale. I got to know him very early in his ESPN career. Dick is a screamer as everyone knows. About twenty-five years ago, before a game at Rupp Arena, we were talking in the media area. I tell him he has all the money in the world, and he's giving me that "what are you talking about?" look.

"If you don't change how you talk, you're going to lose your throat before your career is over," I said to him.

He went from the Dick Vitale who was your friend, who counseled you and loved hearing great things about himself... to a side of Dick I had never seen before. He told me I didn't know what I was talking about.

Excuse me?—I was really upset at that remark.

"Look, here's the deal," I cautioned him. "You need to hire a voice coach. My Aunt Doris was a cantor and a great opera singer. My mom was a great singer. My mom taught me at an early age that you need to talk from your diaphragm. If you talk from your diaphragm instead of your throat, you won't put pressure on your throat."

Me? I can't sing in the shower—but, believe me, until I was thirteen, I had a set of pipes.

Just look at coaches who scream all the time. They have a sore throat all the time because they're talking the wrong way.

The next time I saw Dick, I asked him about the voice coach. He abruptly walked away. And the weird thing is that for the past twenty-five years, since that moment, I've had very few conversations with him. I had zero desire to talk to him. When he comes to Rupp Arena,

411

he's friendly with everybody else in the media. But we basically don't talk to each other—all since I made that suggestion.

Dick eventually lost his voice and ended up having polyps taken off his throat. I'm not a doctor, but I'm convinced that if he listened to me back then, his voice wouldn't sound like it does today.

When you look at somebody who's considered a big star like Vitale, and you take them out of their comfort zone, and their role changes— then their attitude towards you can change just as quickly.

Sour grapes? No—Vitale is a Hall of Famer. What he has done to raise a fortune to help out kids with cancer is a million times better than anything I've ever done. In that case, he used his power for about the best cause on Earth.

It never bothered me that he wasn't smart enough to listen to me— that's his call.

But he has no idea how close I came to ripping him like crazy because of how he treated me.

116

I Love P.J. (Cooksey)

Patricia "Patti" "P.J." Cooksey. I love P.J. I'm going to repeat it. *I love P.J.*
There is a spirit and joy about P.J. that's different—especially when you know what she's gone through. I don't believe women's organizations all across America have given P.J. her due.

Try walking a mile in her shoes. I know I wouldn't be tough enough.

It's interesting and ironic that covering my last Kentucky Derby, on my last day on TV, I ran into P.J. We had a great hug and a great talk, and she was so excited to introduce me to her kids.

In 1979, P.J. won her first race as a jockey. She ended up winning 2,137 races. At one point she was No. 1 all time for a female jockey, until Julie Krone—another great jockey—passed her up.

P.J. was a pioneer in sports like Jackie Robinson was, but in a *much less* amplified form. I know some people won't like me saying that, but it's true. Jackie Robinson paved the way for African Americans and the way our society changed. P.J. paved the way for other women to become jockeys—and get more respect.

P.J. was treated like crap. That's the nicest way I can put it. How about being in many races where the other male jockeys are trying to push you to the rail because they didn't want you in the race?

P.J. had to use her fists to survive. P.J., because she was female, couldn't get mounts. In order to get mounts, she did something that a lot of jockeys do to make extra money—she exercised horses. P.J. offered to exercise horses in the morning just to get in races.

P.J. was the second female to run in the Derby and the first to run in the Preakness. Her last race was in 2004, capping a 26-year racing career.

413

P.J. also survived a bout with breast cancer in 2001.

Pound for pound, there's no doubt in my mind that with all their injuries and what they have to deal with trying to guide a sixteen-hundred-pound animal, jockeys are the toughest athletes in the world.

P.J. quit riding, not because she felt her skills were diminished, but because she couldn't get any mounts...and she didn't want to go through that whole process again.

Forget your ability as a jockey, it's discouraging when you're turning into the stretch, and you know your horse doesn't have a shot at winning. P.J. told me that it got to the point it wasn't fun knowing that when it came to the stretch, she was sitting on a horse that couldn't win. So, she retired.

I love P.J. because she's positive. I wish my mother had P.J.'s attitude.

My mother in her own way was a pioneer. My mother got two master's degrees at a time women weren't going to college. She was working on her doctorate when she decided not to finish. As a child with an amazing voice, she had a chance to go to Europe to study in conservatories. But, since Jewish people were fleeing that part of the world back then because of the way they were being treated in many places like Russia and Germany, there was no way my grandparents were going to allow her to go.

Why is it that women at times have to be twice as good as men? Why is it that to this day it's embarrassing to see the lack of women on the boards of major companies in America?

I got this way by watching my mother get beat down and not getting jobs when she was much smarter and far more qualified than the men who were hired. *IT'S WRONG!* It's always been wrong.

My sister, who's really smart, will tell you that our mother is the smartest person that she's ever known. And yet, my mom never recovered from getting beat down by men.

P.J. got beat down by men...not just from the other jockeys but from so many owners and trainers who didn't want to put a female on their horse. She's survived, and she's thrived, and everybody loves her.

It would be easy for P.J. to be angry and mad at the world because of how she was treated during her daily battle to be a female jockey. But she's so strong and so positive and a living example of how life is all about not what happens to us, but how we deal with it.

And as a pioneer, she paved the way for so many other women to make a living in one of the world's greatest and toughest sports.

117

Fastest Sportswriter in the World

Chip Cosby was one of the fun characters who covered UK Football for a decade starting in 2000. Think about all those crazy stories with four head coaches, six offensive coordinators, and five defensive coordinators.

This is Chip's take on the blazing speed he displayed in front of the entire UK Football team after practice one day.

"So it was 2006...and I was doing a weekly radio show with Alan, and former UK players Dennis Johnson and Joey Couch (rest in peace, Joey).

It must have been a Tuesday, because the Cowboys had played that Monday night, and I'm a big Cowboys fan. Anyway, the Cowboys lost the game, and Drew Bledsoe was the quarterback at that time. He was awful. So I remember saying on air, 'Heck, I could outrun Drew Bledsoe in the 40-yard dash.' And Cutler was like, 'No way. There's absolutely no way you could outrun Drew Bledsoe in the 40.'

So we kept going back and forth about it, and my braggadocio had gotten to the point where I said I could run the 40-yard dash in under 5 seconds, which Cutler thought was ridiculous. Now keep in mind, I was a 32-year old sportswriter who had never played college football and weighed 275 pounds at the time. I knew there was no way in hell I could run a 40 in under 5 seconds. But we were having such a good time with it I decided to just keep rolling with it.

Then comes the next day after football practice. The media had finished all their coach and player interviews, and Rich Brooks walked up to me. He said, 'I heard you on the radio saying you could run the 40 in under 5 seconds.' He reached in his pocket, pulled out a wad of cash (I can't remember how much, but it was at least 200 bucks). He said, 'I'll give you a week to train, and then after practice, you're going to come out here and run the 40. If you run it under 5 seconds, this (he points to the cash) is yours.'

I was like, 'Aww, shit, what have I gotten myself into?' But I figured what the hell, might as well have fun with it.'

I didn't train a lick. In fact, I was sick as a dog the morning I woke up to run the 40. But there was no way I could back out.

It was a Wednesday. It must have been raining because the team was inside at the Nutter Field House. Practice ended. Brooks blew his whistle and called the entire team over to the sideline. He yelled out, 'Alright, Cosby, let's see what you got.'

I lined up. He was at the end holding a stopwatch. On your mark, get set, go...I took off. Now mind you, I felt like I was moving pretty fast. In the back of my mind, I was like, 'I might do this, or at least come close.'

I crossed the finish line and looked over at Brooks.
'5.81.'

I was like, 'No way. I did better than that. Let's do it again.'

I lined up, sprinted, crossed the finish line again.
'5.84.'

OK. I'm done. Keep the money.

The thing I remember the most about the whole experience was the players' reactions on the sideline as I was running.

They loved it. They were hooting and hollering, laughing, having a good time with it. That part made me feel good.

The story blew up bigger than anybody would have imagined. The *Herald-Leader* sent a reporter out to cover it and did a write-up about it. It was picked up the next day by ESPN on *Pardon The Interruption*, and Kornheiser and Wilbon talked about it on the show.

Two days later, Kentucky went out and beat Georgia, who had Matthew Stafford at the time. It was the first signature win of the Rich Brooks era, and it would mark the first of three straight bowl games for Brooks. I had a couple of UK staffers tell me that they thought the whole 40-yard dash experience loosened the players up and helped lighten the mood and pressure going into such a pressure-packed game. Now I don't know about all of that, but the players and coaches did get a kick out of it. I lost the bet, but I'm still waiting on some kind of royalty check from Brooks for the morale boost (half-joking).

Anyway, Alan made the whole thing happen. His radio show provided the forum, and his name and reputation with local viewers brought attention to the story. It was certainly a monumental moment in my career, and something fans still bring up to this day when I'm out and about.

For the past several years, I've thought about reaching out to UK and seeing if I could have another crack at the 40, because I'm about 50 pounds lighter than I was then. But then I realized that I'm also 13 years older, and figured it was better to leave the story as is."

Thanks guys—Chip Cosby

Back to me with a big smile.
I always thought Rich Brooks should have handed out two more game balls—one to Chip, and one to the loud-mouth sportscaster who might have pushed to make it happen.
The wonderful thing is how Rich Brooks had a great sense of hu-

mor about the whole thing.

"I was thinking I should be timing with one of those sand timers," Brooks told me.

Part 13

That's What They Said

118

How Great is Tom Hammond?

*C*lass—that one word describes Tom Hammond. I can't think of ten better network announcers in the history of television than Tom Hammond. His work in the Olympics—in track, in the 100 meters—it's some of the best play-by-play calls in any sport that I've ever heard. It's as good as *anything* I've ever heard.

Tom learned to do all that while he was sports director at LEX18. At that time, he was responsible for doing the replays of the horse races at Keeneland. Tom couldn't go to the races in person because he was anchoring the sports, so they gave him a long sheet that had the horses, their pole positions, the odds, and where they were as the race went on. From that, he would call the race on TV. When I arrived in 1981, Tom was still doing the call. He was *REALLY GOOD*.

To put it mildly, nothing intimidates me—except replacing Tom Hammond. When Tom gave up the call of the Keeneland races, Harry Barfield, the president and general manager of LEX18, calls me into his office and tells me he wants me to take over for Tom. He even offered me extra money. I never asked him how much—I just told him I wasn't doing it. I couldn't follow Tom Hammond. There's *NO WAY!* I knew I was really good at radio-play-by-play, but horse racing to me at that point was different. I didn't want to replace Tom Hammond.

Tom Hammond is really smart. He earned a B.S. in Animal Science from the University of Kentucky in 1967. He specialized in equine genetics and followed after his grandfather, Thomas Poe Cooper, a former dean of the UK College of Agriculture and a former acting president of the university. Tom also has ridiculous vision. I've never seen another human being with vision like his. When I first started working he would do commentaries for LEX18. He had his own typewrite with the tiniest letters I've ever seen. When he handed me the scripts the first thing I said to him was, "Tom, how the hell can you see these things?" I couldn't see it to read it. He just started laughing. He had 20/10 vision—just like baseball great Ted Williams.

Tom Hammond never turned me down anytime I needed him to do an interview or to help. He never big-timed me. He loves Channel 18, and he's an encyclopedia of knowledge. Think about all he's done, all the SEC and national coaches he's interviewed, and all the Olympic greats he's talked to. He and former Rupp's Runts' Larry Conley went on the road for decades broadcasting basketball games. I'm sure they've got a ton of crazy stories from all the coaches they've encountered. Coaches trusted Tom and shared a lot of stories back then— much more than they share today.

Every now and then, Tom will still share a story with me. I'm sixty-seven years old, and if Tom Hammond wanted to talk to me for an hour, I would just sit there and listen. He's an underrated treasure. He was next in line to do the Super Bowl at NBC when they hired Al Michaels.

Here's a funny story about Tom. I'm in Pittsburgh, and I'm working for KDKA. Back then, Tom had never done a football game. However, he was so good doing the Breeders' Cup that his bosses wanted him to branch out and do other things. So, he starts out being the low man on the totem pole doing football for the network. Now, realize that the low man on the totem pole for NBC Sports is still big time.

I'm doing a talk show on KDKA radio. During those days, disgruntled Pittsburgh Steelers fans were angry because the Steel Curtain days were over, and the team was falling apart. They were mad at the world. They lived and died with their team as much as any professional team I've ever been around. I'd put them equal to Kentucky Basketball fans. Steeler fans were mad that Tom Hammond was doing their games because they didn't know who he was. He wasn't famous, like the Dick Enbergs of the world. They were used to having the top network announcers do their games. They weren't necessarily mad at Tom. They were just taking it out on Tom.

I'm getting dozens of calls complaining about Tom. "Who is that Tom Hammond guy, and how come we always get the worst announcer?" they would ask. I did my best to defend Tom. The next time I saw him, I told Tom the story, and he just laughed. Tom was great—he understood they weren't complaining about him. When he told me he had never done football before, I just freaked. He was really good. I listened to his first game and was dumbfounded by how good he already was.

One of the best things at my retirement party was Tom Hammond being there. This gets to me just talking about it. I have so much respect for him.

For him to tell me how much he appreciated what I've done in Kentucky meant the world to me. He said something that no one had ever conveyed to me before. He pinpointed how I dived into, studied the Kentucky culture, and how I made the Kentucky culture like my own. I was shaking afterward. Because that was my game plan. I decided before my first day on TV in Lexington that I was going to be the New York boy who would learn and respect the wonderful sports culture of Kentucky.

If you dive into the culture, people will accept you. Being a big mouth from New York, to me, that was the only way to succeed. In the process, I learned so much about Kentucky that made me want to call it home.

Tom saw what I did, and he thanked me for doing it. I'll never forget it as long as I live.

119

You're Welcome, Kenny Rice

When I think of Kenny Rice, I think of a really good dude. We competed against each other when he was at Channel 36. It's not his fault his station sucked. I thought Kenny was the best part of the station. He did a good job. Kenny got the break of his life because of me. Whether it was pure coincidence or not, to Kenny's credit, he took advantage of it and blossomed.

For a year and a half to two years, I was one of the top stringers for ESPN. A stringer is someone ESPN would call up to send in a story. Any time Kentucky was ranked in the top twenty, they would take a game story from me and run it on the network. Back then, they were desperate for stories. They would take anything.

What always bothered me about the set up was that my TV station always took half the money paid off the top. They said I used their equipment—which was true—but I was also working twenty-five to thirty extra hours a week when I anchored that they didn't pay me.

ESPN back then was paying a hundred dollars a story. After paying my photographer and Uncle Sam, I was only making twenty-five to thirty dollars for doing each story. It just wasn't worth it.

Back then, we couldn't send a story in by satellite. Back then, if Kentucky played a night game, we had to put it on an old tape the station was throwing out. You then had to go to Delta Dash by 6:30 the next morning in order for the tape to make the 7:00 am plane. It would get to New York, and somehow by bus to Bristol, Connecticut by that afternoon. ESPN wouldn't be able to play the game story until 6:00 that night. It was that archaic.

Look at it this way. When I was sending stories to ESPN, CNN, and an independent news service in New York, I didn't leave the TV station until around 1:30 am.

423

There were times the same game story ran the next day on both ESPN and CNN. The only difference was how I tagged out the story. There were times I could watch both stories in the same half hour. I couldn't believe how many times this happened.

One day, ESPN called me up and said you can't do that anymore. My response? "What took you so long?" So I quit CNN because I was doing more stories for ESPN.

I had already turned down a full-time job at ESPN two times. They wanted me to move to New York to be their New York City reporter (which I would have loved)—but they didn't want to pay me a salary, and you couldn't live on what they wanted to pay per story that you did.

One day, they called me for a story, and I told them, "I'm done."

ESPN and ABC are joined at the hip. When I told them I was done, they naturally looked for someone at the ABC affiliate in town. Kenny Rice was at WTVQ TV, so Kenny started doing things for them.

ESPN started doing horse racing around that time. Kenny became the logical person to do it. When NBC got horse racing, Kenny was a natural to start doing that as well. Kenny was all over NBC-TV interviewing triple crown winning trainer Bob Baffert at my last Derby.

Kenny does a terrific job. I've told Kenny how proud I am of him. He handles himself with class.

Here's the best part about Kenny Rice. Kenny goes to the Kentucky Sweet Sixteen high school basketball tournament every year with his father. We're talking decades and decades of games.

Several years ago, I was at the Sweet Sixteen. I'm walking in to cover the championship game, and Kenny yells at me and introduces me to his father. To be able to do that with your father is just a blessing. I've always been happy for them.

I've also always been jealous because that never would have happened with me and my father.

Kenny's a really good dude who's done a great job in broadcasting.

120

Caroline "Killer" Keller

When I came back to work at LEX18 in 1987, John Duvall, then the assistant general manager—at the end of the contract negotiations—said to me, "I have a present for you. Not only am I going to give you your own producer, but I have the perfect producer for you."

John saw my eyes light up because he knew how hard I worked—that I was a workaholic. "I've picked her out for you, but you have to approve her. There's only one bad thing about this. She's never worked in TV, and she's not a sports person, but I think you're going to be really happy."

I asked John if she was efficient. If she was efficient, then I told John, "I'm in."

Her name was Caroline Keller. Caroline turned out great. She still sends Judy and I the best Christmas cards. She finished No. 2 in the Miss Ohio competition twice. Caroline was smart, obviously pretty, and she could think on her feet.

It didn't take her long to fit in because she could *smack talk* sports. One of my big disappointments at the TV station is that they wouldn't put her on TV. After I got to know her and see how she handled herself, she was the most obvious person the station could have put on the air. I wanted to make Caroline a reporter. I was turned down twice, and I was really ticked off.

Back then, news directors didn't want to hire women to do sports. I always thought that was dumb. My feeling was that in a couple of years, Caroline would have left Lexington, perhaps made one other stop, and gone on to ESPN. Pretty... smart...logical...could handle things on a tight deadline...and she could talk sports. It was as obvious as the nose on my face.

Caroline became friends with Judy and me. I was really crazy back then, and Caroline's ability to adjust to me changing things on a dime was absolutely unbelievable. She told me she had a tough time choosing what to write about our time together. Here's what she finally did.

Caroline Keller: My memories of Alan Cutler are as numerous and wildly directed as the hairs on his crazy head (now beard)! When Alan returned to Kentucky from Pittsburgh, one caveat was that he would have his own sports producer, a first in Lexington TV. WLEX upheld its end of the bargain...sort of. What he got was me; a 19-year-old, 5'4, blonde, blue-eyed, soon-to-be pageant contestant, UK co-ed with no editing skills, and sports knowledge limited to an obsession with the Olympics and a crush on Pat Riley. But he didn't balk, at least to me, anyway. Almost immediately, my last name went from Keller to Killer. Now imagine Alan on the phone with a sports figure or contact of some sort. He would say, "My producer, Killer, will come pick you up," or, "I'll send Killer out to get that tape." I cannot tell you how much fun it was to see these often large men looking around and waiting for an equally manly "Killer" to show up, only to see me bop out of a Barry Manilow blaring car. Videographer Norm Kelley, 6'6 and with legs like Alysheba, drew Alan's short straw and was assigned to teach me how to edit. Alan refined it, showing me not to make the cut until the ball was just hitting the air so the video would seem to move faster and the piece more exciting. I practiced that exercise to the tune of "Killer, Killer, come to Edit 5!!!!!" screaming over the intercom until we had TWENTY-THREE tapes in a Friday night sports segment.

We were an unlikely pair bonded by mutual respect. Every once in a while, his blustery, East-coast bravado got out of hand, and he was known to dress down a co-worker or two. I got really mad at him after a particularly harsh tongue-lashing he threw out to someone. I followed him into the edit booth and yelled, "You are not exactly popular in this town. You have one person who likes you; me, and one person who loves you; Judy. If you don't knock it off and get a handle on yourself, you are going to be down to one, and I don't think either of us wants that to happen." I still recall this so vividly because I do not yell at people. Ever. Let alone a boss. He found me in an editing booth and said, "You know, Killer, it took guts to say that. And because you did, I know you do still like me. Thanks." We went back to work, and that was the first and last hint of a cross word spoken between us.

Life in Cutler's world happened fast: We talked fast; we walked fast; we worked fast; we ate fast – if at all. I believe that atmosphere set me up to be able to juggle a lot of things quickly to this day. I also tend to think the potty-mouth I fight almost daily is a direct result of my eight hours a day with Alan. We could both land a joke AND take one like a pro. He brought me Thanksgiving dinner when I was the only one working the holiday. After making me try them, he also never forgot to bring me stuffed banana peppers from DeSha's, where he'd do a Monday night radio show.

I was thrilled to be around him when his daughter, Jenna, was a baby and see that cool, tough persona melt right in front of my eyes – as it also did at the mention of Judy's name. In fact, he got to try out his paternal instincts on me. I was crazy about Mark Grace, first baseman for the Chicago Cubs. Because of this, coupled with the fact that I watched the SNS sports feed and took what we "needed," there were an inordinate amount of Cubs highlights for a Lexington station. Alan would just shake his head with a "Really Killer? My God...." He really was all I could talk about. Just when my ardor was reaching a fever pitch, the Cubs came to play the Reds. Alan was sending a crew to Cincinnati to cover the game, and I begged him to let me go, too. He said no. I couldn't believe it, and the pleading persisted for a couple more days, half thinking he was joking. When game day came and it was clear I really wasn't going, I stood at his desk in anguished amazement asking, "Why?!?!?!" Alan calmly said, "Do you know why? Because I know you are nuts about him and guess what? If he met you, I'm sure he'd fall for you, too. And because he's a baseball player, he'd end up breaking your heart. So that's why you are not going." What could I say to that????? Well, now I know..... Jenna and J.J., you've got a good one. -- Caroline Keller (Killer) Reece

121

Susie Williams Basham

Whether it's Caroline Keller or Susie Basham, I love them both like sisters. I can't begin to tell you how much I care about those two ladies. They always had my back, they always gave great suggestions, they're both smart, they could both adjust on a dime, and they could both do things really quickly. Back then, if something big happened, I would throw everything out the window, and we would just change everything. You have to be really calm and cool putting up with me doing that. Under those pressurized deadlines, I think that's when I excelled—partly because I knew my producers had my back.

Both these ladies saw me in ways my family has never seen me. They saw me in ways the public has never seen me. They saw me in ways that very few people have ever seen me. It's tough for me to describe how much I like both of them.

Susie Williams Basham: My favorite memory is working with Alan during the sanctions on UK and the hiring of Ricky P. Alan would be on hold on one line, talking in another, and typing. I would be yelling, "FIVE MINUTES TO AIR!" Alan would give me copy that I had to run to the booth, and Alan would be putting on a tie as he ran to the studio! Those were crazy times— "cutting" it to the last second, but he always got the story. Those were great times.

122

Robin Lynch

What's interesting is that Robin Lynch, my photographer at the time—a great photographer who's like a little brother—at times drove me crazy while I drove him just as crazy. But, we always had a great deal of mutual respect for each other. When you work with somebody who has as much talent as Robin, you learn to put up with stuff. Robin will get mad at me for saying that, but he's probably also smiling because it's true. I was crazy back then, so he also put up with a bunch of stuff from me. It was an equal deal.

When I think about this, I find myself getting really angry again, so I try not to think about it. LEX18 was going through a period when money was really tight. There was constant talk of people getting laid off. No one was getting a raise. When you're working in the newsroom, you really don't know what's going on because those who are running the company aren't going to tell you.

It's 1992, and Rick Pitino was king in Kentucky as UK's basketball coach. Kentucky was going to the NCAA Tournament. Everyone thought they had a shot to make the Final Four. *Management decides that we're not going to cover the games.*

It's interesting to hear Robin's take on how we missed the 1992 Duke game which is still considered one of the greatest college basketball games of all time. Duke won 104-103 on a great shot at the buzzer by superstar Christian Laettner. It still bothers Robin. It's one of the biggest bunches of garbage that LEX18 ever handed to us. We didn't cover Kentucky. Are you kidding me? This was a dumb decision. It wasn't like sending us would have cost the station thousands of dollars.

Robin Lynch: Of course, to rip WLEX even further than you may already have was the infamous 1992 NCAA Tournament.

429

We offered to drive to Worcester, MA, possibly stay with your brother in NY on the off days, and then drive to Philly to cover UK in the tourney and save money. Of course the powers that be said "no." We STILL couldn't afford it, and we missed what many believe to be the best game in NCAA Tourney history between UK and Duke. I think we were the only Kentucky station to not be at that game...still pisses me off to this day. I tell people that story and they all say, "How the hell can you not cover UK?"

Everybody who has shot video for me at LEX18 and has gone on the road a number of times with me, has unfortunately had similar experiences with my dependence on coffee. Here's one of Robin's numerous accounts of his dealings as my photographer between 1988-1996.

Robin Lynch: Of course there was your coffee drinking and newspaper reading on the road, which made road trips even longer as we had to stop every hour while driving so you could use the bathroom and then get even more damn coffee. I remember leaving Nashville one morning after a UK-Vandy game the night before. You naturally bought a large coffee and set it on top of the newspaper vending machine while you bought a paper. You let the door to the machine slam shut, knocking over the coffee, and spilling it all over your boots. After cleaning everything up, you bought another large coffee and got in the car placing the coffee on the dash. As I backed away from the parking spot, the coffee spilled all over your boots and all over the floor of the car. Once again you cleaned it up and then bought a third large coffee. Hell, we should have been near the Kentucky border, and we hadn't even left Nashville yet. I wish I had seen your expense report for three large coffees at the same location.

I did put in for the three large coffees and expected to get questioned—but no one said a word.

None of us will ever forget the 1990 game where Kentucky shocked LSU at Rupp Arena 100-95. I can't think of five times where Rupp was louder than on that day. I'm not sure there were three times where Rupp was louder in all my time covering sports in Lexington. When i

430

comes to underachieving teams—as much as I personally like LSU coach Dale Brown—that is the biggest underachieving group of basketball players I have ever seen...and there's no number two.

You had Shaquille O'Neal. You had Chris Jackson. You had seven-foot Stanley Roberts. And you had several other players who were great athletes who never really developed into great basketball players the way I think they probably should have.

Kentucky should have lost the game by twenty-five or thirty points easy. Chris Jackson hit seven threes and scored forty-one points. He hit some threes that were Steph Curry-like. He hit some of the longest three-point shots I've ever seen at Rupp Arena.

The only better show I've ever seen at Rupp was when UK star forward Tayshaun Prince hit five in a row against North Carolina. That was better—partially because it was Prince, and partially because he just kept on throwing up threes and moving back each time. On the last one, everyone was anticipating him shooting it, and it seemed like he shot it from thirty-five feet plus. Rupp exploding at that moment was one of the greatest explosions at Rupp I've ever witnessed.

Because Chris Jackson played for LSU, there were only some "oohs and aahs" from the Rupp crowd. I remember him stopping and popping from thirty-five feet like it was nothing. The first time he took one of those shots, I knew he was a great shooter and I knew he had great range, but I'm thinking, "What are you doing?"

I always thought there was something between Jackson—who later changed his name to Mahmoud Abdul-Rauf—and Shaq. Because Shaq only shot the ball eight times that game. He was six of eight. The beauty for Kentucky was that they had six players in double figures. Derrick Miller had 29, Deron Feldhaus had 24, and there were *four others* in double figures. Shaquille O'Neal had 14 points and 21 rebounds. How he only shot the ball eight times, I'll never figure it out!!!! The tallest player on Kentucky, Reggie Hanson, was 6'7". He was skinny, but tough. Stanley Roberts and Shaq were 7'1" or taller. They were huge men. I'm not sure Rick Pitino had a better win at Rupp Arena.

This is Robin's take on us getting an exclusive interview with Shaq the day before the game. I was friends with LSU coach Dale Brown, so we got to see practice when other stations didn't. I got a great one-on-one interview with Shaq. It was a lovely scoop. This is what happened after the game.

Robin Lynch: Lastly I still tell people this story...in February

1990, LSU came to play UK on a Saturday. The night before, Alan and I went to the LSU practice at Rupp, as Dale Brown invited us to come. I think we were the only local TV station there. Shaq was a freshman, and after practice we talked to Dale on camera, and he asked if we wanted to speak with Shaq. Of course we did, and Shaq was great. After the game the following day (which UK won), they brought Shaq to the old media room and sat him on a couch because everyone wanted to talk with him. He sat down, saw Alan and said, "Hey Groucho, good to see you again!" I have run across Shaq a few times years later and always wanted to bring that up to him but never got the opportunity.

123

Larry Vaught

Larry's like my kid brother. You battle with your kid brother every now and then.

When I got here in the early eighties, Larry was working for his father, who was the sports editor of the Danville paper. We would get the Danville paper mailed to us, and it would always be a day or two late. But I started reading the paper because of Larry and his dad. I was impressed how many local stories they were banging out.

Larry's really good. I believe there's nobody in the state of Kentucky that has done more for young people doing feature stories than Larry. I don't think he's ever gotten enough credit—especially early in his career—because he worked for a Danville newspaper. The thinking was that if you're not in Lexington or Louisville, you can't be as good. Growing up the way I did, I always thought that was a bunch of garbage. If you're good, you're good. It doesn't matter who you are or where you're from. I think Larry didn't get enough respect because he wasn't working for the *Lexington Herald-Leader* or the *Louisville Courier-Journal*.

We once did a talk show on TV, which was crazy and almost didn't make any sense. It was a half-hour show, and I wanted to bring somebody else on to help me out. I went to Larry and said, "Here's the deal. There's no money for doing this, but I'm going to tell you why you need to do it. If you will do this, you're going to get exposure on TV, and somehow you're going to start doing some radio and some other things because people will see that you're good, and they'll look at you differently."

Larry agreed to do it. We didn't pay him any money. He did a segment on the show with me, and he did a really good job. Shortly after that, Larry's career changed, and he started doing radio in Lexington.

Larry's very good on radio. That TV show with me changed his career. All kinds of other opportunities then opened up for him. Those were opportunities that should have opened up for him anyway. He was that good.

When the Danville newspaper—which was having trouble—let Larry go, it was a really stupid thing for them to do. He was—and still is—huge there.

I jumped at the opportunity to hire him. I made the suggestion to Bruce Carter, my news director, who agreed it was a very good suggestion. We got the deal done quickly. I consider him a dear friend and have a great deal of respect for what he does.

Here's the wonderful column Larry wrote in preparation for my retirement.

Larry Vaught: He's wanting to just fade away peacefully, but no way can I let Alan Cutler retire on May 5 after 33-plus years with WLEX-TV without making sure you know the real Cutler.

Sure, you've seen him on TV sharing his opinions — and didn't he always have one — but also informing you with his own "exclusive" stories that he worked tirelessly to get.

LEX18 anchor Nancy Cox has worked with Cutler for 25 years. She says she could share a Cutler story from every day.

"What still strikes me the most is the first time I subbed for Mindy Shannon on the 6 p.m. news. I felt like a fish out of water on that set. Did not feel I belonged there with the pros," Cox said. "Then Alan Cutler blew into the studio like a hurricane — a really hairy hurricane. All I could think was, 'I'm sitting beside Alan Cutler! It'll never get any bigger than this!'

"He still storms into the studio and I still sometimes can't believe I work with such an icon. I'll never forget him. And LEX18 will never be the same without him."

Hanna Mordoh now works for the NBC affiliate in Hartford, Conn. She was an intern at LEX18 in 2010 and then got to know Cutler as a co-worker in 2013.

"While we didn't work together often, yes, there are still plenty of fan packages and Friday night football script runs in our past," she said. "I worked as a night-side reporter, so I often helped when I heard the frantic yells – mostly Cutler - among the sports department."

"However, the best Cutler moment I ever witnessed was seeing him become a grandpa. Grandpa Cutler couldn't be prouder, showing off his grandson pictures to the entire newsroom. It was the happiest I have ever seen him. The pride he had in that moment surpassed that of a winning Super Bowl football player or any Kentucky fan after an NCAA Championship win."

"It was fun for me to see such a sports fanatic become the biggest fan of something (someone) new. As much as Cutler's legendary mustache and frank, loud, speech suit him, I have to say his most fitting feature and my favorite 'Bubs' memory is seeing him earn his new title of Grandpa."

Another former co-worker, Mary Jo (Perino) Ford, shares a side of Cutler few see or know from a Thanksgiving morning a few years ago.

"My husband and I went over to the Cutlers' kitchen table. We sat there for hours and ate and drank and laughed. Then we did that all over again," Ford said. "I truly feel like a part of his family and he is a part of mine. It's become an annual tradition on Thanksgiving — and one that will continue beyond his retirement —at least I hope the invite still stands."

It will because that's the soft side Cutler doesn't always show viewers on air. He's mainly all business on air. He's known for asking tough questions and not backing off making tough comments on air when needed.

Jeff Drummond, managing editor for Cats Illustrated, fondly remembers Cutler chasing former UK coach Billy Gillispie trying to get a comment on his job status. Drummond considers it one of the "most memorable and bizarre media moments" he's ever seen — and no one can forget Cutler in those cowboy boots doing all he could to get Gillispie to talk. The coach wouldn't, but it was not for a lack of effort by Cutler.

However, that determination is part of what Drummond will remember best about Cutler.

"There was a moment when I was a greenhorn reporter still in college where I saw a former UK coach get a little nasty and personal with Alan. Cut did not back down and he stood on the moral high ground with his line of questioning, which really impressed me," Drummond said.

"At that time, I was a little in awe of some coaches, and certainly a bit hesitant to ask a tough question. But that moment changed everything for me from a journalistic standpoint. I don't think I've ever shared that with Cut. I hope he can appreciate how influential that was for someone just setting out on his career path."

That's Cutler. He was a trend setter. He did his job the way it should be done. That might not have always made him popular with everyone, but if a tough question needed to be asked, Cutler was often the one asking it of coaches and/or players.

Herald-Leader columnist Mark Story remembers one time Cutler didn't hesitate to ask the tough question. It came after Mason County's Chris Lofton lit up Kentucky in Rupp Arena while playing for Tennessee after not getting a scholarship offer from UK coach Tubby Smith.

"Alan after the game asked Tubby Smith if he regretted not offering Lofton a scholarship," Story said. "It's rarely easy to ask a coach to essentially admit they made a major mistake. On this night, that Lofton question was probably what every Kentucky fan was wondering themselves. It was to Alan's credit he asked it — and to Tubby's credit that he answered it honestly by saying yes."

"Because Alan had such a unique and strong on-air persona, I think that tended to overshadow how hard he worked and the fact he was a reporter willing to ask tough questions."

So do I and that's a big part of why Cutler will be missed by many that he touched in ways he still doesn't realize.

"My favorite Cutler memory was the first time he recognized me and said hello in the press room," Larry Glover of Larry Glover Live said. "I always thought of Alan as one of the stars of Lexington media."

"For him to know who I was gave me a feeling of belonging in this business. That was important to a kid trying to carve out a career in covering the Cats."

That's how Cutler touched so many from those he worked with at LEX18 to others in the UK media to all of you who watched him being Cutler night after night on LEX18.

124

Ryan Lemond

How do I describe Ryan Lemond? We have a strange bond. I really like Ryan. *Please don't tell him I said that.*

He's one of those people that always ends up coming up roses—he just does. He's feisty. He loved our Friday night show. Ryan worked his tail off for our Friday night shows. I can't tell you how many times he put his tie on in the commercial break right before the show started. It would drive me crazy that he wouldn't spend three seconds seeing if his tie was straight—so he never did, just to tick me off. He did a better job at LEX18 than I think he got credit for. But Ryan got tired of working for Bruce Carter, our news director. It got to the point where he couldn't work at LEX18 because he hated Bruce Carter.

Ryan went into real estate, and he didn't hide the fact that he was selling real estate. He took real estate calls in the middle of the afternoon when you're supposed to be doing your TV job. After he left the station, he went into real estate full time. He then falls into the Kentucky Sports Radio job, and he's been very successful doing that—he loves taking his shirt off in public at every opportunity to pump up a crowd of UK fans. And like me, he's not as skinny as he used to be.

Ryan's the kind of guy that if he needs me and calls me at four o'clock in the morning, I'd be over to his house in two seconds. But what's important is that Ryan would do the same for me.

I will always have Ryan's back. We don't go out to lunch or talk much on the phone, but I think the world of Ryan.

Here's something really heart-felt that Ryan wrote for *Vaught's View* about me as part of my retirement from LEX18.

Ryan Lemond: My favorite memories of Cutler involves the

first two times I met him.

Back in 1989, I was working at a TV station in Evansville, Indiana, and I had come over to Lexington to pick up a tape of Rex Chapman from Cutler after a Charlotte Hornets exhibition basketball game at Rupp Arena.

I walked into the WLEX newsroom and saw a very professional well-dressed man sitting at his desk, so I asked him, "Are you Alan Cutler?" The man stared, hysterically laughing at me, and then turned around and said, "Do you see that madman whaling around and screaming back there in the back of the newsroom? That's Alan Cutler!"

Second favorite memory of Cutler involves the very first day I was an employee of WLEX. I walked into that very same newsroom that I had seven years prior, walked up to Cutler, shook his hand and said, "Hey Alan, I'm Ryan Lemond." He said, "Shut up and come in here!"

He had me come in the edit bay where he promptly shut the door and then pointed his finger right at my face and said, "You're going to hear a lot of things about me. You're going to hear a lot of bad things, and you're going to hear some good things. Mostly bad, but do me this one favor. Just make up your decision about me on your own. Don't let somebody else make up your mind about me. You decide for yourself."

From there on, we worked together for almost 12 years (I still hold the record for working with him the longest in the WLEX sports department). There were times I wanted to punch him in his big ol' nose, but he'll never really know how much he means to me and my family. He made me a better man. He made me a better dad. He made me a better husband. He made me a better person.

Lexington sports media will never be the same. Whether you liked him or not, you always tuned in to see what Cutler had to say.

His greatest legacy in this market will be his invention of the "World Famous Prep Report," where for the first time local TV Sports coverage expanded outside the city of Lexington. Cutler started that. Every local community tuned in every Friday night.

One of the highlights of my career was working those Friday nights with the Cut man.

Mazel tov big fella.

125

Kid Sister Mary Jo

Mary Jo Perino is like my kid sister. It's lovely how our relationship has grown and developed over the years. It's not something we could have possibly predicted when we first met each other.

One of the things people don't see about Mary Jo is that she's smart, and she's got a lot of common sense. She's a big fan who has developed a really good understanding of sports.

I've never been close to a lot of people. After work, family, working out, and eating too much—there's no time to socialize. I know there are a lot of people who don't like me, but I don't care about that. *That will probably come out wrong*, but the truth is that I care about the people I care about, and the people that care about me probably care about me more than others realize.

The people I'm close to, like Mary Jo, have my back just like I have theirs. That's been the key to my foundation of the few people that I'm really close to. In today's society, there aren't enough people that really have each other's backs.

Mary Jo Perino: When you first start out in the WLEX sports department, you get the same basic speech. I got that speech.

"Then there's Cutler. He's harmless once you learn how to deal with him."

It was my introduction to him, and a warning. You better learn how to deal with him.

He is like no one I have ever met. Admittedly, I was

intimidated at first. I'm not from Kentucky, so the name Alan Cutler meant nothing to me. But his aura is intimidating. Maybe you've heard, but Cutler has a little bit of an ego :)

I didn't like him at first. I'm not sure anyone does. He called me Bubs. It was endearing until I found out he calls everyone Bubs. It started because he didn't feel the need to learn your name until you'd been around for six months.

He's not the easiest guy to work with. Wait a minute, wasn't this supposed to be a glowing story about Cut???

Anyway, he's not easy to work with. But the advice of "once you get to know him" rings true.

I'm not sure when it happened exactly, but I know it was after I returned from Atlanta in 2007. I started having some issues in my personal life, and Cutler became a sounding board for me. The only reason that was possible was because one time Cut's kids came to the station. They rarely came there together, and they weren't little kids anymore. But I saw how he lit up around them and vice versa. I thought if these seemingly reasonable young people can love him, maybe he's not so bad. So I trusted my gut and confided in him. I cried on his shoulder if you can believe it. And what I discovered is that he cared about me. Like really cared. Over time, we developed a relationship that went beyond TV. We started getting together with each other's families. I went to his house for Thanksgiving. I fell in love with his wife and kids. I was at the baby shower for his first grandchild. I feel like I'm part of his family, and he is part of mine.

I've learned a lot from Cut. I've learned to say no to things - one of the most important lessons out there. I've learned not to care about what others think about you. That's their problem, not yours. He taught me that at the end of the day, you have to do what makes you happy. And laugh. A lot.

Pretty ironic for someone I really didn't want to see every day when I first met him.

And maybe that's the most important lesson of all. Dig deep. Find out who people are and what they love, not just what they do. You might just find yourself a friend for life.

A much much older friend. A less handsome friend. But a friend for life, nonetheless.

126

Keith Farmer

There's a word in Yiddish—it's called being a *Mensch*—and Keith is it. Keith is a gentleman. He's kind, caring, considerate, and really nice. There aren't a lot of people like Keith – there just aren't. When he went to work for LEX18, he didn't get on the air as much as he wanted to. He ended up going to Louisville at WLKY to work for Freddie Cowgill, who's done a really good job as their main sports anchor for about eight thousand years.

I remember when Freddie called me up and told me he was thinking of hiring either Keith or this other guy. He asked if I had a suggestion. I told him I didn't know who the other guy was, but if it's close, I don't care if Keith is No. 2—if you don't hire him, you're an idiot. I told Freddie that Keith is one of the finest human beings he would ever get to know, that he would love working with Keith, and that Keith and he would become really close—and they don't make people like Keith. Freddie hires him, and two weeks later he calls me up and thanks me. He tells me this may end up being the best hire he's ever made. They've been great friends for a long time.

Keith ended up moving up to be the weekend anchor. And then when Mary Jo Perino left, I pushed hard for Keith because he's from here, he knows the area, he works hard, and he's just a great guy. Even though I was the sports director, I did not have the final say—but I pushed hard for him to become our main sports anchor. I think he's doing a terrific job at LEX18.

Keith and I are very different in our styles—I'm really loud and he's not...so?—but our philosophies are a lot closer than people realize.

What Keith said really surprised me.

Keith Farmer: My first real memory with Alan was when I

was in high school, and our team—Madison Central—went to the Sweet Sixteen for the first time ever. Of course, we're getting all this play, and I remember Alan Cutler coming over to our practice. I was wide-eyed and couldn't believe he was standing in my school. This is 1987, and I was a manager for the varsity team. I remember Alan asking my fellow manager to turn around so he could get a shot of the jacket we had made up for us that said 11th Region Champs—after we had knocked Lafayette off in the region. That was my first real experience of being around Alan Cutler and seeing him do his thing and work.

Now you have to fast forward to college—I'm at Morehead State. I haven't even told Cutler this, but he's going to get misty-eyed on me on this one. I was doing some radio work at Morehead State for just a local NPR station that we had. I did sports there along with some other things. While I was finishing up my time there at WMKY, I sat down with the sports director and the general manager, and they asked me what I wanted to do in life. I had done a little bit of TV work as well, so I told them that I really wanted to do TV work. I told them I wanted to start working in Lexington—although I obviously did not. I started in Hazard. When they asked me who I see myself as and what kind of style I liked, I said, "I really like Alan Cutler." The look that these guys gave me was like I had two heads. I guess they expected me to say somebody over at one of the other stations. I told them Alan Cutler because he makes it fun. He has fun. He talks to you in a conversational way, and he makes you smile. That's why I want to be like him.

Needless to say, after I work my first four years in Hazard, I get a chance to come to LEX18, and now I am working with Alan Cutler. That was 1997, and I was just really part time in sports at the time. In 1998, when Kentucky was making the run with the 'Comeback Cats,' they told our photographer Greg "Punk" Gorham that he could either go to Tampa for the Regional, or he could wait and see if they make it to the Final Four and go to the Final Four. You couldn't do both. "Punk" decides to go to Tampa, because no one thought that

team was going to make it to the Final Four. "Punk" chooses
Florida, and Kentucky ends up coming back and winning. So,
LEX18 then tells me I'm going to the Final Four in San
Antonio with Cutler. Now I'm rooming with Cutler. Now I'm
getting to hear what everybody's talking about with the
snoring Cutler, but at the same time, it's also pretty cool—we
got to work together. Here I am cutting all of his stories at the
Final Four. I'll never forget he had to run off and do a live
shot. I kept working, and he and Ryan (Lemond) brought me
back some of the best tacos I've ever had in my life.

We get to the championship game. Kentucky beats Utah, and
Cutler and I go into the locker room. It was a warm locker
room. Here's hot Cutler, sweating away after getting a couple
of interviews, and in comes hot, sweaty Ashley Judd. And the
two of them give each other the biggest hug as if they've
known each other their whole lives—like they're cousins or
something. It was awesome seeing them celebrate the
championship together.

The other thing I remember about that was walking out with
Tubby Smith and doing an interview with him. I'm literally
walking backwards, and Cutler's just interviewing away. We're
getting a one-on-one interview with him because that's the
way Cutler is. He didn't go into the locker room and quit. He
waited and got an interview that nobody else got. I believe we
might have gotten Saul (Smith) as well on his way out. And
maybe Cameron Mills. I definitely remember Tubby and how
loose he was. He had just won the title, and it was one-on-one
rather than in a group setting.

Fast forward to 2013—I come back to Lexington and run
Cutler off. I've run off my idol. I got to be the one around
when he took off and rode off to the sunset.

127

Kyle Scott

Kyle Scott worked for LEX18 from 2015 through 2018 as our weekend sports anchor. Kyle was a wonderful human being who drove me crazy calling me "boss." After I told him a number of times to stop calling me "boss"—he never stopped, even to this day, because he knew I didn't like it. Now I just shake my head when he does it.

Kyle Scott: There were plenty of moments during my 3+ years of working with Alan that I can recall thinking, "This would only happen to Cutler!" Put it this way, how many local TV personalities have had their head shot created as a BIG HEAD for a basketball game? And that BIG HEAD was used for UK basketball games at Rupp Arena...pretty cool!

Another funny moment - also at Rupp Arena - was when Coach Cal stuck his finger in Alan's ear during a stand-up. You read that correctly, John Calipari put his finger in Alan's ear while Alan was delivering his lines! And in typical Cutler fashion, he didn't miss a beat...he acknowledged Cal and finished his thought.

And then there was the time I was driving us back to the station after an early morning at Churchill Downs for Pre-Derby coverage. Alan fell asleep moments after we hit the highway, so I thought it would be funny to take a picture of him sleeping. I sent the picture to the weekday sports anchor, Keith Farmer. Keith thought it was funny, so he shared it with the assistant news director and news director.

Unfortunately, they did not think it was funny, as they noticed Alan was not wearing his seat belt. When we got back to the station, Alan was reprimanded by the higher-ups and would have to take an online safety course for not wearing his seat belt.

After I got in trouble, Kyle felt bad and apologized to me. I told him he had nothing to apologize for because I was the idiot not wearing my seat belt. I now wear my seat belt all the time.

Part 14

Going Out on Top

128

As Good as It Gets

One of the great things about my job is the people I've been able to meet and the moments that are magical. I realize how fortunate and blessed I am. Every now and then, you do something really special—you know it—and appreciate it. The fact that I was able to share and do this special story with Brian Gilbert—a dear friend and our chief photographer—made it even better.

One of the things I'm going to miss are the horse people I would talk to over the years that would tell me about everything going on with all the two and three-year-olds. As you know, I always like to find a story that's off the beaten path.

I found out about Glenwood Farm in Versailles. Tanya Guenther, who runs the farm, is one of the most remarkable women I've run across. As a kid, she was studying bloodlines. She becomes an investment banker in England, decides that she wants to do something special, so she takes over the farm that her father—a stockbroker in Canada—bought.

To do what she did in the 2018 Kentucky Derby is one of the most remarkable things I've seen. If you had ten horses that you took to a sales ring, and one of them wins a graded stakes race—that would be really good. To breed two of your own horses and turn them into Derby horses—with Justify winning the Triple Crown, and Vino Rosso winning the Breeders' Cup Classic in 2019—well, that would be absolutely unbelievable.

Here's the part that's even better. While Brian and I were doing the story, Stage Magic—the mother of Triple Crown winner Justify—had just produced a baby fourteen hours earlier. Tanya lets us in the stall with the mother and baby. You just don't get to do that every day. looked at Brian's face, and he had a grin on from ear to ear. Then o top of that, Tanya suggests they take the baby outside for the first time so we could get some more video.

It was such a cool moment. For Tanya to feel so comfortable with us to include us in such an intimate moment was a spectacular feeling for me. That's the joy of horse racing. At the end of my career, I enjoyed covering horse racing more than I enjoyed covering Kentucky Basketball.

When I'm covering the Kentucky Derby, I can do what I want when I want. As long as I can find really good stories—which luckily I was able to do every year—you can get to know people as people. I had never met Tanya before. And as you'll see in my story, look at how open she is with me. This is a strong, really smart, tough woman who is succeeding tremendously in a sport dominated by men. To do what she has done is absolutely amazing. For me, going out on my last Derby with a story like this is about as good as it gets.

Cutler Narration: You take ten horses to a sale. If one—if one—would make it to the Derby, that would be spectacular. That would be crazy ridiculous. How about taking ten horses to the sale, and TWO make it to the Derby? That's what's going on at beautiful Glenwood Farm, and both have a big-time shot at taking the Roses.

This is Tanya Guenther hanging out with Justify's mother, Stage Magic, who gave birth about fourteen hours ago to this beautiful baby. She's a former investment banker in London who's from Canada. She gave that up to chase the dream that started as a little girl. Horses.

Tanya Guenther: I felt like I wanted something that had meaning for me. Something that I really loved to do. So, coming and doing the horses was just something I was passionate about from a young child basically. It made sense to me.

Cutler Narration: There aren't many kids who are seven that are studying pedigrees. Tanya is not only the matchmaker for the mares but raises them until they're sold. These horses are her babies. As a kid, Vino Rosso was calm. It was easier for them to become close.

Tanya Guenther: I actually cried when we sold Vino Rosso because I'd become a little bit attached to him. Justify was a bit tougher colt, but Vino Rosso was so laid back. You could develop a bit more of a personal relationship in the sense that the colt—I don't know. I can't really explain it. But when we sold him—I was very proud that we achieved a good price—but I was sad at the same time.

Cutler Narration: When you think about it, it's not only spectacular, it's crazy. In this field right behind me, Vino Rosso and Justify were hanging out and playing as kids. And now, they're running for the roses. John Guenther, Tanya's father, a stockbroker who lives in Canada, bought Glenwood Farm in 1986. He gives his daughter a tremendous amount of credit for their success. Their philosophies don't always match, but they make their major decisions together.

Tanya Guenther: I call it sparring matches. We have a fair amount of sparring when it comes to everything on the farm—but in a good way. We kind of spar back and forth on pedigrees if we have horses that we're racing. Hopefully, we come up with better decisions by both standing up for what we think and then somehow coming to a mutual agreement.

Cutler Narration: Can you believe the feeling that Tanya and her father, John, might have if they're neck and neck down the stretch? I talked to a number of horse experts about this specific thing. Even though they played as kids in the same field, if they're neck and neck in the stretch, they probably won't recognize each other. Two mares produce two Derby horses at the same farm.

129

How I Dropped the Mic

It's a typical crazy football Friday night in September of 2017. It's about 10:40 pm, and I'm at the station doing something I've done for parts of five decades. We needed a football score, so I shouted, "HEY, SOMEBODY GET THE SCORE!" I'm not really yelling *at anyone*, we just needed the score. One of the great things about Friday night is that nobody counts, and everybody hustles. We all do the little things to make the show work. Friday nights' success, where we've been named the best sports show in Kentucky more than anyone else, has been all about teamwork.

No TV station in Lexington was covering high school sports the right way when I showed up in 1981. Back then, believe it or not, viewers still wrote me letters. One letter changed Lexington sports forever by telling me how special Paris High School was. Paris High won the state championship in 1981 and 1982. They were in the process of winning thirty-eight games in a row. Back then, I *still* had to ask where Paris High was.

I didn't know at that time that I would grow to love Paris with all the beautiful horse farms that led to many great Kentucky Derby stories in Bourbon County. To me, that part of Kentucky is like a little slice of heaven.

When I first arrived at WLEX, Lexington TV stations were only shooting games in Lexington. I pitched to my boss that Friday night football wasn't just about sports, but it's really about community involvement. John Ray, our news director, told me I was crazy at first, but he eventually bought in, and we doubled the number of photographers to shoot games. We started shooting games all over central Kentucky, and we quickly established the "World Famous Prep Report" as the best Friday night show in the state. Over the years, coaches have told me they did things like bringing a TV to a Pizza Hut to watch our show. I went to the first Paris game we covered, and fans were cheering us like crazy. They were so happy to see a TV station giving them love.

Well, we got the score on that crazy Friday night. I don't even know what game it was, but it was at that moment—it hit me—I didn't want to die at the TV station having a heart attack trying to get a score on a Friday night. Why that hit me at that moment, I have no idea. I'm almost sixty-five, and I'm chasing down high school scores. I used to love the high school show, but I've done it enough. I said to myself at that moment, "*I WANT TO RETIRE!*"

I did the show, and I sat on my decision. I didn't even tell my wife, Judy, because you don't come out and say you're retiring and then change your mind. Besides, there was no deadline for me. I wanted to see if I felt the same way in a month. The feeling not only didn't dissipate, it *got stronger.*

Sometime in October, I talked to Judy, and she was cool with it. I then told my daughter, my son, my son-in-law, my brother, and my sister.

The main thing was that I didn't want this to leak out. It was really important to me that I controlled *ME* leaving. There are too many people who have stayed in the business a long time who weren't able to control their exit and were pushed out. That's happened more than the public knows. Right or wrong or whatever, I wanted to control it, and I wanted to do it on my own terms. The station asked me if I wanted another three-year contract. They asked me about the contract shortly after I decided to retire—but before I made the announcement.

I kept my mouth shut for another reason. I wanted to announce it at the company party. The TV station does this thing—it's really old school, and really cool. I don't know how many other stations do this kind of thing, but we have an Employee Appreciation party after Christmas. Food, drinks…it's a party…people get dressed up, there's music—it's a fun night. In today's world of tight budgets, the company doesn't have to do that. Why spend the money? I'm surprised they still do it, but it's great that they do.

If you work for LEX18, every five years you get honored. This year, it was Nancy Cox's twenty-fifth year. They did a terrific video about her. I tease our wonderful anchor that she's had more hairstyles than me. "No way," says Nancy.

This year, it was the thirtieth year for me since I came back to Lex ington the second time. They put a video together—a nice goofy video, which was cool. I said a couple of things and tried to make people laugh.

As I'm finishing up, I say, "Derby Day is going to be a little different this year. It'll be emotional for me because it's my last day on TV— (pause) I quit."…There was dead silence in the room. No cheering, no booing, no yelling, nobody threw anything at me—it was dead silence. You have to understand that there's a spotlight on, you're in front of all your peers, and there's NO REACTION AT ALL. People later said they freaked. I was telling people I was going to work until I'm sixty-eight—at the time I started saying that—it was my plan—and I was going to collect social security at sixty-six and put it away for retirement for two years. That was my goal.

Talk about dropping the mic! A couple of people have asked me why I didn't really drop the mic. I actually did want to do it, but if you think about it—the reverb, with the speakers going crazy—it would have hurt people's ears. A number of people in the room that night have told me they wished they could retire the same way.

Since my announcement, the response from viewers has been ridiculously overwhelming. If you're at any place for a long time period, you're bound to get some sort of heightened reaction. The specific reactions that I've gotten from people have been profoundly stunning. Whether it was a story I did in the 1980s, or just something I said to encourage someone, or something I did that made them feel important—so many of you have reached out to me. Many of the stories you have shared with me have humbled me and brought me to tears. Just as poignantly, I'm overwhelmed by the number of you who have told me how much you have enjoyed watching me on TV for all those years. I am forever grateful.

Being old school, Frank Sinatra is one of my favorites. I've listened to his famous song "My Way" hundreds of times. You only go through life one time, so you might as well try and do it *my way*.

Mic drop.

Acknowledgments

I'm not sure how I can properly thank the man I call "Doc"—Dr. John Huang. Doc spent countless hours on this project at my kitchen table as I ad-libbed the book into his phone. How he kept his sanity in dealing with me through our hundreds of phone calls, video conferences, text messages, and emails is beyond me. The trust I have for him is off the charts. The main reason I selected Doc to do this book—after he bugged me to write it—was because of his trust, his kindness, and his smarts. And, oh yeah, he can write pretty well also.

To my wife Judy—that poor woman has put up with me for close to four decades. Her guidance through all of this was so much stronger than she realized. Judy's advice and council on a number of touchy topics in the book would have made Wes, her father, very proud. I'm huge on that word "trust"—which could be Judy's middle name.

To my family, who put up with their workaholic Dad not being around nearly enough. My children are the No. 1 reason I did this book. I was hoping they wanted to know what in the world their father was up to during all that time. Having Jenna and J.J. was like winning the lottery twice for Judy and me.

The lottery wins continued with the addition of Jonathan Bickett, our great son-in-law, who also had some timely suggestions for the book.

As former Yankee great Lou Gehrig said in his last appearance at Yankee Stadium—"Today, I consider myself the luckiest man on the face of the earth."

But it gets even better. I hope and pray our wonderful grandkids, Andrew and Eliza—when they can understand this book—are proud of their grandpa.

Hoops—Hoops—Hoops. If I had a wise older brother in this business that has always had my back and who I trust, it would be the Hall of Famer, Dick "Hoops" Weiss. He's one of the great sportswriters in the history of college sports. Hoops has written a gazillion books and just finished another one with Dick Vitale. I called Hoops early on and said, "Don't tell me how the book will succeed—tell me what I need to do so it doesn't fail."

Hoops told me that if the book didn't sound like me, then it would

456

definitely fail. That's why Doc and I spent all those long hours in the morning at my kitchen table getting to know each other *before* we started all the research, phone calls, and banging on the computer to fill in the blanks.

Another special thanks goes to Pat Dalbey, at the time president and general manager of LEX18, who wished me "good luck" and said to "go for it," even after I showed him some of the sensitive chapters in this book—which included our problems due to "the chase" involving former UK basketball coach Billy Gillispie.

As I mentioned in the book, I had problems with my boss, Bruce Carter. After I decided to retire, I was just going to leave the station without saying goodbye and skip the big party. Bruce convinced me to stay and attend. The love I felt from everyone at the end was shocking, overwhelming—and a lifetime memory. Had I just walked out, there would be no book. Plus, Bruce kept me from being fired after "the chase." Thank you Bruce.

David Bryan Blondell did the book's cover art. Wow! David's a native Kentuckian and is known for creating unique prints of star players from the University of Kentucky. When we first talked, David said, "I got this," but he didn't tell me what he was going to do. His cover art captures perfectly that moment between me and Billy G. Do yourself a favor and follow David's work via www.BlondellArt.com, on Twitter @BlondellArt, or contact him by email at David@BlondellArt.com.

Thanks to Marissa Kinsley, J.J.'s girlfriend, and to Greg Gerlach for their fantastic ideas regarding the cover design.

Thanks to Greg and Judy Gerlach for helping us format the book for publishing. Greg and I go way back to our days together at LEX18. He was an outstanding reporter and someone I always respected and trusted. I'm not surprised that his production company is very successful.

A special thanks goes to Arnold and Miller. Charles (Chuck) Arnold and Chris Miller—two respected lawyers in Lexington who helped me tremendously when it was possible that I wouldn't be able to do this book based upon my contract with LEX18. They guided me through a rough patch.

Still another thank you goes to Katie Huang—Doc's daughter—who is already a successful author. She read our entire manuscript, cleaned up a lot of our grammar and spelling, and—as a "non-sports" person—confirmed that the book was indeed an interesting read for everyone.

A slam dunk goes to Cal—Coach John Calipari—for writing the foreword, and being so forward thinking when it comes to student-athletes. An assist goes to Eric Lindsey, Cal's right-hand man, who does the impossible job of being in charge of sports information for the UK basketball team.

I could go on and on thanking many others—just like I could have easily topped a hundred and fifty chapters in the book—but we all know that Dr. John Huang's heart could not have handled that.

So I'll end with this. To all the fans out there who have tuned in over the course of my career—who have watched my sportscasts, or listened to my talk shows, or checked out my interviews, or thanked me for my featured stories, or disagreed with my commentaries—I want to THANK YOU most of all. Without your passion, and interest, and support of your sports teams, I would have never chased down many of these stories.

Thank you True Blue fans. This one's for you!

Alan Cutler

July 12, 2020

About the Authors

ALAN CUTLER'S dream started right out of college at Cortland State, continued on to Farmington, New Mexico doing Little League Baseball play-by-play, and then to the beautiful mountains of western Colorado, where he did more radio play-by-play (while also shocking himself by becoming a successful radio news director). Alan then went on to put his New York face in Boise, Idaho learning a new craft—TV, which led to a stint in Lexington as the popular sports director at LEX18. After moving on to KDKA-TV in Pittsburgh—where he co-hosted a very popular radio show on KDKA-Radio—Alan returned back "home" to LEX18 where he remained for the next three decades covering three Kentucky NCAA championship teams and serving as the host of the Cincinnati Bengals Radio Network. It's been a wild and fun journey.

Growing up in Long Beach, N.Y., where his front yard was a canal two houses from the bay, right by the ocean, Alan always wanted to be a sportscaster. Chasing his dreams was a natural choice. Along the way, he's made some wonderful relationships, met a lot of sports stars, and learned all about the *people* behind the athletes.

Alan is married to Judy, who has been his rock for all these years.

During that time, God blessed them with Jenna and J.J. That led to Jonathan, the perfect son-in-law, and Andrew and Eliza—the two best grandkids in the world.

Cut To The Chase gets right to the point of who Alan Cutler really is—because chasing Billy Gillispie, which made him famous, really wasn't just a chase. It was Alan continuing to go after a big story when others had quit.

"The word 'chase' has been a huge part of my life. I was chasing a dream by becoming a sportscaster. I was chasing a dream while having fun. I was chasing a dream that started with wanting to know who the New York Yankee players were—as people. What was Mickey Mantle like? What were the people I interviewed like? I hustled non-stop in my career, which allowed me to go deep with the many people I've included in this book. I've got strong opinions—that's me. Hope you enjoy the book."

Dr. John Huang is a retired orthodontist and military veteran. He currently covers University of Kentucky sports for *Nolan Group Media* and *JustTheCats.com*. He enjoys writing books in his spare time. You can contact him at www.huangswhinings.com or follow him on Twitter @KYHuangs.